Praise for *Did It Happen Here?*

"Brimming with insights from classic ~~texts~~ ... ~~scholars~~
alike, *Did It Happen Here?* is a ~~must-read for anyone~~ ... ~~in~~ ...
wondering and worrying about the state of American democracy."
—Kevin M. Kruse, professor of history, Princeton University

"Bringing together classic texts and contemporary interventions, this
important volume catalogues the diverse meanings and instantiations
of fascism. The essays think our present anew by probing the uses and
limits of historical analogy and urging a comparative and translational
approach." —Adom Getachew, author of *Worldmaking after Empire:
The Rise and Fall of Self-Determination*

"Going well beyond the question of who or what deserves to be called
a fascist, this unparalleled collection provides an urgently needed
examination of American democracy in critical condition."
—Tara Zahra, author of *Against the World*

"In recent years, there is perhaps no other topic that has sparked spirited
debate among academics, politicians, and journalists. This sharp,
timely, and capacious collection masterfully peels back the layers of
fascism—closely analyzing its historical roots, shifting meanings, global
dimensions, and enduring impact on American society. This is a valuable
contribution to modern political thought." —Keisha N. Blain,
co-editor of the # 1 New York Times bestseller *Four Hundred Souls:
A Community History of African America, 1619–2019*

"The 'fascism debates' of the Trump era say less about fascism or right-
wing politics than the fault lines that divide Trump's enemies on the
liberal left. What do we expect from American democracy, and what
do we fear from it? The Trump debate will fade, but the big questions
explored in this thoughtfully curated volume will linger."
—Matthew Karp, author of *The Vast Southern Empire*

"A timely collection of informed voices." —*Kirkus Reviews*

DID IT HAPPEN HERE?

PERSPECTIVES ON FASCISM AND AMERICA

EDITED BY

DANIEL STEINMETZ-JENKINS

W. W. NORTON & COMPANY

Independent Publishers Since 1923

For information about permission to reproduce selections from this book, write to
Permissions, W. W. Norton & Company, Inc., 500 Fifth Avenue, New York, NY 10110

For information about special discounts for bulk purchases, please contact
W. W. Norton Special Sales at specialsales@wwnorton.com or 800-233-4830

Manufacturing by Lake Book Manufacturing
Book design by Beth Steidle
Production manager: Gwen Cullen

ISBN 978-1-324-11059-0 pbk.

W. W. Norton & Company, Inc., 500 Fifth Avenue, New York, N.Y. 10110
www.wwnorton.com

W. W. Norton & Company Ltd., 15 Carlisle Street, London W1D 3BS

1 2 3 4 5 6 7 8 9 0

CONTENTS

Introduction by Daniel Steinmetz-Jenkins
Making Sense of the Fascism Debate   IX

PART I
CLASSIC TEXTS

REINHOLD NIEBUHR
Pawns for Fascism   3

LEON TROTSKY
Bonapartism, Fascism, and War   11

RAYMOND ARON
The Future of Secular Religions   17

HANNAH ARENDT
The Seeds of a Fascist International   22

ANGELA DAVIS
*Political Prisoners, Prisons,
and Black Liberation*   27

UMBERTO ECO
Ur-Fascism   35

PART II
ON FASCISM ANALOGIES

RUTH BEN-GHIAT
What Is Fascism?   53

JAN-WERNER MÜLLER
Is It Fascism?   58

ROBERT O. PAXTON
I've Hesitated to Call Donald Trump a Fascist.
Until Now   68

VICTORIA DE GRAZIA
What We Don't Understand About Fascism   71

RICHARD J. EVANS
Why Trump Isn't a Fascist   79

PETER E. GORDON
Why Historical Analogy Matters   86

SAMUEL MOYN
The Trouble with Comparisons   106

TAMSIN SHAW
William Barr:
The Carl Schmitt of Our Time   114

DANIEL BESSNER AND BEN BURGIS
What's in a Word?   122

PART III
IS FASCISM AS AMERICAN AS APPLE PIE?

SARAH CHURCHWELL
American Fascism:
It Has Happened Here   135

ROBIN D. G. KELLEY
U.S. Fascism v. Angelo Herndon   149

JASON STANLEY
One Hundred Years of Fascism   154

NIKHIL PAL SINGH
Bellum Se Ipsum Alet   164

KATHLEEN BELEW
There Are No Lone Wolves:
The White Power Movement at War   173

PART IV
GLOBAL PERSPECTIVES

LEAH FELDMAN AND AAMIR R. MUFTI
From Crisis to Catastrophe:
Lineages of the New Right   187

FAISAL DEVJI
Losing the Present to History   198

PRIYA SATIA
Fascism and Analogies—British and American,
Past and Present   211

PANKAJ MISHRA
Narendra Modi and the New Face of India   219

MARLENE LARUELLE
So, Is Russia Fascist Now?
Labels and Policy Implications   237

PART V

HAS FASCISM TAKEN ON A NEW FORM TODAY?

GEOFF MANN
Are We Approaching a New Wave of Fascism?   249

MOIRA WEIGEL
Fighting Fascism in the Twenty-First Century:
The Adorno Algorithm   256

ANTON JÄGER
From Bowling Alone to Posting Alone   270

REBECCA PANOVKA
Men in Dark Times:
How Hannah Arendt's Fans Misread the
Post-Truth Presidency   285

UDI GREENBERG
Gender and the Radical Right's Departures from
Fascism   298

COREY ROBIN
Trump and the Trapped Country   305

Acknowledgments   313
Notes   315
Contributors   337
Credits   341
Index   343

INTRODUCTION

Making Sense of the Fascism Debate

DANIEL STEINMETZ-JENKINS

Debates about fascism in the United States are nearly a century old. Ever since Sinclair Lewis published his dystopian novel *It Can't Happen Here* in 1935, the question of whether fascism could happen here has been posed repeatedly, from one generation to the next. Indeed, an exhaustive new work by the intellectual historian Bruce Kuklick, titled *Fascism Comes to America*, shows that calling political opponents "fascists" constitutes a long-standing American tradition; he points out that American Trotskyists, New Dealers, the Jim Crow South, the civil rights movement, John McCain, Barack Obama, and Donald Trump have all been condemned as "fascist" by their opponents.[1]

Even so, there is something different about the fascism debate today. Beyond the superficial labeling of an opponent, it has generated deep analytical work involving multiple schools of thought (Black radical tradition, Marxism, the Frankfurt School, Cold War liberalism, to name a few), and addressed ultimate concerns (such as race, gender, technology, and the environment). There is also no obvious or stable political axis (progress/centrist, left/center/right) to the debate. Finally, the debate has not been confined to academia. Along with interventions from scholarly experts addressing a popular audience, it has extended into mainstream public discourse, with noted pundits and politicians weighing in.[2]

This anthology brings together classic interpretations and

definitions of fascism as well key writings that have defined the contemporary debate. My main aim in this introduction, though, is to offer an explanation for why it is worth tracing and understanding the dispute. The so-called fascism debate discloses something fundamental about the Western mind-set, culture, and political values—it reveals ultimate, and conflicting, concerns in a time of crisis and change, and how we choose to portray them.

WE LIVE IN A TIME of perpetual crisis—or at least one marked by crisis rhetoric. Since Brexit and the election of Donald Trump in 2016, certain Western politicians, pundits, scholars, and intellectuals have proclaimed the arrival of a new age racked by "the crisis of democracy,"[3] "the crisis of liberalism,"[4] "the climate change crisis,"[5] "the bank run crisis,"[6] "the crisis of higher education,"[7] "the pandemic crisis,"[8] "the crisis of a New Cold War,"[9] and the like. The language of crisis is now omnipresent. "Welcome to the world of the polycrisis," as the economic historian Adam Tooze put it, one in which "it no longer seems plausible to point to a single cause and, by implication, a single fix."[10]

But why is the notion of a polycrisis, coined in the 1970s by a French Marxist, now being revived to describe the current order of things?[11] Whose crisis? Which democracy? Political assumptions drive these questions.

The language of a domestic and international crisis of democracy was also apparent during the Obama administration; but it had yet to seize the imagination of the political mainstream. For voters electrified by his rallies and political homilies of hope and change, Obama had emerged as MLK 2.0, a savior to deliver the country from the bondage of George W. Bush's war on terror abroad, from the shame of Gitmo and Abu Ghraib and from violations of civil rights in the name of national security at home, such as with the Patriot Act. In the midst of the most devastating financial crisis since the Great Depression, Obama's message of hope sought to move the United States beyond the political dead ends of the Bush years. Obama, no doubt, faced a daunting task given what he had inherited from the previous administration. It is worth noting, however, that despite the long shadow cast by 9/11, the political establishment rarely labeled Bush's policies as fascistic—in fact, many liberals who defended Bush's war on terror came close to sharing his view that democracy stood embattled by the threat of "Islamo-fascism."[12] Some of those defending this line would later see fascism in Trump.[13]

It was after Obama's reelection in 2012 that commentators on both sides of the political aisle expressed growing concerns that democracy was entering into a state of crisis. Some argued that the epic failure to bring democracy to Iraq and Libya, and the aftermath of the Arab Spring, indicated a global "democratic recession."[14] Meanwhile, China's political rise and economic advance offered the world a viable political alternative to Western democracy.[15] Global right-wing authoritarianism accelerated during the Obama presidency, as demonstrated by the electoral successes of Recep Tayyip Erdoğan in Türkiye, Narendra Modi in India, Viktor Orbán in Hungary, Vladimir Putin's return to the Russian presidency, and the growth of populist nationalist parties around Europe.

On the domestic front, Obama's policies were creating ideological cleavages long thought politically foreign to U.S. politics. His critics on the left proved hostile to his handling of the financial crisis, believing that certain measures were fixed to the advantage of the wealthy and that, in the words of the historian Eric Foner, "the government was indifferent to the plight of ordinary Americans."[16] They sought a socialist alternative to what they deemed as Obama's "neoliberalism," hence the unexpected traction of Bernie Sanders's 2016 presidential campaign. Meanwhile, on the far right, the white supremacist fringe—marked by the conspiracies of birtherism and racist "replacement theory"—was making its way toward center stage in the Republican Party, a trend that would foretell Trump's future presidency.

Prior to Trump's election, concerns about fascism typically came from the right, and were often directed at Obama. In 2009, for instance, Fox News compared the newly elected president to Mussolini.[17] Tea Party accusations that Obama was a fascist were not uncommon, and charges of fascism soon appeared after the Obama administration's dismissal of General Motors CEO Rick Wagoner, as a part of the government's bailout of the automobile industry.[18]

For their part, establishment Democrats expressed little fear of American democracy being threatened by fascism. After all, despite growing right-wing populist sentiment, the Tea Party, and the intrigues of Senate Leader Mitch McConnell and House Speaker John Boehner, Obama had won, with relative ease, the two proceeding elections against white Republican presidential opponents; and given Trump's nomination as the Republican candidate, most polling and election forecasting indicated that Hillary Clinton would easily win the next.[19] Shocking as it is now, Trump's nomination was encouraged by some liberals, as it would provide Clinton with the easiest path to the White House, insofar that Trump, according to this view, "would almost certainly lose."[20]

But Trump's election ushered in a radical volte-face: terrified by the results, many Democrats, as well as some Republicans, suddenly began affirming that democracy was in profound crisis. A plethora of books intended for mass consumption soon appeared, some written days after Trump's victory,[21] offering prophecies of democracy's imminent demise.[22] Trump's victory emotionally and intellectually deregulated a democratic establishment that eight years earlier had expressed overwhelming joy over something long thought impossible: the election of the first Black president. Meanwhile, Ta-Nehisi Coates (who had arguably become the leading Black intellectual of that time), writing for *The Atlantic*—and long suspicious of the idea that Obama ushered in a postracial America—argued that the country had shown its true colors: Trump proved the norm; Obama had been the exception.[23]

Certain Republicans were shell-shocked by Trump's victory—many left the party, notably Colin Powell, Joe Scarborough, and George Will; some declared themselves to be "Never Trump" Republicans. How could someone as obscenely opposed to cherished political norms ascend to the nation's highest office, they wondered? Who is to blame? What was happening to the country?

For many, Trump's election called into question a core political assumption—perhaps an unconscious one—that had long been in place since the end of the Cold War: the notion that there is no viable political alternative to liberal democracy. The fracturing of this confidence led many Americans to the revelation that their democracy is actually fragile, vulnerable to injury, even death—a point that is powerfully made by Peter Gordon's essay in this volume. But who is to blame for this, they demanded? The age of crisis had arrived but making sense of it proved no easy matter.

For some, its advent had little to do with any inherent shortcomings of the country's long-standing democratic norms and values. Rather, the crisis was the work of sinister forces seeking to undermine democracy at home, or opposing it abroad. "The bad guys are winning," said the centrist Anne Applebaum: illiberal actors were becoming the new norm, a historical reversal of the political direction of the twentieth century, which ended in liberalism's Cold War triumph.[24] But how were these enemies of democracy to be labeled: authoritarians, nationalists, right-wing populists? Or could they even be fascists?

Critics, of course, had been arguing for decades that economic globalization brought about ever more extreme economic inequality, both within the United States and internationally, between Northern countries and the Global South.[25] This, they argued, was bound to cause a global reaction. The 2008 financial crisis and the European sovereign debt crisis amplified the problem, as critics warned that the political center had become too technocratic, too closed off from democratic processes, that is, too cut off from the people. The populist backlash in the United States and Europe against the norms of the day hardly proved surprising. Dissidents from across the political spectrum expressed disdain for the status quo: the Occupy movement protested against the exorbitant wealth of the "one percenters." More generally, those on the left expressed their frustration with a Democratic Party that had swapped the New Deal for neoliberalism. And had not the Black radical tradition warned for decades against white supremacist and fascist forces in America?[26] It is telling that Black Lives Matter movement was alive and well during the Obama administration, but that it took the death of George Floyd for it to receive mainstream political acceptance. Meanwhile, new-right forces were boiling over with nativist bile toward immigrants, the federal government, and "Obamacare."

Trump's election brought the rhetoric of crisis from the periphery to the center of American political life. But what was principally to blame?

Much, but not all, of the new fascism debate that exploded with Trump's election serves as a proxy debate for a larger discussion of what constitutes a thriving democracy both domestically and internationally. To what degree are threats external to the mainstream to blame for the crisis of democracy, and to what extent the internal democratic shortcomings of the political system itself? The latter position in this anthology is on clear display in Corey Robin's essay. We have debated since Trump's election, says Robin, whether Trump would topple democracy. But the problem is, in his words, "not the threat of a tyrannical white majority to the Constitution, but the way in which a minority of mostly white voters depends upon the Constitution to stop the multiracial majority." What is needed, then, is a fundamental overhaul of political institutions that do not reflect the will of the popular majority.

Viewed in this manner, it might be tempting to see the fascism debate as the continuation of the political dispute between those who supported the liberal Hillary Clinton being the Democratic presidential nominee in 2016 versus those who preferred the socialist candidate, Bernie Sanders. Accordingly, those who invoke charges of fascism against Trump are viewed by their critics on the left as part of the political establishment that has dominated the Democratic Party for decades, and whose hegemony is being challenged on the left and the right. In this reading, the leftists who resist applying the fascism label to Trumpism are the true democrats who see in fascism talk a rhetorical ploy that distracts from what is truly ailing American society: growing socioeconomic inequality brought on by the neoliberal policies that the Democratic Party has embraced for decades. This view could be attributed to such leftist thinkers as Daniel Bessner; aspects of it hark back to an older leftist debate, from the 1930s, regarding whether the socioeconomic conditions were in place for a veritable American fascist movement, as texts by Leon Trotsky and Reinhold Niebuhr included in this volume illustrate.

The limitation of this view, however, is that it telescopes the fascism debate into a narrow political perspective that does not do justice to its diverse perspectives and concerns. It also doesn't map onto key figures of the fascism debate when it presumably should. Alexandria Ocasio-Cortez, along with plenty of Marxist thinkers critical of liberalism, for instance, believes that the United States has a real problem with fascism. At the same time, many liberal thinkers, such as Adam Tooze and the political theorist Jan-Werner Müller, and conservatives, such as Tom Nichols, are equally critical of comparing the present to Europe's fascist past.[27] And on the far right, there are the sensationalist views of Dinesh D'Souza. He claims that the fascist threat today comes not from Trump but the Democratic Party, whose policies—"anti-free speech," "anti-religious liberty," etc.—he traces back to National Socialism; a perspective that few if any professional historians support.[28] Viewed in this light, the fascism debate is a Rorschach test for understanding what is truly ailing American society. It involves a variety of ultimate concerns and competing visions of society, which explains why so much of the dispute centers around the use of historical analogies.

———

DURING A TIME OF CRISIS, when the world is made strange, there is an existential need to turn to the past to understand the bewildering confusion of the present—to find meaning in history. Who and/or what we blame for causing the crisis will often influence the historical comparisons we choose to make, as we seek/struggle to make sense of what has occurred, is occurring, and might occur in the future. The presentist component is unavoidable as we project our values and anxieties onto past periods.[29] The historical analogies that intellectuals and scholars have picked to understand what happened with Trump's election or the January 6, 2021, Capitol attack are neither random nor self-evident.

In his best-selling *On Tyranny: Twenty Lessons from the Twentieth Century*, Timothy Snyder predicted that Trump would undermine American democracy just as Hitler had undermined liberal institutions in Germany: by cultivating obsequious civil servants and businessmen who followed his orders, and deceiving the naïve masses by manipulating the truth. Despite constant criticism from his fellow historians for making simplistic and reckless comparisons,[30] Snyder doubled down on his use of fascism analogies by predicting that it was "pretty much inevitable" that Trump would try to stage a Reichstag fire to overthrow democracy.[31] Snyder believed that January 6 vindicated his claims.[32] Whether one agrees with him or not, Snyder's interventions blur the line between history and prophecy. And the Trumpist right has responded by hurling accusations of fascism back at their accusers, as the writings of Dinesh D'Souza demonstrate par excellence.

Given all this inflated rhetoric, fears of a new civil war hardly prove surprising. But as Nikhil Pal Singh notes in his essay in this anthology, worries about an imminent civil war "defer the more daunting fight to salvage a democracy of common purpose and shared flourishing from one that has long subsisted on life support."

Many of the pieces in this anthology—those by Ruth Ben-Ghiat, Peter Gordon, Tamsin Shaw, Richard Evans, etc.—defend using analogies with fascism but in a far more complex fashion than does Timothy Snyder.[33] They have been met by a host of critics, such as Victoria de Grazia, Jan-Werner Müller, Daniel Bessner, Ben Burgis, and others, who offer varying historical objections to the comparison. Perhaps the core complaint of drawing on the darkest moment of Europe's history to explain Trump is summed up by the historian Samuel Moyn: it abnormalizes a presidency that is quintessentially a product of the American system and therefore fails to examine "the status quo ante Trump that produced him." But is it even necessary to make recourse to Europe to explain American fascism?

The historian Robert Paxton claims "that the earliest phenomenon that can be functionally related to fascism is American: The Ku Klux Klan . . . the first version of the Klan was arguably a remarkable preview of the way fascist movements were to function in interwar Europe."[34] One scholar who has put forth a powerful defense of this position is the American cultural historian Sarah Churchwell. Many of her arguments rely on the observations of Black political leaders of the 1930s, such as Langston Hughes and W. E. B. Du Bois, who explicitly interpreted Jim Crow America in a fascist light.

African American thinkers, and often those associated with the Black radical tradition, have long used the term "fascism" to describe numerous features of American politics and society. A classic example of this is Angela Davis's 1971 essay, "Political Prisoners, Prisons, and Black Liberation," which views the disproportionate rate of Black incarceration in the United States through the prism of a fascist political system. The Black radical tradition is represented in this volume by Robin D. G. Kelley and Jason Stanley.[35]

Watching from afar, however, intellectuals from the Global South often view the fascism debate as just another instance of American provincialism. As Faisal Devji explains, "seeing what is happening in the United States and elsewhere today as the struggle of fascism against liberalism or white against Black conceals more than it reveals, because it is a view that refuses to look beyond America or the West in a historical context which has become global." This refusal, says Devji, is even apparent in well-meaning critiques of Eurocentrism that nevertheless focus only on those Western media outlets considered the most high-profile. There is something contradictory and misguided, observes Devji, in thinking about the global in purely Euro-American terms. Contributions to this volume by Priya Satia, Pankaj Mishra, Kathleen Belew, Nikhil Pal Singh, Marlene Laruelle, and Leah Feldman and Aamir R. Mufti bring a much needed global perspective to the fascism debate.

Resisting the comforts afforded by historical comparison is far from easy. "Many historians," observed the British historian Geoffrey Barraclough, "are still emotionally involved in the death-agonies of the old world, which they feel more deeply than the birth-pangs of the new."[36] Barraclough, one of the pioneers of the study of contemporary history, was convinced that historians were so blinded by the past that they could not discern what was new or, as he put it, "the sense of living in a new period."[37] Barraclough's concerns are apropos of the current moment. The Cambridge historian Gary Gerstle has proclaimed that the age of neoliberalism is ending; it has been broken by the 2008 financial crisis, the Trump presidency, "Biden's infrastructure success," and the general economic fallout of the pandemic.[38] What, though, comes after neoliberalism, says the historian Nils Gilman, is "something yet to be named."[39]

A lot of the fascism debate can be reduced to anxieties about the kind of politics that are replacing the old order of things, and the human tendency to fall back on stale historical analogies to grasp the booming buzzing confusion of the present.

For this reason, even as Geoff Mann's piece on climate change and Moira Weigel's essay on media studies and the authoritarian personality accept fascism as an appropriate term for describing contemporary realities, they also believe that historical analogies might obfuscate the present moment as fascism has now taken on new forms. Weigel argues that fascism takes place today not in a mass society, but in a networked one. The same is true of those attempts that connect the authoritarian right's critique of gender fluidity and LGBTQ+ activism to fascism, while failing to see, argues Udi Greenberg, how Trumpism actually breaks with Mussolini and Hitler's gendered thinking about labor and militarism.[40] There is also the tendency to misinterpret classic interpretations of fascism in the rush to apply their insights to the present. This tendency is illustrated by Rebecca Panovka's essay, which explains how Hannah Arendt's contemporary admirers misapply her famous work *The Origins of Totalitarianism* to the post-truth presidency of Donald Trump. Similar judgments can be made about issues and topics that this book does not discuss in substantive detail, such as issues of displacement and migration, artificial intelligence, and conspiracy theory.[41]

MORE BROADLY CONSTRUED, the fascism debate is a glaring example of a larger global phenomenon, namely today's myriad history wars—disputes over how to think about national identity in light of the country past and present—taking place in Canada, Barbados, Mexico, Colombia, South Africa, Australia, throughout Europe, and especially between Russia and Ukraine.[42] As the public tries to sort through questions of national identity, it naturally is turning to the past through popular podcasts, newspapers, television, trade books, and documentaries. Enter the historians, who offer their services for a general audience confused by a brave new world.

This sense of uncertainty explains why historians dominate today's fascism debate. But given the impasse of the debate, the turn to history could be complimented by other methodological approaches. During the early days of the Cold War, for instance, sociology played a key role in explaining both the historical factors that gave rise to fascism and the socioeconomic conditions that needed to be addressed so as to make authoritarianism unappealing and unnecessary. The fascism debate might be enriched by the kind of approach that marked classic works of mid-twentieth-century sociology which sought to explain the modern condition, such as David Riesman's *The Lonely Crowd*, Theodor Adorno's *The Authoritarian Personality*, and C. Wright Mills's *The Power Elite*—as well as pieces by Anton Jäger and Moira Weigel in this anthology.[43]

Nor is there much work on par today with Reinhold Niebuhr's famous theological explorations—most notably his *Moral Man and Immoral Society*—of the distinct ethical nature of modern societies: theological considerations that are often ignored in today's fascism debate or viewed merely through the study of nationalism and, more generally, culture.[44] But as Marlene Laruelle's essay on the question of fascism in Russia reveals, it would be nearly impossible to grasp Putin's decision to invade Ukraine without understanding the political theology of the Russian Orthodox Church.

The fascism debate shows how history has eclipsed sociology in understanding the human predicament. I believe that this has had one unfortunate practical consequence, namely, doom and gloom of political forecasting too wedded to the horrors of the past. Little wonder that historians prophesied that the 2022 midterms would see the GOP win majorities in the House and Senate, allowing Trumpist forces to legally undermine democracy, just as Hitler had undermined the Weimar Republic (a failed prophecy); that Ron DeSantis stands to achieve this victory as a smarter, better educated and more fascistic version of Trump; that Trump, like the Undertaker, will rise again and this time achieve his fascist designs; that if Ukraine doesn't completely defeat Russia the entire free world is in jeopardy; that something must be done to stop China lest the liberal international order enter hospice care.

Anyone concerned about democracy must always take seriously those forces that are hostile to it, especially as generational divides within the Democratic Party over the Israel-Gaza conflict could play a major role in ushering Trump back into the White House. But we should be suspicious of historians moonlighting as prophets of doom and democratic avengers. Their desire to sound the tocsin against the threat of recurrent heresy too often obfuscates, rather than clarifies, the complexity of current events. Being overfixated on the traumas of history can make it difficult to grasp what is new. It also leads to a never-ending blame game as to who is responsible for the collapse of the older order of things. The way forward is to put the fascism debate to rest, even as we try to come to terms with the neurosis it has revealed in us—a purpose that this anthology serves. "The past may live inside the present," observes the historian Matt Karp, "but it does not govern our growth."[45] Instead of letting fears distort politics, the goal now should be to push forward with the hope of building a better society for a new age.

PART I

CLASSIC TEXTS

PAWNS FOR FASCISM

REINHOLD NIEBUHR

Of the various strata of human society the small tradesmen, clerks, white-collar workers and poorer farmers, who constitute the so-called lower middle class, would seem to the casual observer to be least capable of fulfilling a fateful role in contemporary social history. Yet the indications are that they hold a position in modern society of such strategic significance that the fate of modern civilization may well be decided by them. If this should prove true it is also fairly certain that their decision will be an unfortunate one.

The significance of the lower middle class does not derive from its possession of any particular political virtue or capacity. On the contrary it exceeds all classes in political ineptitude. But recent developments in lower middle class politics prove that social desperation may be compounded with political confusion into an independent political impulse of such fanatic power and such ambiguous direction that it may become the chief source of confusion in an age of confusion. Individual life is probably under stricter personal discipline in lower middle class existence than anywhere else in society. In that sense the genteel poor are

In this 1937 essay, Reinhold Niebuhr, the most influential Protestant liberal theologian of the twentieth century, examines the likelihood of a widespread fascist movement taking place in the United States by comparing its lower middle class with that of fascist Italy's and Germany's. American wealth, Niebuhr argues, has curbed the fascist temptation in the United States, unlike in Europe, where the situation is considerably more desperate.

a force for stability in a social structure. But they are least able to find themselves amidst the complexities of a technical civilization and the perplexities of a period of change. They are therefore potentially the chief source of social disease in modern history.

Until the postwar period the lower middle classes have never expressed a political will or fashioned a political instrument of their own. In the struggle between the landed aristocracy and commercial wealth which determined European politics during the past two centuries the lower middle classes were a politically negligible force. In both France and England they were the main constituents of that neutral element in the population which asked only to be left alone and which tended to give its loyalty to any government able to establish itself. The rising industrial workers of the early nineteenth century were more potent allies of the commercial classes in their struggle against feudalism than the poorer brethren of the middle class. They had a truer instinct for the realities of political life and a more natural inclination for collective action.

In the twentieth century the most significant political and social struggles are those in which the workers are pitted against the commercial and industrial classes. Once the workers had helped the business men to destroy the aristocracy or at least to win their freedom from the political and economic disabilities which a decaying feudalism sought to impose upon commercial life, the alliance between the workers and the bourgeoisie tended to dissolve. The business classes, in safe possession of the basic economic power of modern society, naturally exchanged their radical for a conservative role. Their primary concern was to prevent the political liberties, which the workers had won in joint action with them, from becoming a source of peril to their economic power. The history of Spain during the past five years of revolution telescopes into a brief span of a few years the whole social history of Europe with its triangular struggle between landed gentry, business men and workers and its volteface of the upper middle class, once the destruction of feudalism has been accomplished.

It was natural to assume that the struggle between the industrial and financial oligarchs and the workers would determine the history of

European civilization in the next hundred years, as the struggle between finance and land had determined its past. The prophecies based upon this assumption have been rendered fatuous and void by the sudden emergence of the lower middle classes as a distinctive political force. The consequence of this emergence is the rise of fascism. Peculiar national traits and circumstances may contribute to the rise of fascism but the deepest roots of its power lie in lower middle class life. The radical interpretation of fascism as essentially a contrivance for the preservation of a dying capitalistic civilization is inaccurate. Business communities come to terms with fascism because they prefer it to socialism, and without their final alliance with it fascism could not come to power so easily. But the financial oligarchy does not originate fascism. Nor does it enjoy the restraints and restrictions which fascism places upon economic life once it has come to power. The real source of fascism lies in the social resentments and the political confusion of lower middle class life.

Psychologically the basic characteristic of lower middle class life is an individualism which has only indirect contact with the collectivist tendencies of capitalism and frantically fears the collectivist creed of socialism. Economically and socially, the primary determinant of petty bourgeois attitudes is the possession of minimal property in the form of savings, and the possession of a home, small business, or farm. For the petty bourgeoisie the idea of property is therefore related to the idea of security. Property is not, as regards the owners of industry, a source of social and political power; and it is not regarded, so far as the workers are concerned, as the cause of social oppression. Property is the individual family's basis of security. The individualism of this attitude is accentuated by types of employment in which individual capacity, skill, and diligence tend to create so many differentials in wage and income that general levels of income are obscured. As a consequence individual resourcefulness is preferred to common action in securing and protecting social status and economic security.

The reliance upon property and upon individual initiative sharply distinguishes lower middle class attitudes from those of the workers. The social experience of the workers persuades them to regard property chiefly as an instrument of social power in the hands of their opponents and to rely upon common rather than individual action for the improvement of their standards. Thus workers are naturally collectivists both in terms of their immediate trade union experience and in terms of their ultimate social philosophy. This is not quite true of American workers, among whom bourgeois individualism has maintained a considerable influence, but it is becoming increasingly true of them as well as of European workers. The lower middle classes, though sometimes poorer than skilled workers, are consequently inclined to espouse a more conservative political creed than the workers. They imagine the libertarianism of owners is identical with their own and fail to recognize the gulf between property as social power and property as minimal social security.

This social conservatism alone would not, however, have prompted the petty bourgeoisie into an independent political movement. It was, on the contrary, the cause of their long dependence upon the politics of the richer middle classes. Their ambition to establish an independent political force was created by the contraction of modern capitalism with its depreciation of property values and its consequent destruction of their social security. Whether a depression results in the foreclosure of a farmer's mortgage or the bankruptcy of a small trader or the clerk's unemployment, the common consequence is a profound resentment, which is the more bitter for its failure to articulate itself clearly. It is ignorant of the cause of, and confused about the ways of escape from, the social difficulties in which the petty bourgeoisie find themselves. The worker, at least the worker schooled in trade union solidarity, is never purely an individual. A sense of mutual dependence and a common fate binds him to his fellows and thus transmutes social difficulties into a new social hope rather than into pure desperation.

What is most interesting about the middle class situation is that the social desperation and resentment in this class, though at first dissipated in individual attitudes, has been finally molded into a collective force. This has been the work of demagogues, whose method and creed reveal striking similarities in all the Western nations, however great may be the differences between them. Their economic creed, whether expressed in Hitler's idea of "freedom from interest servitude" or Father Coughlin's inflationary program or Townsend's old age pensions or the late Senator

Long's "share the wealth" panacea, looks forward to some form of property equalization without a disturbance of basic property relations. It is profoundly ignorant of the essentially collectivist character of property in a technical society and cannot understand that the centralizing tendencies in capitalism work automatically to the advantage of the owners of big property and against the small owners. It consequently seeks to establish social security by money and credit manipulation and by moratoria upon debts and mortgages. A part of its creed, as for instance inflation, is more perilous to the savings of the lower middle classes than helpful in relieving them of their debts. Other portions of the general program, such as moratoria and credit manipulations, tend to arrest the process of expropriation to which the small owner is subject but cannot finally stop the pitiless logic of centralization.

More important than the economic creed of the demagogue is his appeal to the social resentments and his exploitation of the psychological difficulties of the lower middle classes. Racial prejudice is a common human weakness but the lower middle classes are more prone to it than either the aristocrat, the plutocrat, or the worker. Each of these classes has a cosmopolitanism of its own. In petty bourgeois life a natural parochialism in social experience combines with a sense of individual frustration to create racial and national resentments and prejudices. A sense of racial superiority is a compensation to the little man for his sense of individual inferiority. Thus the "cracker" white of our South is most venomous in his prejudice against the Negro, and anti-Semitism flourishes most violently among the petty traders of Germany.

Up to the present moment petty bourgeois demagogy has fortunately not yet tapped this weakness of lower middle class life in America. The history of our postwar Klan proves how vulnerable our middle class life is in this respect. One may well wait with bated breath for the moment when an artful demagogue will provide an inevitable articulation for the racial resentments of our petty bourgeois life.

National as distinct from racial prejudice is an equally strong force among the poorer individualists. It was the force of national sentiment which helped the financial and commercial classes to defeat the feudal aristocrats. They required national unity for healthy commerce. The business classes thus first supported the king against the nobles and finally democracy against the king in their effort to overcome feudal anarchy. Having succeeded in establishing the nation, the logic of a technical civilization, with its international interdependence, forced them into internationalism. They bequeathed their nationalism, as it were, to their weaker and poorer brethren. The latter were desperately in need of some symbol of social solidarity in an individualistic existence in which the sense of community was atrophied and therefore tempted to morbid compensations. Perhaps this tendency among the genteel poor was accentuated, at least in Europe, by the nationalistic internationalism of the worker, whose Marxian thought tends to perpetuate an eighteenth-century disregard of legitimate national sentiment.

The old conservatism and the new spirit of rebellion in middle class life naturally lead to an ambiguous political program which seeks to combine both bankers and workers in the role of a common enemy. The only justification for such a political orientation is the undoubted fact that skilled workers frequently have the collective power to protect their standards against a contracting economy better than the individualistic poor. The latter consequently feel themselves ground between the upper and the nether millstone and draw the erroneous conclusion that the two millstones are parts of the same system of oppression. Since the only similarity between capitalistic oligarchs and the industrial workers is a rationalistic inclination to disregard traditional national boundaries and sentiments, patriotic passion therefore becomes the only possible basis for opposition to both groups. In Germany fascism has accentuated the power of national sentiment by identifying it with racial solidarity. Since Jews are prominent in both finance and labor organization, though their prominence is not as disproportionate as claimed, they are rather effective foils for this kind of hysteria. Whatever may be said about the ludicrous character of German Nazi anti-Semitism it must be admitted that it is an extremely effective instrument for combining resentments against foes who have nothing in common. The instrument gains in effectiveness because it fits so admirably into the parochial narrowness and the sense of individual inferiority of lower middle class life. The pathetic consequence of the political ineptitude and social confusion of petty bourgeois life is that the most timid portion of a national population should give birth to so violent a social movement and that individualists should, in their effort to escape collectivism, fasten a tyrannical state upon society. The violence of timid people is not as paradoxical as it may seem, since cruelty is a natural temptation to the weak. And desperate. The collectivism into which petty bourgeois individualists become betrayed is particularly defective because it is not suited to the necessities and logic of a technical age. It seeks by powerful state action to desiccate rather than to control the inevitable centralization of economic power in a technical civilization.

Lower middle class politics are consequently a retrogressive force in modern history. Without their confusion modern society would have a much clearer chance of readjusting its political structure to the necessities of its economic life. It is not at all unlikely that this confusion may become the primary cause of disaster in modern civilization. The peril of this confusion is the greater because petty bourgeois politics aggravate the anarchy of international life in the effort to overcome the anarchy within the nation.

It must be added that lower middle class attitudes have not reached the degree of desperation in the more favored nations which they attained in Italy and Germany. In France these classes are for the time being united with the workers in the popular front government of M. Blum. In America Roosevelt claims the allegiance of both workers and lower middle classes for a political program which satisfies both because ultimate issues are postponed in it. The alliance between the genteel and the industrial poor may function for some time in this country because the workers are only slowly disavowing bourgeois political attitudes and asserting the type of radicalism which it is the destiny of workers in Western civilization to assert. Yet this alliance is insecure in both France and America. In France petty bourgeois prejudices restrict the popular front government from carrying through any rigorous policies of socialization. It must content itself with burdening a very sick economic system with additional social services, a program which will soon bring it into fiscal difficulties. The peril of fascism is far from being laid in France, though it may be averted for some time.

The wealth of America is so great, even in a time of depression, that social desperation has not yet reached any such proportions as tempt the lower middle classes of Europe into their confused rebellions. Nevertheless it is true that if Senator Long had lived the peril of American fascism might be an immediate one. Should the present prosperity prove to be a very brief respite in a general tendency of contraction (as many economists predict) lower middle class desperation would undoubtedly express itself in fascistic or semi-fascistic terms in the election of 1940. It may well become the decisive factor in our political life at that time.

It is too early to prophesy, and much too early to write, the tragic social history of our era. Europe is drifting toward a war which it seems powerless to avert. No one can predict what may lie on the other side of that conflict. But it is fairly safe to predict that if modern civilization fails to find a way out of its chaos before the anarchy of its life breeds death and destruction, the chief contributory cause of its failure will lie in the demonic force latent in the lives of all the good little people, so touching in their personal rectitude and individual discipline, who serve us in the shops, who till our soil and who perform all functions in our social mechanism with the exception of industrial labor. If that should prove true it would add a peculiar pathos to the tragedy of modern existence.

BONAPARTISM, FASCISM, AND WAR

LEON TROTSKY

THE POINT AT WHICH FASCISM SUCCEEDS

Both theoretical analysis as well as the rich historical experience of the last quarter of a century have demonstrated with equal force that fascism is each time the final link of a specific political cycle composed of the following: the gravest crisis of capitalist society; the growth of the radicalization of the working class; the growth of sympathy toward the working class and a yearning for change on the part of the rural and urban petty bourgeoisie; the extreme confusion of the big bourgeoisie; its cowardly and treacherous maneuvers aimed at avoiding the revolutionary climax; the exhaustion of the proletariat, growing confusion and indifference; the aggravation of the social crisis; the despair of the petty bourgeoisie, its yearning for change, the collective neurosis of the petty bourgeoisie, its readiness to believe in miracles; its readiness for violent measures; the growth of hostility toward the proletariat which has deceived its

In the 1920s and 1930s, Leon Trotsky was the most important figure in the Marxist opposition against Joseph Stalin. This essay, completed in August 1940, the month he was killed, articulates Trotsky's thesis that, as things currently stood, a veritable fascist movement was not possible in the United States as the country lacked a mass labor party, which was necessary for producing a widespread fascist reaction.

expectations. These are the premises for a swift formation of a fascist party and its victory.

It is quite self-evident that the radicalization of the working class in the United States has passed only through its initial phases, almost exclusively in the sphere of the trade union movement (the CIO). The prewar period, and then the war itself, may temporarily interrupt this process of radicalization, especially if a considerable number of workers are absorbed into war industry. But this interruption of the process of radicalization cannot be of a long duration. The second stage of radicalization will assume a more sharply expressive character. The problem of forming an independent labor party will be put on the order of the day. Our transitional demands will gain great popularity. On the other hand, the fascist, reactionary tendencies will withdraw to the background, assuming a defensive position, awaiting a more favorable moment. This is the nearest perspective. No occupation is more completely unworthy than that of speculating whether or not we shall succeed in creating a powerful revolutionary leader party. Ahead lies a favorable perspective, providing all the justification for revolutionary activism. It is necessary to utilize the opportunities which are opening up and to build the revolutionary party.

PROBLEM OF POWER POSED TO THE WORKERS

The second world war poses the question of change of regimes more imperiously, more urgently than did the first war. It is first and foremost a question of the political regime. The workers are aware that democracy is suffering shipwreck everywhere, and that they are threatened by fascism even in those countries where fascism is as yet nonexistent. The bourgeoisie of the democratic countries will naturally utilize this dread of fascism on the part of the workers, but, on the other hand, the bankruptcy of democracies, their collapse, their painless transformation into reactionary dictatorships compel the workers to pose before themselves the problem of power, render them responsive to the posing of the problem of power.

Reaction wields today such power as perhaps never before in the modern history of mankind. But it would be an inexcusable blunder to see only reaction. The historical process is a contradictory one. Under the cover of official reaction profound processes are taking place among the masses who are accumulating experience and are becoming receptive to new political perspectives. The old conservative tradition of the democratic state which was so powerful even during the era of the last imperialist war exists today only as an extremely unstable survival. On the eve of the last war the European workers had numerically powerful parties. But on the order of the day were put reforms, partial conquests, and not at all the conquest of power.

The American working class is still without a mass labor party even today. But the objective situation and the experience accumulated by the American workers can pose within a very brief period of time on the order of the day the question of the conquest of power. This perspective must be made the basis of our agitation. It is not merely a question of a position on capitalist militarism and of renouncing the defense of the bourgeois state but of directly preparing for the conquest of power and the defense of the proletarian fatherland.

May not the Stalinists turn out at the head of a new revolutionary upsurge and may they not ruin the revolution as they did in Spain and previously in China? It is of course impermissible to consider that such a possibility is excluded, for example in France. The first wave of the revolution has often, or more correctly, always carried to the top those "left" parties which have not managed to discredit themselves completely in the preceding period and which have an imposing political tradition behind them. Thus the February revolution raised up the Mensheviks, the S. R.'s who were the opponents of the revolution on its very eve. Thus the German revolution in November 1918 raised to power the social democrats who were the irreconcilable opponents of revolutionary uprisings. . . .

THE NEWEST CROP OF PHILISTINES

Most of the philistines of the newest crop base their attacks on Marxism on the fact that contrary to Marx's prognosis fascism came instead of socialism. Nothing is more stupid and vulgar than this criticism. Marx demonstrated and proved that when capitalism reaches a certain level the only way out for society lies in the socialization of the means of production, i.e., socialism. He also demonstrated that in view of the class structure of society the proletariat alone is capable of solving this task in an irreconcilable revolutionary struggle against the bourgeoisie. He further demonstrated that for the fulfillment of this task the proletariat needs a revolutionary party. All his life Marx, and together with him and after him Engels, and after them Lenin, waged an irreconcilable struggle against those traits in proletarian parties, socialist parties which obstructed the solution of the revolutionary historical task. The irreconcilability of the struggle waged by Marx, Engels, and Lenin against opportunism, on the one side, and anarchism, on the other, demonstrates that they did not at all underestimate this danger. In what did it consist? In this, that the opportunism of the summits of the working class, subject to the bourgeoisie's influence, could obstruct, slow down, make more difficult, postpone the fulfillment of the revolutionary task of the proletariat. It is precisely this condition of society that we are now observing. Fascism did not at all come "instead" of socialism. Fascism is the continuation of capitalism, an attempt to perpetuate its existence by means of the most bestial and monstrous measures. Capitalism obtained an opportunity to resort to fascism only because the proletariat did not accomplish the socialist revolution in time. The proletariat was paralyzed in the fulfillment of its task by the opportunist parties. The only thing that can be said is that there turned out to be more obstacles, more difficulties, more stages on the road of the revolutionary development of the proletariat than was foreseen by the founders of scientific socialism. Fascism and the series of imperialist wars constitute the terrible school in which the proletariat has to free itself of petty bourgeois traditions and superstitions, has to rid itself of opportunist, democratic, and adventurist parties, has to hammer out and train the revolutionary vanguard and in this way prepare for the solving of the task apart from which there is not, and cannot be, any salvation for the development of mankind.

Eastman, if you please, has come to the conclusion that the concentration of the means of production in the hands of the state endangers his "freedom" and he has therefore decided to renounce socialism. This anecdote deserves being included in the text of a history of ideology. The socialization of the means of production is the only solution to the economic problem at the given stage of mankind's development. The delay in solving this problem leads to the barbarism of fascism. All the intermediate solutions undertaken by the bourgeoisie with the help of the petty bourgeoisie have suffered a miserable and shameful fiasco. All this is absolutely uninteresting to Eastman. He noticed that his "freedom" (freedom of muddling, freedom of indifferentism, freedom of passivity, freedom of literary dilettantism) was being threatened from various sides, and he decided immediately to apply his own measure: renounce socialism. Astonishingly enough this decision exercised no influence either on Wall Street or on the policy of the trade unions. Life went its own way just as if Max Eastman had remained a socialist. It may be set down as a general rule that the more impotent is a petty bourgeois radical especially in the United States the more.

FASCISM HAS NOT CONQUERED IN FRANCE

In France there is no fascism in the real sense of the term. The regime of the senile Marshal Pétain represents a senile form of Bonapartism of the epoch of imperialist decline. But this regime too proved possible only after the prolonged radicalization of the French working class, which led to the explosion of June 1936, had failed to find a revolutionary way out. The Second and Third Internationals, the reactionary charlatanism of the "People's Fronts" deceived and demoralized the working class. After five years of propaganda in favor of an alliance of democracies and of collective security, after Stalin's sudden passage into Hitler's camp, the French working class proved caught unaware. The war provoked a terrible disorientation and the mood of passive defeatism, or to put it more correctly, the indifferentism of an impasse. From this web of circumstances arose first the unprecedented military catastrophe and then the despicable Pétain regime.

Precisely because Pétain's regime is senile Bonapartism, it contains no element of stability and can be overthrown by a revolutionary mass uprising much sooner than a fascist regime.

ESPECIALLY IMPORTANT TO U.S. WORKERS

In every discussion of political topics the question invariably flares up: Shall we succeed in creating a strong party for the moment when the crisis comes? Might not fascism anticipate us? Isn't a fascist stage of development inevitable? The successes of fascism easily make people lose all perspective, lead them to forget the actual conditions which made the strengthening and the victory of fascism possible. Yet a clear understanding of these conditions is of special importance to the workers of the United States. We may set it down as an historical law: Fascism was able to conquer only in those countries where the conservative labor parties prevented the proletariat from utilizing the revolutionary situation and seizing power. In Germany two revolutionary situations were involved: 1918–1919 and 1923–1924. Even in 1929 a direct struggle for power on the part of the proletariat was still possible. In all these three cases the social democracy and the Comintern criminally and viciously disrupted the conquest of power and thereby placed society in an impasse. Only under these conditions and in this situation did the stormy rise of fascism and its gaining of power prove possible.

THE FUTURE OF SECULAR RELIGIONS

RAYMOND ARON

It is more than half a century since Friedrich Nietzsche uttered the famous phrase on which our present ordeals are a diabolical comment: "God is dead; anything goes."

The spiritual conflicts of our own day attack men's souls more deeply than any of those that have divided Europe since the Renaissance. It is not enough to say that spiritual unity no longer exists: It has become inconceivable. Christian churches have congregations of millions, but the greatest crises of conscience, including the present one, take place outside the sphere of traditional belief. The Christians in Germany have fought for their Führer without their pastors telling them, or even dreaming of telling them, that they were fighting in the unjust cause of conquest by the sword. Moreover, Nietzsche's inversion of values has been morally accepted and put into practice by millions of people. Despite their different origins, secular morality and the catechism have joined together to form spiritual families akin to one another in their very opposition. The young barbarians trained by Hitler belong

Raymond Aron is often considered the leading French liberal intellectual of the twentieth century. This piece, written in 1944 during his days as an editor and writer for the French resistance journal *La France libre*, shows Aron defending the view that fascism and communism proved so powerful because they served as secular substitutes for traditional religious beliefs and practices.

to another universe. Can we be sure they will ever be eradicated? What miracle could ever restore peace between them and us?

It is true that men can live without believing in an afterlife. For century upon century, the peasants of every civilization have plowed the earth, bent under the yoke of seasons and myths. How many lives, even today, fail to rise above the unconsciously accepted tradition! How many people are fulfilled, without being driven by atheism into a sense of deprivation and failure! But there are also souls to whom the good news has given a hunger that nothing can satisfy except a plenitude comparable to that which was promised. And even if man can manage to live without expecting anything from God, it is doubtful whether he can live without hope. But there are millions of people, imprisoned in dreary jobs, lost in the multitude of cities, who have no other share in a spiritual community but what is offered them by the secular religions. The crowds who acclaim false prophets bear witness to the intensity of the aspirations mounting to an empty heaven. As Bernanos has said, the tragedy is not that Hitler proclaims or takes himself for a god, but that millions of people are desperate enough to believe him. Any crisis, whether economic or political, that severs the multitudes from their roots will deliver them yet again to the combined temptations of despair and enthusiasm.

At the same time, the secular religions do offer a substitute system of unification. Surprisingly, scientists sometimes discover, as if touched by grace, the virtues of even a watered-down Marxism. Here again it is a matter of an unmet need. When knowledge accumulates ceaselessly but at random, it increases the desire for a system. Charles Maurras owed his prestige largely to the fact that every morning he added some other example or detail to his doctrine as a whole. Whatever one thinks of Marxist materialism, it is certainly better than the ordinary materialism that served as a philosophy for the physicist before he or she was converted. Even Nazi racism supplies a kind of principle on which to base some sort of philosophy of human existence.

It might be said that these spiritual needs are in a sense created by those who exploit them for their own advantage. But there are times and situations when secular religions seem to fill an abyss into which society might otherwise fall. In short, they introduce a supreme principle of authority when all the others are collapsing.

Today's fashionable formula, according to which the world, in the absence of legitimate powers, is given over to fear and violence, does no more than state a fact. If there is to be social stability, men must agree to obey and recognize that their superiors have the right to command. The reasons for obedience vary according to history and circumstance. Sometimes they are to be found in the depths of the past, in the collective unconscious, inherited from ancient custom; sometimes they are rational and self-evident in terms of a particular technique or function (performed in any given instance by a merely temporary incumbent); sometimes, as in an ideal army, the two kinds of reason coexist and reinforce one another.

Nowadays the traditional legitimacy that sustained monarchies and aristocracies is becoming extinct. In addition, the constitutional forms in which the idea of democratic legitimacy was embodied have lost some of their former prestige. The moral and political ideas that guaranteed them have been undermined by the criticism of counterrevolutionary thinkers and the lessons taught by events. The pessimism of mass psychology has repressed the optimistic notion of a general will. How can we believe that truth or the common good could emerge from free discussion when everywhere we see passions unleashed against one another? Moreover, the mechanisms of democracy have been degraded by the uses to which they have been put, and by the way authoritarian parties have caricatured them. National Socialism gained absolute power by means of repeated elections. Where is the dividing line between plebiscite and election, between votes that are genuine and votes that are rigged?

In France, even before the war, one was struck by the way discipline inside an organization like the Communist Party was much better than that among ordinary citizens or even in the army. Officials at all levels were called *responsables*, reflecting the notion, not confined to the military, that whoever gives orders is the one who assumes responsibility. And the *responsables*, conscious of their position, had no difficulty in winning the trust of the activists. There was none of the ill-humor and continual suspicion that Alain recommended toward all wielders of power, and that the French readily manifest toward their rulers.

Since 1940 we French have been through the tragic experience of seeing first the disintegration and then the restoration of our state. When France collapsed under the shock of Hitler's war machine, when the armistice left us with a government that was "half-prisoner," whose words and decisions might at any moment betray the country and serve the enemy, people clung on all sides to flags, standards, and standard-bearers. One saw the most extreme reactions. Some people, in despair because of their love for their country, became suspicious of everything and everybody and no longer believed in or obeyed anything but their consciences. Others, though often motivated by the same fundamental feelings, obeyed all the more implicitly the orders of their superiors because their authority was so flimsy they feared a social vacuum. Here and there some practically isolated pockets of traditional order survived. For a few months, as Spengler prophesied, armies were known by the names of their generals, as if the ultimate loyalty, amid the collapse of all other values, was fidelity to one person. This phenomenon is more natural than may appear. The "depersonalization" of the state comes about at the end of a long process of evolution: Before a state can be recreated it has to pass once again through the original stage, when power was embodied in one man.

The situations we have just been examining, where a regime is based on the ascendancy of a secular religion, on the fraternity between followers of the same cult, and on the prestige of one man, seem to be poles apart from one another. Prestige is something mysterious and incommunicable, linked to the very being of a leader and to the distance that exists or is artificially created between that leader and his fellow men. It does not in itself offer a rational or even a pseudo-rational justification for the doctrine he espouses. The fact is that in our day and age the adventurers brought to power by popular acclamation reinforce their assumed dignity by the myths they claim to fulfill. Though they derive their authority neither from God nor from history, they never rule in their own name, but always by virtue of a "mission."

Men are tired of obeying "officials" and an authority without a face or a name: In reaction to the anonymity of rational organizations, heroes suddenly emerge. Men are weary of submitting to an order that they do not understand and that, in the absence of any moral inspiration, degenerates into force or inevitability. The hope of salvation can transfigure that order by giving it a spiritual significance. The two kinds of aspiration tend to merge: Collective beliefs generate prophets, and Caesars invent their own religions. Even if all images of an earthly paradise vanished, the primal belief in a man of destiny would remain. When their empire was in decline, the Romans made their emperors into gods.

THE SEEDS OF A FASCIST INTERNATIONAL

HANNAH ARENDT

It was always a too little noted hallmark of fascist propaganda that it was not satisfied with lying but deliberately proposed to transform its lies into reality. Thus, *Das Schwarze Korps** conceded several years before the outbreak of the war that people abroad did not completely believe the Nazi contention that all Jews are homeless beggars who can only subsist as parasites in the economic organism of other nations; but foreign public opinion, they prophesied, would in a few years be given the opportunity to convince itself of this fact when the German Jews would be driven out across the borders like a pack of beggars. For such a fabrication of a lying reality no one was prepared. The essential characteristic of fascist propaganda was never its lies, for this is something more or less common to propaganda everywhere and of every time. The essential thing was that they exploited the age-old Occidental prejudice which confuses reality with truth, and made that "true" which until then could only be stated as a lie. It is for this reason that any argumentation with fascists—the so-called counter-propaganda—is so extremely senseless: it is as though one were to debate with a potential murderer as to whether

---

* A Nazi publication. —Arendt's posthumous ed.

Hannah Arendt was a leading mid-twentieth-century political philosopher who is most well known for her studies on the nature and origins of totalitarian regimes. In this piece from 1945, she explains the essential nature of Nazi propaganda and how it transforms lies into realities.

his future victim were dead or alive, completely forgetting that man can kill and that the murderer, by killing the person in question, could promptly provide proof of the correctness of this statement.

This was the spirit in which the Nazis destroyed Germany—in order to be proved in the right: an asset which may be of the greatest value for their future activity. They destroyed Germany to show that they were right when they said the German people were fighting for its very existence; which was, at the outset, a pure lie. They instituted chaos in order to show that they were right when they said that Europe had only the alternative between Nazi rule and chaos. They dragged out the war until the Russians actually stood at the Elbe and the Adriatic so as to give their lies about the danger of Bolshevism a *post facto* basis in reality. They hope of course, that in a short time, when the peoples of the world really comprehend the magnitude of the European catastrophe, their politics will be proved completely justified.

If National Socialism were really in essence a German national movement—like, for instance, Italian fascism in its first decade—it would gain little by such proofs and arguments. In that case success alone would be decisive, and their failure as a national movement has been overwhelming. The Nazis themselves know this very well, and therefore several months ago they retired from the governmental apparatus, separated the party from the state once again, thereby relieving themselves of all those nationalistic chauvinist elements who joined them partly for opportunistic reasons, partly out of a misunderstanding. The Nazis also know, however, that even if the Allies should be so foolish as to implicate themselves with new Darlans, the influence of these groups would remain unavailing simply because the German nation itself no longer existed.

Actually, the National Socialist Party, since the end of the 1920s, was no longer a purely German party, but an international organization with its headquarters in Germany. Through the outcome of the war it has lost its strategic base and the operational facilities of a particular state machinery. This loss of a national center is not exclusively disadvantageous for the continuation of the fascist International. Freed of every national tie and the inevitable extraneous concerns connected therewith, the Nazis can try once more in the postwar era to organize as that true and undiluted secret society dispersed all over the world which has always been the pattern of organization toward which they have striven.

The factual existence of a Communist International, growing in power, will be of great assistance to them. They have been arguing for a long time (for months past their propaganda has been based exclusively upon this) that this is nothing other than the Jewish global conspiracy of the Elders of Zion. There will be many whom they can convince that this global menace can be met only by organizing in the same manner. The danger of such a development will become greater to the extent that the democracies continue to operate with purely national conceptions, renouncing any ideological strategy of war and peace and thereby giving rise to the impression that, in contrast to the ideological Internationals, they stand only for the immediate interests of particular peoples.

In this enterprise, far more dangerous than a mere underground movement of purely German character, fascism will find highly useful the racist ideology which in the past was developed only by National Socialism. It is already becoming obvious that colonial problems will remain unsolved, and that, as a result, the conflicts between white and colored peoples, i.e., the so-called racial conflicts, will become even more acute. Furthermore, competition between the imperialistic nations will remain a feature of the international scene. In this context the fascists, who even in their German version never identified the master race with any nationality but spoke of "Aryans" generally, could easily make themselves the protagonists of a unified White Supremacy strategy capable of out-bidding any group not unconditionally advocating equal rights for all peoples.

Anti-Jewish propaganda will surely remain one of the most important points of attraction for fascism. The terrible losses of the Jews in Europe have made us lose sight of another aspect of the situation: though numerically weakened, the Jewish people will emerge from the war far more widely dispersed geographically than before. In contrast to the pre-1933 era, there is hardly a spot on earth any longer where Jews do not live, in larger or smaller number, but always watched more or less distrustfully by the non-Jewish environment.

As the counterpart of an Aryan fascist International, the Jews, conceived as the ethnic representative of the Communist International, are today perhaps even more useful than before. This is particularly true for South America whose strong fascist movements are sufficiently well known.

The opportunities in Europe itself for a fascist International organization not bound by problems of state and territory are even greater. The so-called refugee population, product of the revolutions and wars of the last two decades, is growing daily in number. Driven from territories to which they are unwilling or unable to return, these victims of our time have already established themselves as national splinter groups in all European countries. Restoration of the European national system means for them a rightlessness compared to which the proletarians of the nineteenth century had a privileged status. They might have become the true vanguard of a European movement—and many of them, indeed, were prominent in the Resistance; but they can easily fall prey, also, to other ideologies if appealed to in international terms. The 250,000 Polish soldiers, who are offered no other solution than the precarious status of mercenaries under British command for the occupation of Germany, are clearly a case in point.

Even without these relatively new problems, "restoration" would be extremely dangerous. Yet in all areas not under immediate Russian influence, the forces of yesterday have placed themselves in the saddle, more or less undisturbed. This restoration, proceeding with the aid of intensified nationalist chauvinist propaganda, particularly in France, is in sharp opposition to the tendencies and aspirations begotten by the resistance movements, which were genuinely European movements. These aspirations are not forgotten, even though for a time they have been forced into the background by the release of liberation and the misery of day-to-day living. At the beginning of the war it was obvious to any student of European conditions, including the numerous American correspondents, that no people in Europe was any longer prepared to go to war over national conflicts. The resurrection of territorial disputes may vouchsafe the victorious governments brief triumphs of prestige and give the impression that the European nationalism of old, which alone could offer a secure foundation for a restoration, has come back to life. It will soon become apparent, however, that all this is merely a short-lived bluff from which the nations will turn with fanaticism redoubled by their embitterment to those ideologies which can propose purportedly international solutions, that is to fascism and to communism.

Under these conditions it may prove an advantage to the Nazis to be able to operate all over Europe at once, without having to be bound to a particular country and rely upon a particular government. No longer concerned with the weal or woe of one nation, they might all the more quickly assume the appearance of a genuine European movement. There is the danger that Nazism might pose successfully as the heir of the European resistance movement, taking over from them the slogan of a European federation and exploiting it for its own purposes. One should not forget that even when it was unmistakably clear that it would mean merely a Europe ruled by Germans, the slogan of a United Europe proved to be the Nazis' most successful propaganda weapon. It will hardly lose its power in an impoverished postwar Europe, rent by nationalistic governments.

These are, in general, the perils of tomorrow. Unquestionably, fascism has been once defeated, but we are far from having completely eradicated this arch-evil of our time. For its roots are strong and they are called—Anti-Semitism, Racism, Imperialism.

POLITICAL PRISONERS, PRISONS, AND BLACK LIBERATION

ANGELA DAVIS

Despite a long history of exalted appeals to man's inherent right of resistance, there has seldom been agreement on how to relate *in practice* to unjust, immoral laws and the oppressive social order from which they emanate. The conservative, who does not dispute the validity of revolutions deeply buried in history, invokes visions of impending anarchy in order to legitimize his demand for absolute obedience. Law and order, with the major emphasis on order, is his watchword. The liberal articulates his sensitiveness to certain of society's intolerable details, but will almost never prescribe methods of resistance which exceed the limits of legality—redress through electoral channels is the liberal's panacea.

In the heat of our pursuit for fundamental human rights, Black people have been continually cautioned to be patient. We are advised that as long as we remain faithful to the *existing* democratic order, the glorious moment will eventually arrive when we will come into our own as full-fledged human beings.

But having been taught by bitter experience, we know that there is

Angela Davis is a noted American Marxist and activist who wrote this piece while in jail in May 1971. The essay argues that a kind of "preventive fascism" had infused the American judicial system as demonstrated by its disproportionate imprisonment of African Americans.

a glaring incongruity between democracy and the capitalist economy which is the source of our ills. Regardless of all rhetoric to the contrary, the people are not the ultimate matrix of the laws and the system which govern them—certainly not Black people and other nationally oppressed people, but not even the mass of whites. The people do not exercise decisive control over the determining factors of their lives.

Official assertions that meaningful dissent is always welcome, provided it falls within the boundaries of legality, are frequently a smokescreen obscuring the invitation to acquiesce in oppression. Slavery may have been unrighteous, the constitutional provision for the enslavement of Blacks may have been unjust, but conditions were not to be considered so unbearable (especially since they were profitable to a small circle) as to justify escape and other acts proscribed by law. This was the import of the fugitive slave laws.

Needless to say, the history of the United States has been marred from its inception by an enormous quantity of unjust laws, far too many expressly bolstering the oppression of Black people. Particularized reflections of existing social inequities, these laws have repeatedly borne witness to the exploitative and racist core of the society itself. For Blacks, Chicanos, for all nationally oppressed people, the problem of opposing unjust laws and the social conditions which nourish their growth, has always had immediate practical implications. Our very survival has frequently been a direct function of our skill in forging effective channels of resistance. In resisting, we have sometimes been compelled to openly violate those laws which directly or indirectly buttress our oppression. But even when containing our resistance within the orbit of legality, we have been labeled criminals and have been methodically persecuted by a racist legal apparatus. . . .

———————

THE OCCURRENCE OF crime is inevitable in a society in which wealth is unequally distributed, as one of the constant reminders that society's productive forces are being channeled in the wrong direction. The majority of criminal offenses bear a direct relationship to property.

Contained in the very concept of property crimes are profound but suppressed social needs which express themselves in antisocial modes of action. Spontaneously produced by a capitalist organization of society, this type of crime is at once a protest against society and a desire to partake of its exploitative content. It challenges the symptoms of capitalism, but not its essence.

Some Marxists in recent years have tended to banish "criminals" and the lumpenproletariat as a whole from the arena of revolutionary struggle. Apart from the absence of any link binding the criminal to the means of production, underlying this exclusion has been the assumption that individuals who have recourse to antisocial acts are incapable of developing the discipline and collective orientation required by revolutionary struggle.

With the declassed character of lumpenproletarians in mind, Marx had stated that they are as capable of "the most heroic deeds and the most exalted sacrifices, as of the basest banditry and the dirtiest corruption." He emphasized the fact that the Provisional Government's Mobile Guards under the Paris Commune—some 24,000 troops—were largely formed out of young lumpenproletarians from fifteen to twenty years of age. Too many Marxists have been inclined to overvalue the second part of Marx's observation—that the lumpenproletariat is capable of the basest banditry and the dirtiest corruption—while minimizing or indeed totally disregarding his first remark, applauding the lumpen for their heroic deeds and exalted sacrifices.

Especially today when so many Black, Chicano, and Puerto Rican men and women are jobless as a consequence of the internal dynamic of the capitalist system, the role of the unemployed, which includes the lumpenproletariat, in revolutionary struggle must be given serious thought. Increased unemployment, particularly for the nationally oppressed, will continue to be an inevitable by-product of technological development. At least 30 percent of Black youth are presently without jobs. In the context of class exploitation and national oppression, it should be clear that numerous individuals are compelled to resort to criminal acts, not as a result of conscious choice—implying other alternatives—but because society has objectively reduced their possibilities of subsistence and survival to this level. This recognition should signal the urgent need to organize the unemployed and lumpenproletariat, as indeed the Black Panther Party as well as activists in prison have already begun to do.

In evaluating the susceptibility of the Black and Brown unemployed to organizing efforts, the peculiar historical features of the United States, specifically racism and national oppression, must be taken into account. There already exists in the Black and Brown communities, the lumpenproletariat included, a long tradition of collective resistance to national oppression. . . .

RACIST OPPRESSION invades the lives of Black people on an infinite variety of levels. Blacks are imprisoned in a world where our labor and toil hardly allow us to eke out a decent existence, if we are able to find jobs at all. When the economy begins to falter, we are forever the first victims, always the most deeply wounded. When the economy is on its feet, we continue to live in a depressed state. Unemployment is generally twice as high in the ghettos as it is in the country as a whole and even higher among Black women and youth. The unemployment rate among Black youth has presently skyrocketed to 30 percent. If one-third of America's white youth were without a means of livelihood, we would either be in the thick of revolution or else under the iron rule of fascism. Substandard schools, medical care hardly fit for animals, overpriced, dilapidated housing, a welfare system based on a policy of skimpy concessions, designed to degrade and divide (and even this may soon be cancelled)—this is only the beginning of the list of props in the overall scenery of oppression which, for the mass of Blacks, is the universe.

In Black communities, wherever they are located, there exists an ever present reminder that our universe must remain stable in its drabness, its poverty, its brutality. From Birmingham to Harlem to Watts, Black ghettos are occupied, patrolled, and often attacked by massive deployments of police. The police, domestic caretakers of violence, are the oppressor's emissaries, charged with the task of containing us within the boundaries of our oppression.

The announced function of the police, "to protect and serve the people," becomes the grotesque caricature of protecting and preserving the interests of our oppressors and serving us nothing but injustice. They are there to intimidate Blacks, to persuade us with their violence that we are powerless to alter the conditions of our lives. Arrests are frequently based on whims. Bullets from their guns murder human beings with little or no pretext, aside from the universal intimidation they are charged with carrying out. . . .

———

THE VICIOUS CIRCLE linking poverty, police, courts, and prison is an integral element of ghetto existence. Unlike the mass of whites, the path which leads to jails and prisons is deeply rooted in the imposed patterns of Black existence. For this very reason, an almost instinctive affinity binds the mass of Black people to the political prisoners. The vast majority of Blacks harbors a deep hatred of the police and are not deluded by official proclamations of justice through the courts.

For the Black individual, contact with the law-enforcement-judicial-penal network, directly or through relatives and friends, is inevitable because he is Black. For the activist become political prisoner, the contact has occurred because he has lodged a protest, in one form or another, against the conditions which nail Blacks to this orbit of oppression.

Historically, Black people as a group have exhibited a greater potential for resistance than any other part of the population. The ironclad rule over our communities, the institutional practice of genocide, the ideology of racism have performed a strictly political as well as an economic function. The capitalists have not only extracted superprofits from the underpaid labor of over 15 percent of the American population with the aid of a superstructure of terror. This terror and more subtle forms of racism have further served to thwart the flowering of a resistance, even a revolution which would spread to the working class as a whole.

In the interests of the capitalist class, the consent to racism and terror has been demagogically elicited from the white population, workers included, in order to more efficiently stave off resistance. Today, Nixon, Mitchell, and J. Edgar Hoover are desperately attempting to persuade the population that dissidents, particularly Blacks, Chicanos, Puerto Ricans, must be punished for being members of revolutionary organizations; for advocating the overthrow of the government; for agitating and educating in the streets and behind prison walls. The political function of racist domination is surfacing with accelerated intensity. Whites, who have professed their solidarity with the Black liberation movement and have moved in a distinctly revolutionary direction, find themselves targets of the self-same repression. Even the antiwar movement, rapidly exhibiting an anti-imperialist consciousness, is falling victim to government repression.

Black people are rushing full speed ahead toward an understanding of the circumstances which give rise to exaggerated forms of political repression and thus an overabundance of political prisoners. This understanding is being forged out of the raw material of their own immediate experiences with racism. Hence, the Black masses are growing conscious of their responsibility to defend those who are being persecuted for attempting to bring about the alleviation of the most injurious immediate problems facing Black communities and ultimately to bring about total liberation through armed revolution, if it must come to this.

The Black liberation movement is presently at a critical juncture. Fascist methods of repression threaten to physically decapitate and obliterate the movement. More subtle, yet not less dangerous ideological tendencies from within threaten to isolate the Black movement and diminish its revolutionary impact. Both menaces must be counteracted in order to ensure our survival. Revolutionary Blacks must spearhead and provide leadership for a broad antifascist movement.

Fascism is a process, its growth and development are cancerous in nature. While today, the threat of fascism may be primarily restricted to the use of the law-enforcement-judicial-penal apparatus to arrest the overt and latent-revolutionary trends among nationally oppressed people, tomorrow it may attack the working class en masse and eventually even moderate democrats. Even in this period, however, the cancer has already commenced to spread. In addition to the prison army of thousands and thousands of nameless Third World victims of political revenge, there are increasing numbers of white political prisoners—draft resisters, antiwar activists such as the Harrisburg 8, men and women who have involved themselves on all levels of revolutionary activity.

Among the further symptoms of the fascist threat are official efforts to curtail the power of organized labor, such as the attack on the manifestly conservative construction workers and the trends toward reduced welfare aid. Moreover, court decisions and repressive legislation augmenting police powers—such as the Washington no-knock law, permitting police to enter private dwellings without warning and Nixon's "Crime Bill" in general—can eventually be used against any citizen. Indeed congressmen are already protesting the use of police-state wiretapping to survey their activities. The fascist content of the ruthless aggression in Indo-China should be self-evident.

One of the fundamental historical lessons to be learned from past failures to prevent the rise of fascism is the decisive and indispensable character of the fight against fascism in its incipient phases. Once allowed to conquer ground, its growth is facilitated in geometric proportion. Although the most unbridled expressions of the fascist menace are still tied to the racist domination of Blacks, Chicanos, Puerto Ricans, Indians, it lurks under the surface wherever there is potential resistance to the power of monopoly capital, the parasitic interests which control this society. Potentially it can profoundly worsen the conditions of existence for the average American citizen. Consequently, the masses of people in this country have a real, direct, and material stake in the struggle to free political prisoners, the struggle to abolish the prison system in its present form, the struggle against all dimensions of racism.

No one should fail to take heed of Georgi Dimitrov's warning: "Whoever does not fight the growth of fascism at these preparatory stages is not in a position to prevent the victory of fascism, but, on the contrary, facilitates that victory."[1] The only effective guarantee against the victory of fascism is an indivisible mass movement which refuses to conduct business as usual as long as repression rages on. It is only natural that Blacks and other Third World peoples must lead this movement, for we are the first and most deeply injured victims of fascism. But it must embrace all potential victims and, most important, all working-class people, for the key to the triumph of fascism is its ideological victory over the entire working class. Given the eruption of a severe economic crisis, the door to such an ideological victory can be opened by the active approval or passive toleration of racism. It is essential that white workers become conscious that historically, through their acquiescence in the capitalist-inspired oppression of Blacks, they have only rendered themselves more vulnerable to attack.

The pivotal struggle which must be waged in the ranks of the working class is consequently the open, unreserved battle against entrenched racism. The white worker must become conscious of the threads which bind him to a James Johnson, Black auto worker, member of UAW, and a political prisoner presently facing charges for the killings of two foremen and a job setter. The merciless proliferation of the power of monopoly capital may ultimately push him inexorably down the very same path of desperation. No potential victim of the fascist terror should be without the knowledge that the greatest menace to racism and fascism is unity!

UR-FASCISM

UMBERTO ECO

In 1942, at the age of ten, I received the First Provincial Award of Ludi Juveniles (a voluntary, compulsory competition for young Italian Fascists—that is, for every young Italian). I elaborated with rhetorical skill on the subject "Should we die for the glory of Mussolini and the immortal destiny of Italy?" My answer was positive. I was a smart boy.

I spent two of my early years among the SS, Fascists, Republicans, and partisans shooting at one another, and I learned how to dodge bullets. It was good exercise.

In April 1945, the partisans took over in Milan. Two days later they arrived in the small town where I was living at the time. It was a moment of joy. The main square was crowded with people singing and waving flags, calling in loud voices for Mimo, the partisan leader of that area. A former *maresciallo* of the carabinieri, Mimo joined the supporters of General Badoglio, Mussolini's successor, and lost a leg during one of the first clashes with Mussolini's remaining forces. Mimo showed up on the balcony of the city hall, pale, leaning on his crutch, and with one hand tried to calm the crowd. I was waiting for his speech because my whole childhood had been marked by the great historic speeches of Mussolini,

Umberto Eco was an Italian medievalist, philosopher, novelist, and political commentator. In this 1995 piece, Eco explains his own firsthand experience with Italian fascism as a boy, and provides an account of what he sees as the "typical features" of fascism.

whose most significant passages we memorized in school. Silence. Mimo spoke in a hoarse voice, barely audible. He said: "Citizens, friends. After so many painful sacrifices . . . here we are. Glory to those who have fallen for freedom." And that was it. He went back inside. The crowd yelled, the partisans raised their guns and fired festive volleys. We kids hurried to pick up the shells, precious items, but I had also learned that freedom of speech means freedom from rhetoric.

A few days later I saw the first American soldiers. They were African Americans. The first Yankee I met was a Black man, Joseph, who introduced me to the marvels of Dick Tracy and Li'l Abner. His comic books were brightly colored and smelled good.

One of the officers (Major or Captain Muddy) was a guest in the villa of a family whose two daughters were my schoolmates. I met him in their garden where some ladies, surrounding Captain Muddy, talked in tentative French. Captain Muddy knew some French, too. My first image of American liberators was thus—after so many palefaces in black shirts—that of a cultivated Black man in a yellow-green uniform saying: "*Oui, merci beaucoup, Madame, moi aussi j'aime le champagne. . . .*" Unfortunately there was no champagne, but Captain Muddy gave me my first piece of Wrigley's Spearmint and I started chewing all day long. At night I put my wad in a water glass, so it would be fresh for the next day.

In May we heard that the war was over. Peace gave me a curious sensation. I had been told that permanent warfare was the normal condition for a young Italian. In the following months I discovered that the Resistance was not only a local phenomenon but a European one. I learned new, exciting words like *réseau, maquis, armée secrète, Rote Kapelle*, "Warsaw ghetto." I saw the first photographs of the Holocaust, thus understanding the meaning before knowing the word. I realized what we were liberated from.

In my country today there are people who are wondering if the Resistance had a real military impact on the course of the war. For my generation this question is irrelevant: we immediately understood the moral and psychological meaning of the Resistance. For us it was a point of pride to know that we Europeans did not wait passively for liberation. And for the young Americans who were paying with their blood for our restored freedom it meant something to know that behind the firing lines there were Europeans paying their own debt in advance.

In my country today there are those who are saying that the myth of the Resistance was a Communist lie. It is true that the Communists exploited the Resistance as if it were their personal property, since they played a prime role in it; but I remember partisans with kerchiefs of different colors. Sticking close to the radio, I spent my nights—the windows closed, the blackout making the small space around the set a lone luminous halo—listening to the messages sent by the Voice of London to the partisans. They were cryptic and poetic at the same time (*The sun also rises, the roses will bloom*) and most of them were "*messaggi per la Franchi*." Somebody whispered to me that Franchi was the leader of the most powerful clandestine network in northwestern Italy, a man of legendary courage. Franchi became my hero. Franchi (whose real name was Edgardo Sogno) was a monarchist, so strongly anti-Communist that after the war he joined very right-wing groups, and was charged with collaborating in a project for a reactionary coup d'état. Who cares? Sogno still remains the dream hero of my childhood. Liberation was a common deed for people of different colors.

In my country today there are some who say that the War of Liberation was a tragic period of division, and that all we need is national reconciliation. The memory of those terrible years should be repressed, *refoulée, verdrängt*. But *Verdrängung* causes neurosis. If reconciliation means compassion and respect for all those who fought their own war in good faith, to forgive does not mean to forget. I can even admit that Eichmann sincerely believed in his mission, but I cannot say, "OK, come back and do it again." We are here to remember what happened and solemnly say that "They" must not do it again.

But who are They?

If we still think of the totalitarian governments that ruled Europe before the Second World War we can easily say that it would be difficult for them to reappear in the same form in different historical circumstances. If Mussolini's fascism was based upon the idea of a charismatic ruler, on corporatism, on the utopia of the Imperial Fate of Rome, on an imperialistic will to conquer new territories, on an exacerbated nationalism, on the ideal of an entire nation regimented in black shirts, on the rejection of parliamentary democracy, on anti-Semitism, then I have no difficulty in acknowledging that today the Italian Alleanza Nazionale, born from the postwar Fascist Party, MSI, and certainly a right-wing party, has by now very little to do with the old fascism. In the same vein, even though I am much concerned about the various Nazi-like movements that have arisen here and there in Europe, including Russia, I do not think that Nazism, in its original form, is about to reappear as a nationwide movement.

Nevertheless, even though political regimes can be overthrown, and ideologies can be criticized and disowned, behind a regime and its ideology there is always a way of thinking and feeling, a group of cultural habits, of obscure instincts and unfathomable drives. Is there still another ghost stalking Europe (not to speak of other parts of the world)?

Ionesco once said that "only words count and the rest is mere chattering." Linguistic habits are frequently important symptoms of underlying feelings. Thus it is worth asking why not only the Resistance but the Second World War was generally defined throughout the world as a struggle against fascism. If you reread Hemingway's *For Whom the Bell Tolls* you will discover that Robert Jordan identifies his enemies with Fascists, even when he thinks of the Spanish Falangists. And for FDR, "The victory of the American people and their allies will be a victory against fascism and the dead hand of despotism it represents."

During World War II, the Americans who took part in the Spanish war were called "premature anti-fascists"—meaning that fighting against Hitler in the forties was a moral duty for every good American, but fighting against Franco too early, in the thirties, smelled sour because it was mainly done by Communists and other leftists. . . . Why was an expression like *fascist pig* used by American radicals thirty years later to refer to a cop who did not approve of their smoking habits? Why didn't they say: *Cagoulard pig, Falangist pig, Ustashe pig, Quisling pig, Nazi pig*?

Mein Kampf is a manifesto of a complete political program. Nazism had a theory of racism and of the Aryan chosen people, a precise notion of degenerate art, *entartete Kunst*, a philosophy of the will to power and of the *Ubermensch*. Nazism was decidedly anti-Christian and neo-pagan, while Stalin's *Diamat* (the official version of Soviet Marxism) was blatantly materialistic and atheistic. If by totalitarianism one means a regime that subordinates every act of the individual to the state and to its ideology, then both Nazism and Stalinism were true totalitarian regimes.

Italian fascism was certainly a dictatorship, but it was not totally totalitarian, not because of its mildness but rather because of the philosophical weakness of its ideology. Contrary to common opinion, fascism in Italy had no special philosophy. The article on fascism signed by Mussolini in the *Enciclopedia Treccani* was written or basically inspired by Giovanni Gentile, but it reflected a late-Hegelian notion of the Absolute and Ethical State which was never fully realized by Mussolini. Mussolini did not have any philosophy: he had only rhetoric. He was a militant atheist at the beginning and later signed the Convention with the Church and welcomed the bishops who blessed the Fascist pennants. In his early anticlerical years, according to a likely legend, he once asked God, in order to prove His existence, to strike him down on the spot. Later, Mussolini always cited the name of God in his speeches, and did not mind being called the Man of Providence.

Italian fascism was the first right-wing dictatorship that took over a European country, and all similar movements later found a sort of archetype in Mussolini's regime. Italian fascism was the first to establish a military liturgy, a folklore, even a way of dressing—far more influential, with its black shirts, than Armani, Benetton, or Versace would ever be. It was only in the thirties that fascist movements appeared, with Mosley, in Great Britain, and in Latvia, Estonia, Lithuania, Poland, Hungary, Romania, Bulgaria, Greece, Yugoslavia, Spain, Portugal, Norway, and even in South America. It was Italian fascism that convinced many European liberal leaders that the new regime was carrying out interesting social reform, and that it was providing a mildly revolutionary alternative to the Communist threat.

Nevertheless, historical priority does not seem to me a sufficient reason to explain why the word "fascism" became a synecdoche, that is, a word that could be used for different totalitarian movements. This is not because fascism contained in itself, so to speak in their quintessential state, all the elements of any later form of totalitarianism. On the contrary, fascism had no quintessence. Fascism was a *fuzzy* totalitarianism, a collage of different philosophical and political ideas, a beehive of contradictions. Can one conceive of a truly totalitarian movement that was able to combine monarchy with revolution, the Royal Army with Mussolini's personal *milizia*, the grant of privileges to the Church with state education extolling violence, absolute state control with a free market? The Fascist Party was born boasting that it brought a revolutionary new order; but it was financed by the most conservative among the landowners who expected from it a counterrevolution. At its beginning fascism was republican. Yet it survived for twenty years proclaiming its loyalty to the royal family, while the Duce (the unchallenged Maximal Leader) was arm in arm with the king, to whom he also offered the title of emperor. But when the king fired Mussolini in 1943, the party reappeared two months later, with German support, under the standard of a "social" republic, recycling its old revolutionary script, now enriched with almost Jacobin overtones.

There was only a single Nazi architecture and a single Nazi art. If the Nazi architect was Albert Speer, there was no more room for Mies van der Rohe. Similarly, under Stalin's rule, if Lamarck was right there was no room for Darwin. In Italy there were certainly Fascist architects but close to their pseudo-Colosseums were many new buildings inspired by the modern rationalism of Gropius.

There was no fascist Zhdanov setting a strictly cultural line. In Italy there were two important art awards. The Premio Cremona was controlled by a fanatical and uncultivated Fascist, Roberto Farinacci, who encouraged art as propaganda. (I can remember paintings with such titles as *Listening by Radio to the Duce's Speech* or *States of Mind Created by Fascism*.) The Premio Bergamo was sponsored by the cultivated and reasonably tolerant Fascist Giuseppe Bottai, who protected both the concept of art for art's sake and the many kinds of avant-garde art that had been banned as corrupt and crypto-Communist in Germany.

The national poet was D'Annunzio, a dandy who in Germany or in Russia would have been sent to the firing squad. He was appointed as the bard of the regime because of his nationalism and his cult of heroism—which were in fact abundantly mixed up with influences of French *fin de siècle* decadence.

Take Futurism. One might think it would have been considered an instance of *entartete Kunst*, along with Expressionism, Cubism, and Surrealism. But the early Italian Futurists were nationalist; they favored Italian participation in the First World War for aesthetic reasons; they celebrated speed, violence, and risk, all of which somehow seemed to connect with the Fascist cult of youth. While fascism identified itself with the Roman Empire and rediscovered rural traditions, Marinetti (who proclaimed that a car was more beautiful than the *Winged Victory of Samothrace*, and wanted to kill even the moonlight) was nevertheless appointed as a member of the Italian Academy, which treated moonlight with great respect.

Many of the future partisans and of the future intellectuals of the Communist Party were educated by the GUF, the Fascist university students' association, which was supposed to be the cradle of the new Fascist culture. These clubs became a sort of intellectual melting pot where new ideas circulated without any real ideological control. It was not that the men of the party were tolerant of radical thinking, but few of them had the intellectual equipment to control it.

During those twenty years, the poetry of Montale and other writers associated with the group called the Ermetici was a reaction to the bombastic style of the regime, and these poets were allowed to develop their literary protest from within what was seen as their ivory tower. The mood of the Ermetici poets was exactly the reverse of the Fascist cult of optimism and heroism. The regime tolerated their blatant, even though socially imperceptible, dissent because the Fascists simply did not pay attention to such arcane language.

All this does not mean that Italian fascism was tolerant. Gramsci was put in prison until his death; the opposition leaders Giacomo Matteotti and the brothers Rosselli were assassinated; the free press was abolished, the labor unions were dismantled, and political dissenters were confined on remote islands. Legislative power became a mere fiction and the executive power (which controlled the judiciary as well as the mass media) directly issued new laws, among them laws calling for preservation of the race (the formal Italian gesture of support for what became the Holocaust).

The contradictory picture I describe was not the result of tolerance but of political and ideological discombobulation. But it was a rigid discombobulation, a structured confusion. Fascism was philosophically out of joint, but emotionally it was firmly fastened to some archetypal foundations.

So we come to my second point. There was only one Nazism. We cannot label Franco's hyper-Catholic Falangism as Nazism, since Nazism is fundamentally pagan, polytheistic, and anti-Christian. But the fascist game can be played in many forms, and the name of the game does not change. The notion of fascism is not unlike Wittgenstein's notion of a game. A game can be either competitive or not, it can require some special skill or none, it can or cannot involve money. Games are different activities that display only some "family resemblance," as Wittgenstein put it. Consider the following sequence:

1	*2*	*3*	*4*
abc	bcd	cde	def

Suppose there is a series of political groups in which group 1 is characterized by the features *abc*, group 2 by the features *bcd*, and so on. Group 2 is similar to group 1 since they have two features in common; for the same reasons 3 is similar to 2 and 4 is similar to 3. Notice that 3 is also similar to 1 (they have in common the feature *c*). The most curious case is presented by 4, obviously similar to 3 and 2, but with no feature in common with 1. However, owing to the uninterrupted series of decreasing similarities between 1 and 4, there remains, by a sort of illusory transitivity, a family resemblance between 4 and 1.

Fascism became an all-purpose term because one can eliminate from a fascist regime one or more features, and it will still be recognizable as fascist. Take away imperialism from fascism and you still have Franco and Salazar. Take away colonialism and you still have the Balkan fascism of the Ustashes. Add to the Italian fascism a radical anticapitalism (which never much fascinated Mussolini) and you have Ezra Pound. Add a cult of Celtic mythology and the Grail mysticism (completely alien to official fascism) and you have one of the most respected fascist gurus, Julius Evola.

But in spite of this fuzziness, I think it is possible to outline a list of features that are typical of what I would like to call Ur-Fascism, or Eternal Fascism. These features cannot be organized into a system; many of them contradict each other, and are also typical of other kinds of despotism or fanaticism. But it is enough that one of them be present to allow fascism to coagulate around it.

1. The first feature of Ur-Fascism is the *cult of tradition*. Traditionalism is of course much older than fascism. Not only was it typical of counterrevolutionary Catholic thought after the French Revolution, but it was born in the late Hellenistic era, as a reaction to classical Greek rationalism. In the Mediterranean basin, people of different religions (most of them indulgently accepted by the Roman Pantheon) started dreaming of a revelation received at the dawn of human history. This revelation, according to the traditionalist mystique, had remained for a long time concealed under the veil of forgotten languages—in Egyptian hieroglyphs, in the Celtic runes, in the scrolls of the little known religions of Asia.

   This new culture had to be *syncretistic*. Syncretism is not only, as the dictionary says, "the combination of different forms of belief or practice"; such a combination must tolerate contradictions. Each of the original messages contains a sliver of wisdom, and whenever they seem to say different or incompatible things it is only because all are alluding, allegorically, to the same primeval truth.

   As a consequence, there can be no advancement of learning. Truth has been already spelled out once and for all, and we can only keep interpreting its obscure message.

   One has only to look at the syllabus of every fascist movement to find the major traditionalist thinkers. The Nazi gnosis was nourished by traditionalist, syncretistic, occult elements. The most influential theoretical source of the theories of the new Italian right, Julius Evola, merged the Holy Grail with *The Protocols of the Elders of Zion*, alchemy with the Holy Roman and Germanic Empire. The very fact that the Italian right, in order to show its open-mindedness, recently broadened its syllabus to include works by de Maistre, Guenon, and Gramsci is a blatant proof of syncretism.

If you browse in the shelves that, in American bookstores, are labeled as New Age, you can find there even Saint Augustine who, as far as I know, was not a fascist. But combining Saint Augustine and Stonehenge—*that* is a symptom of Ur-Fascism.

2. Traditionalism implies the *rejection of modernism*. Both Fascists and Nazis worshipped technology, while traditionalist thinkers usually reject it as a negation of traditional spiritual values. However, even though Nazism was proud of its industrial achievements, its praise of modernism was only the surface of an ideology based upon Blood and Earth (*Blut und Boden*). The rejection of the modern world was disguised as a rebuttal of the capitalistic way of life, but it mainly concerned the rejection of the Spirit of 1789 (and of 1776, of course). The Enlightenment, the Age of Reason, is seen as the beginning of modern depravity. In this sense Ur-Fascism can be defined as *irrationalism*.

3. Irrationalism also depends on the cult of *action for action's sake*. Action being beautiful in itself, it must be taken before, or without, any previous reflection. Thinking is a form of emasculation. Therefore culture is suspect insofar as it is identified with critical attitudes. Distrust of the intellectual world has always been a symptom of Ur-Fascism, from Göring's alleged statement ("When I hear talk of culture I reach for my gun") to the frequent use of such expressions as "degenerate intellectuals," "eggheads," "effete snobs," "universities are a nest of reds." The official Fascist intellectuals were mainly engaged in attacking

modern culture and the liberal intelligentsia for having betrayed traditional values.

4. No syncretistic faith can withstand analytical criticism. The critical spirit makes distinctions, and to distinguish is a sign of modernism. In modern culture the scientific community praises disagreement as a way to improve knowledge. For Ur-Fascism, disagreement is treason.

5. Besides, disagreement is a sign of diversity. Ur-Fascism grows up and seeks for consensus by exploiting and exacerbating the natural *fear of difference*. The first appeal of a fascist or prematurely fascist movement is an appeal against the intruders. Thus Ur-Fascism is racist by definition.

6. Ur-Fascism derives from individual or social frustration. That is why one of the most typical features of the historical fascism was the *appeal to a frustrated middle class*, a class suffering from an economic crisis or feelings of political humiliation, and frightened by the pressure of lower social groups. In our time, when the old "proletarians" are becoming petty bourgeois (and the lumpen are largely excluded from the political scene), the fascism of tomorrow will find its audience in this new majority.

7. To people who feel deprived of a clear social identity, Ur-Fascism says that their only privilege is the most common one, to be born in the same country. This is the origin of nationalism. Besides, the only ones who can provide an identity to the nation are its enemies. Thus at the root of the Ur-Fascist psychology there is the *obsession with a plot*, possibly an international one. The followers must feel besieged. The easiest way to solve the plot is the appeal to xenophobia. But the plot must also come from the inside: Jews are usually the best target because they have the advantage of being at the same time inside and outside. In the United States, a prominent instance of the plot obsession

is to be found in Pat Robertson's *The New World Order*, but, as we have recently seen, there are many others.

8. The followers must feel humiliated by the ostentatious wealth and force of their enemies. When I was a boy I was taught to think of Englishmen as the five-meal people. They ate more frequently than the poor but sober Italians. Jews are rich and help each other through a secret web of mutual assistance. However, the followers must be convinced that they can overwhelm the enemies. Thus, by a continuous shifting of rhetorical focus, the enemies are at the same time too strong and too weak. Fascist governments are condemned to lose wars because they are constitutionally incapable of objectively evaluating the force of the enemy.

9. For Ur-Fascism there is no struggle for life but, rather, life is lived for struggle. Thus *pacifism is trafficking with the enemy*. It is bad because *life is permanent warfare*. This, however, brings about an Armageddon complex. Since enemies have to be defeated, there must be a final battle, after which the movement will have control of the world. But such a "final solution" implies a further era of peace, a Golden Age, which contradicts the principle of permanent war. No fascist leader has ever succeeded in solving this predicament.

10. Elitism is a typical aspect of any reactionary ideology, insofar as it is fundamentally aristocratic, and aristocratic and militaristic elitism cruelly implies *contempt for the weak*. Ur-Fascism can only advocate a *popular elitism*. Every citizen belongs to the best people of the world, the members of the party are the best among the citizens, every citizen can (or ought to) become a member of the party. But there cannot be patricians without plebeians. In fact, the Leader, knowing that his power was not delegated to him democratically but was conquered by force, also knows that his force is based upon the weakness of the

masses; they are so weak as to need and deserve a ruler. Since the group is hierarchically organized (according to a military model), every subordinate leader despises his own underlings, and each of them despises his inferiors. This reinforces the sense of mass elitism.

11. In such a perspective *everybody is educated to become a hero*. In every mythology the hero is an exceptional being, but in Ur-Fascist ideology, heroism is the norm. This cult of heroism is strictly linked with the cult of death. It is not by chance that a motto of the Falangists was *Viva la muerte* (in English it should be translated as "Long live death!"). In nonfascist societies, the lay public is told that death is unpleasant but must be faced with dignity; believers are told that it is the painful way to reach a supernatural happiness. By contrast, the Ur-Fascist hero craves heroic death, advertised as the best reward for a heroic life. The Ur-Fascist hero is impatient to die. In his impatience, he more frequently sends other people to death.

12. Since both permanent war and heroism are difficult games to play, the Ur-Fascist transfers his will to power to sexual matters. This is the origin of machismo (which implies both disdain for women and intolerance and condemnation of nonstandard sexual habits, from chastity to homosexuality). Since even sex is a difficult game to play, the Ur-Fascist hero tends to play with weapons—doing so becomes an ersatz phallic exercise.

13. Ur-Fascism is based upon a *selective populism*, a qualitative populism, one might say. In a democracy, the citizens have individual rights, but the citizens in their entirety have a political impact only from a quantitative point of view—one follows the decisions of the majority. For Ur-Fascism, however, individuals as individuals have no rights, and the People is conceived as a quality, a monolithic entity expressing the Common Will. Since no large quantity of human beings can have a common will,

the Leader pretends to be their interpreter. Having lost their power of delegation, citizens do not act; they are only called on to play the role of the People. Thus the People is only a theatrical fiction. To have a good instance of qualitative populism we no longer need the Piazza Venezia in Rome or the Nuremberg Stadium. There is in our future a TV or internet populism, in which the emotional response of a selected group of citizens can be presented and accepted as the Voice of the People.

Because of its qualitative populism Ur-Fascism must be *against "rotten" parliamentary governments*. One of the first sentences uttered by Mussolini in the Italian parliament was "I could have transformed this deaf and gloomy place into a bivouac for my maniples"—"maniples" being a subdivision of the traditional Roman legion. As a matter of fact, he immediately found better housing for his maniples, but a little later he liquidated the parliament. Wherever a politician casts doubt on the legitimacy of a parliament because it no longer represents the Voice of the People, we can smell Ur-Fascism.

14. Ur-Fascism speaks Newspeak. Newspeak was invented by Orwell, in *1984*, as the official language of Ingsoc, English Socialism. But elements of Ur-Fascism are common to different forms of dictatorship. All the Nazi or Fascist schoolbooks made use of an impoverished vocabulary, and an elementary syntax, in order to limit the instruments for complex and critical reasoning. But we must be ready to identify other kinds of Newspeak, even if they take the apparently innocent form of a popular talk show.

On the morning of July 27, 1943, I was told that, according to radio reports, fascism had collapsed and Mussolini was under arrest. When my mother sent me out to buy the newspaper, I saw that the papers at the nearest newsstand had different titles. Moreover, after seeing the headlines, I realized that each newspaper said different things. I bought one of them, blindly, and read a message on the first page signed by five or six political parties—among them the Democrazia Cristiana, the Communist Party, the Socialist Party, the Partito d'Azione, and the Liberal Party.

Until then, I had believed that there was a single party in every country and that in Italy it was the Partito Nazionale Fascista. Now I was discovering that in my country several parties could exist at the same time. Since I was a clever boy, I immediately realized that so many parties could not have been born overnight, and they must have existed for some time as clandestine organizations.

The message on the front celebrated the end of the dictatorship and the return of freedom: freedom of speech, of press, of political association. These words, "freedom," "dictatorship," "liberty"—I now read them for the first time in my life. I was reborn as a free Western man by virtue of these new words.

We must keep alert, so that the sense of these words will not be forgotten again. Ur-Fascism is still around us, sometimes in plainclothes. It would be so much easier, for us, if there appeared on the world scene somebody saying, "I want to reopen Auschwitz, I want the Blackshirts to parade again in the Italian squares." Life is not that simple. Ur-Fascism can come back under the most innocent of disguises. Our duty is to uncover it and to point our finger at any of its new instances—every day, in every part of the world. Franklin Roosevelt's words of November 4, 1938, are worth recalling: "I venture the challenging statement that if American democracy ceases to move forward as a living force, seeking day and night by peaceful means to better the lot of our citizens, fascism will grow in strength in our land." Freedom and liberation are an unending task.

PART II

ON FASCISM ANALOGIES

WHAT IS FASCISM?

RUTH BEN-GHIAT

Are you confused about the meaning of fascism? If so, you're not alone. Benito Mussolini, the creator of fascism, famously did not define it until 1932.[1] With Nazis once again making news in America and a neo-Fascist as Italian head of state, I will offer some thoughts on how the meaning of fascism has changed over a century.

———

"EVERYONE IS SURE they know what fascism is," writes Robert Paxton in his 2004 *The Anatomy of Fascism*.[2] Paxton gives perhaps the most comprehensive definition I have found, collapsing into one *very long* sentence many traits of fascism:

> Fascism may be defined as a form of political behavior marked by obsessive preoccupation with community decline, humiliation, or victimhood and by compensatory cults of unity, energy, and purity, in which a mass-based party of committed nationalist militants, working in uneasy but effective collaboration with traditional elites, abandons democratic liberties and pursues with redemptive violence, and without ethical or legal restraints, goals of internal cleansing and external expansion.[3]

The January 6 coup attempt changed Paxton's mind about whether Donald Trump and Trumpism can be called fascist.[4] That brought Paxton into line with scholars such as Jason Stanley, who deems fascism "a political method" that can appear anytime, anywhere, if conditions are right.[5] This line of thought risks emptying the term of its historical specificity but is essential for understanding our new authoritarian age and the risks we face in America today.

THE FASCIST YEARS (1922–1945)

"Does Fascism aim at restoring the State, or subverting it?" Mussolini teased his followers before the 1922 March on Rome that brought him to power, playing on his movement's ideological ambiguity.[6]

Fascism, as a word, has its roots in the Latin term *fasces*, or bundle. In the late nineteenth century, groups of Sicilian peasants rising up against their landlords were known as the *fasci Siciliani*. This radical tradition found an echo in the *fasci di combattimento*, or fascist combat leagues, which Mussolini founded in 1919.

In creating fascism, Mussolini, a former leftist revolutionary, confused many by "bundling" things that were supposed to be opposite: nationalism and imperialism with socialist elements.

Mussolini's paradoxical definition of fascism as a "revolution of reaction" is perhaps the most accurate.[7] Fascism aims at radical change brought about by violence and backed up by law to shut down political and social emancipation and take away rights. Soon nothing much beyond rhetoric remained of Mussolini's leftist past, and indeed leftists were the first and most consistently persecuted targets of fascism. This pleased his powerful conservative backers, as did his prompt privatization of the insurance and other industries.

Fascism spawned antifascism, and the Communist International's early 1930s definition of fascism as "the open terrorist dictatorship of the most reactionary, most chauvinist and most imperialist elements of finance capital" captured the logic of expansion and plunder that led

Italian fascism and Nazism into war (while ignoring communism's own repression).[8] By the time it was defeated in 1945, fascism had become synonymous with racism, imperialism, and genocide.

THE COLD WAR (1945–1990)

The new geopolitical climate of the Cold War influenced the use of the fascist label. The Spanish dictator Francisco Franco is a good example. He was a fascist ally of Mussolini and Hitler who during the Spanish Civil War deployed colonial warfare techniques against leftists. By 1940, 250,000 Spaniards were dead, 300,000 were in exile, and 600,000 were imprisoned in concentration camps.

Franco stayed out of World War II, and soon became an American Cold War client, which made it necessary to clean up his fascist reputation. With assistance from American lobbyists and PR firms like McCann Erickson, Franco was rebranded as a "soft authoritarian."[9] No matter that he made Spain a haven for fascists who had to flee their democratizing countries, as I recount in *Strongmen*.[10] The war criminals and terrorists he financed and refused to extradite (he harbored more than a thousand Nazis) knew he was "one of them."

The Cold War also favored the "totalitarian" paradigm for analyzing dictatorship. German émigré scholars like Hannah Arendt saw Stalinism, not Italian fascism, as Nazism's kindred spirit. Arendt was one of many who downgraded Mussolini's regime to "semi-totalitarian" status.[11] Over time, this failure to take Il Duce seriously eased the path to the rehabilitation of fascism, allowing Italy to become a laboratory of far-right politics once again.

THE NEW AUTHORITARIAN AGE (1990–PRESENT)

When communism fell in Europe and the Cold War ended, it created the conditions for the rise of a new right. In 1994, Silvio Berlusconi's center-right government brought Italy's neo-Fascist party (rebaptized as the National Alliance, or AN) to power for the first time in Europe since 1945. That meant fascism had to be redefined.

To appeal to a mainstream public, AN head Gianfranco Fini wore business suits, shunned Fascist salutes, and made Mussolini into a Churchill-like figure: "the greatest statesman of the twentieth century."[12] Berlusconi helped out by claiming in 2003 that "Mussolini never killed anyone, he sent people into confinement to have vacations," referring to Fascist prisons on islands like Ponza where torture had been practiced.[13]

Cleansed of its violence, fascism could now become "post-fascism," as Fini called it—just another form of patriotic and conservative politics. This is a line that the neo-Fascist Italian prime minister Giorgia Meloni is now using to whitewash her extremist-filled government.

That's why we must call fascism out today where we see it. Knowing its history makes that easier. Timothy Snyder makes a convincing case that Russian president Vladimir Putin, who is engaged in a genocidal war against Ukraine, can be considered a fascist, and that we should not "limit our fears of fascism to a certain image of Hitler and the Holocaust."[14]

In fact, fascism operates differently today, which is why its definition is in flux once more. As in Viktor Orbán's Hungary, right-wing one-party states have given way to "electoral autocracies" in which elections continue but threat and detentions, voter suppression, and domestication of the media produce the results the leader needs to stay in office.

Orbán's name for his governance, "illiberal democracy," is his way of escaping the fascist label. Yet there are profound continuities between the policies and platforms of leaders like Orbán and those of historic fascists, from personality cults to racist demographic policies designed to protect "white Christian civilization," to anti-Semitism and persecution of LGBTQ+ populations.

As I observed in a recent *Lucid Magazine* essay, Trump has long kept the fascist flame burning in America.[15] He started his 2016 campaign by retweeting a racist meme from the Nazi outlet *The Daily Stormer* (the publication of Andrew Anglin, whose Twitter account was restored on December 2, 2022, by Elon Musk).

Trump brought Mussolini admirer and far-right operative Steve Bannon into the White House to launch his own "revolution of reaction." In 2017 his administration gave Holocaust deniers a big gift: a Holocaust Remembrance Day statement that made no mention of Jews.

The GOP politicians who now feign outrage at Trump's association with Nazis such as Nick Fuentes had no problem with his mainstreaming of extremism, perhaps because some of them are extremists themselves (Paul Gosar and Marjorie Taylor Greene have appeared with Fuentes).

It's time to accept that the GOP, which was complicit with Trump's January 6 attempted authoritarian take-over, has become a party that furthers fascist values and practices. That means the hate crimes that have skyrocketed in America since 2016 will likely continue to expand.

However we define fascism, remembering that its essence is violence is more important than ever.

IS IT FASCISM?

JAN-WERNER MÜLLER

References to "fascism" have played an increasingly important role in trying to make sense of the present, and also to mobilize various constituencies—from elites who listen to former secretaries of state such as Madeleine Albright warning about fascism to on-the-ground activists who view Antifa as "an illiberal intervention that in resisting fascism does not rely on the state, the justice system or any liberal institution."[1] I want to suggest that it is ultimately implausible to designate today's forms of autocratization as involving anything plausibly called fascism— with the possibly, and evidently not trivial, exception of the most recent versions of Putinism. I suggest that, for the most part, we stick with the concept of far-right populism to make sense of a trend of our times— with "far-right" specifying ideological content and "populism" referring to a claim by actors uniquely to represent what they often call "the real people." This diagnosis can meet two criteria that have been implicit in the debates around the applicability of the concept of fascism. First, that a diagnosis must not create blind spots such that we no longer see the ways in which actually existing liberal democracies—and actually exist- ing liberal democrats—might be complicit in the rise of antidemocratic actors. And second, that diagnoses properly mobilize citizens for the defense of democracy.[2] I cannot engage these quasi-strategic consider- ations in great detail here, and, in any case, they should obviously not all by themselves determine the choice of conceptual frames to comprehend the present (this has arguably been the mistake of those who think that only the f-word can ever shock people out of complacency). But they are also not illegitimate to take into account.

At some point toward the end of the second decade of the twenty-first century, it seemed to become easier to name historical figures to whom Donald Trump had *not* been linked than ones which he has been said to resemble (from more or less mad Roman emperors to—of course—Adolf Hitler). By the same token, there has been an inflation of articles pointing to thinkers who supposedly predicted something like Trumpism, from Richard Rorty to Theodor Adorno and Robert Musil.[3] Arguably, this ever more outlandish search for analogies and prophetic theories was itself without precedent; it has been enabled by a media environment where attention is scarce, but publication space on the web virtually unlimited, attracting not just pundits, but academics subject to the imperative of relentless self-promotion ("Democracy will die, unless you buy my book!," more recently replaced by "Democracy will die, unless you subscribe to my Substack newsletter!"). In a previous era, with not much going on beyond the printed oped page, editors might not have made it a priority to feature musings about whether "Martin Luther was the Donald Trump of 1517."[4]

Among the clamoring for the most counterintuitive and hence most click-worthy comparison, there have been more serious voices linking Trump and other recent leaders suspected of authoritarianism with what remains arguably the concept retaining most potential to mobilize citizens: fascism. It is not difficult to see why this concept has proven attractive for American figures who otherwise share little, if anything, ideologically: neoconservatives labeling Trump a fascist could join a broad antifascist coalition, in the process changing the subject away from embarrassing questions about how they themselves may have paved the road to Trumpism with supposedly good intentions about military interventions, torture, etc.; at the same time, a left that sought a wider indictment of liberal capitalism could claim that Trump had merely made latent fascist tendencies in American life manifest.

The more serious contributors to the debate have usually conceded that, as of 2022, there is no coherent fascist movement in the United States and that Trump and his allies never succeeded in establishing anything that plausibly could be called a fascist regime; *grosso modo*, similar qualifications apply to autocrats or aspiring autocrats in Hungary, Turkey, Poland, Brazil, and India (though in India collective violence de facto encouraged by the ruling party is becoming much more prominent, moving the Modi regime closer to governing practices recognizable as fascist).[5] That is not the end of the discussion, of course; it would be foolish to start reflecting on fascism only when it is fully fledged. But can one even meaningfully speak of strong intimations of fascism?

My suggestion is to distinguish a discussion about causes and conditions (as well as historical constituencies) for fascism on the one hand and one about the characteristics of fascism on the other.[6] Clearly, one is not reducible to the other; moreover, one can possibly conclude that, while a number of contemporary political phenomena have enough of a family resemblance with historical forms of fascism to merit the application of the term, the conditions for an actual triumph of fascism are still not there. Conversely, it might also be the case that our conjuncture is actually quite favorable for fascism, and that we must brace ourselves for much worse to come—especially if economic conditions were to deteriorate further and fascists were to improve their capacities for propaganda in a new media environment that is partly based on what has been called "incitement capitalism": business models that prioritize hate to maximize "engagement" and hence profits.[7]

Let me start with historical conditions. As many historians have reminded us in recent years, it is impossible to comprehend the emergence of fascism (a heading under which I include Italian fascism and German National Socialism) without taking into account two background conditions in particular. One is the experience of mass violence and death in the First World War (and its aftermath): Mussolini's celebration of *combattentismo* and "trenchocracy" appealed to a particular audience not just of veterans; the same is broadly true for the Weimar Republic.[8] As the British historian Geoff Eley has pointed out, that commitment to violence was translated directly into political strategies against the postwar left; as he puts it, "killing socialists rather than just arguing with them, or at most legally and practically restricting their rights, was the most startling of departures. The brutality of that break can never be exaggerated."⁹

The other background condition was of course the perception of a serious Communist threat, and, irrespective of the accuracy of that perception, a reality of working-class power and broad left-wing mobilization. Fascists did not come to power in the interwar period without the collaboration of, broadly speaking, liberal and conservative elites; as Robert Paxton has pointed out in his masterly summary of decades of research about fascism: "The fascisms we have known have come into power with the help of frightened ex-liberals and opportunist technocrats and ex-conservatives, and governed in more or less awkward tandem with them."¹⁰ Mussolini did not really march on Rome; he arrived by sleeper car from Milan, called in by the king and assorted liberal leaders who rather happily governed with him in subsequent years.

Neither condition—war experience, Communist threats—obviously holds today. The military has been creeping back into the politics of seemingly consolidated democracies; no doubt, this is a disturbing trend (think of Brazil as an obvious example, or also the attempt by Trump to turn military men into props for his political spectacles in the summer of 2020, when, as so often with Trump, stagecraft replaced actual statecraft). But this is all different from a collective experience of violence affecting political life in the way that was the case in interwar Europe. "Living dangerously" might still be an ideal for some, but it's lived by means of bungee jumping or adventure holidays; few of us think that mortal combat is an indispensable part of the good life, and while one can imagine all kinds of possible futures for the military (especially ones based on different technological innovations), a return of the draft would have to figure among the least likely. None of this is to diminish the dangers of veterans becoming active in far-right groups ready for violence, a pattern clearly visible in the United States.¹¹

The question of a comprehensive threat motivating a turn to fascism is more complicated. Clearly, no revolutionary left is on the march comparable to the Comintern or even broadly successful Social Democratic parties (quite the opposite, at least until recently); and even nominally left-wing governments have been operating under what one can still call a broadly neoliberal hegemony. But what hovers in the background is a post-9/11 sense that liberal democracies are endangered from without and, crucially, also from within by "radical Islamism" (or, as a number of intellectuals would claim, "Islamo-fascism"). Less obviously: while 9/11 and the Iraq and Afghanistan wars are hardly analogous to losing the First World War (or being frustrated by paltry gains from the war, as in post-1918 Italy), or Versailles, for that matter, it is not implausible to see the early twenty-first century as one of humiliation for at least parts of "the West"—and to think that a feeling of victimhood and indignation can be used to mobilize for, and justify, various forms of aggression.

The far right has benefited enormously from being able to invoke this supposed threat, as well as any associated desires for revenge. Not equally everywhere of course, but as a frame, this threat remains widely available; less obviously, it has been crucial in allowing the center-right (and sometimes even the center-left, as in Denmark) to mainstream far-right talking points and larger agendas.[12] One need only remember Valérie Pécresse, the onetime standard-bearer of the French Republicans (the latest name for the Gaullist Party), in effect legitimizing the conspiracy theory of the "great replacement" to see that fear of Islam—and an appeal to citizens as victims—remain part of the strategic repertoire of supposed mainstream actors.

Such forms of mainstreaming point to another background condition of fascism for which it might in fact be more plausible to imagine functional equivalents in the present: elites willing to collaborate with fascists or, for that matter, today's far-right parties and movements. In the twenty-first century, no far-right figure has come to power in any North American or West European country (Italy being the obviously not trivial exception) without the collaboration of much more traditional elites and, more specifically, parties that would conventionally be seen as center-right.[13] Such collaboration also has been normalized in ways unimaginable not that long ago: when Austrian Christian Democrats entered a coalition with the far-right Freedom Party in 2000, Europe (or at least leading EU governments) were scandalized; when they did so again in 2017, hardly anyone bat an eyelid.

But then again, the far right is not the same as fascism. Which brings us from the question of causes, conditions, conjunctures, and constituencies to one about characteristics of the family of fascist phenomena. Violence was not just a background experience for fascism; fascists also explicitly celebrated violence as a force giving meaning to individual and collective life; the latter came to be dominated by military or paramilitary regimented mass movements for a reason.[14] Mortal combat was not an occasional necessity, but an active moral choice for fascists; and it is not an accident that all fascist regimes eventually went to war (or were constructed under wartime conditions, as in Croatia). This need for expansion, confrontation, and an overall sense of dynamism of course also explains for some observers why fascism appeared to have a self-destructive tendency and in the end failed as a regime everywhere it was tried.[15]

It is crucial to remember that fascism presented itself as a genuine revolution (a point that would be conceded also by those who argue with Antonio Gramsci that fascism constituted a "passive revolution" which served to preserve crucial elements of capitalist modernity). Fascists advanced a systematic idea about how to mobilize as well as profoundly restructure society (in line with imagined racial hierarchies). Fascism is unthinkable apart from mobilized mass movements devoted to a "rebirth" of what Roger Griffin calls an imagined "ultranation" (homogeneous and racialized).[16]

All of which is not to say that every manifestation of fascism must feature some kind of more or less coherent thought system: as is well known, the self-appointed philosophical leaders of fascism, be it Giovanni Gentile or Alfred Rosenberg, were completely sidelined within the regimes; a figure like Göring proclaimed proudly that he joined the party because he was a revolutionary, not because of the *ideologischer Kram*, the ideological stuff; evidently, plenty wanted revolution but could not be bothered with revolutionary philosophy.[17] Nor is it to say that a regime will in practice, empirically, have to make good on the claim of totally dominating a collective of "new men."[18] But without anything resembling such ambitions on the part of influential actors, it is difficult to see how we can meaningfully speak of fascism. Terms like "semi-fascism," "para-fascism," "fascist tactics" or "performative fascism" invoke a family resemblance (and pocket the surplus shock value of the f-word), while at the same time hinting that the relatives might be so distant as in the end to have very little to do with one another.

True, Trump himself and plenty of his followers have been committed to an ideal (if that's the right word) of complete social domination (and something similar is true of other far-right leaders today).[19] The former businessperson and reality TV actor, together with his collaborators, made politics and the administrative state into a theater of cruelty (the actions of the Department of Homeland Security were only the most conspicuous).[20] It is also true that Trump and his supporters sought to shore up gender and racial hierarchies, and that social domination was not arbitrarily targeted at individuals and groups, but with a view to reinforcing these hierarchies and, in particular, reasserting what Eley has called "visceral presumptions of masculine entitlement."[21]

This brings us to a second complication in matters of both conditions and content. The glorification of violence in the interwar period was inseparable from ideals of male brotherhood. As the German historian Klaus Theweleit has shown in his seminal study *Male Phantasies*, the world that men organized in militias strove for was ultimately one entirely without women.[22] Evidently, one cannot simply generalize this point; the actual regimes did not persecute women but, for the most part, subordinated them in the name of natalism (a feature shared with plenty of nonfascist regimes). Still, what Virginia Woolf at the time referred to as "unmitigated masculinity" played a central role in fascism, and still plays a role in paramilitary groups in, for instance, the United States and Brazil today.[23] But, overall, the gender politics of parties and movements suspected of fascism by some today is rather different: that is not just because some have female leaders like Marine Le Pen and Giorgia Meloni; it is also because they mobilize women specifically by invoking rights, usually against supposedly threatening Muslim men. Highly selective feminism can be incorporated into what some scholars have called "femonationalism";[24] this is categorically different from the occasional concession to female agency one could witness in Nazi Germany and Fascist Italy.

One might say that, if it is not fascism, authoritarianism is still the right designation, and far-right authoritarianism in particular. As historians of the twentieth century have long taught us, not every dictatorship was fascist; losing the distinction between revolutionary fascism committed to a mobilization and reformating of society as a whole and relatively static authoritarianism (which can also be violent, of course) is simply to diminish our capacity for political judgment.[25]

What's more, not all authoritarianisms have the same public justification. What is particular about Trump—and plenty of other far-right populist leaders today—is the claim that he, and only he, represents the people and implements its true will; this is something proponents of bureaucratic authoritarianism, for instance, would not have said. I have suggested in a number of writings that the concept of populism—and authoritarian right-wing populism in particular—can be of help here (though, arguably, less so in the American context where, for historical reasons, "populism" is often primarily imagined as bona fide grassroots pressure on oligarchies, as defending Main Street against Wall Street, etc.).

Populism, I submit, is not so much about antielitism, but about *antipluralism*: populists hold that they, *and only they*, represent what they often call "the real people," or also "the silent majority." As a consequence, they declare all other contenders for power fundamentally illegitimate. This is never just a disagreement about policies, or even values, for that matter; after all, such disputes are entirely normal, ideally even productive, in a democracy. Rather, populists malign other politicians as traitors, as corrupt and "crooked." Less obviously, they insinuate incessantly that all those among the people who do not share their particular symbolic conception of the people—and hence do not support the populists politically—might not properly belong to the people at all. Right-wing authoritarian populists ultimately reduce all political questions to questions of belonging: Trump does not answer his critics with arguments, but condemns them as un-American.

This is indeed a politics of dividing people, of "us against them," as the Yale philosopher Jason Stanley has encapsulated in his definition of fascism. But not every division in a democracy spells danger (in fact, if there were no differences and disagreements, it is not clear why we would need democracy as a means of peacefully processing conflicts in the first place); "normal" democratic conflicts can also pit "us against them," but in such conflicts, actors do not deny the legitimacy of adversaries and find compromise with them in principle acceptable. Less obviously, conflicts conducted within democratic parameters can end up strengthening social cohesion (and democracy as a whole). By contrast, the specific political business model of right-wing populists is to suggest that some people do not properly belong at all, are fundamentally illegitimate, or pose an outright threat to the integrity of the polity. But they do not openly encourage collective violence against such threats. They also do not impose an ideal of the good life on society as a whole, in the way typical of many twentieth-century authoritarians.

Still, their antipluralism has pernicious consequences on the ground, so to speak. My insistence that we are dealing with, in Trump's case, far-right populism, and not fascism, is in no way to belittle the pernicious effects of the failed businessman-turned-entertainer (or, according to Simon Schama, "entertainment fascist") occupying the Oval Office:[26] populist talk results in what the Australian philosopher Kate Manne has called "trickle-down aggression."[27] It is hardly an accident that the number of hate crimes in the United States has risen dramatically, and that many Republicans are now ready to "take the law into their own hands" to defend the country against the threat supposedly posed by what will appear to them as un-American American citizens (not to speak of what they will see as illegal, threatening aliens, what the Trump administration incessantly called "criminal aliens").[28]

Those who are skeptical of the applicability of the concept of fascism do not have to be committed to some notion of American exceptionalism, as in: *it could never happen here.*[29] On the contrary: what is so striking is precisely the family resemblances of what I would call a "populist art of governance" in various countries, from the United States and Turkey to Brazil and India, not to mention Hungary and Poland, the European pioneers of far-right-populism-in-power (what we thought would turn out to be exceptions became examples of a new authoritarian quasi-normal). These similarities do not prove that far-right populism has the same causes everywhere, tempting, and comforting, as it can be to pinpoint one universal macro-cause such as "resentment of the losers of globalization"; rather, it shows that the populist art of governance can be appropriated across borders and that the relevant actors are busy learning from each other. Best—or rather worst—practices of "autocratic legalism" (examples abound: legitimate-sounding laws against "foreign agents" designed to harass NGOs; strategic litigation against journalists and news media organization with a view to bankrupting or at least intimidating them) can easily be copied across borders.[30]

None of this should be taken as a reason to be less concerned, let alone to ease up in the fight for democracy: far-right populism really does destroy democracy, as is evident in Hungary, for instance. It can also always radicalize further in its racism. Even those who somehow don't feel bothered by all this unsavory stuff right now might eventually suffer the consequences: Trump gave a preview of his carelessness and cruelty during the pandemic when, in the fall of 2017, he frivolously tossed paper rolls at the inhabitants of a Puerto Rico devastated by hurricane Maria (another instance, one might say, of the "boomerang effect" discussed by Hannah Arendt and Aimé Césaire: whatever is tried out in the colonies on noncitizens or second-class citizens eventually hits the metropolis).

Far-right militias remain marginal in the United States for now (unlike the RSS in India, for instance, where fascism is becoming a more plausible designation). But the "ethnic antagonism," as Larry Bartels puts it rather delicately—de facto: fear of Black and brown people destroying white Christian America—keeps being stoked not just by Trump, but by plenty of more polite-sounding people in the GOP[31]; it can pave the way for something much worse. "Weimar" on the one hand and democratic normality on the other are not the only paths into the future.

I'VE HESITATED TO CALL DONALD TRUMP A FASCIST. UNTIL NOW

ROBERT O. PAXTON

I resisted for a long time applying the fascist label to Donald J. Trump.[1] He did indeed display some telltale signs. In 2016, a newsreel clip of Trump's plane taxiing up to a hangar where cheering supporters awaited reminded me eerily of Adolf Hitler's electoral campaign in Germany in July 1932, the first airborne campaign in history, where the arrival of the Führer's plane electrified the crowd. Once the rally began, with Hitler and Mussolini, Trump mastered the art of back-and-forth exchanges with his enraptured listeners. There was the threat of physical violence ("lock her up!"), sometimes leading to the forceful ejection of hecklers. The Proud Boys stood in convincingly for Hitler's Stormtroopers and Mussolini's *squadristi*. The MAGA hats even provided a bit of uniform. The "America first" message and the leader's arrogant swagger fit the fascist model.

But these are matters of surface decor. How did Trump relate to more profound social, political, economic, and cultural forces in American life? Like Hitler, among the first political leaders to master radio, Trump mastered electronic media like Twitter and won the support of America's largest television chain, Fox News. Like the fascist leaders, Trump understood the deep disaffection of parts of society for traditional leaders and institutions, and he knew how to exploit a widespread fear of national division and decline. Like Hitler and Mussolini he knew how to pose as the only effective bulwark against an advancing left, all the more fearful because it took on cultural forms unfamiliar to provincial rural America—feminism, Black power, gay rights.

But Trump and Trumpism also differ in some important ways from the historical fascisms. The circumstances are profoundly different. Although the United States has its problems, these are minor compared to those of the defeated Germany of 1932, with over 30 percent of workers unemployed, or the divided Italy at the brink of civil war in 1921. Most Americans are employed, or were until the pandemic, while those lucky enough to own stocks are in clover. American political institutions are not deadlocked, as were those of Germany in 1932, when President Paul von Hindenburg believed that only Hitler could stop the rapidly growing Communist Party. American circumstances are unlike those of Italy in 1921, where the king believed that the only way to stop the runaway take-overs of Italian cities by Mussolini's new nationalist and antisocialist mass movement, which he called fascism, was to invite its leader into office. The crisis created by Trump's refusal to accept a legitimate electoral outcome seems almost trivial by comparison.

A further fundamental difference is Trump's relation to the world of business. Whereas Hitler and Mussolini, at least at the beginning, won their mass audiences with promises to shake up capitalist power, and whereas, once in power with the support of the same businessmen against labor, the fascist leaders had subjected businessmen, often against their preferences, to the demands of forced rearmament, Trump gave American business what they wanted: the relaxation of regulations and access to world markets. It seemed to me better to avoid one more facile and polemical use of the fascist label in favor of a more unemotional term, such as oligarchy or plutocracy.

Trump's incitement of the invasion of the Capitol on January 6, 2021, removes my objection to the fascist label. His open encouragement of civic violence to overturn an election crosses a red line. The label now seems not just acceptable but necessary. It is made even more plausible by comparison with a milestone on Europe's road to fascism—an openly fascist demonstration in Paris during the night of February 6, 1934.

On that evening thousands of French veterans of World War I, bitter at rumors of corruption in a parliament already discredited by its inefficacy against the Great Depression, attempted to invade the French parliament chamber, just as the deputies were voting yet another shaky government into power. The veterans had been summoned by right-wing organizations. They made no secret of their wish to replace what they saw as a weak parliamentary government with a fascist dictatorship on the model of Hitler or Mussolini.

Unlike the demonstrators in Washington on January 6, the French demonstrators of February 6, 1934, did not succeed in penetrating the parliament building. But the outcome was much graver. The French government, fearing that the demonstrators, crossing the bridge leading from the Place de la Concorde, were going to break in to the chamber, authorized the police to shoot. Fifteen demonstrators and one police-man were killed. The French Third Republic had blood on its hands. The ensuing bitter division helps explain why the French prepared only haltingly before 1940 for Hitler's attack, and why the French defeat that June led to the replacement of the Third Republic with the authoritarian Vichy regime.

Curiously, it seems the Washington demonstrators' success at breaching the Capitol gives them less support in American society today than the unsuccessful French demonstrators of February 1934 acquired in their country. In France, elections in June 1936 had a highly con-tested outcome: the installation of a Jew and a Socialist, Léon Blum, as prime minister. French fascists remained active opponents of Blum until opportunity came for them again in June 1940 with Hitler's defeat of the French army, and the replacement of the French parliamentary republic with the authoritarian Vichy regime. In the United States, after the ignominious failure of a shocking fascist attempt to undo Biden's election, the new American president can begin his work of healing on January 20. Despite encouraging early signs and the relative robustness of American institutions, it's too soon for a responsible historian to say whether he'll be more successful in sustaining our republic than Euro-pean leaders were in defending theirs.

WHAT WE DON'T UNDERSTAND ABOUT FASCISM

VICTORIA DE GRAZIA

At the moment, fascism has to be the most sloppily used term in the American political vocabulary. If you think fascists are buffoonish, racist, misogynist despots, the people who support them are deplorable, and a political leader who incites paramilitary forces against protesters is not much different from Mussolini unleashing his black-shirted thugs against unarmed workers, you may be tempted to call the current president of the United States a fascist. But then the president, too, has taken to labeling his enemies fascists. And who wants to argue about semantics in that company?

Make no mistake: understanding what fascism meant in its time, 1920 to 1945, is absolutely crucial to understanding the gravity of our own current national political crisis—as well as to summoning up the huge political creativity we will need to address it. But we won't get close to that understanding if we keep confusing fascism, the *historical phenomenon*, with fascism, *the political label*.

If you grew up as I did, in the United States after the Second World War, everyone seemed to be an antifascist, at least at first. America had fought the good fight, and triumphed. I ached at my father's war stories about the misery of the newly liberated Italians, studied army snapshots of him in front of a mound of corpses at Dachau, and suffered nightmares at learning what the Nazis and the Fascists did to the Jews.

But the picture grew complicated. From my Jewish American mother, a New Dealer and later a Communist fellow traveler, I learned that McCarthyism was the form fascism took in America. After my study abroad in Italy during the 1960s, where I had joined student and worker demonstrations against that country's still vivid authoritarian streak, I came home rhetorically armed to denounce fascists. America seemed riddled with them—starting with those "fascist pigs" in the Princeton, New Jersey, police force who hauled the Black kids (and my little brothers) into custody for Halloween pranks and held them indefinitely, as if habeas corpus didn't apply to juveniles. My Smith College dorm mother was a fascist for enforcing fascistic-patriarchal rules in loco parentis, as were a couple of professors who argued that fascism and communism were opposite sides of the same coin. The ranks of the fascists included LBJ for Vietnam, Nixon and Kissinger for many reasons, and even my father (who also supported the Vietnam War) for his haywire libertarian politics.

Calling people "fascists" has been as American as apple pie for as long as I can remember. But, after becoming a scholar of fascism, I came to see the phenomenon of fascist labeling very differently.

This is especially true now, twenty years into the twenty-first century, heading up to the 2022 centenary of Mussolini's March on Rome.

It's been seventy-five years since the coalition of armies—spearheaded by the United States, the Soviet Union, and Great Britain—crushed the Axis belligerents, Germany, Italy, and Japan. And it's been thirty years since 1990, when the relatively stable Cold War world order, ruled by the two superpowers, broke up with the dissolution of the Soviet bloc.

I now see the fascist phenomenon with new context—the crumbling of the liberal norms that were constructed to save the world from a recurrence of authoritarianism after World War II; the social inequities and financial crises arising from globalization; the failures of American unilateralism; and the obsolescence of domestic and international institutions in the face of new challenges, from climate change to the COVID-19 pandemic, which are posed to wreak even greater global disorder.

In this twenty-first-century light, fascism and its horrific trajectory in the second quarter of the twentieth century look at once inexorable and global, awful and attractive, even understandable. Fascism, its early-twentieth-century proponents claimed, had all of the answers to the political, material, and existential crises of the British-led imperialist world order in the wake of World War I: It would mobilize the militarism generated by World War I to reorder civilian life. It signaled a third way between capitalism and socialism by imposing harmony between labor and capital. And fascism would establish new racial hierarchies to defend the West against soulless American materialism, Judeo-Bolshevism, and the inexorable advance of Asia's "yellow masses." It would knock the hypocritical British Empire off its plutocratic pedestal, destroy the puppet League of Nations, and carve out new colonial empires to let the proletarian nations of the world get their just deserts.

It makes sense that Italy was home to the first fascist take-over. After surviving well enough as a second-order power through the end of the nineteenth century, the country's retrograde monarchy eschewed undertaking needed social reforms and instead got swept up in the competition for colonies, empowering a flamboyant young nationalist right. These activists dominated debates in the piazzas and ultimately pushed the country to enter World War I, believing it would be richly rewarded with new lands.

But that vision was not to be. Mobilizing at a grand scale to fight the Austrians and Germans unhinged Italy's political system. The country divided into interventionist and antiwar camps. After fighting ended, the old political class secured a few new territories out of the Versailles peace conference, but not enough to satisfy the imperialist expectations of the pro-war factions. Nor could elites deliver a substantial program of reforms that would have made war sacrifices seem worthwhile to the ever larger, ever more exasperated movements of workers and peasants spearheaded by socialist and Catholic opposition parties.

By 1921, the liberal political elite calculated that if it opened its electoral coalition to Benito Mussolini's burgeoning *fasci di combattimento* movement, it could co-opt this vigorous political upstart, punish the left and Catholic opposition, and shore up its own power.

Who better than the brilliant, unscrupulous journalist Mussolini, a leading socialist turned radical nationalist, to offer a new way? Lover and tutee of brilliant cosmopolitan women, with a facile ear for big ideas and overweening self-confidence in his political intuition, Mussolini claimed to be both a revolutionary and a reactionary—and positioned his anti-party's armed squads as the only bulwark against the Reds' advance. Avowedly opportunistic, he seized every moment to bash the opposition, ingratiate himself with the old elites, stymie alternative solutions, and woo the military and the police by stressing their shared struggle to restore law and order against the Bolsheviks.

Called by the king to form a coalition government, Mussolini embarked on a restoration more than a revolution. He established an unshakable political majority by outlawing opposition parties. He revived the economy through austerity measures, outlawing nonfascist unions, and renegotiating war debts to prompt U.S. capital to pour into Italy. He restored national prestige by swagger and bluff, no longer a junior partner to Great Britain in the Mediterranean and East Africa, but a freebooting statesman with the ambition to reestablish Italy's Roman Empire.

Fascists spoke of the state as something alive, with a moral personality of its own, and justifiably predatory to survive in a Darwinian world. They celebrated people as energetic animals—New Men and Women who needed hierarchy and a true leader to harness their vigor. The males could become more virile breed stock, the women more fertile, all for the purposes of the state.

Between 1920 and 1930, as Mussolini turned his onetime radical-populist social movement into a giant party-militia, seized power, and transformed his government into totalitarian dictatorship—in his words, "Everything in the State, nothing outside the State, nothing against the State"—fascism established itself as an international reference point for a wide array of like-minded political entrepreneurs and collaborating movements. With the Great Depression, Adolf Hitler's seizure of power in Germany, and Fascist Italy's alliance with the Third Reich, fascism would transform into a multipronged global force. Militarily, Mussolini conquered Ethiopia and Hitler rearmed, both in defiance of the League of Nations. They intervened to help General Francisco Franco overthrow the Spanish Second Republic and formed their anti-Bolshevik Axis with Imperial Japan.

Economically, fascism appealed during a worldwide depression because it seemed to have found a winning model to confront it: closed economies, big state spending, and tightly controlled labor organizations and markets to control wages and inflation. Revved up by rearmament spending, Germany was becoming the new engine of Europe and the leading trade partner for most of its neighboring nations. Germany boasted that it had no unemployment, and Italy had at least suppressed the visibility of out-of-work citizens by recruiting them for its ever growing volunteer militia, sending them back to their rural hometowns, settling them in its new empire in Libya and Ethiopia, or offering them assistance through winter help funds. In both regimes, leaders claimed, capital and labor cooperated in the national interest.

Political enthusiasm displayed itself in whole peoples, uniformed and integrated into mass organizations, their distinctions effaced, united in their cult of the leader. By 1938, propagandists were speaking of the Nazi-Fascist New Order as the true heir to European culture. It launched a counter-Hollywood in the form of UFA, the giant German-dominated film production and distribution cartel, and financed joint film productions with the Japanese as well as a dazzling film festival at Venice to counter the one at Cannes.

The Nazi-Fascist New Order championed the new sciences of demographics and race hygienics in scientific congresses and exchanges. It fostered debates over how to revive jurisprudence and political science by differentiating between friends and enemies in legal codes and in international law and how to build more totalizing welfare states by incorporating sports and healthy eating, in addition to eugenic measures to prevent "useless" lives from detracting from the social good. And it portrayed itself as a pioneer in geopolitics, striking a new balance so that all of the world's great powers would have their so-called vital spaces or lebensraum. Just as the United States would rule Latin America through its Monroe Doctrine, fascist geopoliticians said, Italy would have Eur-Africa, Japan its Co-Prosperity Sphere in Asia, and Germany its Ost-Plan for colonizing Eastern Europe and Russia. On that basis, fascism had a right to make war and for the winning regimes to redistribute chunks of colonial empire to the "deserving."

It's scary to look at a map of the world in 1941: continental Europe conquered for the New Order, the Nazi war machine at the gates of Moscow; Italy in the Balkans, its armies in the field from Benghazi to British Somalia; Japan occupying much of East Asia. The war was a true crusade, driven by its dictators' furies, as well as old-fashioned imperialism: for the fascists, winning meant not just territorial conquest, but population elimination including the global eradication of the Jews, wholesale pillage, and capturing prisoners for slave labor. The tyrants had few qualms about immolating their own peoples to salvage their lost cause. Rather than capitulate to the Allies in June 1943, Mussolini abandoned Italy to German military occupation and two more years of bombardment, invasion, and civil war. Refusing to capitulate as Soviet forces encircled Berlin, Hitler summoned his people to continue the "sacrifice" and "struggle," then killed himself.

Americans may think we know this history, but we have oversimplified its complexity. Boasting about defeating fascism, and declaring it our duty to police the world against any recurrence, we have lost sight of the global crises of the early twentieth century, born of World War I and the Great Depression, that fascism was invented to address.

Over time, we have become accustomed to political leaders of both parties turning the history of fascism into a set of political hobgoblins to legitimate new wars. Never again a Munich, where the great powers capitulated to Hitler, to justify intervention in Vietnam. Never again the Holocaust, to justify intervention in the Balkans and Libya. Never would we bow to an Arab Hitler, to justify invading Iraq and overthrowing Saddam Hussein.

We also have gotten used to Hollywood turning the U.S. encounter with Nazi-fascism into mawkish images of good and evil, and to facile evocations of the Holocaust making anti-Semitism practically the sole measure of what it meant to be fascist. "Fascinating fascism" is the term Susan Sontag, the literary critic, once used to call out American culture's superficiality at being beguiled by fascism's kitschy aesthetics and by the sadomasochistic pleasure of thinking of fascism as chains and shackles that, once shaken off, reinvigorate the meaning of being whole and free.

By cultivating such a jejune view of what fascism was historically, we have struggled to understand the highly relevant story of why it took two decades between the world wars to develop a coalition powerful enough to fight it. Fascism always had opponents, of course, but they—dyed-in-the-wool conservatives, old-fashioned liberals, Catholic centrists, social democrats, Communists, and anarchists—were deeply divided. Mussolini got points from his men when, after outlawing the opposition, he brushed off its leaders as "antifascists," meaning they had no program except to contest his.

It is no disrespect to the hard-fought struggles of antifascist forces to underscore how hard it was to win, much less sustain, electoral victories once the right in polarized political systems aligns itself with forces identifying with fascism. In Spain, the left-wing coalition known as the Popular Front won in February 1936, only to be overthrown by a military coup, backed by international fascism. In France, the May 1936 victory of the Popular Front was reversed in short order as capital took flight for fear of a Red revolution, the economy stalled, and the coalition dissolved.

Most places sought to immunize themselves from fascism by becoming more conservative. Nearly everywhere, the interwar years were a time of nationalism, red-baiting, and eugenics. Anti-Semitism and race-mongering were normal. There was only one place in Europe that fended off the fascist turn with substantial social reforms: the kingdom of Sweden, where the Social Democratic Party won the vote in 1932. Of course, this solid left regime could thrive only as a neutral power, as a niche at the edge of the New Order, supplying the German war machine with coal and steel.

Ultimately, it was the rising hegemons, the United States and the Soviet Union, that had the strongest interests in battling Nazi-fascist hegemony: the Soviet Union because it was in the direct line of Nazi aggression; the United States because it opposed German and Italian expansionism, allied with Japanese expansionism around the globe. But it still took years for New Deal America, the troglodyte British Empire, and Stalin's walled-off USSR to overcome their differences and forge a functioning antifascist military alliance.

Fascism was not fully vanquished by the military victories of World War II alone. Preventing its revival required a big rethink of economic and political principles around the world. It called for big projects, for huge investments, and for government planning to bring about economic recovery. How could a nation's subjects be citizens if they were excluded by their poverty, and by castelike differences in their education, standards of living, and life prospects? How could enhanced productivity, and big profits from new mass-industrial technologies like cars and radios be more equitably distributed? Capitalism had to accept regulation. Old-fashioned liberalism had to accept labor reform and state spending on social benefits. Europe, if it was to end its warring divisions, had to accept some kind of federalism. The Catholic Church had to resolve its theological ambivalence and champion human rights universally, not only for Christians. Socialism (and communism) had to become more patriotic and reformist. World government had to become stronger, fairer, and more universal.

The substance, then, of fascism, but also of antifascism, is what mattered about fascism—not the label of "fascism" that obsesses so many people and dominates our politics today. That focus on substance is what we need now in the United States as we face not fascism, but rather a crisis of a kind that historic fascism invented itself to address, in the most awful ways. In this crisis, we need to summon up the terrifying honesty to address our nation's responsibility for the crumbling of the liberal international order, and, if history serves, to create Popular Front forms of collective action nationally and globally with the power to confront our many challenges—ideally, well short of new wars.

WHY TRUMP ISN'T A FASCIST

RICHARD J. EVANS

A number of prominent commentators, including the historians Timothy Snyder and Sarah Churchwell, the former U.S. secretary of state Madeleine Albright, and the Berkeley public policy professor Robert Reich, have been arguing for some time that Donald Trump is a fascist.[1] The writer Rebecca Solnit has even called Trump's supporters "Nazis."

Look at his contempt for democracy, they say; his attacks on the press and the judiciary, his rabble-rousing, his intolerance of all who oppose him, his authoritarianism, his self-identification with foreign dictators and strongmen, his nationalism and "America first" foreign policy. Look at the way he spurns international organizations, treaties, and agreements, his racism and encouragement of white supremacist groups, his incitement to violence on the streets of the United States.

Certainly, these carry strong echoes of fascism. Hitler and Mussolini attacked the free press, poured scorn on the judiciary, urged their followers to attack and kill their opponents, and put a murderous racism at the heart of their ideology. They tore up treaties, abandoned international organizations, undermined and ultimately destroyed parliamentary democracy, and promoted a cult of their own personality that seduced millions of citizens into accepting them as great redeemers.

The temptation to draw parallels between Trump and the fascist leaders of the twentieth century is understandable. How better to express the fear, loathing, and contempt that Trump arouses in liberals than by comparing him to the ultimate political evil? But few who have described Trump as a fascist can be called real experts in the field, not even Snyder. The majority of genuine specialists, including the historians Roger Griffin, Matthew Feldman, Stanley Payne, and Ruth Ben-Ghiat, agree that whatever else he is, Trump is not a fascist.

Fascism and Nazism were the creation of the First World War, which militarized society and—in the minds of their leaders and supporters—discredited liberal democracy by associating it with armed defeat. In Germany, the defeat was catastrophic, entailing large territorial losses, the emasculation of the country as a great power, and the payment of huge financial reparations to the Allies. Italy was on the winning side in 1918, but the expected gains from banding together with Britain, France, and the United States failed to materialize, and the country left the war with what historians have called "the mentality of a defeated nation."

What drove fascism and Nazism was the desire to refight the First World War, but this time to win it. Preparing for war, arming for war, educating for war, and fighting a war defined fascist theory and praxis. Hitler's aim of conquering territory was put into effect immediately in 1933, as he rearmed Germany and set it on a path to invade neighboring countries. By mid-1940, Nazi Germany had conquered Poland, Austria, Czechoslovakia, and most of Western Europe. The Third Reich lived for war, breathed war, and promoted war without limits. Similarly, Mussolini's central aim was to create a new "Roman Empire," beginning with the conquest of Ethiopia in 1935–1936 and continuing with less successful attempts to subjugate areas around the Mediterranean, disastrously in the cases of Yugoslavia, Greece, and North Africa.

For all of Trump's hostility toward countries he perceives as enemies of the United States, notably Iran, there is no indication that he sought a war with any foreign power, still less that he has been consumed by a desire for foreign conquest and the creation of an American empire. He is an isolationist, busy withdrawing U.S. troops from foreign adventures, from Syria to Afghanistan. "America first" is not about launching foreign wars but disengaging from them.

TRUMP'S ENCOURAGEMENT OF violence against his opponents at home has been unsystematic. He has told his supporters to rough up reporters and suggested during the 2016 election campaign that his followers might like to make use of the Second Amendment of the U.S. Constitution (the right to bear arms) against Hillary Clinton. He has also described white supremacists as "good people." But this bears no comparison to the hundreds of thousands of armed and uniformed Stormtroopers and *squadristi* that the Nazi and Fascist leaders deployed on to the streets daily in the 1920s and early 1930s to intimidate, beat up, arrest, imprison, and often kill political opponents.

Hitler and Mussolini sought to transform their countries into perma-war states: a combination of education and propaganda on the one hand and street-level violence and intimidation on the other aimed to forge a new kind of citizen, one that was aggressive, regimented, arrogant, decisive, organized, and obedient to the dictates of the state. G. M. Trevelyan poured scorn on Mussolini's efforts to turn Italians into second-rate Germans, as the historian put it; but even in Germany this endeavor failed, except with a minority of Hitler's most ardent followers.

The society Hitler wanted was portrayed in the final minutes of Leni Riefenstahl's *Triumph of the Will* (1935), with endless serried ranks of uniformed SS troops marching across the screen like well-oiled automata. The reality was different, as the majority of Germans retreated from this dehumanizing prospect into their own private lives.

Trump by contrast has encouraged a warped vision of personal freedom: a society in which people aren't subject to government regulation or supervision, where anarchy and confusion reign, self-restraint is abandoned, violence is unchecked, and self-aggrandizing corruption permeates politics.

Trump has regard only for those he considers to be "winners," and cannot bear the idea of defeat. Refusing a visit to a war cemetery in Paris in September 2020, he remarked that soldiers who died for their country on the field of battle were "losers" and "suckers."

This mentality contrasts strongly with the central role of self-sacrifice in fascist ideology. Hitler regarded himself as a gambler: "I always go for broke," he told Hermann Göring in 1939. There could be nothing but either total victory or total defeat. Suicide in the event of failure was always an option in his mind. Hitler and his propaganda chief Joseph Goebbels constructed a cult around Nazi "martyrs" such as Horst Wessel, the twenty-two-year-old Stormtrooper killed by Communists three years before the Nazi seizure of power. They also honored the men shot dead by police in the beer hall putsch of 1923, parading the "blood flag" brandished by the would-be putschists at ceremonial commemorations every year.

Self-sacrifice for the nation was so central to Nazi ideology that when it became clear at the end of the Second World War that Nazism had been defeated, a wave of suicides swept the entire Nazi establishment, beginning with Hitler, Goebbels, Heinrich Himmler, and Göring, and cascading down the ranks.

BEYOND DIFFERENCES in ideology and temperament are the contrasts in state organization. In Germany and Italy during the 1930s and 1940s, businesses became helpmeets of the "corporate state." Unions and labor organizations were crushed, while firms and captains of industry generated vast profits, only so long as what they produced served the party and the army.

Both Hitler and Mussolini ensured a near total "coordination" of social institutions and voluntary associations, as everything from football clubs to male voice choirs was absorbed into the structures of the fascist state. This social policy was maintained by huge bureaucratic regimes, providing jobs for thousands of their followers hungry for income and status after years of hardship and privation.

During Trump's disastrous four years in the White House, government posts have been left unfilled, senior officials have been routinely fired and the commander in chief has spent much of his time playing golf. The kind of hyperactive dynamism that characterized fascist regimes was entirely absent. Congress has prevailed over Trump's attempts to sideline or undermine it, and judges, including his own Supreme Court appointees, have adhered to and interpreted the law in ways that have sometimes thwarted Trump's ambitions, notably rejecting his legal challenges to the presidential election. Election officials, among them longterm Republicans, have resisted his attempts to intimidate them, while the mainstream media has refused to broadcast his falsehoods, lies, and misleading claims unchecked.

The damage Trump has done to American democracy is considerable, but the past four years of mayhem have demonstrated the resilience of American institutions, the law, and the Constitution. American democracy is damaged, but it survives.

Democratic culture in the European countries where fascism prevailed after 1918 had shallow roots. The German judiciary was overwhelmingly hostile to the Weimar Republic, and the idea of an unbiased, nonpartisan press was too new to establish itself as an accepted feature of political life. The legitimacy of the German political system in the 1920s and early 1930s was weak, and the corrupt Italian polity was widely discredited.

A substantial portion of the American population—and, indeed, a majority of members of the Republican Party—refuses to accept the election of President-elect Joe Biden. But that does not mean they want the Constitution to be overthrown, merely that they don't think it's been employed fairly.

The shocking scenes at the Capitol on January 6, and the spectacle of Trump lauding those who attacked police and trashed Democratic Party congressional offices as patriots, underlined the real threat he and his followers pose to democratic norms and the rule of law. Armed insurrections are threatened by ultra-right groups across the country for Biden's inauguration.

But January 6 was not an attempted coup. Nor is one likely to occur on January 20. For all of Trump's inflammatory rhetoric, the attack on Congress was not a preplanned attempt to seize the reins of government. Trump is too chaotic and undisciplined to prepare and execute any kind of organized assault on democracy.

The storming of the Capitol has been compared to Hitler's infamous beer hall putsch on November 9, 1923. On that occasion, Hitler gathered his armed and uniformed supporters in a beer hall in Munich, from where they marched toward the city center. Germany was in crisis: inflation was out of control and the French had occupied the Ruhr earlier that year.

Hitler thought the conditions were favorable for a coup d'état, and he proclaimed the formation of a "national dictatorship" headed by himself. But the coup went wrong, the putschists were met by a hail of police bullets, and Hitler was arrested and imprisoned for five years of "fortress confinement" (he served only nine months). The original intention was to seize the government in Munich and, as Mussolini had done in Rome in 1922, march on the capital. But the putsch was confused and chaotic and doomed to failure before it had begun.

HITLER DREW TWO LESSONS from the debacle. First, seizing power by force in an open and direct confrontation with the government was not going to work; the ballot box not the bullet was the way to power. The second lesson was just as important: the beer hall putsch was unsuccessful not least because Hitler had failed to secure the support of the political elite, the army, business, the civil service, and the police.

He would not make the same mistake again. Between 1932 and 1933, he used his electoral success, which had elevated the Nazis to become the largest party in Germany, as a basis for negotiating with these groups to secure their backing for a coalition government that he would head. A vital factor was the redundancy of the legislature: disrupted by warring factions of uniformed Nazis and Communists, the Reichstag met on only a handful of occasions in 1932, and the government legislated by decree. Exploiting this situation and unleashing his violent Brownshirts on to the streets, Hitler transformed the chancellorship into a dictatorship within a matter of months.

Is the storming of the Capitol on January 6, like the beer hall putsch, a beginning rather than an end? It seems clear that Trumpism as a political force in American life isn't going away soon. Many of Trump's supporters will continue to dispute the legitimacy of Biden's election and to regard Donald Trump as the real president of the United States. But there are signs that the events of January 6 have shocked many Republicans into abandoning Trump and his most fanatical supporters. The GOP may split; Trump may become the leader of a hard-right third party run from Mar-a-Lago. Time will tell.

But time is against Trump. Hitler and his followers were young men in 1923. They could afford to wait. Trump is in his seventies and can't. A successor may emerge, but it seems unlikely that he would match Trump's crowd appeal. Questions are being asked about the failure of the police to prevent the storming of the Capitol, but there is little evidence that the forces of order—the administrative and legal arms of the state, as well as the military—will prevent a peaceful transfer of power on January 20. The situation in the United States today is more like Munich in 1923 than Berlin ten years later.

To state these obvious facts is not to encourage complacency. It means that rather than fighting the demons of the past—fascism, Nazism, the militarized politics of Europe's interwar years—it is necessary to fight the new demons of the present: disinformation, conspiracy theories, and the blurring of fact and falsehood.

Banning dangerous and irresponsible figureheads like Trump from social media is a start—they incite violence and purvey misinformation to a degree that makes Goebbels look like George Washington (the first American president, who was said never to tell a lie). Trump's incessant and false claims that the election was rigged have convinced many Americans that their votes no longer count for anything. This lack of democratic faith, not a violent seizure of power, is the real threat to the American republic.

Whether the United States and its citizens succeed in preserving democracy and its institutions depends to a large extent on whether they succeed in identifying what the real threats are and developing appropriate means to defeat them. Imagining that they are experiencing a rerun of the fascist seizure of power isn't going to help them very much in this task. You can't win the political battles of the present if you're always stuck in the past.

WHY HISTORICAL ANALOGY MATTERS

PETER E. GORDON

On June 24, 2019, the United States Holocaust Memorial Museum issued a formal statement that it "unequivocally rejects the efforts to create analogies between the Holocaust and other events, whether historical or contemporary." The statement came in response to a video posted by Alexandria Ocasio-Cortez, the Democratic congresswoman from New York, in which she had referred to detention centers for migrants on the U.S. southern border as "concentration camps." If the historical allusion wasn't already apparent, she added a phrase typically used in reference to the genocide of European Jewry: "Never again." Always a favorite target of right-wing politicians, Ocasio-Cortez drew a scolding retort from Liz Cheney, the Republican congresswoman from Wyoming, who wrote on Twitter: "Please @AOC do us all a favor and spend just a few minutes learning some actual history. 6 million Jews were exterminated in the Holocaust. You demean their memory and disgrace yourself with comments like this." In the ensuing social media storm, the statement by the Holocaust Memorial Museum against historical analogies gave the unfortunate appearance of partisanship, as though its directors meant to suggest that Cheney was right and Ocasio-Cortez was wrong.

Much of this might have been a tempest in a tweet-pot were it not for the fact that, on July 1, 2019, an international group of scholars published an open letter on *The New York Review of Books* website expressing their dismay at the Holocaust Memorial Museum's statement and urging its director to issue a retraction.[1] "The Museum's decision to completely reject drawing any possible analogies to the Holocaust, or to the events leading up to it, is fundamentally ahistorical," they wrote. "Scholars in the humanities and social sciences rely on careful and responsible analysis, contextualization, comparison, and argumentation to answer questions about the past and the present." Signed by nearly six hundred scholars, many working in fields related to Jewish studies, the letter was restrained but forthright. "The very core of Holocaust education," it said, "is to alert the public to dangerous developments that facilitate human rights violations and pain and suffering." The museum's categorical dismissal of the legitimacy of analogies to other events was not only ahistorical, it also inhibited the public at large from considering the moral relevance of what had occurred in the past. Granting the possibility of historical analogies and "pointing to similarities across time and space," they warned, "is essential for this task."

I was neither an author of this letter nor an original signatory, but like many others, I later added my name, as I felt the issues it raised were of great importance. The debate involves an enormous tangle of philosophical and ethical questions that are not easily resolved: What does it mean when scholars entertain analogies between different events? How is it even possible to compare events that occurred in widely different circumstances? The signatories of the open letter to the Holocaust Memorial Museum were entirely right to say that analogical reasoning is indispensable to the human sciences. But it's worth turning over the deeper, more philosophical question of how analogies guide us in social inquiry, and why they cannot be dismissed even when some comparisons may strike critics as politically motivated and illegitimate.

JOSEPH PRIESTLEY, the eighteenth-century chemist and theologian, once observed that "analogy is our best guide in all philosophical investigations; and all discoveries, which were not made by mere accident, have been made by the help of it." While it seems improbable that all scientific inquiry must rely on analogy, analogical reasoning does play a central role in much empirical inquiry, in both the natural and the social sciences. (There's an important difference between analogy and comparison but I'll ignore that difference here.) The philosopher Paul Bartha has written that analogy is "fundamental to human thought and, arguably, to some non-human animals as well." Indeed, chimpanzees that learn to associate a certain sound with a particular reward are making analogical inferences: if a sound at time X announces food, then a comparable sound at time Y should also announce food. This same logical structure recurs throughout the empirical sciences. Bartha, citing the philosopher of science Cameron Shelly, offers the example of analogical reasoning among archaeologists in the Peruvian Andes. Unusual markings that were found on old clay pots remained mysterious until researchers noticed that contemporary potters used similar marks to identify the ownership of vessels baked in a communal kiln: they inferred that the old markings had a similar purpose. Similar habits of analogical inference guide scientists in their speculations about features of the cosmos. Even if they cannot empirically verify that a remote corner of the universe exhibits a certain pattern of astronomical phenomena, analogy permits them to infer that the laws that obtain in our galaxy most likely obtain elsewhere, too.

The first thing to note about such analogical inferences is that they commit us to a basic view that the two distinct phenomena in question belong to the same world. Famously, the first line of British writer L. P. Hartley's novel *The Go-Between* declared that "the past is a foreign country, they do things differently there." And historians, along with anthropologists, are often eager to say that humanity exhibits an astonishing variety of habits and moral codes, and that the standards that apply in one case may not apply in another. Historians are especially keen to argue that historical inquiry alerts us to difference: things that we might have assumed were eternal features of the human condition are in fact specific to their time and may have changed, sometimes in drastic ways, over the course of history.

But claims about difference should not be confused with claims about incommensurability. When I say that A is like B, I presume that there is a common standard (or language or culture) by which I could legitimately raise the matter of similarities or differences at all, since otherwise the task of comparison could not even get off the ground. Just because A is dissimilar to B in certain respects does not imply that there can be no common measure by which they might be compared. When applied to the human sciences, the incommensurability thesis—the claim that discrete phenomena are unique in themselves and cannot be compared to anything else—has some very odd consequences, since it leaves us with a picture of human society as shattered into discrete spheres of time or space, as if A belonged to one world and B to another.

Notwithstanding its manifold difficulties, however, this picture still enjoys some popularity in the human sciences. It has gained a special authority in anthropology, a discipline that has been seized by the anxiety that it had imposed patronizing or distorting standards on other cultures and had made false assumptions about what a given cultural practice meant. Tied to this methodological anxiety was the more explicitly political concern that anthropology had not rid itself of its imperialist origins. The incommensurability thesis offers a welcome release from this problem, as it enables the anthropologist to reject all claims of Western supremacy.

The incommensurability thesis also enjoyed a particular prestige among scholars in the Anglophone world, especially in the 1980s and 1990s when French post-structuralist ideas were ascendant in the human sciences and in some precincts of philosophy. Michel Foucault believed that notions of rupture or discontinuity would eventually displace conventional themes of linear progress. Following philosophers of science such as Gaston Bachelard and Georges Canguilhem, Foucault argued that one could properly understand modern science only if one abandoned the commitment to "great continuities" in thought or culture and turned instead to "interruptions" or "thresholds" that "suspend the continuous accumulation of knowledge." He admitted that the notion of discontinuity was riven by paradox, since it "enables the historian to individualize different domains but can only be established by comparing those domains." But he nevertheless was tempted to defend a theory of "epistemes" (or frameworks of knowledge) as radically distinct.

When one episteme yields to another, he argued, it is as though the fundamental schema by which the world is intelligible suddenly gives way, and the resulting shift is so abrupt that we must give up nearly any notions of continuity between them. This controversial idea bears a note-worthy resemblance to Thomas Kuhn's theory of scientific revolutions, since Kuhn, like Foucault, saw the history of science as a jagged rather than linear path, marked by abrupt shifts in paradigms. Kuhn went so far as to say that in the wake of such a tectonic shift the scientist lives "in a different world."

Whether Michel Foucault or Thomas Kuhn held such views in earnest is a matter of some dispute. Foucault eventually abandoned his "archaeological" method and adopted a method of genealogy that restored a sense of continuity across long stretches of time, charting, for instance, a path from the Christian confessional to modern psychoanalysis. What Kuhn actually meant with his talk of different worlds is still anyone's guess, but the philosopher of science Ian Hacking suggests that Kuhn was at heart a rationalist who (unlike radicals like Paul Feyerabend) did not really mean to endorse the full-blown theory of incommensurability. More recently, philosophers and historians enchanted by poststructuralism will still declare that the past is discontinuous with the present, that its very reality is not something we can affirm, and that insisting on things being one way or another is a sign of ontological naïveté. To such historians, it may suffice to say that at least some facts are certain: the dead are truly dead.

Though scholars may continue to disagree about who most deserves the credit or the blame for popularizing the idea of historical incommensurability, at least one thing seems clear: if this idea is right, then analogical reasoning in history becomes an impossibility. If I sincerely believe that a given event in the past belongs not just to a foreign country but to a world so different from my own as to break all ties of communication between them, then I have no license to speak about the past at all. If I am bound by the rules of my own time, then the past and all its events become in effect unknowable. A past that is *utterly* different is more than merely past; it has no claim on my knowledge and it might as well blink out of existence altogether. This is more than merely a matter of logic; it has political consequences. If every crime is unique and the moral imagination is forbidden from comparison, then the injunction "Never again" itself loses its meaning, since nothing can ever happen "again."

Among historians, however, the rush to say that the past is a foreign country typically has a more prosaic meaning. It is often just an extravagant way of warning against the bias of "presentism," namely, the belief that current conventions obtained in the past precisely as they do today. Needless to say, this warning falls far short of the incommensurability thesis: saying that a given event was in some specific way different from a present event is no reason to say they cannot be compared at all. Unfortunately, historians—especially in the anglophone world—often receive little training in the philosophy of the social sciences, and they tend to muddle this point. They conflate difference with incommensurability, making different countries into different worlds.

But if comparison is clearly legitimate, then why the worry about historical analogy? Part of the answer is that historians, by methodological habit, are inclined to see all events as unique, rather than seeing them, as a political scientist might, as a basis for model building or generalization. The nineteenth-century German philosopher of the social sciences Wilhelm Windelband once argued that natural scientists typically strive for "nomothetic," or rule-governed, explanation, while historians and other scholars of the human world are more invested in "idiographic" understanding—that is, they wish to know something in all its particularity. This is why historians more often than not will specialize in discrete epochs and individual countries, and why they tend to resist drawing from history any grandiose lessons regarding constants of human nature. Still, nothing about this idiographic method actually prevents the historian from comparing one event to another.

WHEN IT COMES TO the horrors of the Third Reich, however, trusted habits of historical understanding are often cast aside. Especially in Western Europe and North America, the genocide of European Jewry has taken on the paradoxical status of a historical event beyond history. Although most historians would, of course, insist that the genocide is a human event that can be known just as other human events are, in the popular imagination the idea has taken hold that the Holocaust represents the ne plus ultra of human depravity. Its elevation into a time-less signifier of absolute evil has had the effect of making it not only incomparable but, in a more troubling sense, unknowable.

There is, after all, at least one common element in every trauma: it belongs to the shared record of human events. Hannah Arendt's descrip-tion of Nazism's evil as "banal" was not meant to diminish its horror but to magnify it, by reminding us that its perpetrators were not mon-sters but ordinary men. She feared that, in the public mind, the sheer magnitude of the Nazis' crime would remain so opaque that it would be depoliticized and lifted free of political history, as if it had not been perpetrated by human beings at all.

But all human atrocities are indeed human acts, and as such all are candidates for comparison. The twentieth century alone has given us instances enough of mass murder to occupy historians of comparative genocide for many years to come. Between 1904 and 1908, the German Empire murdered an estimated 75,000 Herero and Nama people in ter-ritories along the western coast of South Africa—an event that scholars typically call the first genocide of the twentieth century. The Arme-nian genocide, between 1915 and 1923, took an estimated 700,000 to 1.5 million lives (the exact figure is still a matter of dispute). The Rwan-dan genocide in 1994 involved the mass slaughter of Tutsis, Twa, and Hutus—the number of deaths has been calculated at between 500,000 and 1 million. To disallow comparisons of these atrocities with the Holocaust risks the implication that some human lives are less precious than others, as if the murder of mass populations in the European sphere should arouse greater outrage than the murder of mass populations in Armenia or Rwanda.

But if all atrocities are comparable, then why did the Holocaust Memorial Museum issue such a categorical statement against the pos-sibilities of comparison? My surmise is that the statement was not log-ical at all but political: its officials harbor the fear that the Holocaust will become little more than a polemical weapon in ideological contests between left and right. In a short paper posted on the museum website in 2018, "Why Holocaust Analogies Are Dangerous," Edna Friedberg, its resident historian, warned of politicians and social media commentators who "casually use Holocaust terminology to bash anyone or any policy with which they disagree." She condemned "sloppy analogizing," and Holocaust analogies that she called "grossly simplified" or "careless." Such analogies are dangerous, she explained, because "[t]he questions raised by the Holocaust transcend all divides."

But this just prompts the question of whether there might be legitimate analogies that are not grossly simplified or careless. Friedberg does not entertain this question, but it merits consideration. Like common law, the moral imagination works by precedent and example. We are all equipped with an inherited archive of historical events that serves as the background for everything that occurs. Especially when we are confronted with new events that test the limits of moral comprehension, we call upon what is most familiar in historical memory to regain our sense of moral orientation. We require this archive not only for political judgment, but as the necessary horizon for human experience.

Even the term "concentration camp" (not to be confused with "death camp") has historical origins well before the Nazi era, as Andrea Pitzer laid out in an essay for the *New York Review of Books Daily*.[2] Although, in the popular imagination, we may associate the term "concentration camp" mostly with the forced internment of ethnic, national, and political enemies during the Third Reich, the term was already in use in South Africa from around 1900. Such examples remind us that human beings are thoroughly historical; we inherit our nomenclature from the past, and even our highest moral standards are carved from the accumulating bedrock of past collective experience. To consider any event as being literally without comparison would violate our sense of history as a continuum in which human conduct flows in recognizable ways. Not all comparison is careless; as a form of moral reasoning, it is indeed indispensable.

Looming behind today's debates over the treatment of migrants in U.S. detention centers and its historical antecedents is a larger question: Is the present administration descending into fascism? The question is hardly impermissible. Even if we regard Trump himself as a laughably unserious person whose own ideological convictions lack depth or consistency, the enthusiasm he has inspired among white nationalists would suggest that we take the comparison seriously.

Fascism, after all, is not only a historical term; it describes a modern style of authoritarian rule that seeks to mobilize the masses by appealing to nationalism, xenophobia, and populist resentment. Its trademark is the use of democratic procedure even as it seeks to destroy the substantive values of democracy from within. It disdains the free press and seeks to undermine its credibility in the public sphere. During World War I, German nationalists attacked the *Lügenpresse* (or lying press), a term that was later revived by the Nazis. The U.S. president's endless assault on what he calls "fake news" recapitulates this slur, and in his use of Twitter, he has shown great skill in circumventing the news media by speaking directly to his political base.

When we speak of fascism, the term can name both a historically distinctive ideology and a general style. Skeptics like Jan-Werner Müller reject contemporary analogies to twentieth-century fascism as mistaken in part because new authoritarian-populist regimes—such as Orbán's Hungary, Erdoğan's Turkey, Modi's India, or Trump's America—are aware that the term bears an intolerable stigma: today's antidemocrats, Müller writes, "have learned from history" that "they cannot be seen to be carrying out mass human rights violations."[3] But this argument doesn't refute the analogy; it confirms it. The new regimes can find ways to adopt the strategies of the past even as they publicly disavow any resemblance.

To be sure, no historical comparison is perfect. The differences between Trumpism and fascism are legion: the GOP has no paramilitary wing, and its party loyalists have not managed to capture the media or purge the political opposition. Most important of all, the White House has so far failed to promulgate a consistent ideology. But we hardly need to "equate," as Müller puts it, contemporary right-wing populism with fascism to discern their similarities. The analogy permits a more expansive appeal to the political past. The fascism in Trumpism is largely aspirational, but the aspirations are real. This is one of the lessons of Jason Stanley's recent book *How Fascism Works,* in which fascism assumes a very broad (if rather impressionistic) meaning, alerting us to commonalities across time and space that we might otherwise have missed.

The émigré philosopher Ernst Cassirer identified fascism's method as the modern use of political "myths."[4] It imagines the masses not as a pluralistic citizenry but as a primal horde whose power can be awakened by playing upon atavistic feelings of hatred and belonging. Its chosen leader must exhibit strength: his refusal to compromise and readiness to attack are seen as signs of tough-mindedness, while any concern for constitutionality or the rule of law is disdained as a sign of weakness. The most powerful myth, however, is that of the embattled collective. Critics are branded as traitors, while those who do not fit the criteria for inclusion are vilified as outsiders, terrorists, and criminals. The pugnacious slogan "America first," brought to prominence by Woodrow Wilson during World War I and then, in the late 1930s, by Charles Lindbergh, and now revived by Trump, functions as an emotional code, tightening the bonds of tribal solidarity while setting sharp limits on empathy for others.

"The most telling symptom of fascist politics," writes Stanley, "is division. It aims to separate a population into an 'us' and a 'them.'" A skeptic might say that this definition tells us nothing terribly special about fascism since the strategy of dividing the world into enemies and friends is a commonplace of politics everywhere. But this may be the most sobering lesson: fascism may be less a distinctive mode of political organization than the *reductio ad malum*, the dark undertow of modern society carried to an extreme. This was Cassirer's view: fascism, he warned, was a latent temptation in democracy, a mythic form that could reawaken in times of crisis.

Our political nomenclature is always adaptive, attaching itself to new events as history unfolds. Consider, for instance, the term "racism." When we speak of different institutions or practices as racist, we understand that this term maps onto reality in different ways: the institutions of American slavery and Jim Crow differ in a great many respects from the institutionalized racism of our own day. But historians of African American history know very well that making use of a common terminology can alert us not only to differences but also to continuities. The manifold techniques of systemic racism—mass incarceration, discriminatory impoverishment, disenfranchisement through gerrymandering, and other modes of subordination, both subtle and overt—cannot be understood if we fasten only on the particular and somehow imagine that the past was a "different country."

In the popular imagination, the belief persists that history involves little more than reconstruction, a retelling of the past "as it actually was." But historical understanding involves far more than mere empiricism; it demands a readiness to draw back from the facts to reflect on their significance and their interconnection. For this task, analogy does crucial work. By knitting together the present with the past, the analogy points in both directions and transforms our understanding not only of the present but also of the past. Contemporary analogies to fascism can also change how we think about fascism itself, stripping it of its unworldly singularity and restoring it to our common history.

But this is not a liability of historical analogy, it is its greatest strength. Our interpretations are always in flux, and the question of whether a given analogy is suitable can only be answered by making the analogy to see if it casts any light, however partial it may be. All historical analogies are interpretative acts, but interpretation is just what historians do. Those who say that we must forgo analogies and remain fixed on the facts alone are not defending history; they are condemning it to helpless silence.

Meanwhile, some of my colleagues on the left remain skeptical about the fascism analogy because they feel it serves an apologetic purpose: by fixing our attention on the crimes of the current moment, they fear that we will be blinded to longer-term patterns of violence and injustice in American history. On this view, cries of alarm about the rise of fascism in the United States are implicitly calls to defend the status quo, since the real emergency is nothing new. But this argument is specious. Those who reject the analogy from the left have merely inverted the idea of American exceptionalism, a convenient trick that relieves them of the need for more differentiated judgment. After all, the fact that things have always been bad does not mean they cannot get worse. Ultimately, this skepticism is a game of privilege: those who would burn the whole house are not the ones who will feel the flames.

Among all the terms that are available to us for historical comparison today it is hard to see why "fascism" alone should be stamped as impermissible. No differently than other terms, fascism now belongs to our common archive of political memory. Exceeding its own epoch, it stands as a common name for a style of institutionalized cruelty and authoritarian rule that recurs with remarkable frequency, albeit in different guises. In the United States, it would no doubt take a different form. As the historian of European fascism Robert Paxton has observed, "the language and symbols of an authentic American fascism would ultimately have little to do with the original European models."⁵ In an American fascism, he writes, one would see not swastikas but "Christian crosses" and "Stars and Stripes."

The true signs of fascism's resurgence, however, would not be merely the symbols it deploys in its propaganda but its treatment of those who are most vulnerable. This is why the spectacle of migrants in cages should alarm us all, and why we cannot take comfort in the thought that things are not as bad as they once were. The phrase "Never again" can be used in a restrictive sense as a summons to the Jewish people alone that it should never permit another Holocaust to occur. But if the phrase contains a broader warning, it must apply across time and space to other people as well. By forbidding all comparison, this more expansive meaning is vitiated. The moral imperative that such an atrocity should never again be visited upon any people already implies the possibility of a reprisal— with all of its terrifying consequences.

POSTSCRIPT

When the above essay was first published Donald Trump was still president of the United States—a circumstance that, like many on the left, I found highly distressing. To be sure, the essay was not written chiefly as an indictment of Trumpism, nor did it occur to me that it would lend itself so easily to the dualistic polemics that were then dominant in public discussion. The question that seemed so urgent to a great many at the time—is Trumpism a species of fascism, or is it not?—was not the question that most aroused my interest. Unlike many interlocutors on the left today, I have never arrogated to myself the authority to speak with certainty about contemporary political controversies, nor would I ever claim that such pronouncements are my strength. The question that was of concern for me was chiefly philosophical, and it addressed a basic problem of reasoning in the social sciences. But in the atmosphere of polarized debate it was altogether expected that the essay would elicit responses from scholars who were eager to offer correctives that only betrayed their own penchant for dualistic thinking. In retrospect I can readily understand why the need for polemic overwhelmed careful reflection. But it is worth revisiting a few of the methodological and philosophical problems that I considered central.

To me the question "Is this fascism or not?" is already a question *mal posée*. As I noted in the original version of my essay, the differences between Trumpism and fascism are legion, and these differences merit our attention: the Republican Party has no organized paramilitary wing, it possesses no state monopoly over the media, nor did it even come close to purging its ranks of opposition critics. Members of rival parties were never subjected to orchestrated campaigns of intimidation, nor were they stripped of their citizenship, nor were sent off into internment camps for political enemies. The list of such differences is so obvious and extensive one may find it absurd to belabor the self-evident point that any attempt to *equate* Trumpism with fascism is bound to fail. The exercise in differentiation would no doubt prove instructive, however, if only for the very simple and logical reason that no two political events are ever identical. But of course this was something that careful readers of my essay could have easily grasped.

Because the lesson was apparently lost in the ensuing debate, however, it is worth stating again. The point of an analogy is *not* equation. It is to discern similarity across dissimilarity, continuity across discontinuity. The very concept of analogical reasoning, at least in the human sciences, is to further our understanding of how distinct phenomena might nonetheless warrant comparison without losing sight of the many points at which they diverge. To insist that we simply banish all comparison would make sense only if we supposed that each and every event in human history is identical only to itself. On this supposition nothing would ever admit of comparison because each event would appear as if it were a singularity—a gravity well that collapses upon itself and escapes any of the conceptual tools by which we typically seek to understand human conduct. To see the world this way, however, represents a species of nominalism that is so extreme and so implausible that it would defeat not only comparison but the very possibility of description as such. For understanding always involves conceptualization, and concepts by definition are universals rather than mere particulars. Ever since Plato, philosophers have faulted nominalism as a doctrine that founders in self-contradiction. It wants to declare that every event is a mere particular, but it cannot even begin to make itself intelligible without appealing to categories that have validity across a range of cases.

The nominalist may further object that comparison must always fail because no two events are alike in *every respect*. But this objection forgets the well-known argument from Wittgenstein, that everyday language consists in terms that do not require exhaustive definitions; we compare events not by applying rules but by recognizing family resemblances across a wide variety of distinctive phenomena. To insist that two events are comparable only if they share *all* essential features in common is simply to repeat the old Leibnizian dictum that two things that are indiscernable in all respects are simply identical. But surely even the most empirically minded historian is not so mindless as to insist that every event is comparable only to itself.

All of these considerations, unfortunately, seem too rarefied for historians who wave aside problems of philosophical method and assign to themselves a privileged role as guardians of the past. But it is hardly obvious that the discipline of history alone should be granted this authority, nor do the rules of historicist understanding stand uncontested in the court of political judgement. There is, for example, an entire discipline of comparative political science that begins with the premise that distinct political phenomena admit of comparison across time and space. In their 2018 book, *How Democracies Die*, my colleagues Daniel Ziblatt and Steven Levitsky (both skilled in comparative politics) laid out an empirically scrupulous analysis of creeping authoritarianism across the globe. So far as I know, few critics felt that they had transgressed the sacred rules of scholarship by comparing apples with oranges, or that they simply lumped too many disparate phenomena together in their effort to explain why so many democratic states today seem at risk of collapse. It may be that they did themselves a great favor simply by avoiding the term "fascism," a word that obviously carries a greater rhetorical punch even when it is deployed more or less synonymously alongside terms such as "right-wing populism" or "illiberal democracy."

But perhaps we should consider another reason as to why some historians began to raise the cry of alarm when the analogy to fascism emerged in public debate. In the historical profession, perhaps more than in any other precinct of the modern academy, the accusation of "presentism" will often suffice to silence one's opponents, since collapsing differences across time is supposed to be the greatest of all methodological crimes. So it was all the more surprising when, in the summer of 2022, a prominent member of the historical profession wrote a rather flat-footed critique of presentism and was roundly condemned for his failure to appreciate the continuities between past and present. The truth, however, though one barely mentioned in his critique, is that the accusation of so-called presentism seldom captures the complex ways in which the historical profession seeks to police its boundaries. There is a simple reason for this: not only do historians alert us to historical difference, they also alert us to hidden patterns of continuity over time. Historians who study poisonous and long-persisting phenomena such as racism or sexism or anti-Semitism may be rather more charitable about presentism, for the simple reason that they discern in the record of human conduct as much continuity as change. When they look upon the long and lamentable history of human hatred, they recognize that (to repeat a point made famous by Michel Foucault) all history is a history of the present, and that the past is not so foreign after all.

This is one reason we should reject the sober-sounding pronouncement of the historian that we must respect the "alterity" of the past. I am not entirely certain that I know what this means, but it strikes me as an obvious exaggeration, a dogma of metaphysics that has little to do with the way in which historians typically go about writing history. Even Max Weber, whose name is habitually heard whenever the conversation turns to worries about "presentism" or "politicizing the past," did not really endorse the impossible talisman of so-called value-freedom, at least not in the manner that some may imagine. Weber recognized that all social understanding of the past is conditional upon evaluative schemes that are made rather than found. This is why he was a partisan of *interpretative* sociology. He knew that in the human sciences a certain kind of naturalistic posture is impossible, since the world we are studying is not a meaningless array of objects; we are studying ourselves. When we set about trying to understand the past we are guided by our own criteria of what is significant—and what we find significant is inevitably born out of our own evaluations and concerns.

Let me now address a further and quite different objection to the analogy that has little to do with problems of metaphysics or epistemology. This objection seems to have arisen among colleagues on the political left for reasons that pertain more to political strategy than scholarship. Stated simply, the argument seemed to be that entertaining *any* analogies to fascism would serve as mere distraction from the more urgent task of defeating Trumpism. Notice that this not really an argument about the descriptive accuracy of our political language; it is an argument about its political effects. The two arguments are logically distinct; somebody might find the analogy descriptively helpful but still object that promoting the analogy in public would be strategically disadvantageous. Now, the question of whether allusions to fascism might distract public attention would appear to be a matter of empirical psychology, and it's not at all obvious that raising the specter of fascism turns our attention away from more pressing political concerns. Nor am I aware of any studies in social psychology that have addressed this question. I am inclined to say that the analogy is typically used not to distract us but to *enhance* public feelings of alarm. When the analogy is used in this way, of course, it is seldom more than a rhetorical gesture, a way of expressing maximalist moral outrage. And this is probably what drove Alexandria Ocasio-Cortez to compare the cages for migrants at the southern U.S. border to concentration camps. Unlike my critics, however, I do not find this analogy unacceptable or irresponsible simply because it is used in an emotive register to express heightened condemnation. Expressive speech is one legitimate mode of political speech, and it's not at all clear to me why any single critic should arrogate to himself the authority to wave aside our expressive speech as inappropriate.

But there is a different and more interesting question that arises in connection with the charge that the fascism analogy is a "distraction." This is the question as to whether the fascism label covers up the deeper, more enduring and systemic problems that afflict American society. Calling Trumpism "fascist" (or so the argument runs) implies that our moral panic is confined *only* to the current political crisis, and this means that we are implicitly stating our approval for the system as it was before Trumpism came along. Denouncing Trumpism is therefore an instance of "liberal hysteria" (a rather incautious phrase that was used in the title of one editorial in *The New York Times*) and this hysterical reaction is typical among liberals who never found any reason for objecting to the widespread corruption and racism of the political status quo.

Unlike the other objections mentioned above, I find this objection rather compelling. But readers who are familiar with the Frankfurt School of critical theory will not be surprised to hear that this was more or less what its foremost representatives had in mind when they warned of a fascist resurgence in the postwar era. Critics such as Theodor Adorno, Max Horkheimer, and Walter Benjamin permitted themselves to use "fascism" as a generalized diagnostic for a broad variety of political and psychological patterns. In the classic 1950 work of social psychology, *The Authoritarian Personality* (co-authored by Adorno et al.), "fascism" becomes a highly elastic term, one that applies to characterological features that have their roots in attitudinal and personal styles, most of which are traceable (using psychoanalytic metrics) to early childhood development and primary scenes of sexual and familial socialization. Several years later, following his return to Germany, Adorno warned that fascism had never been truly defeated but endured in everyday habits and political conventions. It was fascism in this capacious sense that he had in mind when he observed in 1967 that "the social conditions for fascism continue to exist."

Today's historians have little patience for those who resort to such expansive language. They use the term "fascism" in an exceedingly narrow and purely descriptive sense, based on the conviction that all more expansive uses are untethered from history and irresponsible. The dispute may strike us as rather ironic when we consider that the first-generation members of the Frankfurt School who promoted the expansive use were themselves refugees from fascism (or, in Benjamin's case, its victim) and they devoted their lives to developing critical instruments for explaining both its emergence and its consequences. By contrast, today's gatekeepers against comparison deny that contemporary events are in *any* meaningful sense analogous to fascism. By their own reckoning, however, they have little personal experience of fascism and what they know of it is derived chiefly through academic study. This is not necessarily a disadvantage. Historians have long argued that there is a great divergence between academic study of the past and personal experience, and many historians feel entitled to dismiss first-person accounts of the past as merely anecdotal. The true irony, however, concerns the odd charge that any expansive use of the fascism analogy would be a sign of liberal apologetics. When it comes to the Frankfurt School this charge misses the mark entirely. Forged in the crucible of rising fascism in the midtwentieth century, the Neo-Marxist Institute for Social Research saw fascism not as a pathological departure from bourgeois liberalism but as a development internal to the history of bourgeois society itself. If the Frankfurt School understood fascism in an expansive sense, this was not because they were afflicted with "liberal hysteria," it was because they had developed a serious and comprehensive theory concerning the political pathologies that pervade late-capitalist society. Nor is the Frankfurt School the only intellectual formation on the left to speak of fascism as an ongoing and systemic threat internal to bourgeois society. Throughout the twentieth century Marxist and neo-Marxist historiography has seldom disputed this idea. Fascism is not dismissed as a historical curiosity that has no bearing on current political events; it is understood as an authoritarian solution to instabilities that are endemic to the normal operations of the late-capitalist order.

We may find it perplexing that some historians apparently feel that this entire school of neo-Marxist analysis is without merit. But even for those who have little sympathy for Marxist historiography, the question of the fascism analogy might still warrant our consideration for a rather more general reason. As I wrote in my original essay, analogical reasoning works in two directions: to say that "X is *like* Y" may shed some light on both X *and* Y. The proposition that Trumpism is like fascism may prove helpful not only if it teaches us something about Trumpism; it may also assist us in recalling an essential lesson about fascism itself. One of the most important insights about fascism, typically credited to Hannah Arendt, is that the worst crimes of the twentieth century were due not to the actions of a handful of fanatics but to the great mass of average citizens who were not motivated by extreme ideologies but were simply willing to ignore the excesses committed in their name. When it comes to modern mass-political regimes, inaction and indifference may suffice as explanatory variables.

This historical lesson is not one that we can blithely dismiss as irrelevant to the precarious democracies of our own time. After all, it is the rule in politics that tribal loyalty typically wins out over principle. We might consider, for instance, the sobering fact that very few of the so-called moderates in the Republican Party ever had the temerity to criticize the policies of the Trump administration, and only when he lost the election did a small handful break away from their invertebrate colleagues to speak out against the excesses of the preceding years. And now that he is no longer in power, we cannot ignore the ironic fact that the Biden administration has not yet dismantled the brutal policies concerning migrants at the southern border that moralists in the Democratic Party were quick to condemn just a few years before. Fascism, in other words, is far more capacious in its reach than is typically supposed. If the analogy has any legitimacy today, I would suggest that it is chiefly due to the fact that it alerts us to enduring patterns of authoritarianism and cruelty that are systemic rather than exceptions to the operation of modern democratic states.

Although some may object that this interpretation sets the parameters too broadly and detaches the term from its mid-twentieth-century referents, I would suggest that we relax these historicist scruples and permit the term to enter the accumulating lexicon of political judgment. To claim that our language is wholly bound to the moment of its origin and cannot travel beyond its temporal or geographic borders is to betray a cramped provincialism in relation to our past. The language that we inherit from past events is not fixed in its meaning, nor does it lose its grip as we move forward in time. Our moral language, not unlike the language of art, is always labile and available for reappropriation. We do not cease reading Shakespeare simply because we are not Elizabethans, nor do we cease reading Marx simply because we are not his nineteenth-century contemporaries. The Greeks first used the word τὕρᾰννος, tyrant, in reference to Gyges, the Lydian king; but long after his death the aspiration to tyranny persists.

So, too, the aspiration to fascism. The unsettling truth is that America cannot claim any exception to the patterns of authoritarianism and right-wing populism that are now insurgent in states around the world. American exceptionalism ranks among our most enduring political myths, but it is simply that—a myth. The 1935 novel by Sinclair Lewis, *It Can't Happen Here*, was meant as a satire, but not as an unrealistic fantasy. Its antihero, an aspiring demagogue named Berzelius "Buzz" Windrip, appears far too plausible, especially at a time when Donald Trump succeeded in winning the presidency and then refused to concede electoral defeat. On January 6, 2021, a motley assortment of militias and self-declared right-revolutionary groups (such as the Proud Boys, the Oath Keepers, and other groups, many of them avowed white supremacists) pledged loyalty to the President and stormed the Capitol with the intent of bringing down the elected government and executing those they considered traitors. To be sure, when judged by past instances of fascist rebellion the mob in Washington was a small and absurd bunch, but their absurdity does not mean that they were any less dangerous; and we now know how close they came to murdering members of both the House and the Senate. If that eruption of violence taught us anything at all, it was that there are no guarantees about the survival of our current political order. Democracy is not an eternal form, but an impermanent and embattled experiment that could collapse in the States just as it has elsewhere. And that is the most historical lesson of all. To believe otherwise would betray a true failure of political imagination.

THE TROUBLE WITH COMPARISONS

SAMUEL MOYN

In the 1980s, German intellectual life was very much agitated by something called the "historian's dispute" (*Historikerstreit*). It began when Free University of Berlin professor Ernst Nolte—an unknown high school teacher before he wrote a brilliant comparative study of fascism in the 1960s—insulted Holocaust historian Saul Friedländer at a dinner party.

As it unfolded, the dispute concerned many things. It started with Nolte's pernicious suggestion that the Zionist leader Chaim Weizmann had declared war in 1939 on Germany on behalf of the Jewish people, as if that licensed what Germany did next. The dispute proceeded through Nolte's contention that Adolf Hitler had acted in response to Joseph Stalin's prior atrocities, as if two wrongs could make a right. But a major part of the dispute turned on the propriety of comparison. It was about the plausibility of analogizing National Socialism to other phenomena before and after.

When Michiko Kakutani famously made an analogy between the days of January 1933 and what might transpire in January 2017, and others argued that Trump's Reichstag fire was only months away, no historian's dispute took place.[1] No wonder: Germany's conservative historians had unleashed analogies to "normalize" their country's history, as they put it. By contrast, America's resistance after the election of Donald Trump turned to analogy to abnormalize him: the United

States teetered on the edge of fascism, and with a Hitler on the make now at the helm.

That comparison requires a careful ethic is the lesson three years on, for the sake of understanding and mobilization alike. It is surely fodder for some future ironist that, after our era of fearing Trump's actions, he appears set in the current pandemic to go down in history for a worse sin of inaction. For all his abuses of the powers accorded the presidency in the prior generation, his failure to deploy them now seems more glaring. His hijinks in flouting the rule of law, though inexcusable, have not concealed the continuity of American governance, for good and for ill. (The Republicans have gotten their conservative judges and tax cuts, just as before.) William Barr is the reincarnation of Carl Schmitt, the evil genius of National Socialism, wrote Tamsin Shaw in *The New York Review of Books*, except that our attorney general has done his worst by letting some louts out of their lies and pursuing causes with roots deep in American history.[2] No analogy to Hitler or fascism is needed to explain these results.

In 2016, the impulse to draw comparisons to some of the worst episodes in European history may have been understandable and even useful. The future was opaque and elites were shaken by the election results. And there were strategic uses to such warnings. The horrors coming were likely, though no one knew their exact form. Sometimes, the sky does not fall in precisely the way the chickens fear, but it is still the right move to cluck.

Yet people forget that analogy had commonly seemed noxious, not necessary, in the previous century. The Weimar syndrome has often led to bad things, and the comparison to fascism had normally been agreed to be dubious. Nolte, for example, had made his name with *Three Faces of Fascism* (1963), a proposal to use comparison promiscuously, and precisely when it came to the nebulous concept of "fascism." Not merely did it apply to Benito Mussolini's Italy, Nolte insisted, but also to the French reactionary monarchists of Action Française of the turn of the twentieth century, as well as to Hitler's later movement and regime.

In the midst of the German dispute in 1986, that comparison led him to intolerable excesses, both intellectually and politically. Comparison excused, rather than indicted. Martin Broszat of the Munich Institute for Contemporary History, an *éminence grise* among German historians, insisted that it was essential to regard National Socialism as comparable to other regimes. He wondered if the time had come to treat Hitler's Germany as a state in many respects like other states, analogizing its welfare policies to those taking shape farther west in the middle of the twentieth century. Didn't the German Labor Front program resemble what William Beveridge devised for Britain: a modern welfare state?

One of the deepest American critics of such apologetic comparisons at the time was the Harvard University historian Charles Maier. Comparative exercises were crucial, Maier observed, but they were potentially misleading, too—especially when analogies were made without the balance provided by its obverse, disanalogy. "Any genuine comparative exercise emphasizes uniqueness as much as similarity; it establishes what is common in contrast to what is distinctive," Maier, as master of comparative analysis himself, concluded. "Comparison must be a two-edged sword."[3] Indeed, as one of the greatest modern historians, the Frenchman Marc Bloch, had argued fifty years earlier, the whole point of comparison, when responsible, is to isolate what is singular and thus in need of new attention. A comparison cannot be about ignoring distinctions, but must isolate them, or it is negligent or reckless.

The Nazi regime did indeed resemble other regimes. It was just that the similarities that conservative Germans cited were trivial. In Germany after 1933, the conductors "von Karajan and Furtwängler produced music; the post office delivered mail,"[4] Maier conceded. So what? Of course, Nazi Germany was similar in some respects to other examples, but that is true of everything in the world—and banal. Everything, after all, shares an indefinite number of traits with everything else, and differs just as much. No two items one might connect are entirely identical, nor utterly distinct. What matters in responsible comparison are the reasons you want to stress one or another similarity—and whether you take seriously major differences. Without acknowledging differences, comparison is partisanship, and not always in a good cause.

For Maier, the conservative Germans were obfuscating the fact that their ancestors, and no one else, had built the death camps. This made the Nazi project distinctive. In saying so, he wasn't appealing to some mystical notion that things in general are "incommensurable" in the world, sharing nothing in common with one another. He wasn't contending at all that comparison itself is never allowed. In fact, almost no one trades on that notion. There is no ban on analogy, which sits at the heart of human reasoning. If there is any risk in our public discussion, indeed, it is the opposite one of a surfeit of comparisons so thick that a day on the internet does not pass without the shades of multiple pasts haunting every new event. Rather, Maier's point was that analogy only works responsibly in tandem with disanalogy. The two depend on each other. And too much of the one without enough of the other, Maier insisted, is deceptive and ideological.

Now, on one level, our analogies since 2016 are very different from those made in the historian's dispute thirty years earlier. Far from relativizing what made Hitler's Germany special by comparison to other states, we have feared that precisely the distinctive evil of his regime, or of fascist horror generally, was back in our time. And so, one might assume that abnormalizing Trump is innocent of the same intellectual mistakes that normalizing Nazism involved in the historian's dispute. It isn't. It has turned out that riotous analogy without disanalogy is an error for those who want to impose stigma, and not only for those who seek to lift it.

For those doubtful about the fascism analogy for Trumpism—and I count myself as one of them—the point is to appreciate both continuity and novelty better than the comparison allows. Abnormalizing Trump disguises that he is quintessentially American, the expression of enduring and indigenous syndromes. A response to what he represents hardly requires a restoration of "normalcy" but a questioning of the status quo ante Trump that produced him. Comparison to Nazism and fascism imminently threatening to topple democracy distracts us from how we made Trump over decades, and implies that the coexistence of our democracy with long histories of killing, subjugation, and terror—including its most recent, if somewhat sanitized, forms of mass incarceration and rising inequality at home, and its tenuous empire and regular war-making abroad—was somehow less worth the alarm and oppro-brium. Selective outrage after 2016 says more about the outraged than the outrageous.

It is no contradiction to add to this qualm that comparing our cur-rent situation in America to fascism also spares ourselves the trouble of analyzing what is really new about it. For all its other virtues, compar-ison in general does not do well with the novelty that Trump certainly represents, for all of his preconditions and sources. It is true that in the face of novelty, analogy with possible historical avatars is indispensable, to abate confusion and to seek orientation. But there is no doubt that it often compounds the confusion as the ghosts of the past are allowed to walk again in a landscape that has changed profoundly. Comparison is always a risky tool; it leads to blindness, not just insight.

But keeping us honest is not the only reason that contrasts are essen-tial at every turn. The politics of comparison are routinely bad. The best defense of analogy is that it could help improve our situation, by attract-ing crucial allies, and plotting next steps. Arguably, comparison served some of those functions in the early Trump years. I confess I found the *reductio ad Hitlerum* annoying even then, not least because it already seemed to me the definition of irresponsibility: if you say the world is about to end, either it will grimly confirm your prophecies or you will say your warning saved it. Heads, you win; tails, I lose. But if it was rea-sonable not to demand an ethics of comparison in those early days, three years on our situation is radically different. For what we have learned is that our politics of comparison *doesn't do the work we hoped it would.*

A friend of mine and another Harvard historian, Peter Gordon, sug-gested in *The New York Review of Books* a few months ago that "skepti-cism" of the usual comparisons is complacent.[5] I'm not sure how. The fact that things can get worse than Trump has already made them—as Gordon rightly observes they can—hardly means that the popular anal-ogy to fascism helps create a better world for the victims we care about. Insisting that it does raises the political question of what the most pro-ductive response is to avoid constant ruin, visited most grievously on the worst-off, as always. Does seeing Hitler reincarnated in Trump, or the Gestapo in Immigration and Customs Enforcement, stave off that result? Does branding our enemies as fascists sap their legitimacy? On their own, not much, so far as I can see. Comparison doesn't help victims; and if contrast is inescapable in any responsible comparison, then either both are part of the same parlor game of the privileged, or neither is.

Another colleague and friend, Jason Stanley, has argued judiciously in his book *How Fascism Works* (2018) for identifying Trump and many other features of contemporary politics as fascist.[6] Stanley himself doesn't depend on comparisons; nothing in his treatment turns on there ever having been fascist regimes before. And, of course, no one could deny that fascism involves ideological trends that are pervasive in modern American history, and that are bad enough in their own right and in their present form, even if an actual fascist regime remains far off. And no one should have trouble critiquing all of the things that Stanley says constitute fascism: appeals to a mythic past, attacks on intellectualism and intellectuals, hierarchies of race and gender, calls for law and order, and so forth.

The only real question is whether, when the stirrings of fascism are redefined *as the thing itself*, there is an analytical cost. If Stanley is right, most of modern political history is fascist, latently or openly. Perhaps it is. But Stanley does not recognize that the far more popular allegation of fascism—in Madeleine Albright's bestseller *Fascism: A Warning* (2018), for example—is precisely about *suppressing* our understanding of all the forces Stanley is rightly concerned about in order to scapegoat Trump, as if he were an alien in our midst. But Trump will never die for our sins.

Stanley's project, precisely because it is so open to the depravities of American history, is also open to political doubts. The choice of the word "fascist" to describe them both trades on the extraordinary horror people feel when that allegation is made and at the same time undermines it by making fascism so quotidian and ordinary in human affairs as to become something like their essence. And while there is no doubt that identifying the oppression at the heart of most U.S. politics to date is worthwhile, it is unclear what the label of fascism adds in practical terms.

It may be unfair to worry that analogies to the collapse of Weimar or the coming of fascism are actually harmful. True, around the world and constantly in American life since the 1940s, politicians have used such comparisons to justify the worst preemptive steps, from ghastly suppressions of local student opposition to even ghastlier responses to global Communist threats. Acts in the name of preserving democracy, not just scuttling it, have been a nasty business. And there is room to argue that, this time around, American analogies with regime collapse have had grievous consequences. Not only have they helped rehabilitate some of those most responsible for Trump himself—like neoconservatives who found a new audience among liberals after losing control of the Republican Party—but they have also helped determine the fate of the Democratic Party, which chose a "Never Trump" candidate over a transformational one.

But the more devastating truth is that bad analogies have been less harmful than useless. Occluding what led to the rise of Trump (who posed as a victims' candidate) and "Trump-washing" the American political elite before him who led to so much suffering are less serious mistakes than delaying and distorting a collective resolve about what steps would lead us out of the present morass. In no sense have the fascist comparisons made a productive difference in devising them. Charging fascism does nothing on its own. Only building an alternative to the present does, which requires imagining it first.

If, as seems likeliest, Joe Biden wins the presidency, Trump will come to be treated as an aberration whose rise and fall says nothing about America, home of antifascist heroics that overcame him just as it once slew the worst monsters abroad. Those who warned against the coming of fascism will congratulate themselves for saving the home of the free and redeeming the land of the brave, which somehow lurched toward the brink. They will cordon off the interlude, as if it was "an accident in the factory," as Germans after World War II described their twelve-year mistake. Far from recognizing Trump as not just the product of and verdict on what came before, they will see his passing as the confirmation of the need to restore it. A few will wonder what happened to the discourse of fascism, and remember the disquieting possibility that fascist tendencies lurk everywhere in modern politics. But their books will sell in smaller numbers. Most will consider the danger past. This is, after all, America.

Comparison, even when controlled by the ballast of contrast, is a political act to be judged successful or not. We must clarify not just what is common when we compare, but also what is distinctive. And, in doing so, we must participate in bringing about a better future, not a worse one, if we can. Analogy and disanalogy with the past can assist in analyzing our present, but not if they allow indulging in a melodramatic righteousness, and luxuriating in our fears, all while preparing a terrifyingly normal future.

WILLIAM BARR

The Carl Schmitt of Our Time

TAMSIN SHAW

U.S. Attorney General William Barr's defense of unchecked executive authority in his November 5, 2019, speech to the Federalist Society had an unpleasant familiarity for me. It took me back to a time in my life—during the late 1990s, as a graduate student in England, and the early 2000s, teaching political theory in the politics department at Princeton University—when I seemed to spend altogether too much time arguing over the ideas of a Nazi legal theorist notorious as the "crown jurist" of the Third Reich.

Carl Schmitt's work had then become popular in universities, and particularly in law schools, on both sides of the Atlantic. The frequent references to his "brilliance" made it evident that in the eyes of his admirers he was a bracing change from the dull liberal consensus that had taken hold in the wake of the Cold War. Schmitt's ideas thrived in an air of electrifyingly willed dangerousness. Their revival wasn't intended to turn people into Nazis but to rattle the shutters of the liberal establishment.

Schmitt was supposed to be a realist. For him, laws and constitutions didn't arise from moral principles. At their basis, there was always a sovereign authority, a decision maker. Schmitt stipulated that the essential decision was not a moral choice between good and evil but the primally political distinction between friend and enemy. And that distinction, in order to be political in the most important sense, had to generate such intense commitment that people would be prepared to die for it. He set out this view in a brief work, *The Concept of the Political*, in 1932. Only a few years later, he and many of his fellow Germans showed that they were prepared to kill for it. And kill and kill and kill.

In spite of his ideas' serving this dismal role in recent history, I found that there were always one or two students for whom the simplicity of Schmitt's dualistic choice was appealing. All the complex reflections and reasoning that enter into responsible political judgment could be dismissed in favor of one very simple binary opposition. We all want our justifications to end somewhere, to bring an end to the process of providing reasons for our beliefs, values, and actions, and those prepared to listen to an authority telling them exactly where that should be are unburdened. I liked to think that most of the students who embraced Schmitt's work were attracted to the view merely as a theoretical position and were as lacking in real enmity as the anemic liberals whom Schmitt despised.

But in the same period that I encountered these tousle-haired Schmittians in flip-flops, there was in the United States a tremendous craving for action to avenge the terror attacks of September 11, 2001, and prevent further loss of American lives. Impatience at endless diplomatic wrangling, including the United Nations' failure to take seriously the Bush administration's case for invading Iraq, made simple decisionism and the idea of the unchecked executive ferociously appealing in U.S. political life. The concept of the "enemy combatant" became sufficiently vague for the executive branch to apply it more or less at will to whatever person it pleased. And for many of those advocating preemptive war, or rendition and torture, on the grounds that terrorists might attack us with weapons of mass destruction, the sense of "it's them or us" developed a new and ugly intensity.

The problem of containing the terrorist threat was not construed as one of detection and policing. It was a war. And for prominent thinkers and politicians on the right, it was a civilizational battle for "Judeo-Christian values" against "Islamo-fascism," a friend-enemy distinction that remains deeply rooted in parts of American society today. This ill-defined enemy is the specter constantly evoked by the people Trump has chosen as his advisers and officials. Their mythic world-historical struggle has become detached from the actuality of counterterrorism operations. General Michael Flynn, a veteran of the "global war on terror," wrote in his 2016 book *The Field of Fight*:

> We're in a world war against a messianic mass movement of evil people, most of them inspired by a totalitarian ideology: Radical Islam. But we are not permitted to speak or write those two words, which is potentially fatal to our culture.[1]

The idea that "evil people" might destroy "our culture" is alarmingly bellicose rhetoric, but one that is evidently persuasive for certain people. Steve Bannon uses it, too. He made a speech via Skype at a Vatican conference in 2014 in which he stated that "we are in an outright war against jihadist Islamic fascism." These are just the beginning stages "of a very brutal and bloody conflict." He called upon the "church militant" to fight this "new barbarity." In the White House, Bannon's main initiative was the racist and deeply harmful travel ban on people from Muslim countries. Trump's Executive Order 13769 restricted entry to the United States for citizens of Iraq, Iran, Libya, Somalia, Sudan, Syria, and Yemen on the grounds—disputed by most counterterrorism experts—that it was an essential counterterrorism measure.

So the views expressed in Barr's Federalist Society address were not new ones. Not only has this Schmittian approach to constitutional doctrine come to be accepted as one respectable view among others in law schools, it has become increasingly accepted as a feature of American politics as well. Barr described the travel ban as "just the first of many immigration measures based on good and sufficient security grounds that the courts have second guessed since the beginning of the Trump Administration." The president, when acting, or claiming to act, in the interests of national security, should be allowed unlimited scope for decision-making. Barr told his audience that the Framers' view of executive power

entailed the power to handle essential sovereign functions—
such as the conduct of foreign relations and the prosecution
of war—which by their very nature cannot be directed by a
pre-existing legal regime but rather demand speed, secrecy,
unity of purpose, and prudent judgment to meet contingent
circumstances. They agreed that—due to the very nature of
the activities involved, and the kind of decision-making they
require—the Constitution generally vested authority over these
spheres in the Executive.[2]

Constitutional experts have denounced this view of the unchecked
executive not only as a misinterpretation of Article II of the Constitution, but as a dangerous attempt to place the president above the law.

Barr's view is the final *reductio ad Schmitt* of our political era. As
attorney general, at the head of the Justice Department, he is charged
with upholding the rule of law, but he admires only lawlessness in
moments of crisis. He claims in his Federalist Society speech that America's greatness has been achieved through its most savage conflicts, from
the Civil War, through "World War II and the struggle against Fascism,"
to, most recently, "the fight against Islamist Fascism and international
terrorism." Barr even folds into this narrative "the struggle against racial
discrimination," while using his office to defend a blatantly racist president. These "critical junctures" when the country has been most challenged, he claims, are the moments that have brought the Republic "a
dynamism and effectiveness that other democracies have lacked." Such
moments of decision gained that significance precisely because this was
when the presidency "has best fulfilled the vision of the Founders." By
this, Barr means the urgent, secret decisions that forge a strong and vital
sovereign authority.

This is not just a theoretical position for Barr. He previously supported President George H. W. Bush's pardoning of Caspar Weinberger,
Reagan's secretary of defense, who was charged with obstruction of federal investigations and lying to Congress about the Iran-Contra affair.
That reckless criminal enterprise presumably represented the kind of

"dynamism and effectiveness" that the liberal rule of law tries to suppress. Barr admires action.

He also fears that the commitments motivating sovereign decisions and actions will become etiolated if removed from the sustaining light of Christian faith. Religion is the only basis, he has claimed, for the kind of commitment that is conducive to greatness. In an address at Notre Dame given on October 11, 2019, Barr poured contempt on the "high-tech popular culture" that distracts us from our fundamental commitments. Willfully disregarding the First Amendment's establishment clause, he told his audience that "as Catholics, we are committed to the Judeo-Christian values that have made this country great."

Barr claims to have extremely high-minded motivations.[3] Unlike the frivolous and profane culture that surrounds him, he has understood how to lead a dignified human life:

> Part of the human condition is that there are big questions that should stare us in the face. Are we created or are we purely material accidents? Does our life have any meaning or purpose? But, as Blaise Pascal observed, instead of grappling with these questions, humans can be easily distracted from thinking about the "final things."

The "militant secularism" rampant in America, he insists, endangers this spiritual vocation. Will Barr be remembered, I wonder, for his determination to confront important and intractable theological and philosophical problems? Surely not.

He will be remembered, rather, for defending an impeached president who tried to bribe a foreign power to dig up dirt on his domestic political rivals. And for mischaracterizing Robert Mueller's report into Russian interference in the 2016 election, then lending his support to the bizarre view, promoted by Donald Trump and Vladimir Putin, that Ukraine was responsible for the electoral meddling. Barr may also be remembered for eccentrically jetting around Italy, Britain, and Australia, in an effort to gin up support for a baseless conspiracy theory about the "deep state" involving George Papadopoulos, a junior adviser to the Trump campaign and convicted felon. He will be remembered, too, for accusing the FBI of "spying" on the Trump campaign and for dismissing the inspector general's report that vindicated the FBI on the substantive issues on the same day that the President called the agency's officers "scum."[4]

Like Barr, Carl Schmitt held a moralizing view of secularism and liberalism as inadequate to the true seriousness of life. But commentators have been puzzled by what this "seriousness" consists of and whence the demand for such deep enmity arises. The political philosopher Leo Strauss criticized Schmitt for implicitly resting "the political" on moral foundations, even as Schmitt claimed the realm of politics was entirely distinct from morality. One prominent German scholar, Heinrich Meier, made a very influential argument that this moral basis was supplied by Schmitt's Catholic faith. The "ultimate values" that demand the "ultimate sacrifice" must derive from the hidden theistic basis of this thought. Is this what Schmitt has in common with Barr?

A more obvious explanation for Schmitt's demand for enmity, for his condemnations of a liberal culture that weakens that hostile will and of the rule of law that obstructs it, is racism. He was, after all, not just a Catholic but a Nazi. His actions and unpublished writings betray a virulent anti-Semitism. We do not need to invoke an esoteric theism to account for what can be sufficiently explained by bigotry. And many would argue that in our own time the mythic crusade against the civilizational threat of "Islamo-fascism," and the manufactured fear of the supposed barbarian hordes who must be prevented from flooding in from the south by an impregnable border wall, are barely disguised manifestations of a similar racism. It has nothing at all to do with the meaning of human existence, or "final things," or anybody's God.

The reality of the "war on terror," though, is becoming further and further detached from the mythic crusade against "Islamo-fascism." The greatest terrorist threat America now faces comes from domestic terrorists. And national security policy has pivoted away from the Islamic world toward more traditional geopolitical rivals such as Russia and China. We're not engaged in a binary civilizational battle. As the myth becomes unsustainable, Barr and his allies will have to find a new enemy to justify their view of the president as the indispensable, unitary sovereign at the head of an executive branch that is perpetually on a war footing. They will be forced to ramp up the rhetoric of apocalyptic conflict—as Barr is indeed doing.

This doesn't mean, of course, that they will need a foreign war (though, as the escalating confrontation with Iran shows, this may remain an option); all authoritarian regimes create their own internal enemies. No one should doubt Barr's capacity and will to do this. In his original tenure as attorney general, from 1991 to 1993, Barr disbanded the counterintelligence team of the FBI that had been focused on the Soviet Union during the Cold War but whose expertise and Russian language skills seemed less relevant in 1992. He instead turned the FBI's attention to gang-related crime and violence and became a leading advocate of the mass incarceration policies that have since so disproportionately affected America's Black population.[5]

And today, during his second tenure leading the Justice Department, in December 2019, he returned to these themes—apparently disputing the right of Americans of color to protest police violence. Law enforcement must be respected, he said, adding ominously that "if communities don't give that support and respect, they might find themselves without the police protection they need."[6] In effect, he reserved the right to make decisions about who should and should not be afforded the protection of the rule of law, a notably Schmittian reflex.

Barr is not just another craven defender of Trump. Just as Carl Schmitt's identification of parliamentary democracy's weaknesses in the 1920s and his increasingly authoritarian rhetoric in that period had a basis that was quite independent of the cult of Hitler, so William Barr represents a cast of legal thinking (or perhaps, more accurately, antilegal thinking) that has its own origins and supporters. One clear ally is John Durham, whom Barr has placed in charge of his inquiry into the FBI's conduct in the Trump-Russia investigation.

Durham's colleagues have constantly assured us of his integrity, but his natural tendency, too, is to speak in the crudest terms of friends and enemies. In a lecture to the Thomistic Institute at Yale University in November 2018, Durham was discussing his investigation into the destruction of tapes showing CIA torture (an investigation that resulted in no indictments) when he chose to describe the alleged malfeasance revealed by the tapes as no more than "the unauthorized treatment of terrorists by the CIA."[7] This is a troubling description: as Durham must know, not all of the young Muslim men subjected to torture *were* terrorists. At least twenty-six of them were found to have been wrongfully detained.[8] He also chose a bizarre analogy to describe his deeper motivations: he compared himself to the 1970s movie cop *Dirty Harry*, a white officer with little respect for due process who often shoots to kill Black criminals and displays a sociopathic lack of conscience about doing so. Durham told his audience a story about Harry Callahan encountering a "Black militant" who can't comprehend Callahan's unselfish motivation "to serve."

Durham now serves a master who views lawless conflict—the "critical junctures" that "demand speed, secrecy, unity of purpose, and prudent judgment"—as the most important engine of progress, the vital heart of American power, that will bring a wider reckoning with "final things." Independently of Trump and this presidency, William Barr, his henchmen, and his Federalist Society supporters represent a powerful threat to the fundamental values of liberal democracy.

WHAT'S IN A WORD?

DANIEL BESSNER AND BEN BURGIS

Since Donald Trump came down his escalator in 2015, a debate has raged on the left about whether Trump is a "fascist" who threatened the existence of political democracy in the United States. Since Joe Biden decisively won the 2020 presidential election, a closely related debate has broken out about whether Trump's many efforts to hold on to the presidency could reasonably be considered a "coup."

Last week's storming of the U.S. Capitol, which appears to have been undertaken by a loose mob of ragtag QAnon conspiracy theorists, has sparked another round in this great, endless debate. Those who argued that Trumpism is a form of fascism saw in this "insurrection" a genuine threat to the United States' democratic institutions.

But for those who, like us, considered Trumpism a manifestation of extant American trends, and Trump himself to be an ineffectual leader, the events of January 6—while a disturbing escalation in the violent and erratic tendencies of Trump and his most hard-core supporters— were ultimately important because they demonstrated the *weakness* of Trump's position.

It was the last and strangest episode in a series of increasingly desperate attempts to somehow reverse the results of the election. When Republican state legislatures, Trump's own appointees to the Supreme Court, and even Vice President Mike Pence had all refused to follow the President off that cliff, the only card he had left to play was encouraging a violent mob that seems to consist primarily of online conspiracy theorists and insurrectionary fantasists.

Even if the QAnon-ers at the Capitol thought they could overthrow the government and ensure Trump remained in power, a deranged action that had no chance of succeeding cannot reasonably be called a coup. Otherwise, any bizarre event, from Charles Manson's attempt to foment a race war that would transform the United States to the bombings carried out by the many tiny organizations in the 1970s that considered themselves to be carrying out a revolutionary war against the government, could be classified as a "coup."

This becomes especially clear when one compares what happened on January 6 to genuine coups, like the United States' overthrow of Mohammad Mossadegh in Iran in 1953 or Jacobo Arbenz Guzmán in Guatemala in 1954, or what happened in Venezuela in 2002, when military generals tried and failed to remove the elected government.[1]

What happened in Washington, D.C., last week was a violent spasm of impotent rage by a mob mostly made up of civilians and a president who egged them on and talked out of both sides of his mouth about whether he supported what they were doing, but who also made no real attempt to mobilize the power of the state to back them up.

To point this out is not to minimize the horrors of an attempted mob action designed to intimidate Congress. But the good news is we don't need to choose between taking these events seriously and being accurate and careful about what kind of danger the mob represented.

To many, these might appear as semantic questions: If everyone on the left agrees that what happened on January 6 was horrifying, who cares what we call it? If Trump is a deranged reactionary demagogue, does it matter what we label him?

This debate is further complicated by the fact that there's a long history of leftists either casually using "fascist" as an expressive way of insulting particularly appalling politicians or calling attention, as many Black radicals have done, to oppressive features of the American system, especially the police and carceral state. Suffice to say that we have no quarrel with anyone who uses the term in either of these ways, or who affirms that "this is a coup!" in order to viscerally object to the antidemocratic nature of Trump's many ineffectual attempts to stay in power. The latter are real, and, though quixotic, shouldn't be ignored.

Our point is that there is the potential for very real, and very negative, political consequences if the fascism and coup narratives become the dominant frameworks through which leftists and liberals understand the threat posed by Trump and QAnon. In our opinion, these narratives distort how many of our friends and comrades on the left think about the Democratic Party, tech censorship, and police power, while also providing a sop to those who would like the incoming Biden administration to increase the authority of an already far too powerful national security state.

CLASSICAL EUROPEAN FASCISM

Before getting to these larger concerns, let's talk about the merits of the case. Is Trump a fascist? And what does that mean?

Since World War II's end in 1945, political thinkers and critics alike have deployed the term "fascism" to describe right-wing authoritarian regimes like Augusto Pinochet's in Chile or the apartheid government in South Africa. More dubiously, the term "fascism" was also widely applied, on the left, to the administrations of Richard Nixon, Ronald Reagan, and George W. Bush, and, on the right, to the administrations of Bill Clinton and Barack Obama (the latter of whom was regularly portrayed at right-wing protests sporting a Hitler mustache).

In all of these cases, the political point was to draw an analogy with Classical European Fascism (CEF). The core examples of CEF were the movements and then governments led by Benito Mussolini and Adolf Hitler, though in the American context—where Nazi Germany became the existential enemy whose defeat justified the existence of the U.S. empire—most of the time, the implicit analogy was to the Nazis and not the Italians.

What anyone makes of any particular diagnosis that a post–World

War II movement or government is "fascist" depends on what they take to be the most important and distinctive features of CEF. If one wants to focus on how right-wing governments suppressed freedoms and democratic institutions, Pinochet was most certainly a fascist (although Nixon was not). If one wants to emphasize that right-wing movements lacked a commitment to democracy, then the Watergate break-in and *Bush v. Gore* suggest that both Nixon and Bush were fascists. If one wants to emphasize the commonalities between certain conservative tropes and the rhetoric of CEF, then not only Nixon and Bush but Herbert Hoover and Dwight Eisenhower, and for that matter Clinton, might also count as fascists.

Since Trump's election in 2016, a variety of thinkers across the political spectrum, from Timothy Snyder to Jason Stanley to Madeleine Albright, have argued that the Trump administration was either fascist itself or embodied elements of fascist philosophy.[2] Many of these thinkers pointed to Trump's rhetoric, his authoritarian style, and policies like the grotesque "Muslim ban" to justify their claims.

In contrast to these thinkers, we insist that what made CEF unique was not the presence of rhetorical tropes common to many right-wing movements before and after, but its ability to dominate many of the most important institutions of a society.

When Hitler was appointed chancellor, for example, he set about destroying democracy, outlawing opposition parties and independent labor unions, murdering and incarcerating political enemies, and legally stripping Jews of their rights. Hitler and Mussolini also both came to power at the head of street-fighting mass movements that were filled with combat veterans and that cut their teeth terrorizing Jews, socialists, Communists, and trade unionists. Once in power, both fascist leaders proceeded to abolish the normal institutions of capitalist democracy.

While parts of the American state—particularly its security forces, from the police to Immigration and Customs Enforcement (ICE) to the military—embody some fascistic elements, neither Trump, nor any other modern American president, has tried to initiate a process of *Gleichschaltung* (coordination) in which the U.S. state and society were reoriented along fascist lines. Nothing in the recent American experience approaches what happened in Nazi Germany or Fascist Italy, although there certainly are precedents in slavery and Jim Crow.

Moreover, as people writing in the United States in 2021, we must also be aware of how the fascist analogy has been historically deployed, and where it has been most effective and resonant. While there is a long and noble tradition of left-wing antifascism, it was liberal antifascism that has had the most consequential impact on U.S. history. And liberal antifascism, from its beginnings, has been defined by a skepticism of mass politics, a skepticism that directly led to the creation of a post–World War II American state defined far more by technocratic than representative governance.

Indeed, the most important institutions of this state—the National Security Council, the Council of Economic Advisers, the Central Intelligence Agency, the modern Federal Bureau of Investigation, the Department of Defense—were designed, at least partially, to limit ordinary Americans' impact on public and foreign policy.

Thus, while all leftists must be antifascist, and while important critics of the U.S. state have used the fascist analogy in the past, our argument that the analogy is not only inaccurate but politically counterproductive for the left rests on our belief that liberal antifascism has been of far more consequence than left-wing antifascism, and, given that Biden is about to become president, will likely be of more consequence in the coming years.

For us, the most salient issue is not how strongly we should condemn right-wing leaders. Whether you think that Trump counts as a "fascist" or not, there's no denying that, by any reasonable metric, George W. Bush inflicted far more damage on the world. The Patriot Act, the drone program, the widespread use of "extraordinary rendition," the global torture program implemented from Guantánamo Bay to "black sites" in Eastern Europe, and the assertion of a wildly lawless right to "indefinitely detain" anyone, including American citizens like José Padilla, were monstrous assaults on the rights of criminal defendants and terrifying extensions of state power.[3]

The wars Bush started in Afghanistan and Iraq spilled oceans of blood, engendered decades of chaos, and strengthened a military establishment that destroys the lives of Americans and foreigners alike. Any minimally decent society would have long since extradited Bush to The Hague. And while Trump hasn't matched that record, his handling of the COVID crisis certainly counts as "monstrous" in its own way.

As such, our question isn't whether any of these figures deserve the harshest labels we can throw at them, but whether applying these labels is, first, accurate, and second, politically useful. We have doubts on both counts.

TRUMP AND THE FASCISM ANALOGY

That the small number of genuine fascists in the United States mostly support Trump, and that he's often shown a disturbing eagerness to welcome their support, is not in dispute. During the 2016 election, he initially pretended not to know who David Duke and the Ku Klux Klan were in order to dodge a question about repudiating their endorsement. In 2017, Trump also infamously remarked that there were "very fine people" on both sides of a confrontation between neo-Nazis and Antifa in Charlottesville, Virginia. Furthermore, during the 2020 election, he told the Proud Boys to "stand back and stand by." And, of course, Trump encouraged the storming of the Capitol on January 6.

Frightening as these events are, it's important to put them in their proper perspective. The highest estimates of the attendance at the nationwide gathering of white supremacists in Charlottesville was a few hundred people. The total nationwide membership of all such organizations, plus the multiracial but fascistlike Proud Boys, is likely a tiny fraction of the total membership of, for example, the Democratic Socialists of America (DSA)—and the DSA is still (unfortunately) an extremely small organization on the periphery of American politics. Moreover, many of those who stormed the Capitol appear to have been members of QAnon, a cultlike movement motivated by conspiracy theories as opposed to any genuine political program.

As such, when people talk about Trump as a fascist threat to

American democracy, they can't really be talking about the forces discussed above. That Trump and his coterie tolerated them as much as they did is certainly a profound moral indictment of Trumpist politics, but it's not as if Trump governed especially differently from a "normal" GOP president. The issue in dispute in the "fascism" debate therefore isn't primarily about Trump's willingness to accept the support of cosplaying CEF supporters. It's about Trump himself and the movement he leads.

Which brings us to one of our major questions: Is it accurate to label Trump a fascist? We don't think so. Trump didn't ride to power at the head of some street-fighting mass organization like Mussolini's Black-shirts or Hitler's Brownshirts. Trump stumbled into the Republican nomination for president because the GOP establishment was unable to consolidate against him in the way the Democratic establishment successfully consolidated against Bernie Sanders. Trump admittedly encouraged supporters to assault hecklers at rallies, though he backed off when he started to worry about his personal legal liability—a pattern of bluster and retreat that defined his presidency.

When the peculiarities of the Electoral College and the deep incompetence of the Democratic nominee allowed him to slip into office, Trump didn't proceed to unleash an army of paramilitary supporters in an American Kristallnacht or take dramatic action to remake the American state in his image. In fact, as Corey Robin has repeatedly and helpfully emphasized, Trump was a weak president.[4]

The Muslim ban and his many attempts to escalate the war of ICE (an organization founded by Bush and used by Obama) on undocumented immigrants were disgusting and led to a great deal of avoidable human misery, but it's also striking that, despite his best efforts to ramp up that machinery of repression, the overall number of deportations declined during Trump's presidency. To the extent that Trump succeeded in governing at all, he mostly governed in the way that Mitt Romney or John McCain probably would have: cutting taxes, appointing union-busters to the National Labor Relations Board and social conservatives to the Supreme Court, and generally acting like a standard-issue Reaganite Republican.

For its part, Trump's foreign policy was neither that of a "right-wing isolationist" in the mold of Charles Lindbergh or Pat Buchanan or a hypermilitaristic conqueror in the mold of Hitler or Mussolini. Instead, he erratically zigzagged between escalating preexisting tensions with countries like North Korea and Iran and making occasional, unpredictable, and halfhearted attempts to de-escalate the use of U.S. force abroad.[5] He appointed generals like H. R. McMaster and James Mattis before falling out with them. He also appointed neocons like John Bolton before falling out with them.[6]

And Trump's rhetoric was strikingly free of the constant invocations of the glory of war that were central to the rhetoric of CEF (possibly because Trump himself never served in the military), and he certainly never made any grand attempts at conquest on the CEF model. Instead, Trump continued in the mold of Obama, pursuing "clean," drone-centered warfare in places like Yemen, where he doubled the rate of drone strikes.[7] If Marco Rubio had won the Republican nomination and then the presidency, it's likely that quite a few of the same moves would have been made, if without Trump's characteristic unpredictability.

To say all of this isn't to minimize the dangers that Republicans like Trump actually represent. As distant as it may be from CEF, mainstream Republicanism has done profound damage to the United States, and the rest of the world, in the last forty years. Democrats and Republicans are not exactly the same. One of us lives in a swing state and reluctantly voted for Biden on the grounds that NRLB appointments, for example, are important to the socialist left. But hyperbolic talk that identifies Trump as a "fascist" who represents a unique threat to the core institutions of American democracy does not help the left. Instead, it creates a constant pressure on socialists to deemphasize our own program, and our own profound conflict with the neoliberal center, in order to force us to unite with that center as well as neoconservative "Never Trump" Republicans, big tech companies, and even "the intelligence community" in a grand reenactment of the Popular Front against fascism assembled in the 1930s and 1940s. After all, if a rising tide of fascism poses an imminent threat to democracy itself, shouldn't we put everything else aside to defeat that threat?

Never has this pressure been as intense as in the aftermath of January 6.

WHAT'S A "COUP" AND WHY DOES IT MATTER?

An "attempted coup," in the usual way that phrase is used, refers to a coup attempt that *might have succeeded*. Without this criterion of demarcation, any bizarre, radical action that has as its goal the overthrowing of the government can be defined as a coup. If this were the case, then we in this (or any other) country would be under constant threat of coups.

Given what we know now, it was simply impossible for the bizarre group that gathered in Washington, D.C., on January 6 to have achieved its goal of ensuring that Trump remained president. Most important, the group didn't have the support of the uniformed military, the sine qua non of most successful coup attempts.

But, again, does it really matter what we call the storming of the Capitol, especially given that we agree it was a bad thing? Why not, in fact, call it a coup to highlight the dangers posed by QAnon and the ever more radicalized American right?

There are three answers to these questions. First, we do not believe that the Trump far right has any real chance of overthrowing the U.S. government. While this loose coalition of forces is no doubt capable of spectacular acts of grotesque violence, this does not mean that they pose a genuine structural threat to American democracy. Indeed, the riots were put down within hours, and Congress successfully certified the presidential election soon after the Capitol was secured. The events of January 6 thus do not approach Mussolini marching on Rome or Hitler effectively abolishing the Reichstag.

Second, while we believe that the far right must be taken seriously, the most dangerous potential consequence of the Capitol storming is the overreaction of an emboldened security state.

Two decades ago, the American state and society responded to another singular act of violence by trampling on civil liberties and invading two countries. There's serious reason to fear that a new focus on "domestic terrorist groups" will provide succor to the politicians and security bureaucrats who see monsters everywhere. Put simply, identifying the events of January 6 as a coup does little but play into the hands of an already too powerful security state.

There have already been calls for new domestic terrorism legislation.[8] There's a great danger that any such laws will be used against the left. Just as Israeli laws against "incitement" passed in the wake of Prime Minister Yitzhak Rabin's assassination in 1995 were later deployed against pro-Palestinian, antioccupation activists, it's all too easy to imagine any new antiterror legislation being used to crack down on left-wing radicals.

Third, as the historian Samuel Moyn has pointed out, some Republicans have begun to distance themselves from Trump and the "insurrectionists" in an attempt to "Trumpwash" themselves and reenter a reconsolidating American center.[9] Exaggerating fears of a coup will only aid in this twisted effort.

The most shocking aspect of January 6 was that the rioters were able to enter the Capitol. Though we're still finding out what, exactly, happened, judging by the outrageous image of a Capitol cop taking a selfie with rioters, it's likely that at least some elements of the Capitol police were initially reluctant to crack down on protesters they instinctively considered comrades.[10] This is a major problem upon which leftists must focus.

But it's simultaneously crucial that we refuse to give in to the temptation to exaggerate the riot by identifying it as a potentially successful "coup" that could have replaced capitalist democracy with fascism. It's just not true, and pretending that it is plays into the hands of our enemies.

PART III

IS FASCISM AS AMERICAN AS APPLE PIE?

AMERICAN FASCISM

It Has Happened Here

SARAH CHURCHWELL

As militarized police in riot gear and armored vehicles barreled into peaceful protesters in cities across America, and its president emerged from a bunker to have citizens tear-gassed on his way to a church he'd never attended, holding a Bible he'd never read, many people recalled a famous saying often misattributed to Sinclair Lewis's 1935 novel *It Can't Happen Here*: "When fascism comes to America, it will be wrapped in the flag and carrying a cross." Because Lewis's novel is the best remembered of the many warnings against American fascism in the interwar years, he has latterly been credited with the admonition, but they are not Lewis's words.

The adage probably originated instead with James Waterman Wise, son of the eminent American rabbi Stephen Wise and one of the many voices at the time urging Americans to recognize fascism as a serious domestic threat. "The America of power and wealth," Wise cautioned, is "an America which needs fascism." American fascism might emerge from "patriotic orders, such as the American Legion and the Daughters of the American Revolution . . . and it may come to us wrapped in the American flag or a Hearst newspaper." In another talk that year, he put it slightly differently: American fascism would likely come "wrapped up in the American flag and heralded as a plea for liberty and preservation of the constitution."

An American fascism would, by definition, deploy American symbols and American slogans. "Do not look for them to raise aloft the swastika," Wise warned, "or to employ any of the popular forms of Fascism" from Europe. Fascism's ultra-nationalism means that it works by normalizing itself, drawing on familiar national customs to insist it is merely conducting political business as usual. As José Antonio Primo de Rivera, the leader of Spain's proto-fascist Falange Party, proclaimed in 1934, all fascisms ought to be local and indigenous:

> Italy and Germany . . . turned back towards their own authenticity, and if we do so ourselves, the authenticity which we find will also be our own: it will not be that of Germany or Italy, and therefore, by reproducing the achievement of the Italians or Germans we will become more Spanish than we have ever been. . . . In fascism as in movements of all ages, underneath the local characteristics there are to be found certain constants. . . . What is needed is a total feeling of what is required: a total feeling for the Fatherland, for life, for History.[1]

Samuel Moyn recently argued in *The New York Review of Books* against comparing Trump's policies to fascism, because his administration is "pursuing causes with roots deep in American history. No analogy to Hitler or fascism is needed to explain these results."[2] But this presumes that fascism does not have its own deep roots in American history. It is arguable—not to say, exceptionalist—to presuppose that anything indigenously American cannot be fascist; this begs the question of American fascism rather than disputing it. Experts on fascism such as Robert O. Paxton, Roger Griffin, and Stanley Payne have long argued that fascism can never seem alien to its followers; its claims to speak for "the people" and to restore national greatness mean that each version of fascism must have its own local identity. To believe that a nationalist movement isn't fascist because it's native is to miss the point entirely.

Historically, fascist movements were also marked by opportunism, a willingness to say almost anything to get into power, rendering definitions even murkier. Trying to identify its core, the unsplittable fascist atom, has proved impossible; we are left with what Umberto Eco called fascism's "fuzziness," others its "hazy and synthetic doctrines." There are good arguments against attempting through taxonomies to establish what's become known as a "fascist minimum," as if a checklist could qualitatively differentiate fascism from other authoritarian dictatorships. Some think anti-Semitism is a litmus test; others genocide. Does colonialism count? Aimé Césaire, C. L. R. James, and Hannah Arendt, among many other notable thinkers who lived through the first fascisms, certainly thought it did, arguing that European fascism visited upon white bodies what colonial and slave systems had perfected in visiting upon Black and brown bodies.

Paxton has argued influentially that fascism is as fascism does. But conspicuous features are recognizably shared, including: nostalgia for a purer, mythic, often rural past; cults of tradition and cultural regeneration; paramilitary groups; the delegitimizing of political opponents and demonization of critics; the universalizing of some groups as authentically national, while dehumanizing all other groups; hostility to intellectualism and attacks on a free press; antimodernism; fetishized patriarchal masculinity; and a distressed sense of victimhood and collective grievance. Fascist mythologies often incorporate a notion of cleansing, an exclusionary defense against racial or cultural contamination, and related eugenicist preferences for certain "bloodlines" over others. Fascism weaponizes identity, validating the *Herrenvolk* and invalidating all the other folk.

Americans of the interwar period, though they could not predict what was to come in Europe, were nonetheless perfectly clear about one fact we have lost sight of today: all fascism is indigenous, by definition. "Fascism must be home grown," admonished an American lecturer in 1937, "repeating the words of Benito Mussolini, that fascism cannot be imported," but must be "particularly suited to our national life." Logically, therefore, "the anti-Negro program" would provide "a very plausible rallying cry for American fascists," just as anti-Semitism had for Germans. Others recognized that the deep roots of anti-Semitic evangelical Christianity provided equally plausible rallying cries for an American fascism. Wartime patriotism and the Allied triumph soon gave Americans permission to regard fascism as an alien and uniquely European pathology, but "the man on horseback," the despot who could ride reactionary populist energies to power, had been a specter in American politics since at least as early as the presidency of Andrew Jackson in the 1830s.

ONE OF THE LAST, and most horrific, public lynchings in America took place in October 1934, in the Florida Panhandle, where a crowd of as many as five thousand gathered to watch what had been advertised hours earlier in the local press. Claude Neal was burned and castrated, had his genitals stuffed into his mouth, and was forced to tell his torturers that he enjoyed their taste. After he was finally dragged to his death behind a car, his mutilated corpse was urinated upon by the crowds, and then hung from the Marianna courthouse. The German press, quick to capitalize on reports of American lynching, circulated photographs of Neal, whose horrific death they described with "sharp editorial comments to the effect that America should clean its own house" before it censured other governments' treatment of their citizens. "Stop Lynching Negroes is Nazi Retort to American Critics," read the *Pittsburgh Courier* headline reporting German accounts of American racial violence.

The *Courier* was one of many African American papers that not only saw affinities between Nazi Germany and Jim Crow America, but also traced causal connections. "Hitler Learns from America," the *Courier* had declared as early as 1933, reporting that German universities under the new regime of the Third Reich were explaining that they drew their ideas from "the American pathfinders Madison Grant and Lothrop Stoddard," and that "racial insanities" in America provided Nazi Germany with "a model for oppressing and persecuting its own minorities." The African American *New York Age* similarly wondered if Hitler had studied "under the tutelage" of Klan leaders, perhaps as "a subordinate Kleagle or something of the sort."

The Nazis themselves saw a clear kinship. Recent histories have demonstrated that Hitler systematically relied upon American race laws in designing the Nuremberg laws, while the Third Reich also actively sought supporters in the Jim Crow South, although the political leadership of the white South largely did not return the favor. But the correspondence between the two systems was perfectly evident at the time, on both sides of the Atlantic. A Nazi consul general in California even tried to purchase the Klan, with the idea of plotting an American putsch. His price was too low—the Klan was nothing if not mercenary—but, as journalists remarked after the story came to light in 1939, the Klan could not afford to seem foreign; "to be effective," its nativist agenda had to be pursued "in the name of Americanism."

In 1935, African Americans organized around the country in mass protests against Mussolini's slaughter of Ethiopians across the sea. "American Fascism Already Has Negroes," declared the Jamaican American journalist and historian Joel Augustus Rogers. Langston Hughes agreed: "Give Franco a hood and he would be a member of the Ku Klux Klan, a Kleagle. Fascism is what the Ku Klux Klan will be when it combines with the Liberty League and starts using machine guns and airplanes instead of a few yards of rope." "In America, Negroes do not have to be told what fascism is in action," Hughes told another audience. "We know."

At the same time, in 1935, W. E. B. Du Bois published *Black Reconstruction in America*. This foundational work of African American revisionist historiography appeared amid the tumult of the Scottsboro Nine's persecution and as Jesse Owens's medal haul at the Berlin Olympics was seen as both a joke against Hitler and a rebuke to Jim Crow America. In no way coincidentally, then, Du Bois implies in his study more than once that the white supremacism of Jim Crow America could indeed be regarded as "fascism." A half century later, in a neglected but remarkable essay, Amiri Baraka made Du Bois's notion explicit, arguing that the end of Reconstruction "heaved Afro America into fascism. There is no other term for it. The overthrow of democratically elected governments and the rule by direct terror, by the most reactionary sector of finance capital. . . . Carried out with murder, intimidation and robbery, by the first storm troopers, again the Hitlerian prototype, the Ku Klux Klan, directly financed by northern capital."³ It would take another decade or so for white American historiography to absorb the argument, when, in 2004, Paxton observed in *The Anatomy of Fascism* that a strong argument could be made for the first Ku Klux Klan's in the Reconstruction South being the world's earliest fascist movement:

> [The first Klan was] an alternative civic authority, parallel to the legal state, which, in the eyes of the Klan's founders, no longer defended their community's legitimate interests. By adopting a uniform (white robe and hood), as well as by their techniques of intimidation and their conviction that violence was justified in the cause of their group's destiny, the first version of the Klan in the defeated American South was arguably a remarkable preview of the way fascist movements were to function in interwar Europe.

After the KKK was resurrected in 1915, the second Klan claimed as many as five million members by the mid-1920s, a degree of proliferation in American society that represented one out of every three or four white Protestant American men. When Mussolini burst onto the world stage in 1921, many Americans across the country instantly recognized his project, as newspapers from Montana to Florida explained to their readers that "the 'Fascisti' might be known as the Ku Klux Klan," and "the klan . . . is the Fascisti of America." Comparisons between the homegrown Klan and Italian fascism soon became ubiquitous in the American press; the resemblance was not superficial.

The second Klan disintegrated in the late 1920s under the taint of corruption and sex scandals, but some of its erstwhile leaders soon began cutting their bloodstained cloth to fit new political fashions. The majority of the American fascist groups of the interwar period, more than one of which self-identified as fascist, began not as branches of Nazism, but as offshoots of the Klan. Their Christian nationalism was inextricable from their anti-Semitism, although it also led to a sectarianism that may have kept them from forging stronger alliances.

Many of these groups shared the fondness of their European counterparts for dressing up in "colored shirt" uniforms, to suggest organized force and militaristic might, to intimidate and exclude, including Atlanta's Order of Black Shirts; the White Shirts, militant "Crusaders for Economic Liberty," founded by George W. Christians, who cultivated a toothbrush mustache and Hitlerian lock of flopping hair; the Gray Shirts, officially the Pioneer Home Protective Association, founded in upstate New York; the Khaki Shirts (also "U.S. Fascists"); the Silver Shirts, which William Dudley Pelley modeled on Hitler's "elite Nazi corps"; and the Dress Shirts. By the end of 1934, American journalists were mocking the growing list. "Gray Shirts Make America No. 1 Among Shirt-Nations," read one sarcastic headline, noting that unless other countries began cheating by combining colors, "it will be impossible to out-shirt us."

But others took the threat more seriously. As James Waterman Wise repeatedly explained, "the various colored shirt orders—the whole haberdashery brigade who play upon sectional prejudice," were "sowing the seeds of fascism" in the United States. The Black Legion was an offshoot of the Klan that flourished in the Midwest, whose leader spoke of seizing Washington in a revolutionary coup, called the New Deal a Jewish plot "to starve the Gentiles out," and espoused the extermination of American Jews by means of poison gas dispensers in synagogues on Yom Kippur. Anyone wondering "what fascism would be like in this country" should look to the Black Legion, with its "odor of Hitlerism," its "anti-Catholic, anti-Jewish, anti-Negro, anti-labor platform, its whips, clubs and guns, its brazen defiance of law and order and the due processes of democracy," warned a widely syndicated 1936 editorial. "These are the attitudes and equipment of fascism."

The short-lived Friends of the Hitler Movement soon transformed into the more acceptable Friends of New Germany in 1933, before becoming the Bund. It held several large rallies in Madison Square Garden, including its 1939 "Mass Demonstration for True Americanism," where a giant banner featuring George Washington was flanked by swastikas, and twelve hundred "storm troopers" stood in the aisles delivering the Nazi salute; footage from the rally was restored in 2019 as the short film *A Night at the Garden*. By 1940, the Bund claimed membership of a hundred thousand and had established summer camps in upstate

New York, New Jersey, and Long Island where it trained American Nazi youth. The Bund's propagandist, Gerhard Kunze, reported at the time that "the swastika is not foreign but one hundred per cent American. The Indians always used it," while the emblem of another group, "the American National-Socialist Party," was "an American Indian, arm outstretched in salute, poised against a black swastika." The Bund admitted to working to naturalize Nazism, seeking consanguinities with American symbolism.

Then, too, there was Father Coughlin. "I take the road of Fascism," he said in 1936, "before forming the Christian Front," whose members referred to themselves as "brown shirts." His virulently anti-Semitic radio program, regularly transmitting claims from the fabricated *Protocols of the Elders of Zion,* reached almost thirty million Americans at its height—the largest radio audience in the world at the time. Those listeners tuned in at the end of 1938 as Coughlin was justifying the violence of Kristallnacht, arguing that it was "reprisal" against Jews who had supposedly murdered more than twenty million Christians and stolen billions of dollars in "Christian property"; Nazism, he said, was a natural "defense mechanism" against the communism financed by Jewish bankers. Coughlin's weekly newspaper, *Social Justice,* which had an estimated circulation of 200,000 at its height, was described by *Life* magazine at the time as probably the most widely read voice of "Nazi propaganda in America."

But the American leader most often accused of fascist tendencies was Huey Long. As Louisiana governor (and senator), Long imposed local martial law, censored the newspapers, forbade public assemblies, packed the courts and legislatures with his cronies, and installed his twenty-four-year-old lover as secretary of state. Long was a racketeer, but his "Share Our Wealth" program did improve local conditions, building roads and bridges, investing in hospitals and schools, and abolishing the poll tax. His economic populism was also not predicated on furthering racial, ethnic, or religious divisions; he subordinated his white supremacism to his redistributionist political message. "We just lynch an occasional nigger," he breezily declared when dismissing antilynching laws, though he also recognized "you can't help poor white people without helping Negroes," and so was prepared for his rising tide to lift all boats. When Long set his sights on the 1936 presidential election, Franklin D. Roosevelt was sufficiently alarmed to inform his ambassador to Germany: "Long plans to be a candidate of the Hitler type for the presidency," predicting that by 1940 Long would try to install himself as a dictator.

Roosevelt was hardly alone in fearing that Long sought to be an "American Fuehrer"; Long's political career gave plenty of reason for doubting his democratic bona fides. He inspired Sinclair Lewis's Buzz Windrip in *It Can't Happen Here*, the president-dictator who promises Americans $5,000 a year if they vote for him, as Long had done. But the name Windrip also suggests Reverend Gerald B. Winrod, the "Kansas Hitler" who led the "Defenders of the Christian Faith" and had been touring the nation lecturing on the millenarian role of Hitler, Stalin, and Mussolini in biblical prophecy since the late 1920s. That Lewis also viewed the Klan as a fascist movement is clear from an extended denunciation that opens the novel, in which Lewis rips through a genealogy of American proto-fascist tendencies, including anti-Semitism, political corruption, war hysteria, conspiracy theories, and evangelical Christianity, before ending on the "Kentucky night-riders," the "trainloads of people [who] have gone to enjoy lynchings. . . . Not happen here? . . . Where in all history has there ever been a people so ripe for a dictatorship as ours!"

President Windrip himself is "vulgar, almost illiterate, a public liar easily detected, and in his 'ideas' almost idiotic." His fascist regime, driven by Christian nationalism and a desire for ethnic homogeneity, turns both African Americans and Jews into enemies of the state, decreeing that all bankers are Jewish. *It Can't Happen Here* suggests that in America, fascism's most dangerous supporters would be those "who disowned the word 'Fascism' and preached enslavement to Capitalism under the style of Constitutional and Traditional Native American Liberty." It would be "government of the profits, by the profits, for the profits." Fascism's cancerous version of nationalism means that an

American fascism will always graft American pieties about individual liberty onto realities of systemic greed, printing "liberate" on flags waved by a huckster.

Dorothy Thompson, the celebrated journalist and antifascist campaigner (and Sinclair Lewis's wife at the time), similarly earned the sobriquet of "Cassandra" for prophesying that fascism in the United States would look all too familiarly American when it arrived. (Thompson enjoyed the riposte that Cassandra was always proven right in the end.) "When Americans think of dictators they always think of some foreign model," she said, but an American dictator would be "one of the boys, and he will stand for everything traditionally American." And the American people, Thompson added, "will greet him with one great big, universal, democratic, sheeplike bleat of 'O.K., Chief! Fix it like you wanna, Chief!'" A year later, in 1938, a Yale professor named Halford Luccock was also widely cited in the press when he told an audience: "When and if fascism comes to America it will not be labeled 'made in Germany'; it will not be marked with a swastika; it will not even be called fascism; it will be called, of course, 'Americanism.'" And Luccock went on: "The high-sounding phrase 'the American way' will be used by interested groups, intent on profit, to cover a multitude of sins against the American and Christian tradition, such sins as lawless violence, tear gas and shotguns, denial of civil liberties."

In 1941, Thompson wrote again in similar terms, saying she was reminded of what Huey Long himself had once explained to her: "American Fascism would never emerge as a Fascist but as a 100 percent American movement; it would not duplicate the German method of coming to power but would only have to get the right President and Cabinet." FDR's vice president, Henry Wallace, issued his own warning. "American fascism will not be really dangerous," he wrote in *The New York Times* in 1944, "until there is a purposeful coalition among the cartelists, the deliberate poisoners of public information, and those who stand for the K.K.K. type of demagoguery."

Wallace's warning came amid the Roosevelt administration's misguided prosecution on sedition charges of many of these figures, including Winrod, Pelley, Elizabeth Dilling (of the so-called Mothers'

Movement), and James True (who founded a group called America First, Inc., and called for an American pogrom). This constellation had orbited around the America First Committee of 1940–1941 and its figurehead Charles Lindbergh, the celebrated aviator who, for a time, lent their conspiratorial anti-Semitism a veneer of legitimacy until he was met with disgrace in September 1941 for a speech widely condemned as anti-Semitic and "un-American." As the United States entered World War II, the meaning of "America first" underwent an abrupt volte-face from patriotic to seditious, becoming a byword for anti-Semitic Nazi sympathies.

That did not stop Huey Long's former deputy, the Reverend Gerald L. K. Smith—who had built his own political career on denunciations of presumptively Jewish "international bankers"—from running for president in 1944 on a promise to fix the nation's "Jewish problem." Smith's party was called America First.

———

NOW, IN 2020, we find ourselves with an America First president. Arguments that Donald Trump can be understood only in relation to the modern conservative movement in America, best framed by the turn to the right under Barry Goldwater or Lee Atwater's famous southern strategy, assume a rupture with American politics of the interwar period that was not necessarily evident at the time. To give just one example, Goldwater was described more than once during his presidential run in 1964, by both his supporters and his critics, as an "America First" politician.

Nor is it only Trump's critics who see fascist tendencies in his administration's rhetoric glorifying violence and disregarding the rule of law, democratic processes, and civil liberties; the President and his supporters regularly embrace traditions of American fascism themselves. "America first" was initially the favorite slogan of American xenophobic nativist movements and politics from 1915 to 1941, starting with Woodrow Wilson's loyalty test, demanding that immigrant "hyphenate Americans" prove they were for "America first," followed by its use as a rallying cry to keep America out of the League of Nations and from ratifying the

Treaty of Versailles. Warren G. Harding also ran on an America First campaign in 1920, even as the slogan was being appropriated by the second Klan, which regularly marched with the legend on banners and used it in recruitment ads. It was invoked on the floor of Congress by supporters of the nativist and eugenicist Immigration Act of 1924. Then it was assimilated by self-styled American fascist groups of the 1930s, including the German American Bund and the virulently anti-Semitic America First, Inc., before it was adopted by the America First Committee of 1940–1941, when Lindbergh used it to convince Americans that "Jewish interests" were seeking to manipulate the United States into taking part in a European war.

Trump himself has echoed the "Nordicist" rhetoric of interwar Klansmen and American fascists when he said he would prefer more immigrants from Norway and fewer from "shithole" places like Haiti and Africa. He has praised the "bloodlines" of Henry Ford, who circulated the series of articles titled *The International Jew*, which promulgated *The Protocols of the Elders of Zion* across America during the 1920s. In that same decade, Fred Trump, then a young man (later, father of Donald), was arrested after a brawl involving Klansmen broke out at a Memorial Day Parade in Queens.[4] Donald Trump was reported to own the speeches of Hitler during the 1990s; he denied ever reading them—but then he is also incapable of telling the truth.

And lately, in response to the killing of George Floyd in the spring of 2020 and the Black Lives Matter protests that swept the nation and then the world, Donald Trump announced that he would hold a rally for his supporters in Tulsa—one year short of the centenary of the worst antiblack pogrom in American history, which left as many as three hundred African Americans dead, eight thousand homeless, and that city's Black community destroyed.[5] Trump's rally was to have taken place on June 19, a day known as Juneteenth that has come to be celebrated as an anniversary marking the end of slavery in the United States and the emancipation of African Americans. For complex historical reasons, the deferral of liberty and the franchise, the belatedness of free and full citizenship under the law, the active suppression of Black rights, all resonate in the Juneteenth celebration. (After widespread outrage at the clear provocation, Trump's rally was postponed a day, to June 20, still in Tulsa. Trump proceeded to take credit for educating the country about Juneteenth.)

Trump is no student of history, but someone around him clearly is. But it is also true that Trump's thundering ignorance does not mean he doesn't understand the racist and fascist rhetoric he deploys. We need not argue that he is a mastermind plotting a fascist coup to recognize that Trump has a demonstrable sense of how white supremacism works in America, without ever having troubled to organize his thoughts, such as he has, about it.

And this, too, was how fascism always operated in practice: it was nothing if not opportunistic. What Paxton calls its "mobilizing passions" catalyze fascism, which is propelled, as he notes, more by feelings than by thought. Only "the historic destiny of the group" matters to fascists, he adds: "their only moral yardstick is the prowess of the race, of the nation, of the community. They claim legitimacy by no universal standard except a Darwinian triumph of the strongest community." Its "hazy and synthetic doctrines," combined with its ultra-nationalism and anti-intellectualism, means that fascism is never a coherent set of ideological doctrines. Force takes the place of ideology, as the fascist strongman performs for his followers their sense of rightful dominance and rage that other groups, in embracing equality, reject their entitlements.

American fascist energies today are different from 1930s European fascism, but that doesn't mean they're not fascist; it means they're not European and it's not the 1930s. They remain organized around classic fascist tropes of nostalgic regeneration, fantasies of racial purity, celebration of an authentic folk and nullification of others, scapegoating groups for economic instability or inequality, rejecting the legitimacy of political opponents, the demonization of critics, attacks on a free press, and claims that the will of the people justifies violent imposition of military force. Vestiges of interwar fascism have been dredged up, dressed up, and repurposed for modern times. Colored shirts might not sell anymore, but colored hats are doing great.

Reading about the inchoate American fascist movements of the 1930s during the Trump administration feels less prophetic than proleptic, a time-lapse montage of a para-fascist order slowly willing itself into existence over the course of nearly a century. It certainly seems less surprising that recognizably fascistic violence is erupting in the United States under Trump, as his attorney general sends troops to the national capital to act as a private army, armed paramilitary groups occupy state capitols, laws are passed to deny the citizenship and rights of specific groups, and birthright citizenship as guaranteed under the Fourteenth Amendment is attacked. When the President declares voting an "honor" rather than a right and "jokes" about becoming president for life, when the government makes efforts to add a new question of citizenship to the decennial census for the first time in the nation's history, and when nationwide protests in response to racial injustice become the pretext for mooting martial law, we are watching an American fascist order pulling itself together.

Trump is neither aberrant nor original. Nativist reactionary populism is nothing new in America, it just never made it to the White House before. In the end, it matters very little whether Trump is a fascist in his heart if he's fascist in his actions. As one of Lewis's characters notes of the dictator in *It Can't Happen Here*: "Buzz isn't important—it's the sickness that made us throw him up that we've got to attend to."

U.S. FASCISM V. ANGELO HERNDON

ROBIN D. G. KELLEY

The fascist racketeers were no fools. They understood the psychology of their starving victims. Their appeal to them was irresistible. It went something like this: "Run . . . the niggers back to the country where they came from—Africa! They steal the jobs away from us white men because they lower wages. Our motto is therefore: America for Americans!"

Anyone living in Donald Trump's America will find these words eerily familiar; the author's name, not so much. When Angelo Herndon penned this passage over eight decades ago, the twenty-four-year-old with a sixth-grade education was one of the most famous Black men in America. He had spent almost three years in a Georgia jail cell, about five years in southern coal mines, and at least two years as a Communist organizer in the Deep South.

Herndon's conviction under Georgia's insurrection statute and his subsequent defense made the handsome young radical a cause célèbre. His story upends typical Great Depression images of despondent men and women in breadlines and soup kitchens, waiting for Franklin D. Roosevelt's New Deal to save the day.

Instead, the story of thousands of Angelo Herndons is a story of Black antifascism.

As American finance capital eagerly floated loans to the Italian dictator Benito Mussolini, and *Fortune*, the *Saturday Evening Post*, and *The*

New Republic ran admiring spreads on Italian fascism, Black radicals
called out and resisted homegrown fascism in the form of lynch law, the
suppression of workers' organizations and virtually all forms of dissent,
and the denial of civil and democratic rights to Black citizens. As this
was the state of affairs in much of the United States long before Mussolini's rise, Black radicals not only anticipated fascism, they resisted before
it was considered a crisis. As Herndon aptly put it, his case was "a symbol
of the clash between Democracy and Fascism."

Born Eugene Angelo Braxton on May 6, 1913 or 1914, he and his
seven siblings grew up poor mainly in Alabama, though by his own
account he was born in Wyoming, Ohio. His parents, Paul Braxton
and Harriet Herndon, both hailed from the Black Belt town of Union
Springs, just southeast of Montgomery, in Bullock County, Alabama.
Angelo was barely five years old when Paul Braxton succumbed to "miners' pneumonia" and his death sent Harriet and her children back to
Union Springs, where she sharecropped to make ends meet. In 1926
Angelo (then about thirteen) and his brother Leo (fifteen) worked in
the coalfields of Lexington, Kentucky, before moving in with their aunt
Sallie Herndon in Birmingham, Alabama.

In 1930 Angelo was working for the Tennessee Coal and Iron
company in Birmingham when the fledgling Communist Party began
organizing there. He was primed for its message of militant class struggle and racial justice, having once dreamed of organizing "some kind
of a secret society that was to arm itself with guns and ammunition
and retaliate against the Ku Klux Klan and the American Legion."
On May 22, he attended his first Communist-led mass meeting and
listened to party leaders denounce racism, segregation, and lynching,
and demand that Black people have the right to equality and national
self-determination—that is, the right of the subjugated Black majority in the South to secede from the United States and form a truly
democratic government if they so desired. This position, adopted by
the Communist International in 1928, promoted not separatism but
rather the rights of a subjugated nation to choose. Consequently, the
policy led the party to greater support for civil rights and racial justice. Impressed with the Communists for fighting for all workers and

for advocating openly for "Negro rights," teenaged Angelo joined the party that night.

Using his birth name, Eugene Braxton, he immediately threw himself into the work, organizing coal miners, the unemployed, and sharecroppers, and spending many a night in an Alabama jail cell. The political situation heated up in March 1931, when nine young Black men were pulled from a freight train near Paint Rock, Alabama, and falsely accused of raping two white women. Following a hasty trial, all the defendants except the youngest were sentenced to death. The Communist-led International Labor Defense (ILD) built an international campaign to defend the "Scottsboro Boys," eventually leading to their release. Meanwhile, in the fall of 1931, the party dispatched Herndon to Atlanta. The reputedly liberal city had become a hotbed of fascism. Between March and May 1930, Atlanta police arrested six Communist leaders: Morris H. Powers, Joseph Carr, Mary Dalton and Ann Burlak, who were all white, and African Americans Herbert Newton and Henry Storey. The state charged the Atlanta Six, as they came to be known, under a nineteenth-century statute that made it potentially a capital crime for anyone to incite insurrection or distribute insurrectionary literature.

Liberals across the country objected to this arcane law largely on the grounds that it violated free speech. Most white Atlantans, however, were less concerned with the party's incendiary literature than with its interracialism. That white women and Black men had attended an anti-lynching meeting together was an egregious violation of southern conduct and the primary reason for their arrests.

Unemployment fueled the party's growth in Atlanta, which in turn fueled the fascist movement. During the summer of 1930, about 150 Atlanta business leaders, American Legionnaires, and key figures in law enforcement founded the American Fascisti Association and Order of Black Shirts. Their goals were to "foster the principles of white supremacy" and make the city (and its jobs) white. The Black Shirts held a march on August 22, 1930, carrying placards that read "Niggers, back to the cotton fields—city jobs are for white folks."

Since the Black Shirts were of the better class, the anti-insurrection statute did not apply to them, though they earned the ire of merchants and housewives who feared losing access to cheap Black labor, and of unemployed white men who got black shirts but no jobs. By 1932, the city began denying Black Shirts parade permits and charters, though racial terror and discrimination continued unabated.

As the Atlanta Six appealed their case, Angelo Herndon became the next victim caught in the web of Georgia's insurrection statute. On June 30, 1932, he led a march of over one thousand Black and white workers to city hall that forced the city to add $6,000 to local relief aid. Twelve days later Herndon was arrested while picking up his mail, and police searched his room without a warrant. They discovered a small cache of leaflets, pamphlets, Communist newspapers, and books by George Padmore and Bishop William Montgomery Brown.

Initially charged simply for being a Communist, on July 22 Herndon was indicted for violating the insurrection statute. The ILD retained two local Black lawyers, John H. Geer and Benjamin Davis Jr., the latter a scion of a prominent Black Republican family who would go on to become a national leader in the Communist Party.

The rabidly anti-Communist prosecutor, John Hudson, sought the death penalty for Herndon for possessing the material. But Davis and Geer showed that the material in Herndon's possession was readily available in the public library. And Davis turned the tables by insisting that "lynching is insurrection" and that the systematic exclusion of Black people from the jury pool was a violation of Herndon's rights, rendering any indictment against him invalid.

On January 18, 1933, an all-white jury found Herndon guilty but spared him execution by sentencing him to eighteen to twenty years on the chain gang. After securing his release on bail in October 1934, the ILD sent Herndon on a national tour to talk about his case in the larger struggle against class oppression, racial injustice, and fascism. "Today, when the world is in danger of being pushed into another blood-bath," he warned in one of his stump speeches, "when Negroes are being shot down and lynched wholesale, when every sort of outrage is taking place against the masses of people—today is the time to act."

The tour ended after the U.S. Supreme Court rejected his appeal, sending him back to prison in October 1935. His legal team then turned to the insurrection statute itself and succeeded in convincing a Fulton County Superior Court judge that the law was unconstitutional. Herndon was released again on bond three months after he returned to prison. Predictably, the Georgia Supreme Court rejected the lower court's ruling, setting the stage for a second appeal to the U.S. Supreme Court, which in 1937 in a 5–4 decision finally struck down Georgia's insurrection statute, vacating Herndon's conviction for good.

But in 1935, as Herndon crisscrossed the country fighting for his life, the Nazis consolidated power in Germany, Japan occupied Manchuria, Britain and France tightened their grip on the colonies, and Mussolini invaded Ethiopia. Black radicals heeded Herndon's plea "to act," mobilizing in defense of Ethiopia, resisting lynch law in the South, organizing a global anticolonial movement, and defending Republican Spain from the fascists.

Angelo's brother Milton Herndon died fighting Franco's troops in the Spanish Civil War. He told his men why he was there: "Yesterday, Ethiopia. Today, Spain. Tomorrow, maybe America. Fascism won't stop anywhere—until we stop it." His words still ring true.

ONE HUNDRED YEARS OF FASCISM

JASON STANLEY

When Fascist Blackshirts marched through the streets of Rome at the end of October 1922, their leader, Benito Mussolini, had just been installed as prime minister.[1] While Mussolini's followers had already organized into militias and begun to terrorize the country, it was during the 1922 march, historian Robert O. Paxton writes, that they "escalated from sacking and burning local socialist headquarters, newspaper offices, labor exchanges, and socialist leaders' homes to the violent occupation of entire cities, all without hindrance from the government."[2]

By this point, Mussolini and his Fascist Party had been normalized, because they had been brought into the center-right government the previous year as an antidote to the left. The government was in disarray, its institutions delegitimized, and leftist parties were squabbling among themselves. And Fascist violence had fueled disorder that Mussolini, like a racketeer, promised to resolve.

But while Mussolini presided over fascism's first real taste of political power, his movement was not the first of its kind. For that, one must look instead to the United States. As Paxton explains, "It may be that the earliest phenomenon that can be functionally related to fascism is American: The Ku Klux Klan . . . the first version of the Klan was arguably a remarkable preview of the way fascist movements were to function in interwar Europe."

THE GREAT RACE TO THE BOTTOM

As important as these functional parallels between movements and organizations were, it is at the level of ideology that one finds the common denominator shared by American and European (especially German) variants of fascism. In 1916, the American eugenicist Madison Grant published *The Passing of the Great Race*, which decried the supposed replacement of whites in America by Black people and immigrants, including "Polish Jews."³ According to Grant, these groups posed an existential threat to the "Nordic race"—America's "native class."

While Grant did not object to the presence of Black people in America, he insisted that they must be kept subordinate. His book was an exercise in scientific racism, arguing that "Nordic whites" are superior to all other races intellectually, culturally, and morally, and thus should command a dominant position in society. At the core of his worldview was a racialized version of American nationalism: Nordic whites were the only "real" Americans, but they were at risk of being "replaced" by other races.

Grant tapped into a powerful political current of his time. In the years that followed, the "America First" movement would emerge to oppose "internationalism" and immigration. As Sarah Churchwell of the University of London notes in her brilliant 2018 book, *Behold, America: The Entangled History of "America First" and "the American Dream,"* in February 1921 Vice President-elect Calvin Coolidge "wrote an essay for *Good Housekeeping* called 'Whose Country is This?'"⁴ Coolidge's answer, as Churchwell recounts, was unambiguous: "'Our country must cease to be regarded as a dumping ground' and should only accept 'the right kind of immigration.'" By that, he explicitly meant "Nordics."

It was also in 1921, Churchwell notes, that the second Ku Klux Klan adopted "America first" as part of its official credo. With its fevered commitment to white supremacy and traditional gender roles, the second Klan focused its efforts on spreading paranoia about Jewish Marxists and their attempts to use labor unions to promote racial equality. Meanwhile, the industrialist Henry Ford had been financing the publication and distribution of *The International Jew*, a compilation of articles that placed Jews at the center of a global conspiracy.[5] Jews, Ford claimed, controlled American media and cultural institutions, and were bent on destroying the American nation.

One finds the same kind of racialized nationalism running through *Mein Kampf*, Adolf Hitler's 1924 prison manifesto. Hitler was incensed by the presence of foreigners, and especially Jews, in Vienna, but he made clear that his hatred was not for the Jewish religion. Before arriving in Vienna, he writes, Hitler had rejected anti-Semitism, because he saw it as a form of discrimination against Germans on the basis of religion.

But Hitler came to see Jews as the ultimate enemy, portraying them as members of a foreign race who had become assimilated in Germany in order to take it over. This, he claimed, would be achieved by loosening immigration laws to "open the borders," encouraging intermarriage to destroy the Aryan race, and using control of the media and culture industries to destroy traditional German values. According to Nazi propaganda, Jews were the force behind international communism and the source of the mythical "stab in the back" that had supposedly caused Germany to lose World War I.

Hitler drew inspiration from the United States, which, following the rise of the America First movement, had adopted immigration policies that strictly favored northern Europeans.[6] Looking to the early American settlers' genocide of the continent's native peoples in the name of Manifest Destiny, he found a model for his own later actions in pursuit of lebensraum (territorial expansion).[7] And as the historian Timothy Snyder shows in his 2015 book, *Black Earth: The Holocaust as History and Warning*, Hitler hoped to recreate the American antebellum South's slavery regime in Ukraine.[8]

THE MISRULE OF LAW

The fact that American racialized nativism and German fascism embodied shared practices, not just shared beliefs, merits closer attention. As the American legal theorist Kimberlé Crenshaw has shown, legal practices historically have enforced and perpetuated unjust hierarchies of value in ways that often go unnoticed.[9] Hence, the point of antidiscrimination laws is not to offer special protections for any specific group—say, Black women; rather, it is to ensure that the law does not reproduce discriminatory social, political, and historical hierarchies of value.

This is one of the central insights of critical race theory (CRT), which evolved from the work of Crenshaw, Derrick Bell, and other scholars who have explored how legal practices perpetuate discrimination— sometimes as a side effect of motivated reasoning by those in power, and sometimes as a policy's explicit intent.[10] And, because CRT has become one of the most important theoretical tools in antifascist practice, it is also the new bugbear of the white nationalist right.

CRT urges us to recognize law as the core manifestation of a political ideology. In the case of fascism, citizenship is based on racial identity, which in turn rests on a founding myth of hierarchy and superiority.[11] While a race-based conception of national identity was not central to Italian fascism, it was the driving force behind Nazism. With the 1935 Nuremberg laws, German citizenship came to be based on Aryan superiority.[12] Only those of "German blood" could be German citizens with political rights. Jews, by dint of being non-Aryans, were excluded from citizenship and therefore stripped of political rights.

Not by coincidence, Black Americans had long suffered similar treatment in the post–Civil War American South. As James Q. Whitman of Yale Law School documents in *Hitler's American Model: The United States and the Making of Nazi Race Law*, Nazi ideology borrowed straightforwardly from the Jim Crow regime's use of legal practice to structure the nature of citizenship.[13] While the Allied victory eventually ended German racial fascism in 1945, America's Jim Crow regime would survive for another generation.

FASCIST BIG TENTS

The defeat of Nazi Germany had required America to overcome the power of the isolationist America First movement at home. But the draconian immigration policies that the movement had inspired in the 1920s were still in place in the 1930s, when America infamously turned away many Jewish refugees attempting to flee Europe ahead of the Holocaust.[14]

In a 1939 *Reader's Digest* essay titled "Aviation, Geography, and Race," the leading spokesman of America First, the aviator Charles Lindbergh, wrote: "It is time to turn from our quarrels and to build our White ramparts again. This alliance with foreign races means nothing but death to us. It is our turn to guard our heritage from Mongol and Persian and Moor, before we become engulfed in a limitless foreign sea."[15] Lindbergh advocated neutrality in the war between Britain and Germany, regarding both as allies against open immigration into Europe and the United States by nonwhite peoples.[16]

In Germany, fascists had entered government as a result of their rapidly rising popularity in electoral politics, starting in 1928.[17] The German economy had experienced a series of terrible shocks, from hyperinflation to soaring unemployment.[18] Hitler's Nazis, naturally, blamed these problems on Jews, communism, and international capitalism. Like Mussolini's Blackshirts, they violently attacked leftists and provoked open street fighting—and then presented themselves as the only force that could restore order.[19]

Nazi ideology appealed to multiple constituencies. With its promise to strengthen the nation by supporting traditional gender roles and the creation of large Aryan families, it appealed to religious conservatives.[20] And with its hostility toward communism and socialism, it promised to protect big business from organized workers.[21] The Nazis opposed capitalism only as a *universal* doctrine—that is, as one that granted Jews the right to property—and portrayed themselves as the protectors of Aryan private property against "Judeo-Bolshevism."[22]

On the cultural front, it bears emphasizing that fascist parties have always been violent defenders of a strictly binary conception of gender. In the 1920s, Berlin was a cultural boomtown and a center of emerging European gay life, which Nazi ideology associated with Jews.[23] The city was also the site of Magnus Hirschfeld's Institut für Sexualwissenschaft, a vast library and archive housing a wide variety of gender expression.[24]

That made him one of the Nazi Party's main enemies.[25] When the Nazis started burning books, Hirschfeld's library was among the first targets.

It is no surprise that fascists have always found common cause with religious conservatives. While fascism and Christianity forged an alliance of convenience in Italy and Germany, they all but fused into a single ideology elsewhere. In Romania, for example, the Legion of the Archangel Michael was both the most Christian and the most violently anti-Semitic of the European fascist parties.[26]

In Brazil, a Catholic integralist form of fascism was imported directly from Italy by Plínio Salgado.[27] The role of Christianity is also obvious in the structure of the Russian fascism that is ascendant today.[28] Russians and Russia are depicted as the last defenders of Christianity against the heathen forces of decadent Western liberalism and gender fluidity. And, of course, Christianity has always animated American fascism, with its ideological core of white Christian nationalism.[29]

FROM PUTSCH TO PARLIAMENT

By the end of the 1920s, the Nazis had managed to appeal to multiple groups that did not regard themselves as Nazis. And owing to the widespread distrust of more mainstream political parties and institutions, they became the second-largest parliamentary party after the 1930 election, and then the leading party following the election in 1932.[30]

Though German conservatives looked askance at the Nazis, they regarded Hitler as preferable to any option on the left. Thus, with the support of the conservative establishment, Hitler was appointed chancellor by Germany's president in 1933.[31] While Hitler had made his virulent opposition to democracy abundantly clear in his statements and writings, German conservatives handed him power anyway, demonstrating—at best—unforgivable naïveté.

In fact, every canonical example of European fascists' success in the twentieth century involved political parties coming to power through the normal electoral process, after having broadcast their antidemocratic sentiments and sometimes even their express intentions. Conservative leaders and voters chose fascism over democracy, believing that they would win out in the end.

For a fascist party to triumph, it must attract support from people who, if asked, would loudly deny that they share its ideology. This need not be so difficult: voters merely have to be persuaded that democracy is no longer serving their interests.

FASCISM TODAY

If we think of fascism as a set of *practices*, it is immediately evident that fascism is still with us. As Toni Morrison pointed out in a 1995 speech, the United States has often preferred fascist solutions to its national problems.[32] Consider, for example, the Prison Policy Initiative's findings on global incarceration rates in 2021: "Not only does the U.S. have the highest incarceration rate in the world; every single U.S. state incarcerates more people per capita than virtually any independent democracy on earth."[33]

This is a burden that falls disproportionately on the formerly enslaved population of the country. And unlike in many other democracies, prisoners in forty-eight U.S. states cannot legally vote.[34] In Florida, strict disenfranchisement laws strip one million people—enough to shift the state's partisan leaning toward Republicans—with *past* felony records of their voting rights.[35] And under the state's current Republican governor, Ron DeSantis, an election police force has been created to address a nonexistent epidemic of voter fraud.[36] In the run-up to the 2022 midterm elections, there have been highly publicized arrests of Black people with felony records who thought they could vote (and who, in some cases, had received confusing messages about the matter from the state).[37]

We should recognize this for what it is: the return of Jim Crow tactics designed to intimidate Black voters. Unlike the Third Reich, the Jim Crow regime never suffered defeat and elimination in war. Instead, its practices have quietly persisted in varying forms, often serving as a model for laws like those in Florida. In most cases, racist laws are made to appear racially neutral. Literacy tests for voting, for example, are ostensibly neutral but discriminatory in fact.[38]

Nor is this tactic confined to the United States. In India, the Hindu nationalist ruling party has created a national registry to codify citizenship and expel "illegal immigrants," cynically exploiting the fact that a significant number of Indian Muslims lack official documentation.[39] Hindu nationalists can now target Indian Muslims and threaten them with deportation to Bangladesh. At the same time, the 2019 Citizenship Amendment Act gives non-Muslim migrants from Afghanistan, Bangladesh, and Pakistan a fast track to citizenship.[40]

The manipulation of citizenship laws to privilege one group as the true representatives of the nation is a feature of all fascist movements. As Tobias Hübinette of Karlstad University has pointed out, the Sweden Democrats, Sweden's far-right party, has "a direct organizational lineage tracing back to World War II-era Nazism." Its platform asserts a racially homogeneous Swedish national identity, and its candidates have "campaigned openly for the installation of a repatriation program with the explicit purpose of making non-Western immigrants move back to their countries of origin."[41] In the September 2022 election, the Sweden Democrats became the second-largest party in parliament—echoing the Nazi Party's achievement in 1930.[42]

Far-right leaders elsewhere in Europe have also been openly campaigning against multiracial democracy, though Muslim minorities have been substituted for the massacred Jewish population as the fifth column in their "great replacement" theory.[43] In Hungary, Prime Minister Viktor Orbán has used the courts and the law to silence opposition media and peddle a Christian nationalist nostalgia for a lost greater Hungary.[44] By stoking fears of sexual and religious minorities, he has shown how a leader can win elections time and again while openly campaigning against the press, universities, and democracy itself.

A NEW WAVE?

In the century since Mussolini's March on Rome, leaders and parties who openly run against democracy have all too easily prevailed in elections. In Brazil, President Jair Bolsonaro called for removing democratic

institutions and repeatedly praised the country's former military dictatorship.[45] And despite his disastrous first term, he stands a decent chance
of winning in the second-round vote on October 30, 2022.[46] And in the
United States, the Republican Party has become a cult of personality
beholden to a white nationalist leader who led an effort—most of which
he plotted in the open—to overthrow American democracy.

Fascists can win when social conservatives decide that fascism is
the lesser evil. They can win when enough citizens decide that ending
democracy is a reasonable price to pay for achieving some cherished
goal—like the criminalization of abortion. They can win when a dominant cohort chooses to end democracy in order to preserve its cultural,
financial, and political primacy. They can win when they attract votes
from those who merely want to thumb their noses at the system or lash
out in resentment. And they can win when business elites decide that
democracy is just a substitutable input.

Fascist parties feed a longing for national innocence, which is why
they run on narratives of national glory that erase past crimes. Hence,
some parents will support fascist parties—while vehemently disclaim-
ing the label of fascism for themselves—to prevent their children from
learning about the racist legacies that underpin the persistence of
racist outcomes.

Today, as in the past, fascist movements often have a powerful symbolic dimension that makes them contagious internationally. In the figure of Giorgia Meloni, Italy has its first far-right leader since Mussolini.
Having long promoted admiration of Mussolini's legacy and hatred of
immigrants and sexual minorities in her pursuit of party and government positions, Meloni's ascension to the Italian premiership is a potent
symbol for global fascism.[47]

Finally, the world has its most openly fascist leader since Hitler in
the figure of Russian president Vladimir Putin, who has demonstrated
why we must never become complacent about this ideology and its implications. Putin's genocidal war against Ukraine shows that he is not a
pragmatic actor, but rather a fanatic seeking to recreate a lost Russian
empire. In mustering such effective resistance, the Ukrainians have con-
firmed the ancient truth suggested in Pericles's famous funeral oration:

democracies fight better than tyrannies, because democratic citizens fight by their own choice.[48]

When institutions have been delegitimized for presiding over enormous economic disparities, cronyism, and generational crises, massive social change becomes possible. Sometimes, that change is positive, as when the labor movement helped establish the weekend, improve workplace safety, and abolish child labor. But such moments are inherently perilous. Fascism is the dark side of liberation, and history shows that it is often what democratic polities will prefer.

BELLUM SE IPSUM ALET

NIKHIL PAL SINGH

Since the election of Donald Trump and the events of his presidency, political discussion in the United States has circled the drain of dystopian speculation. The United States, we are told, is gripped by irremediable political polarization that augurs "the death of democracy." "I can't say this more clearly," Thomas Friedman wrote in September 2020: "our democracy is in terrible danger, more danger than it has been in since 1861." Published in the wake of the riotous invasion of the Capitol on January 6, 2021, books by journalist Stephen Marche and scholar Barbara Walter alternatively contrive scenarios for how civil conflict is likely to unfold, and forensically scour the planet for characteristic features of civil wars emerging "on our own soil." Endorsing this work in the *Financial Times*, Edward Luce similarly attests to the "alarmingly persuasive case that warning lights are flashing redder than at any point since 1861."

Political analysis in these times of rolling economic and public health crises, heightened political risks and threats, is difficult to assess in a fair, clear-minded way. Combining fabulation and fact, and presenting loose prognostication in an idiom of predictive science, it often defies the most cursory sense of historical context and complexity. This work invites blithe dismissal or vigorous assent, gaining traction upon current discussion by bidding up worst-case scenarios, implying that only a fool or miscreant could ignore the warnings. Such arguments achieve greatest success when they ratchet the common sense of rising polarization. "The genre of civil war fantasy," Marche observes, "is almost exclusively right

wing." Now gentle reader, please enjoy my book filled with fanciful scenarios of the imminent civil war that you will need to anticipate in order
to stop it happening. If pornography is a perverse prophylaxis for sexual
indulgence, these criers of our interregnum invite similar frisson, incitement, and passivity at the scenes they conjure of civilization's demise.

When people toss around references to 1861, they are referring to the
great "bellum" ("war") that organizes all of U.S. history into two distinct
"before" and "after" periods. This industrial-scale armed slaughter killed
2.5 percent of the entire U.S. population, still the largest mass casualty
war in American history. So, it is important to begin by establishing
a sense of proportion. The United States is a large, impossibly diverse
country. At this moment in its history, it is probably no less difficult to
govern effectively than it would be to divide into well-organized camps
battling for supremacy, precinct by precinct. The conventional red-blue
election maps distort not only the marbled grain of U.S. political contention, but also much of the ordinary, if grudging comity of everyday
life in a society where most people work day in and day out with others
to make their lives livable. The consequences of the staggering loss of
life from the pandemic will unpredictably roil our politics for years to
come. That reliable bellwethers of elite, middlebrow common sense now
imagine that the United States is on a path toward a civil war, however,
is a good indicator that we are in the presence of a shallow or hyperbolic
reading of our predicament.

That said, the preoccupation with civil conflict directs us to a crucial
set of questions. The idea of war among people who acknowledge their
enemies as members of the same political community tells us something
significant about the societies in which we live. Use of this concept, as
the historian David Armitage suggests, generates contests over its proper
meaning and disagreements about the character of societal contention:
Is it a riot or revolution, an insurgency or a reactionary backlash, a protest or a criminal action? Walter and Marche try to add rigor and objec-
tivity by employing the minimalist, low-threshold definition of civil war
as "major armed conflict" resulting in more than one thousand fatalities
per year. But given that U.S. police forces kill approximately one thousand people per year, it might be fair to say that the country already

subsists in a state of low-grade civil war.[1] The recurrence and scope of popular protest, including rioting and property destruction after the murders of Michael Brown and George Floyd by police in 2014 and 2020 respectively, lends credence to this suggestion: in the zones of precarity where many people dwell, impoverished, unsheltered and overpoliced, civil war is ongoing.

Complicating matters further, the interpretation of the meaning of the actual U.S. Civil War constitutes an aporia at the heart of U.S. political history. Historical interpretation of the meaning of the "antebellum" period remains contested by what we call the left and the right, where it is alternatively understood as beginning in 1619, with the crime of racial slavery, whose baleful legacies continue today, or in 1776, with the compact of self-governing republics whose founding constitutional design is supposed to transparently constrain all positive law. Similarly conflicted is interpretation of the postbellum politics of a newly industrializing national society and its reformed constitutional order, whose centralized state, racially inclusive citizenship, extensions of immigration and naturalization, and substantive due process rights have been repudiated by political opponents on the right ever since. From certain intellectual and partisan standpoints, the historical Civil War either settled nothing of consequence or never really ended.

How then should we assess the case that the United States is devolving into a period of sustained factional conflict that is likely to worsen? Partisan animus is real, and politically consequential; thresholds for civic violence and police abuse in U.S. society are shockingly low relative to other rich countries. The United States accounts for almost 40 percent of total global military spending, the single largest component of federal discretionary spending, and more than the total amount of discretionary expenditures on civilian health, transportation, housing, and education.[2] The country has sustained military conflict around the world for the past two decades, and throughout a history of continental expansion, hemispheric dominance, and global military intervention. The United States manufactures and exports most of the world's arms and contains more privately owned guns than people. Mass shootings at concerts, schools, churches, malls, mosques, and synagogues occur with regularity, often betraying a resurgence of racist and nativist animus behind a veil of individual madness.

Perhaps these long-standing features of U.S. society and government policy should make us even less sanguine about the prospects of avoiding descent into armed civil conflict. One of the more prevalent concerns, for example, is the infiltration and exfiltration of U.S. military and police forces into and out of white supremacist and far-right organizations, as well as the cultivation of links between armed militia and vigilante groups and mainstream GOP politics. There is ample evidence that this occurs, and is perhaps even on the rise. At the same time, few commentators who dwell on these matters pause to consider the far greater significance of the metastatic growth of the legitimate U.S. military, carceral, and border security apparatus over the past four decades, or the existence of massive, death-dealing U.S. arms industries that flood the country and the world with weapons with little dissent or fanfare. How should we weigh the size and political stability of these consensually validated institutions of organized violence against the dramaturgy of polarization and civil war?

That civil war talk invariably enters into speculation about the dispositions, loyalties, and competency of the national security state may be one of its most telling contradictions. Walter begins her book with an account of an alarming militia plot to kidnap Michigan governor Gretchen Whitmer in 2020.[3] "That a kidnapping attempt by a group of far-right extremists is a sign of impending civil war may strike you as preposterous," she admits. "But modern civil wars start with vigilantes such as these—armed militants who take violence directly to the people."

Her first instinct may well prove to have been closer to the truth. Of the twelve conspirators who engaged in surveillance of the governor's home as a prelude to the kidnapping idea, at least four were either FBI agents or government informants. Infiltrating the group online, the FBI used a total of twelve informants, involving themselves in some measure to incite the otherwise hapless plotters. Six defendants eventually stood trial, with one taking a plea in exchange for a lighter sentence and testimony against his codefendants. The first federal trial against the remaining five conspirators fell apart as two defendants were acquitted and the others subjected to a hung jury (though you do not learn that from reading Walter's book). All plotters were convicted in subsequent trials.

Like the Capitol riot of January 6, these are serious matters and indicative of the emergence of more militant and violent forms of dissent from the far right. At the same time, to see this as prelude to civil war significantly overreaches and thus misreads the current balance of forces and threats. That U.S. security professionals who once strategized about stopping "terror," or starting the next U.S. war overseas, now see themselves preparing for counterinsurgency at home may be less suggestive of the potential for civil war in the United States than of deeper, more long-standing institutional pathologies of a national security state that generates insecurity by design and as a business model.

Indeed, a tendency to imagine that contemporary political struggles and disagreements are on the verge of decomposing into violent conspiracies is not only a polarizing feature of the current moment but also, paradoxically, a stabilizing one. American political development over the past several decades has not merely been divided into opposing camps, around, for example, questions of race and gender equality, reproductive rights, or gun ownership; it has also been locked into a dynamic of partisan competition that encourages threat inflation, yielding important contributions from both parties to expansively coercive institutionalizations in the name of collective security.

From the early Cold War, U.S. partisanship revolved around which party was better prepared to fight communism, leading to covert actions, proxy wars, and full-scale military invasions, culminating in a disastrous, immoral war in Vietnam. By the 1970s, this morphed into a question of which party was tougher on crime; a policy orientation that delivered a regime of mass incarceration unprecedented in world history. The attacks of 9/11 raised the question of which party would keep the American "Homeland" safe from foreign predators, leading to two more decades of fruitless war in the Middle East and West Asia, and a deportation delirium that has swept up millions. What if the banal revelation at the end of U.S. wars on communism, crime, and terror and of relentless pursuit of other-directed nemesis is simply that Americans are their own worst enemies?

The specter of civil war might be better understood as a metaphor for waning confidence in the (liberal) U.S. empire. The breakdown of the "rules-based international order" as a regulative ideal is part and parcel of an attrition of what the political philosopher Raymond Geuss has called the "sheltered internal space of . . . *homo liberalis*" fashioned during the post-1945 golden age of American pluralism, rising affluence, increasing tolerance, and expanding civil rights.[4] The "Great Society," the name that was given to the expansive policy effort to institute social democratic liberalism inside the United States, and the civil rights revolution that made the United States a formal multiracial democracy for the first time in its history, was its high watermark. With the war in Vietnam raging, and eruptions of impoverished Black residents and rising crime roiling American cities, however, President Lyndon Johnson concluded that the United States now faced a "war within our own boundaries," before abdicating, instead of pursuing a second term. Americans have been talking about civil war at greater volume and frequency ever since.[5]

In these same years, a conception of politics as civil war by other means captured the imagination of the modern U.S. right on its own ascent to power. The politician and GOP presidential candidate Barry Goldwater laid down the gauntlet in the 1960s with a famous declaration that "extremism in defense of liberty is no vice."[6] Ronald Reagan was his successful heir, rising to the presidency while declaring himself a "state's righter" against an overweening federal government while attending a county fair in Mississippi near the site of the infamous 1964 murders of three civil rights workers. Shrinking the welfare state would go hand in hand with expanding the carceral state: "running up the battle flag," as Reagan put it, against a feral, drug abusing, Black "underclass." Forging the first GOP congressional majority in four decades in 1994, Newt Gingrich made these inner war analogies explicit. Our politics is a "war that has to be fought with the scale and duration and savagery that is only true of civil wars," he argued.[7] "We are lucky in this country that our civil wars are fought at the ballot box, not on the battlefield; nonetheless it is a true civil war."[8] Trump's "American carnage" was something of a belated echo.

The modern GOP has avidly fought Gingrich's version of civil war

at the ballot box and in the courts, leveraging countermajoritarian institutions and using the individual states as laboratories for reactionary
politics: advancing model legislation against public regulations, period-
ically mobbing local school boards, gerrymandering congressional districts, undermining public unions, funneling federal spending on health,
welfare, and police via block grants to maximize state discretion, defending a right of fetal personhood that trumps a woman's right to bodily
autonomy, making it more difficult to register to vote and to cast a vote,
stimulating white revanchism and moral outrage against expressions of
public disorder and antinormative behavior at every opportunity. In the
process, they successfully captured commanding heights of the judiciary,
and have now successfully rolled back landmark, fifty-year old national
civil rights gains: striking down federal voting rights protections, ending
a national right to abortion, and overturning legal protections for criminal suspects in police custody. Winning two of the last five national
presidential elections with a minority of the popular vote, and rigor-
ously deploying the Senate filibuster during periods in the congressional
minority, civil war by other means has proven to be a well-honed and
effective GOP strategy.

In the face of this challenge, it is difficult to judge the Democratic
Party as much more than a feckless, mildly recalcitrant partner. Over
the past forty years, it has alternatively sought to ratify, in gentler tones,
GOP-driven projects and demands to lower corporate taxes, get tough
on crime, end welfare as we know it, expand the ambit of deportation,
and sustain open-ended military authorizations. It has sought to placate
vulnerable constituents with forms of symbolic recognition and modest
regulatory action, often undergirded by weak executive authority and
moral sentiment. It is the undeniably saner and more constructive of the
two electoral options Americans are forced to choose between. But it
also operates an effective pincer movement against alternatives further
to the left that seek to transform skewed imbalances in the power of
capital and labor, police authority, and public safety. When constituents choose to fight, for example, against police abuse or for labor rights,
Democrats are often missing in action, or else warning against unpopular opinions that will awaken the scary monster on the right. Forever

counseling that we choose the lesser evil, they have instead grown habit-uated to living with the fox inside the chicken coop.

One of the biggest challenges facing political analysis in the United States today is to sort through the distortions of cynical politics, a hyper-trophied security state, and a degraded information ecology. Much of it now succumbs to a vicious feedback loop that links inflated threats and viral mobbing on social media to party operatives and opportunistic pun-dits trolling for outrages to serve as campaign fodder for the next elec-tion. A right-wing grievance factory (embodied by outlets like Fox News) stokes fears about loss of status and order resulting from attacks on racial hierarchy, normative sexuality and gender roles, and traditional emblems of authority like the police, as liberals and progressives warn of fascism descending, but struggle to distinguish between what is merely impoli-tic and offensive, and existential dangers or genocidal threats. The GOP leverages judicial and state-level power to construct a future built on decentralized despotism, while progressives seek to leverage the powers of surveillance capitalism and federal policing authorities to forestall a right-wing insurgency that won many of its most substantive victories long ago. The right sees itself as representative of a true national majority whose pat-rimony has been stolen by globalists and the beneficiaries of artificial rights. Leftists and progressives present a more plausible appeal to the thwarted potential of an urban, multiracial majority. Yet, they govern via rear-guard administrative rule making tailored to fractioned constituencies, rather than fighting for a politically ambitious agenda to redistribute political power and material resources to the diverse, nonwealthy multitude.

What we see is less the play of two parties to a civil war than two parties locked in attritional struggle over an increasingly predatory state. If history is any guide, the likely outcome will be continued governmen-tal incontinence and societal decay. What is apparent at the end of a long arc of right-wing ascendancy and progressive neoliberal policymaking is the shape of a long interregnum defined by a series of fanciful and failed solutions to the denouement of U.S. capitalism's post–World War II golden age. The essential truth of this era was not occulted—at least at the outset: "The standard of living of the average American has to decline," the Fed chair Paul Volcker intoned in 1979 as he embarked upon monetary policies that would crush high inflation and with it the last vestiges of organized labor. "I don't think you can escape that."[9] The hoped-for restoration of corporate profitability that would trickle down, the mastery over diminishing petroleum resources captured by despotic powers, and the political management of declining standards of living has defined the task of elite governance in the United States ever since.

The results speak for themselves. We might characterize the last two and a half decades in the world's most affluent states—and the United States in particular—as a period of crisis compression and rising fatalism. The onset of the millennium did not bring about the apocalyptic big bang foretold by Y2K fantasists, but yielded instead to slow rolling catastrophe with endemic features. We are people stalked by periodic financial collapse, destructive weather events, imminent civic violence, and airborne death. Region-wasting hurricanes and wildfires are the backdrop to daily life on our warming planet. Riotous mass protests against governing authority persistently expose the illegitimate face of ostensibly democratic forms of rule. Americans who learned to bowl alone, faced rising midlife mortality, self-medicated with opioids, got locked up and gunned down in the old deindustrialized urban core, struggled to make rent, stockpiled guns, and trolled for the next Columbine, Sandy Hook, or Uvalde in the suburbs and hinterlands in turn conjured Trump as a kind of perverse mirror.[10]

The promise to "Make America Great Again," unlike Obama's enjoining "Hope and Change," or even Bush's dream of "a new American Century," represented a conscious involution—a not entirely inadvertent mockery of the pretensions of those prior idealistic schemes, confirmation that the liberal patrimony has been spent. It is the darkness of this vision that has given rise to a cottage industry of criers warning of the death of democracy and impending civil war. From across the political spectrum, a characteristically American politics of anticipatory fear has served up a dismal record of misdiagnosing fundamental problems and prescribing toxins as cures. Luxuriating in anxious expectation of the next catastrophe, it defers the more daunting fight to salvage a democracy of common purpose and shared flourishing from one that has long subsisted on life support.

THERE ARE NO LONE WOLVES

The White Power Movement at War

KATHLEEN BELEW

On April 19, 2020, in the grip of social distancing and fear about the novel coronavirus that inexorably changed our world, the United States quietly passed the twenty-fifth anniversary of the Oklahoma City bombing. With its death toll of 168 people—including 19 young children—and the injury of hundreds more, the bombing was the largest deliberate mass casualty on American soil between Pearl Harbor and 9/11. It was a cataclysm, a shock, a horror in the heartland of America. Yet despite its historical significance, people remember the bombing as the work of a lone wolf or a few bad apples. People who visit the memorial in Oklahoma City, view documentaries on Netflix, or read more casually about the 1990s might easily come away with no story of the white power movement: a generations-long groundswell with a complex ideology that continues to propel mass violence in the present.

Our eyes are turned on other horrors. Our news is full of hate crimes, exclusions legal and illegal, cruelty and violence in speech and in action. But the historical context can illuminate the whirlwind of the present.

The problem of understanding the Oklahoma City bombing and other acts of political violence as "lone wolf" attacks derives partly from the movement itself, which has successfully disguised its degree of coherence and organization. But it also results from failures that we can repair by telling better stories. The lone wolf myth rests on journalistic accounts that fail to capture social connections between and ideology of white power actors; activist accounts that fail to take seriously the violent and organizational capacity of white power groups; policy makers and law enforcement officers who use piecemeal, rather than systemic, response mechanisms for a broad and transnational problem; and a general public that has no frame of reference to understand these acts of violence. Indeed, the most common story seems to be one about individual communities that would break us from one another.

The Oklahoma City bombing, in other words, was not the act of a lone wolf. This phrase is misleading and damaging, directing our attention away from long histories and complex relationships, away from systemic inequality and organized ideology in order to focus on individual perpetrators. Instead, the bombing was a culminating action of the white power movement. It was carried out by a broad and organized social movement supported by decades of networking, deep belief, and a shared sense of the coming end of the world.

What would it mean to know that story, to teach it in our history textbooks, to recognize its repercussions in the present? My hope is that the history of organized hate could have a utility in confronting the present and imagining a different future.

Our moment, indeed, gives us opportunities to think deeply about what it means to study and write the history of the present. In one sense, this is simply about the urgent project of contributing to public discourse. In another, it follows the Foucauldian mandate of understanding a genealogy of the present such that we might decode the moment in which we find ourselves.

But I find the most useful model in Lisa Lowe's *The Intimacies of Four Continents*, in which she situates her pursuit as a way of troubling and revealing what she calls "the politics of knowledge that give us the received history of our present," and thereby revealing different possibilities of response and action.[1] In other words, the project of "history of the present" isn't just decoding or explaining, but is fundamentally about creating space for new courses of action. It's about expanding the realm of the possible, about broadening our shared imaginary. History of the present might not only decode and explain, but also lay bare the assumptions of "received knowledge" and perhaps reveal a different path.

Because let me be perfectly clear: without a different response, today's wave of white extremist violence will certainly crush beneath it the lives of more victims, their families, and their communities, and may indeed seep further into governance.

My first book, *Bring the War Home*, presents a history of the white power movement from its formation after the Vietnam War to the 1995 Oklahoma City bombing.[2] It reveals a broad-based social movement united through narratives, symbols, and repertoires of war. This movement connected neo-Nazis, Klansmen, and skinheads; people in every region of the country; people in suburbs and in cities and on mountaintops. It joined men, women, and children; felons and religious leaders; high school dropouts and aerospace engineers; civilians and veterans and active-duty troops. It was a social movement that included a variety of strategies—but its most significant legacies have evolved from its 1983 revolutionary turn to declare war against the federal government and other enemies. The strategies that stem from that pivotal turn include, first, the use of computer-based social network activism, beginning in 1984, which has only amplified in the present, and second, "leaderless resistance."

That strategy, perhaps most easily explained as cell-style terror, was implemented in large part to foil the many government informants who infiltrated Klan groups in the 1960s and to stymie court prosecution. But it has had a much more durable and catastrophic effect in its clouding of public understanding. It has allowed the movement to disappear, leaving behind a fiction of supposed lone wolf terrorists, bad apples, and errant madmen.

The 1983–1995 period featured many episodes of white power coordination, social networking, and spectacular violence, but at no point in this period was there a meaningful stop to this movement's organizing. Even in the wake of the Oklahoma City bombing, there was no durable shift in public understanding, no major prosecution that hobbled the movement. There was no meaningful and permanent response to white power activism in surveillance organization and resources, juror education, prosecutorial strategy, or military policy. The piecemeal responses in each of these areas utterly failed to contain white power as a growing and broad-based social movement. Not even lawsuits, which were in many ways the most effective measure attempted, delivered a full stop to white power organizing and violence.

In the two years since the release of *Bring the War Home*, it has become more urgent than ever to think carefully about the terminology that shapes and delimits understanding of this movement. My use of the term "white power" here is meant precisely to do the work of recognizing both the revolutionary ideology put forward by this movement and the links between groups and belief systems too often understood as disparate.

White power should not be confused with white supremacy. Although this certainly was a white supremacist movement, the activists we consider here today are one very small and violent component of that broad and complex category. White power should not be called "white nationalist," which carries with it a distortion that threatens to contribute to public misunderstanding: people hear this term and think of overzealous patriotism. But the nation in white nationalism since 1983 was not the United States, but rather a transnational "Aryan nation" that connected white people around the world. The interests of white nationalism were and are fundamentally opposed to those of the United States, at least insofar as the United States is imagined as an inclusive constitutional democracy.

Nor should we confuse white power with the alt-right, a specific and recent subset of organizing with large overlaps into the white power movement. The alt-right is new; white power is decades, even generations old.

White power—which was also the most common phrase used by these activists in self-description—most accurately conveys this movement. White supremacist extremism, which has come into more frequent use in the aftermath of Charlottesville—especially among scholars who study this groundswell outside of the United States—also conveys both its seriousness and its specificity, but was not used by white power activists or their opponents in the earlier period.

This linguistic clarification is necessary because academics, journalists, and activists alike are late to the study and understanding of white power ideology and activism. We have failed to listen to the deadly intent of these actors. This is part of a broad misunderstanding of this violence that emerges from the urge to categorize and contain belief systems that people find fringe, shocking, or oppositional. Thus we see stories about the Tree of Life synagogue attack as anti-Semitic violence, the Christchurch shooting as Islamophobic violence, the El Paso shooting as anti-immigrant violence, the attempted assassinations by a Coast Guard officer as political violence, and the militias on our border and parading armed through our capital cities as neutral. They are, of course, acts of anti-Semitic, Islamophobic, anti-immigrant, and political violence. But they are also actions motivated by a common white power ideology. Understood through a focus on perpetrators, they are part of the same story. Seeing them together, instead of as lone wolf actions, we can begin to see a trend, a wave, a rising tide.

We have also failed to understand perpetrators on their own terms. For example, a large part of the scholarly work on the white power movement, already divorced from that on other kinds of perpetrators, has attempted to categorize and quantify the various branches of the movement—attempting to establish how many Klansmen, how many neo-Nazis, how many skinheads, etc. In fact, this question is often irrelevant to the way that white power activists understood their own participation in the movement. The historical archive reveals that people regularly circulated between groups and belief systems, that they often held concurrent memberships, and that they used a wide variety of flexible and interchangeable symbols and ideologies.

Indeed, the white power movement is distinct from earlier mobilizations of the Klan and earlier neo-Nazi movements because of its ideological, generational, and religious diversity. Leaders wrote about the imperative of accepting members that people found shockingly different (like Christian Identity rural survivalists banding together with urban skinheads).

The white power groundswell was certainly a fringe movement, but it was comparable with better-known mobilizations such as the anti-Communist John Birch Society. Membership numbers are a poor measure of white power activity, with records often distorted or destroyed. Nonetheless, scholars and watchdog groups who seek an aggregate count of the movement's varied branches—one that includes, for instance, both Klansmen and neo-Nazis rather than only one of these often overlapping self-designations—estimate that in the 1980s the movement included around 25,000 "hard-core members"; an additional 150,000 to 175,000 people who bought white power literature, sent contributions to groups, or attended rallies or other movement events; and another 450,000 who did not themselves purchase materials or participate, but who read the literature.[3] The John Birch Society, in contrast, reached 100,000 members at its 1965 peak and, while much less violent, has garnered much more public awareness and scholarly attention.[4]

So: why don't we have a story of Oklahoma City? Why didn't people understand white power, when Birch still comes up so regularly? In fact, we knew about white power activism as it happened. The episodes I cover in *Bring the War Home* appeared in major newspapers, on public access television, on talk shows and morning shows, and on the radio. But nevertheless, white power activism was misunderstood by many Americans, and unconfronted and unresolved such that the movement could resurface in our present moment. I argue that this comes down to three things.

The first is a change in movement organizing strategy. Beginning in 1983, a new strategy, leaderless resistance, depended upon the action of independent cells without direct contact with movement leadership. The strategy, which had the specific aim of preventing prosecution, was distributed through movement literature and adopted widely throughout the underground. Leaderless resistance changed recruitment goals, emphasizing the importance of a small number of fully committed activists rather than large memberships of less-committed followers.[5] Because of this change, membership numbers could not forecast activity or the movement's capacity for violence.

The second was a number of failed trials. The Department of Justice attempted a large-scale trial of thirteen white power activists and leaders in 1987–1988 in Fort Smith, Arkansas, on federal charges including seditious conspiracy. This involved the fruits of several smaller stings by FBI and Bureau of Alcohol, Tobacco, and Firearms agents that had resulted in plea bargains, and several people testified against their fellow activists in order to shorten their own sentences, keep their families together, or assure their protection. Their descriptions of the race war were vivid: thirty gallons of cyanide seized just before it could be used to poison the water of a major city; assassinations of a talk radio personality, fellow group members, and state troopers; a reign of paramilitary training, parading, and harassment of various enemies; and two huge laundry hampers of military-grade weapons pushed through the courtroom. Seditious conspiracy was wholly evident, declared outright in the writings and speeches of the movement, and outfitted with semi- and fully automatic rifles, machine guns, rocket launchers, antitank M72s, and grenades. Witnesses described how white power separatist compounds manufactured their own Claymore-style land mines and trained in urban warfare.

However, the Fort Smith trial failed; all thirteen activists walked free. A historical analysis of the trial raises several questions about its efficacy. Two jurors had romantic pen-pal relationships with two defendants, and one of these couples married after the trial, casting doubt upon the impartiality of the jury. Defendants, representing themselves, gave lengthy character testimony about their tours in Vietnam, arguing that those who had served their country in wartime could not possibly be seditious conspirators against it (the historical record does not support this argument). Large swaths of evidence were excluded, as were jurors familiar with white power activity in the area (which had been widely reported in local news sources). One juror later spoke of a white supremacist view, though common to the region, that the Bible prohibited race mixing. And white power women did enormous performative work in the courtroom to attempt to establish the good character of the defendants. Their actions led to sympathetic journalistic and scholarly accounts that clouded the movement's violent record and allowed it to appeal to the mainstream.

Finally, the third and last element was the large-scale and durable forgetting of everything we knew about white power activism. The sedition trial represented such an embarrassment that it—along with the tragedies that were also public relations disasters at Ruby Ridge and Waco in the early 1990s—would impact the investigative strategies used in Oklahoma City. The acquittals at Fort Smith made the Department of Justice and some agents in the FBI reluctant to try an investigative and prosecutorial strategy that would attempt to portray the Oklahoma City bombing as the work of a movement. Indeed, the Bureau had institutionalized a policy to pursue only individual actors in white power violence, with "no attempts to tie individual crimes to a broader movement."[6] This strategy not only worked to obscure the bombing as part of a social movement but, in the years following bomber Timothy McVeigh's conviction and execution, effectively erased the movement itself from public understanding.

The evidence of McVeigh's involvement in the white power movement is too extensive to document at length here, but a few highlights include his choice of a building that had been a movement target since the early 1980s, the use and distribution of a movement novel titled *The Turner Diaries* in formulating his plan for the bombing, his presence as high-level security for movement leadership in the Michigan militia, his membership in a Klan chapter, his contacts and attempted contacts with the white power groups Arizona Patriots, National Alliance, and the separatist compound at Elohim City, Oklahoma, and the date of the bombing on the anniversary of not only the Waco siege but the execution date of a prominent white power activist who had once targeted, yes, the federal building in Oklahoma City. Additional evidence abounds, and not at the level of conspiracy theory: a simple social geography of McVeigh's life prior to the bombing places him decisively in the white power movement as a follower of the strategy of leaderless resistance.

All this is to say that white power activity in the United States is not new, nor has it been as shadowy as we may have imagined. It was known, and then forgotten, and it is this process of forgetting that directs our attention to the parameters of public debate and public memory, and to what might be different in our current moment that might open the way for confronting racist formations in our society.

A history focused on perpetrators reveals that many of the

purportedly inexplicable acts of violence in the present are motivated by a coherent and deliberate ideology. The March 2019 attack on two mosques in Christchurch, New Zealand, which left fifty-one people dead and scores more injured, was not a lone wolf attack or the work of a few isolated radicals. It was, again, part of the white power movement, a broad groundswell that has joined people together in common purpose, social relationships, and political ideology. This movement formed in the United States after the Vietnam War, using narratives of violence and the symbols and weapons of that conflict to bring together Klansmen, neo-Nazis, skinheads, and other white radicals.

The materials left behind by the alleged Christchurch attacker—not just the manifesto, but also social media posts and the white messages scrawled on the weapon and magazines used in the attack—definitively locate his ideology in this movement. He references the Fourteen Words, a slogan written by the U.S. white power activist David Lane, who was incarcerated in the late 1980s after his participation in a white power terror cell called the Order. That group stole millions of dollars from armored cars and department stores to distribute to white power cells around the country, assassinated enemies, and attacked infrastructure targets in an attempt to foment race war.

The Fourteen Words refer to the central mission of the white power movement, which is to ensure a white future and the birth of white children. The Christchurch gunman also refers to a "future for our people," expressing the apocalyptic fear of racial annihilation that has animated white power activism for decades. The manifesto ends with highly stylized, idyllic images of white mothers and children. This focus on women is also a mainstay of the white power movement and its intense emphasis on white reproduction, worries about the hyperfertility of people of color, and the fear of racial extinction.

These ideas about genocide and population replacement aren't new, nor do they constitute a conspiracy theory responding only to growing populations of Muslim immigrants. White power activists share views with other conservatives on many social issues, but they understand these issues as deeply related to racial extinction. They have written about this in precisely this way for decades. They opposed interracial marriage, abortion, and gay and lesbian movements, they said, because these would decrease the white birthrate; they opposed immigration because they feared they would be overrun. They framed these issues with ideas about the purity of white women—who, they said, would have to bear three children each in order to avoid racial extinction—and with hateful invective about hyperfertile racial others.

The white power movement was profoundly transnational, motivated by ideas that have long roots in the United States and elsewhere but are not bounded by nation.

As with many transnational movements, white power was both shaped by inflows from other places—like skinhead culture from Great Britain—and exported as a specific white power ideology, shaped by U.S. paramilitarism, abroad. Groups like Aryan Nations sent their materials around the world in the 1980s and 1990s, and activists in Australia and New Zealand could read white power newspapers from the United States and send for materials. White power groups like Wotansvolk and the World Church of the Creator even set up chapters and memberships in other countries. Wotansvolk had representation in forty-one countries by 2000, and World Church of the Creator had chapters in a multitude of places including New Zealand, Canada, Norway, and South Africa. The language and strategy of white power also spread through books like *The Turner Diaries*, a novel-turned-manual-turned-lodestar that appeared in places like apartheid South Africa and sold more than fifty thousand copies in the few decades after it was released. The places white power activists chose to pollinate map onto an idea of whiteness that transcends national boundaries.[7]

Understanding these acts of violence as politically motivated, connected, and purposeful would fundamentally change the way we understand, speak, and write about such attacks—a crucial first step toward a different response.

The future envisioned by the white power movement is also profoundly radical, and not just the overzealous patriotism that many people think of when they hear the word "nationalism." Indeed, the mass casualties wrought by this movement are not, in themselves, the movement's goal. They are means to an end, a way to awaken a broader white public to what white power activists see as obvious: the threats posed to the white race by immigration and racial others. The violence is meant to mobilize white people around the world to wage race war.

The Christchurch manifesto talks about just this strategy. In a section about the use of guns, the attacker writes about how he hopes to spur a seizure of guns that would then enrage the right in the United States and provoke further conflict. This strategy is directly out of *The Turner Diaries*.[8]

Indeed, that novel is the crucial text in understanding the way futurity works in the white power movement. It sets out to answer the question that undergirds the entire project: How could a tiny fringe movement hope to overthrow the most powerful, militarized superstate in the history of the world?

In *The Turner Diaries*, the narrator describes the problem as "a gnat trying to assassinate an elephant." The novel then lays out a plan in which white power cells and undercover operatives carry out assassinations, attacks on infrastructure targets, and sabotage to awaken a broader white public to their cause. Through guerilla warfare and cell-style terror, they are able to seize an air force base with nuclear weapons, provoke a nuclear exchange between the United States and the Soviet Union (and Israel), and take over first the nation and then the world in its aftermath. The details are worth understanding, and I have explored them elsewhere. Here I want to focus first on the inherent apocalypticism braided through these beliefs, and on the role of the white bystander/ broader white public in the future imagined by the movement.

In the period of my study, apocalypticism was enormously important not only to the white power movement but in broader political culture. In the rising evangelical congregations of the 1980s and 1990s, the ones that read Tim LaHaye's Left Behind novels and planned for the rapture, the fears of the Cold War became intertwined with faith belief. After the fall of the Berlin Wall in 1989, I argue, there was a fundamental crisis of narrative—people with these ingrained fears of the end of the world still held them, but now operated without a clear narrative enemy or agent of the end.

This worked in an even stronger and more direct way in the white power movement, where activists connected ideas of a radical political future with their belief in imminent apocalypse. Christian Identity, one of the movement's two most prominent theologies, foretold the imminent end of the world. But whereas evangelical belief offered the promise of the rapture—in which the faithful would be peacefully transported to heaven before the bloodshed of the tribulations—Christian Identity called its adherents to arms. The faithful either would have to outlast the tribulations to see the return of Christ, becoming survivalists, or would have to take up arms to clear the world of nonbelievers in the End Times. Nonbelievers, in Christian Identity, included all nonwhite people. In other words, Christian Identity transfigured race war into holy war.[9]

These views of the world—encroaching threats on the white population, the idea of demographic transformation as racial extinction, and the looming fear of the coming end of the world—have come to impact mainstream political formations in all sorts of new and imbricated ways in the 2000s, and not just in the aftermath of the 2016 election.

Historical context could pave the way to better reporting, more sound activism, and better public understanding. There are no lone wolves. There are, from time to time, people who carry out acts of violence that are not motivated by political ideology, as in the case of the 1999 attack on Columbine High School. It would not be correct to attribute the Columbine attack to the white power movement. But in the attacks on the Tree of Life synagogue, the Anders Breivik attack in Norway, the El Paso shooting, and Dylann Roof's attack on AME worshippers in Charleston, we need look no further than the manifestos to see that even those people who have never met another activist in real life can find themselves radicalized by a social network, imbricated in an ideology, and motivated by decades of history.

The grain of hope is that connecting these stories together could make possible a new coalition politics between the many communities impacted by exclusion, hate, and violence—that in our moment we might see a knitting together of people that could create different possibilities of response and action.

PART IV

GLOBAL PERSPECTIVES

FROM CRISIS TO CATASTROPHE

Lineages of the Global New Right

LEAH FELDMAN AND AAMIR R. MUFTI

This project first began to be conceived in the months after Donald Trump's victory in 2016, and this introduction was written as part of a special issue for *boundary2* entitled "From Crisis to Catastrophe: Lineages of the Global New Right" the year following his removal from office, in 2022. In the interim, we found ourselves increasingly immersed in the development of the so-called alt-right and white nationalism more broadly. We quickly realized that we were seeing the emergence of an assemblage of individuals, movements, ideas, memes, and motifs that was worldwide in its reach, scope, and significance. American white nationalists and self-described national socialists were showing up in neo-Nazi videos in Greece, writers belonging to the Nouvelle Droite in France were receiving standing ovations at conferences of white nationalists in the United States, and an idea like the "great replacement" was clearly able to travel from a fourteenth-century castle near the Pyrenees in France to Christchurch, New Zealand, and to Pittsburgh, El Paso, and Buffalo in the United States.

As we continued our expansive research into contemporary forms of the far right, we also, not surprisingly, began to delve more and more into the literary, political, theoretical, and philosophical archives of Euro-American fascisms of an earlier era. As our research and teaching acquired this new direction, and as we began to realize the enormity

188 | GLOBAL PERSPECTIVES

of the political, social, and cultural transformations under way, we also confronted with some dismay the seeming indifference of our profession to the catastrophes unfolding in the world around us, reflected in a whole series of evasive and self-destructive tendencies, many of them mutually contradictory—"postcritique" sentimentalism, big-data-obsessed digital humanities, a renewed hyperspecialization, and "new formalism," to name just a handful. We began to recognize that the new right's attack on critical humanities scholarship (which extends beyond its crusade against critical race theory and queer theory) has accompanied a longer institutional turn toward defunding and eventually eliminating humanist study as the failing (degenerate) arm of the ascending corporate university brand. These aligned shifts within our profession and beyond expose how a late capitalist veneration of an all-knowing market serves to conceal the forms of patriarchal white supremacy that continue to shape our political and social world.

Since the emergence of the Trump coalition in 2015, "fascism" returned to the political vocabulary of the times suddenly and without much intellectual preparation. As events hurtled us forward—or was it backward?—toward some indiscernible catastrophe, many seemed to grasp spontaneously at this relic in the hope that it might deliver an understanding of the present and how we got here, or at the very least give us a stability of orientation as we tried to survive this unsettling and dangerous historical process. But this return of an old concept immediately raised the possibility that this hoary specter from and of another time could easily lead to intellectual paralysis and political ineffectiveness, leaving us permanently lamenting the return of the 1930s in the 2020s. (The meme makers of the white nationalist right have a mocking name for this ubiquitous feature of center-left culture—"the current year.") The fact that this concept has entered the political landscape does not guarantee its analytical effectiveness, but it does mean that this efficacy (or lack thereof) is itself a genuine and viable object of analysis. The effort here is not concerned with developing a global definition of fascism, a concept to encompass a wide range of far-right politics around the world or even just in the Euro-American world. But some things it ought to be possible to say. Between the "fascist maximum" of a radical and militarized state and what Robert Paxton calls the "elusive 'fascist minimum'" lies a broad landscape of ideas, individuals, movements, political parties, and even state forms.[1] The rush to identify the fascist nature of the Trump phenomenon has sometimes produced facile results—the spectacle of his political rallies being seen through the lens of Nuremberg, for instance, and even through Walter Benjamin's notion of the aestheticization of politics. But in various actions and statements before and after Trump's ascent to the presidency, and in various elements of his movement, aspects of the classic fascism complex have been clearly discernible: both authoritarian and (in Max Weber's sense) "charismatic" leadership of the movement, the followers' cultlike veneration of the person of the leader, the populist identification with "the people" against variously defined elites—Trump as the "blue collar billionaire"— the presence of a frankly white nationalist element—anti-Black, anti-immigrant, and anti-Semitic—within the base of the GOP's electoral coalition, to list merely the most obvious ones.

But what has also begun to be clear over the course of the last six years is that far-right and white nationalist culture in Europe and the United States now not only takes organized political form but also extends across vast areas of culture and society, forms of extension and dissemination made possible by the ecologies of the new media landscape and the growing precariousness of more and more lives lived in the wealthiest zones of global capitalism. From social media forums such as 4chan, 8chan, Stormfront, Reddit, Gab, and the Russian messaging service Telegram to textual and graphic science fiction in all its online variety, an enormous cacophony now characterizes the culture of the far right. Until very recently, far-right content was also available with complete impunity on more mainline platforms like Facebook and YouTube and still often manages to evade their algorithmic restrictions. (And outside the Global North, nationalisms and fascisms of the most violent sort—far-right Hindu nationalism, for instance—still seem to have near complete impunity on these global platforms.) Ideologically, this space is some sort of soup-kitchen slop of antiliberalism, antimodernism, white supremacy, southern nationalism, neo-Nazism, anti-Semitism, "social nationalism," Holocaust "revisionism," white nationalism, white "advocacy," white "identitarianism," "race-realism," antifeminism, "anti-poz" homophobia, heterosexual and homosexual "manosphere" misogyny, traditionalism, varieties of mysticism, alt-right hipsterism, "Orthodox nationalism," and Nordic paganism, to name just some of the more prominent tendencies. In addition to these ideological contents, however, questions of style and form are equally important in understanding this cultural space—irony, parody, satire, and a generalized self-conscious assertion of "joyfulness" and jouissance are among the preeminent stylistic tendencies in this space in which varieties of racism, anti-Semitism, misogyny, homophobia, and xenophobia can be freely expressed in mocking repudiation of the pieties of what is derided as "woke" liberal political correctness and multiculturalism.

The ongoing debates about the applicability of the concept of fascism to our historical moment must not only take all these aspects of the contemporary reality into account but also address the retooling of nativist, settler colonial, and blood and soil narratives of white supremacy. This introduction is meant as a small contribution in this direction and proposes to put on a firmer *conceptual* as well as *historical* footing the possibility of understanding the present political and social crisis as the "return" of the far right as a political culture across the Euro-American world—the United States, Western Europe, Russia—but also in India under the rule of Narendra Modi and the Bharatiya Janata Party. Wherever possible, we are also interested in examining the links between these regional spaces, links that are organizational, ideational, historical, or socioeconomic, or combinations of several of these. In many cases, from the (now defunct) Traditionalist Worker Party or the Proud Boys in the United States to Génération Identitaire in France, Skandza Forum in the Nordic countries, Jobbik in Hungary, Golden Dawn in Greece, and Neo-Eurasianism in Russia, these far-right groupings increasingly see themselves as not merely fraternal organizations but rather as local elements of an assemblage of "white" advocacy across the world, even if the racial concept is often concealed within explicitly territorial, linguistic, or cultural imaginaries. But this growing sensibility and experience of "a worldwide white nation," as the late French neofascist thinker Guillaume Faye put it in front of an American audience in 2012, is at least in tension with the ubiquitous political and social imaginary of the "ethnostate," which revives the term coined by Wilmot Robertson in his book of that name.[2] Some of Faye's most influential work is an attempt to defuse this tension and bridge this contradiction. This much ought to be clear: this political and cultural space marks distinct and powerful tendencies in contemporary society that have survived Trump's loss in the 2020 election, and the struggle against them is just beginning. In what ways can an antifascist left be created and mobilized against this diffuse movement and social imaginary, which (for now at least) eschews institutional state politics, preferring the symbology of tribal and occult rites, conspiracies about high finance and the deep state, the social possibilities of the commune, and the organicism of ethnonationalism as the ideological foundations of its alternative to the liberal international order? The possibility of an organized and popular left that is adequate to this historical task at different levels of society remains, we fear, very much an open question.

Many of the analyses of fascism that come to us from the early decades of the twentieth century—for instance, those by Emmanuel Levinas, Georges Bataille, Arthur Rosenberg, Theodor Adorno and Max Horkheimer, Wilhelm Reich, Hannah Arendt, and even Erich Auerbach, to name only some of the most well-known cases—perform various balancing acts between historical explanations and what we might call transhistorical ones, such as psychological (and psychosexual), ethical, or civilizational-spiritual accounts. Against the brutal contextualism and "vulgar" economic determinism of the official Comintern position—"Fascism is the power of finance capital itself"—these early observers of fascism offer deeper indictments of the historical development of the Western bourgeois world over the *longue durée* and its collapse into barbarism in the twentieth century.

But, of course, no analysis of fascisms as historical formations can bypass the question of their relation to the crises of capitalism, a broad question that can itself be reconfigured into a number of more circumscribed ones. With regard to our contemporary moment and to the attempt to reanimate the concept of fascism for analyses of present-day politics, this means at the very least a reconsideration of neoliberalism as a set of economic theories and policy positions and the structural arrangements that have emerged from the interaction of the theories (and theorists) with policy around the world over the last several decades.[3] It hardly needs pointing out that the two biggest moments in the history of the far right over the last century coincide exactly with the two biggest crises of world capitalism in the same time period, namely, the Great Depression and the Great Recession (the latter taking the form of an outright depression in some regions and countries). Trump's protectionist expostulations during his first campaign and some of the policy decisions that followed during his term in office, such as the abandonment of the Trans-Pacific Partnership and the "cold" trade war with China and even the European Union, led some commentators, including such fervent Trumpistas as Pat Buchanan, to declare too early the end of neoliberal "free trade" and "Washington consensus" globalism. In this ideological inversion, the GOP, whose base now consists of the white nationalist right in the country, appears as the party of the (white) working class, whereas the party of the center-left, namely, the Democrats, appears as the party of "special interests" and neoliberal globalization.

The truth of course is quite otherwise, namely, that a host of major policies of the Trump administration and his party in Congress—the relentless (if mostly failed) attacks on Obamacare, the multipronged attack on (primary, secondary, and tertiary) public education, the massive transfer of wealth to the superwealthy through the signature tax bill, and perhaps most catastrophically of all, the chaotic outsourcing of the pandemic response to the private sector, reducing states, cities, and even hospitals in the same city to ruthless competition with one another for the most basic medical supplies, to name just a few of the most disastrous policies—are instances of neoliberal consolidation par excellence in their brutally unrelenting worship of market-centered politics. Against all the talk of antiglobalism and disdain for multilateralism, it would be more accurate to speak of alternative forms of globalization, less multilateral, certainly, but all the more committed to neoliberal arrangements of economies and states. The successful packaging of perhaps the most ostentatiously corrupt crony capitalist and huckster in America as a man of the people bent on clearing out "the swamp" at the nexus of business and politics is a remarkable historical event that needs to be understood in deep sociological, semiotic, and psychological terms. And Trump's uncanny ability to mobilize a crowd to attack the Capitol and send senators and representatives of both parties scurrying for their physical safety makes crystal clear that he remains at the head of the right-wing mob. Only a fool or a charlatan would now deny that fascism is a mass presence in this country, even if it is not as yet a mass movement.

Much of the post-2016 literature on fascism has taken up the logic of definition and diagnosis, counterposing a schematic ordering of populist and authoritarian movements against the possibility of their creative capacities of reinvention.[4] Thus, while fascism appears immediate and present in a series of spectacular events—from the Charlottesville rally and riot, resulting in the murder of the young antifascist Heather Heyer, to the massacres perpetrated by white nationalists—it also, at the same time, remains peripheral, unorganized, ever flailing, and failing. This is hardly a historical novelty, because ascendant fascist movements typically fabricate their mass power precisely from this structural position of peripherality and precariousness in relation to the state apparatus—from their "heterogeneity" to the market and the state, as Bataille already argued in the 1930s.[5] Up to and even including the moment of the seizure of state power, they appear as exogenous to the state apparatus, taking power from the outside through a crisis of party representation, growing militarization, and, more generally, a process of economic, political, and social destabilization.[6] In our present historical conjuncture this enabling peripherality is expressed in the narrative of "white" societies' (and especially their men's) victimization under the sign of the "great replacement."

Among the recurring motifs of a great deal of the culture of the contemporary far right are cataclysm and catastrophe. The "ecopocalyptic" visions elaborated by writers of the far right in France since 1968, from Jean Raspail in *Camp of the Saints* (1973) to Guillaume Faye in *Archeofuturism* (1999) and *Convergence of Catastrophes* (2004), have available to them the work of the older avant-garde of fascio-modernism, including the Italians Julius Evola and Filippo Marinetti, and its veneration of war and a violent hypermodernity.[7] And in the United States, the influence on the contemporary right of such early-twentieth-century proponents of eugenics and environmentalism as Lothrop Stoddard and Madison Grant is wide and palpable—and of course these two had also influenced the official raciology of the Third Reich through the work of Alfred Rosenberg. John Tanton, founding figure of the anti-immigrant and ecological movements in this country, was the publisher who brought Raspail's novel to English-speaking audiences and helped establish it in its present unassailable position in the literary canon of the white nationalist right. The right-wing apocalyptic imaginary has a quality of "accelerationism" to it, the notion that the only way out of the morass of capitalism and liberalism is a speeding up of their destructive tendencies. As Benjamin Noys writes, accelerationism "is not merely a historical curiosity, but an aesthetic and political attitude that continues to exert a gravitational pull on the present. . . . The political vagaries of these aesthetic forms of accelerationism do not fall on the tired tropes of fascism and 'totalitarianism,' but rather on this difficult and tense imbrication with the dynamics of capitalism."[8] Aleksandr Dugin's philosophical crusade in Russia against the post-Soviet incursion of Satanic Western capitalism and liberalism, while traditionalist rather than modernist in its impulses and ideological contents, also carries the imprint of accelerationism in the traces of the constitutional crisis of 1993 and Boris Yeltsin and Yegor Gaidar's violent shock therapy reforms.

A transnational approach to reading the contemporary rise of a new right, especially in the United States and Europe, can in part be framed by two historical nodes—1968 and 1989—both crucial moments in the hegemonic institutionalization of neoliberal socioeconomic and political ideas and practices. The historiography of the intellectual scene in France after May 1968 often does not give sufficient attention to the fact that the period saw the emergence of a vibrant intellectual right as well, not just the left. These new right-wing formations often saw themselves as ideologically distinct from the midcentury right, from Catholic monarchism, for instance, and some of their thinkers, above all Alain de Benoist, were influential more than two decades later in post-Soviet Russia in the 1990s. The French Nouvelle Droit saw itself as a response to what it considered the "Marxist revolution" of 1968.[9] But it quickly became aligned with the National Front in its focus on postcolonial immigration and, with the collapse of the Soviet Union and the disappearance of its satellite states in Eastern Europe, turned its attention to what it correctly saw as the stunning expansion to hegemonic status worldwide of U.S.-led neoliberalism, which its thinkers condemned for its reducing of a rich tapestry of human populations to an undifferentiated mass of producers and consumers.

In turn, the fall of the Soviet Union led to a distinct process of the rise of the new right in its former zone—former Communists morphing into right-wing nationalists in the midst of the application of neoliberal shock therapy to entire populations as a matter of routine policy. The aggravation of the class struggle that accompanied these violent economic transformations contributed to the rise of antiliberal ethnonationalisms in the post-Soviet world, often armed with "postsecularist" critiques of Western liberalism and secularism. To a significant extent this development of the right alongside the left from the late 1960s on was an international development, with resurgent neoreactionary movements and parties emerging to respond to the political, social, and cultural protest movements of the previous decade, in some cases leading to the overthrow of democratically elected progressive governments in military coups d'état more or less supported by the Western powers—Chile and Pakistan immediately come to mind.

Russia and the former Soviet states have particularly come to be associated with a resurgence of authoritarianism, which has only accelerated with Putin's invasions of Ukraine in 2014 and 2022. However, despite these renewed encroachments, transformations of the right-wing and nationalist sort across post-Communist Eastern Europe have been accompanied by unexpected geopolitical realignments. For instance, despite the living memory of the Soviet invasion of Budapest in 1956 and Putin's recent invasion of Ukraine, which has only enlivened the already persistent presence of anti-Russian sentiment in Hungary's political culture, Hungary's resurgent nationalist right displays a marked political warming toward Russia. Viktor Orbán's celebration of "illiberal democracy" is politically aligned with Putin's internal vision for Russia and his geopolitical vision of an alternative political and social axis to the forces of Western liberalism and globalism. Hungary in fact has emerged as a global beacon for white nationalists—many Americans have chosen to move there—and Arktos, the main English-language translator and publisher of the works of the European and Russian right, including those by de Benoist, Faye, and Dugin, was founded there in the second decade of this century. It briefly even drew to its senior staff a representative of the "neo-Aryan" tendency in the monarchist Iranian diaspora. The dissemination of these materials to the anglophone reading public has played no small role in disseminating the social imaginary of "the worldwide white nation" to white nationalists in the Anglo-Saxon world. The three figures mentioned above are routinely cited by such individuals in the U.S. alt-right as Richard Spencer, Matthew Heimbach, Jared Taylor, and Matthew Raphael Johnson as major influences.

The question for us is not whether or not Donald J. Trump, Vladimir Putin, or Narendra Modi (or even Steve Bannon, Stephen Miller, Aleksandr Dugin, Alain de Benoist, or any one of a host of other more macabre acolytes) *is* a fascist but whether and to what extent fascist tendencies in U.S. culture and society have emerged and coalesced around Trump's 2016 campaign, then his presidency, and now his conspiracy-driven grievance crusade, and whether and to what extent these social forces are in a position to redefine aspects of social relations—race and gender relations, for instance—and of culture. What answers we find to such questions, which are the domain of the critical humanities, will also help us understand whether and to what extent these social and political forces are capable of again seizing control of the presidency or of elements of the state despite the liberal-constitutional regime of "checks and balances," which has been put under severe pressure repeatedly since 2017, although it also has clearly survived that onslaught. Fascism may not be *in power* in the United States, or in any European country, but at the very least it has been *empowered* by a whole series of political developments, including Brexit, the Trump phenomenon, Putin's invasion, the reelection of Orbán, and the near election of Marine Le Pen. Equally remarkable and disturbingly closer to home is the apparently seamless appropriation by the far right of aspects of the contemporary humanities—ideas linked to postcolonial critique, cultural studies, queer studies, and minority rights discourse: immigrants and their children are routinely spoken of as a colonial occupation force; whites are viewed as a marginalized minority in their own homelands; queerness is envisioned through violent ritual performances of white masculinity; and, recently, whites have even come to be referred to as stateless, peoples without a state that they can call their own. It is a fundamental task of the critical humanities in these times to understand these acts of appropriation of their ideas and formulate adequate responses to them.

As we confront this new social, cultural, and political landscape, it becomes dismally apparent that the humanities in the academy have been too often oblivious to these social, cultural, and political forces in recent years—including the appropriation of parts of their own discourse by white nationalists. Clearly, some of the most vaunted new trends in the literary profession—world literature, big-data-driven literary history, or postcritique, for instance—aim to depoliticize the practice of criticism and scholarship in their distinct ways, often explicitly so. Seeking to build a broad critical-intellectual approach to the crisis of the present moment, we take up the call outlined by Edward Said for a worldly orientation for criticism as an intellectual practice and form of writing, which he elaborated as an agile, alert, and skeptical orientation of thought in the world, seeking to expose the hierarchies of Culture and Value, on the one hand, and, on the other, the false comforts of critical-ideational systems, political or theoretical positions worked out fully in advance, merely awaiting their "application" to this or that context or body of material.

Exposing some of the ways in which the violence of neoliberal capitalism has been absorbed by our own institutions and profession in this moment of fascist returns, like the corporatized remaking of an entrepreneurial humanities, we are reminded of the necessity to return to criticism and to the possibilities of understanding the human through poetry and literature. By drawing our collective attention to the globalization of a new-right political culture, we call for a skeptical and worldly criticism and pedagogy against some of the most powerful tendencies in the profession as well as the wider world.

LOSING THE PRESENT TO HISTORY

FAISAL DEVJI

Those who would defend and those who criticize histories of the present often switch places during their debate. By choosing to focus on the past on its own terms and without reference to their own times, partisans of the latter position recognize the autonomy of the present far better than those who support the former. By breaking genealogical narratives in imagining a world governed by a quite different logic, they also, if sometimes inadvertently, refuse to naturalize the present and so make it a truly historical phenomenon. The effort to think differently about the past can be understood as a counterintuitive experiment that brings the present into much sharper relief.

The votaries of a history of the present, for their part, adopt the oldest role in the profession by composing a genealogy or record of contemporary power even if only to hold someone responsible for its evils. The historical precedents that have been adduced for recent events ranging from the 9/11 attacks and the war on terror to the financial crisis of 2008, the pandemic of 2020, and the Black Lives Matter campaign suggest, if anything, a flight to the past resulting from an inability to grasp the new. And indeed, it is extraordinary how the rush to history serves as a way of refusing to think about the present and so the future it produces in anything but the most hackneyed ways.

The legitimization of racism or populist authoritarianism in our day, for instance, puts us in mind of European fascism and totalitarianism, just as fears of Muslim ideologues in Europe bring to mind the battles of Christendom, the Wars of Religion or the separation of church and state. In public life these histories often result in explicit efforts to repeat the past, in such ways as reforming Islam as Christianity was reformed or reaffirming Enlightenment values. But even among historians there is little sense of the novelty these phenomena might represent. The remarkable Eurocentrism of the genealogies invoked also suggests an anxiety to reconstitute the West as the center of world history.

No history of the present takes non-Western peoples, places, or powers as its origin unless it is to include them in the making of Euro-American societies. But even such efforts at diversification play into the universal enterprise of the West's history in more benevolent and effective ways than the exclusionary narratives of times past. It is not a question of distinguishing between the historical narratives of Eastern and Western countries, or Southern and Northern ones to use another set of directions, since they all look the same. Few histories can be written without the West being central to them in phenomena like capitalism, colonialism, modernity, the world wars, bipolar politics, and so on.

It might be the case that national histories in countries like China absorb the West within their own narratives and terms of reference, though it is unlikely that these can account for the Euro-American past or present. The only case I know of is a conceptually and empirically thin one deriving in part from Western histories. This is the narrative of Islam as Christendom's great rival, one able to match it at what Marshall Hodgson called a hemispheric scale. During the Cold War, for example, it had been possible for Muslim ideologues to see the superpowers as latter-day versions of the Byzantine and Persian empires, each as evil as the other and doomed to be replaced by Islam.

With the end of the Cold War, it became popular to imagine the Soviet Union as having been destroyed by an Islamic movement in Afghanistan, while the United States waited to take the place of Byzantium with the emergence of Al-Qaeda and later ISIS. Osama bin Laden even went so far as to reverse the usual narrative of historical derivation by claiming that the American leadership took its Middle Eastern clients as models for corruption, violence, and illegality during the war on terror.[1] And this, of course, was simply another sign of their country's imminent collapse as a democracy. Looking at America today, who is to say he was entirely wrong?

Histories of the present tend to make the new familiar, if not less fearsome, by joining rather than separating historical periods in such a way as to maintain a dominant role for the West, even if only to castigate its imperialisms, racisms, or genocides. And in this sense, there is not much difference between pro-Western and anti-Western narratives. Histories of the present are therefore also conservative by definition, especially when they seek to warn us of something we or our ancestors have already experienced. There are far too many such forebodings among historians at the moment, who insist on imagining our time as a new 1848, a new 1914, a new 1933, or a new 1947.

But such Eurocentric, if occasionally inclusive, histories have not been the only ones available to us in modern times. Anticolonial histories from Asia and Africa, for instance, tended to focus on breaking rather than joining narratives in which Europe was the only real subject for good or ill. Decolonization depended upon breaking the hold of the past rather than returning to a precolonial golden age and was focused on a radically open future. Gandhi repudiated historical consciousness itself as a modality of empire, one that allowed people to be classified as modern rulers or traditional subjects who required the pedagogical attention of colonialism to achieve their freedom.[2] He also knew how history allowed empires to understand and control their subjects.

Gandhi is one of the few political thinkers of the twentieth century to disdain history in a modernity defined by utopias and revolutions that sought its fulfilment. He pointed out that history as commonly conceived was a narrative of conflict to whose violence alone did historians attribute any real change, regardless of whether this was to be praised or condemned. Yet societies could sustain and reproduce themselves only in nonviolent ways, by quotidian and unexceptionable practices that didn't deserve the name of history. For it was not the violence either exercised or prevented by law and the state that provided the parameters for nonviolence, but rather the reverse.

Instead of trying to expand the reach of historical knowledge by including everyday life within its ambit, in other words, the Mahatma insisted upon describing the historical record as providing an account of violence as well as its justification. After all, since narratives of persecution and revenge, peace and war, crime and justice, stood on the same historical footing and indeed overlapped one with the other, none was innocent of violence. And by this token nonviolence was not merely unable to provide a subject for history; it was incapable almost by definition of possessing one.

By suggesting that nonviolence had no history, Gandhi did not mean that it was entirely removed from the world of violence. On the contrary, he held that violence was present in every aspect of life, from eating to giving birth, so that even reflexive processes like blinking or digestion, which preserved life, also ended up wearing down the body and finally destroying it. Nonviolence therefore could not possibly imply the more or less successful avoidance of violence, something that the Mahatma would in any case have considered cowardly, but rather entailed an intense engagement with it.

In keeping with the negative or unhistorical character of nonviolence, such engagement consisted of withdrawing one's implicit or complicit support for violence understood as a positive and so historical phenomenon. This involved the recourse to a whole range of negatively defined acts, from nonviolence itself to noncooperation, nonpossession, and nonattachment, each conceptualized as forms of non-doing or undoing whose very logic of absence was what made change possible. Deliberately forsaking the privilege given to action in historical narrative, Gandhi also envisioned the task of negation as being not the enemy's repudiation so much as conversion.

Violence had to be seduced from itself and converted into its opposite by acts of love and practices of sacrifice. And this had to be done not by posing one historical narrative against another but instead by disregarding such narratives altogether. Only by refusing to situate present-day moral and political action within a historical account that could only constrain it might new possibilities for the future emerge. Nonviolence, in other words, worked by breaking up narrative histories and thus freeing human action, though it did so not by opening some dazzling new future for it, but rather by focusing exclusively on the present as a site for moral life.[3]

Gandhi's idea of the present, therefore, had nothing to do with a narrative either of historical continuity or of change that is manifested in ways like distinguishing one period from another. The present was not qualitatively distinct from the past or the future. Instead, he disaggregated such periodization by envisioning a temporality whose similarities and differences could not be historicized, since they always enjoyed a potential existence depending on the actions of individuals. His task was rather to free the present from being determined by the past, and in turn from coming itself to determine the future as a kind of self-fulfilling prophecy.

The Mahatma's efforts to question the linear and homogeneous form that historical temporality took was common to anticolonial thinkers. His contemporary Mohammad Iqbal, the most important Muslim poet and philosopher of the twentieth century, drew upon medieval Persian and Arabic texts to disaggregate time by considering the possibility that different kinds of bodies produced or were part of distinctive temporalities. He cited Bergson's pure duration and Einstein's space–time continuum to imagine new ways of thinking about time, dismissing the historian's vision of serial time as naïve. Like Gandhi, he was interested neither in historicism nor in temporal continuity.[4]

More than altering our perspective on history, Gandhi asks us to distrust it as a form of knowledge and even recommends forgetting the past. By this he doesn't mean we should tolerate violence or banish all that has happened from our memory, but should refuse to identify with either the victims or the perpetrators of historical violence. The Mahatma was aware that nations, races, religions, and other collective categories of belonging were in his time being forged by such vicarious identifications with the past. Repelled by the alternating forms of resentment and fear he saw emerging from these practices of historical recovery, Gandhi wanted nothing to do with them.

Gandhi criticized history because he understood it as betraying the present. A history of the present, therefore, was capable of restricting future possibilities only by tying them to fears and desires from the past. The effort to determine this future by reference to the past, he thought, was an absurd fantasy that risked inviting unexpected outcomes even when its desired goal was forcibly fulfilled. This entailed sacrificing virtuous means in the present only to poison the future ends they were meant to bring about. It also reduced the number of possible ends available to us in the future. A historical understanding of the present seeks, therefore, to control the future by eliminating the very contingency that historians otherwise prize. It is history in the service of power.

If Gandhi questioned history's claims to understand the present in the struggle against imperialism, it is because he realized that it was guided by moral and political aims. But however virtuous these aims, he suggested, they could not be accomplished by historical knowledge, which was fitted out to exacerbate rather than reduce violence. While it was necessary for those engaged in moral and political action to learn from past experience, in other words, this did not require historical consciousness and certainly not a collective identification with the winners or losers of past conflicts. Myth offered a deeper and more philosophical way of thinking about the present than history.

While Gandhi was concerned primarily with the hubris of historical knowledge and its efforts to sacrifice the present to the future in the name of the past, another appreciation of the past's radical limitation in grasping the present emerged during the Cold War. Reflecting upon the destructive role of technology in the development of nuclear weapons, thinkers like Karl Jaspers, Gunther Anders, and Hannah Arendt often wrote about the historically unprecedented future they made possible. This, indeed, was a commonplace assertion at the time, one that very deliberately broke historical genealogies apart precisely to envision a present without a past.

In an essay on Jaspers, for instance, Arendt writes,

> It is true, for the first time in history all peoples on earth have a common present: no event of any importance in the history of one country can remain a marginal accident in the history of any other. Every country has become the almost immediate

neighbor of every other country, and every man feels the shock of events which take place at the other side of the globe. But this common factual present is not based on a common past and does not in the least guarantee a common future.[5]

This way of imagining a global present without a shared past, one in which destruction can be visited upon peoples and countries lying completely outside the history that brought it about, made their potential fate into the result of a natural rather than human history. The problem posed by the novel emergence of the globe as an object rather than simply a context of human action was that its would-be subject, the human race, could be grasped only posthumously. Jaspers and Arendt thought the vision of nuclear extinction brought about a new kind of present separated even from the history that had produced it.

It was the attempt to attach this global present to a history, or at least mediate its inhuman or posthumous reality through the past, that gave meaning to the Cold War's world histories, from Arnold J. Toynbee to Marshall Hodgson and William H. McNeill. Hodgson, for example, defined the global present in terms of a general civilizational ungrounding and borderlessness, one that had to be reconnected to the past or its vestiges in the present to make it meaningful for human beings. And to do this he turned to older forms of historical universality, of which he saw Islam as the chief alternative to the West.

What interested Hodgson about Islamic civilization as a universal form was the possibility it offered of not only constructing another genealogy of the global present, whose absence he thought was what made the latter literally unthinkable and so sublime in its technological dominance, but also of imagining an alternative trajectory of the global. He thought that the historical memory of civilizations like Islam, but also the lived reality of religions more generally, permitted them to mediate and ground the global present, if only because they represented older ideas of universality.

Here is how Hodgson described the role of religion and civilization in mediating the global present:

The basis of community allegiance needs to be reformulated in a society where the religious community is but one of several, none serving as foundation for their common culture. There are many possibilities; I shall suggest one: in such a world, religious communities may play a crucial role, that of communities inter-mediate between the individual and the global mass of four billions, all potentially watching the same television programmes and buying the same products.[6]

For Hodgson, Islam was especially important because it provided the only universal form that a non-Western civilization took before the global present inaugurated by the West, and thus became capable of serving both as its antecedent and as its alternative. Crucial to both Islam and the West as universal categories was the fact that they had become detached from any particular region, culture area, or polity. But this meant that they were faced with a new kind of problem, of how to attach themselves to and be at home in the particular. And this is what they could teach the denizens of the global present.

Unlike Gandhi's nonhistoricist vision of temporality, such Cold War concerns about the global present were dominated by strong ideas about periodization and historical breaks. Indeed, they may even be said to mimic the original notion of such a break, that of modernity or a modern age seen as being qualitatively distinct from all that came before and radically open to an unknown future. Of course, this future was never understood in the old modernist fashion as being either heroic or utopian, though it remained teleological in a deeply pessimistic way. But Cold War history's questioning of temporal scale and limits continues to be intellectually productive.

The questions asked during the Cold War about the global present and its deprivation of history have evaporated in its aftermath. It is perhaps not accidental, then, that the Cold War tends not to be part of today's histories of the present, at least in their popular variants. These have forsaken the global present without a history of its own and returned to national or at most civilizational narratives about histories of the present. Only environmental histories dealing with issues like the Anthropocene have inherited Cold War concerns about the radically ahistorical character of the global present and the posthumous agency of the human race.[7]

Public debate in Euro-American societies, as among its historians, is dominated by genealogies going back to the Reformation or the Enlightenment, liberalism or imperialism, and, of course, the ever popular world wars. What has been lost is any consideration of the present not only as an autonomous and newly global temporality but also as an opening to the unknown future. This was evident with the outpouring of historical analysis following the attack on the Capitol by President Trump's supporters. Much of it was dominated by debates about whether we were witnessing fascism, a coup, an insurrection, or merely a protest.

Apart from the bizarrely legalistic, if not entirely semantic, character of much of this debate, curious were the remarkably provincial if also typically exceptionalist parameters within which it placed a global power like the United States. We have been offered genealogies for which neither the Cold War nor the war on terror that succeeded it in militarizing democracy and decimating civil liberties is crucial. Instead, we are treated to disquisitions about slavery, the Civil War, Reconstruction, and Jim Crow. All important events, but none as recent as 9/11, with its unprecedented empowerment of the presidency and corresponding disempowerment of citizens.

Viewed from outside the charmed circle of Euro-American universities, journals, and think tanks, such talking points seem to represent fantasies of historical regression. They are incapable of recognizing the global nature of either the precedents of, or of the problems posed by, the attack in Washington. The very apocalypticism on display in some of the historical analysis, in other words, might deliver comfort by its sheer familiarity. To see fascism in what happened is one thing, but invoking Weimar is an absurdity. Could it be that America is not so much repeating either its own or the European past as joining the global present it has done so much to bring about?

Even a preliminary consideration of the language deployed by the crowd in Washington, whether in utterance or displayed on signs and items of clothing, makes it clear that its two most important historical and political references were to the American Revolution and the Civil War. The former has, of course, been important from the very early days of the populist right, as evident in the very name of the Tea Party. And the latter has been ubiquitous in the use and criticism of the Confederate flag and other symbols of the defeated South. Both are crucial terms in American history, though they were played out at the Capitol in globally rather more familiar ways.

It was not lost upon those observing these events from other parts of the world that the revolution they represented had more in common with recent precedents from the color revolutions of Eastern Europe and the Arab Spring in the Middle East than with eighteenth-century America or France. With their mixed genders, generations, classes, and even ethnicities, these live-streamed protests organized over social media must be taken together in a way that fractures any singular genealogy of American history. Predictably Eurocentric analogies have also been offered, from the storming of the Winter Palace by sympathizers of the attack to the Reichstag fire by its critics.

There has been much commentary on the irony of America having to face an example of the kind of revolution it encourages, if not instigates, elsewhere. But the importance of this comparison goes beyond blowback or schadenfreude and must be analyzed by historians as part of the global present that Arendt or Hodgson described. This does not mean that a properly national history played no role in the attack or in what brought it about, but it is no longer sufficient to account for the present. It may be that America's revolutionary history played the role of myth in the arguments and identifications of the protesters—a myth whose conspiratorial vision of distant origins and long continuities holds up a mirror to histories of the present.

Like revolution, civil war, too, is an important part of contemporary politics the world over. The United States has been involved in either inflaming or assuaging many of these recently, from Iraq and Syria to Libya and Yemen. But it would be a mistake to think about civil war only in the neocolonial and arguably racist terms of armed hostilities and proxy wars in failing, undemocratic, or incompletely modern states. Even without such violence, a situation resembling civil war can be observed in the unprecedented polarization of politics in countries like Britain, Spain, and the United States, leading to administrative gridlock, militia violence, or separatist movements.

A number of similarities characterize the discursive as much as real occurrence of civil war in different parts of the world. These include the hollowing out and capture of political parties by outsiders in countries like India, the United States, and Britain. Or the sudden emergence of new parties and the collapse of old ones in places like France or Pakistan. It is not that political interests have diverged so much as to become irreconcilable in such nations, but that parties seem no longer to represent stable social or economic interests at all. This may be why we see such a significant global turn to racial, religious, sexual, and other ascribed identities instead.

The liberal politics of interest and contract seems to be faltering along with the party form that serves to represent it. This likely has something to do with the rendering virtual as well as global of the property regimes that had once made interests possible in national contexts. Also important might be the disintegration in advanced economies of manufacturing and with it the working class that was its product. With the end of the Cold War we have also seen the disintegration of what Carl Schmitt called a nomos (or normative order) of the earth, with the war on terror unable to put another one in place. There has been an upswing in civil wars after each of these conflicts in the Balkans, the Caucasus, Central Asia, and the Middle East, with other regions like Eastern Europe also being drawn in.

There is a global pattern here, visible at the Capitol in the display of Iranian, Indian, Israeli, French, and other flags among the Stars and Stripes. Each represented other kinds of civil war, whether between Hindus and Muslims, Jews and Palestinians, royalists and republicans, or Europeans and Africans. Signaling a small if multiethnic immigrant presence at the Capitol organized by a Black man of Arab and Muslim descent, these flags show that American history cannot contain its meaning. Such symbols were not only tolerated but welcomed by white demonstrators assumed to be exclusive in their world of historical, racial, and religious references. And yet the founder and leader of the Proud Boys, the most apparently white among them, is himself Afro-Cuban.

The nonwhite immigrant presence in American public life can no longer be assimilated within the inherited racial and religious categories of national history, with its binary black-and-white structure. Unlike white immigrants, including President Trump's mother, grandparents, and wife, those from Asia, Africa, and Latin America bring their own histories and identities with them to whichever political side they choose. The increased support for Trump among ethnic minorities, including Muslims, cannot simply be attributed to fantasies of white identification. And this non-American history makes them both more suspect and more acceptable, something we have seen with the rise to power of figures like Barack Obama and Kamala Harris, whose African American identity derives from recent immigration rather than historical slavery.

Obama was accused throughout his presidency, not least by Trump himself, of being a Muslim immigrant born outside the United States rather than being identified as an African American. But it may have been these very accusations that also made him more acceptable than an African American to be the country's first nonwhite president. Without diminishing the role that race plays in the country's politics, in other words, the increasing power and influence of nonwhite immigrants has forced open its history to other genealogies and made a new shuffling of identities possible there. Are we seeing the reassertion of America's old race conflicts today, as historians of the present tell us, or their last stand in the face of such a transformation?

Even a cursory look at the attack in Washington tells us how conservative, provincial, and Eurocentric most histories of the present are. The point of such a history should be to demonstrate not the continuity of old problems but the differences that radicalize them, and in doing so to denaturalize our own experience in order to think the future anew.

This was what anticolonial histories in Asia and Africa sought to do in the era of decolonization. Seeing what is happening in the United States and elsewhere today as the struggle of fascism against liberalism or white against Black conceals more than it reveals, because it is a view that refuses to look beyond America or the West in a historical context which has become global.

FASCISM AND ANALOGIES—
BRITISH AND AMERICAN, PAST AND PRESENT

PRIYA SATIA

Navigating uncertain times, it is tempting, and helpful, to search the past for precedents that might help guide understanding and action—inevitably with the risk of drawing false equivalences. Comparing Trumpism to 1930s fascism, especially, has struck some historians and political theorists as likely to blind us to the longer trajectories of Trump's reactionary politics—his quintessential Americanness.[1]

The question of historical analogies has also defined the United Kingdom's memory wars. With respect to Britain's imperial past, Boris Johnson's government has rejected all fascist implication. Britain's schools, museums, and country houses, it insists, must not reflect on restitution, statue removal, or the idea of white privilege;[2] these worries are the province of nations that truly have something to apologize for—namely, Germany. As *The Times* explained on February 10, 2020, the moral case for returning colonial artifacts is unlike that of returning artworks stolen by the Nazis.[3] After all, Britain, led by Johnson's hero Churchill, defeated the Nazis—the finest hour of its proud past. The National Trust's efforts to explore country houses' ties to colonialism and slavery similarly outraged the Churchill biographer Andrew Roberts by implying a "moral equivalence between colonialism and slavery," as if the empire was not founded on slavery and did not continue to depend on forms of bonded labor well after abolition in 1833.[4]

Johnson's government instead calls for unapologetic pride in Britain's past to fortify the nation's capacity to endure today's political challenges, from lockdown to Brexit, when, the prime minister promises, the United Kingdom will once again emerge as "the greatest place on Earth."[5] The past must redeem the present, not the other way around. The leader of the House of Commons, Jacob Rees-Mogg, calls on Britain to "be proud to have spread overseas the liberty it so valued at home," while the Tory MP Iain Duncan Smith celebrates the "prospects" Brexit creates for British youth "to be out there buccaneering, trading, dominating the world again."[6] Rather than redress the imperial past, Britons ought to revive it.

This nostalgia testifies to an urgent need to come to terms with the unpleasant reality of Britain's imperial past. But the anxiety to distance that past from the moral abyss of Nazism and slavery frustrates efforts to do so. To urge Britain to reckon with its imperial past through reparations, school curriculum, restitution, memorialization, or other methods that Germany has also employed in confronting its Nazi past does not automatically imply an equation of British imperialism with Nazism. Different kinds of violent and racist pasts may yet share a common need for redress. We might also, for example, look to South African efforts to address the legacies of apartheid or American attempts to deal with slavery. American thinkers, too, such as Susan Neiman, enlighten conversations about healing American racial divisions by "learning from the Germans"—the title of Neiman's 2019 book. Others put these cases into conversation as counterpoints, for instance Joan Wallach Scott's *On the Judgment of History* (2020).

That said, other thinkers, such as Isabel Wilkerson in *Caste* (2020), go beyond comparing forms of healing, analogizing America's racial divides to Nazism itself; critics analogize Israeli policies in the Occupied Territories to apartheid.[7] Kehinde Andrews's *The New Age of Empire* (2021) likens the genocide of Australia's Aborigines to the Holocaust. The British debate about colonial reparations intensified a decade ago also thanks in part to an effective historical analogy: the Harvard historian Caroline Elkins titled the U.K. version of her 2005 account of British concentration camps in 1950s Kenya *Britain's Gulag*, a Pulitzer

Prize–winning work that helped launch a spate of successful reparations suits by Kenyan survivors.[8] In protesting the camps in the 1950s, the Labour MP Fenner Brockway went further, comparing the camps' communal labor punishments to Nazi slave labor policies.

Historical and local specificities mean all analogies are ultimately inaccurate in ways that historians must always make clear. The point of such comparisons, however, is to uncover darker historical truths obscured by prevailing, more flattering comparisons. Historical analogies played a central role in the making of modern history, including its ugliest episodes; new comparisons allow us to shift the paradigms through which we have long understood the past so that we might make new history in the present.

British imperialism was often justified by comparisons to earlier empires. In South Asia, for instance, the British avoided the charge of harmful conquest by both analogizing their presence to the Mughal Empire that ruled much of the subcontinent before the British and claiming to offer a more enlightened form of imperial rule than what they denigrated as "oriental despotism." As Indian critics pointed out even in the eighteenth century, by refusing to indigenize their rule and extracting India's resources and shipping them out of the country, the British had introduced a wholly destructive form of rule radically unlike the land-based imperium of the Mughals. In fact, Mughal trends in managing food security and water were better. The deadly famines that followed British conquest, up to the Bengal famine of 1943, ceased after Indian independence in 1947, testifying to the particular rapacity of British imperial administration.

The British also disguised their new kind of empire as another Rome. In the eighteenth century, the historian and MP Edward Gibbon narrated the story of Rome's rise and fall as a cautionary tale: Britain would succeed where the Roman Empire had failed. British officials could launder their consciences by reference to Rome's example. What was the destruction of rebellious Indian cities next to the Roman sack of Jerusalem? The British adapted the Roman model in ways that those against racial prejudice today would stomach with difficulty. Blaming Rome's fall on corrupting contact at the margins of its empire, the British determined to ensure against that fate by maintaining racial boundaries. Even then, critics noted the darker implications of the "new Rome" cover story. During the Indian rebellion of 1857, Karl Marx observed that the British had subjugated India by engaging in a "Roman *Divide et impera*," manipulating "races, tribes, castes, creeds and sovereignties" against one another to secure British supremacy. How then can we say that there is no reason to condemn the British Empire because it was simply another empire like Rome or the Mughals?

When the contest between European empires led to World War I, the British styled their conquest of the Middle East as a chance at redemption, where they would emulate ancient "improving" empires in the region—the Persians, Seleucids, Parthians. These flattering analogies helped defend their invention of air control, a cheap but devastatingly violent policing regime, as an improvement scheme for interwar Iraq. An RAF wing commander explained in 1928: "The cheaper the form of control the more money for roads and development and the sooner it will be no longer necessary to use armed forces to do with explosives what should be done by policemen and sticks." As the British Empire fell apart after 1945, Gibbonian analogies—the idea that Britain, like Rome, had become too enfeebled to retain its colonies—helped Britons forget their destructive stand in colonies such as Kenya.

The British were not alone in using historical analogies to legitimize territorial conquest and violent subjugation. Such analogies enabled some of the worst episodes of modern history. The Nazis found inspiration in American race laws and the genocide of Native Americans—as recently examined in James Q. Whitman's *Hitler's American Model* (2017) and Mahmood Mamdani's *Neither Settler nor Native* (2020). If, as Richard Evans argues, "real experts" in European fascism agree that Trump is not a fascist (whatever the mutual support between him and avowed neo-Nazi groups), they may be doing so without equivalent expertise in American history.[9] Lost in this tedious debate is what European fascism itself owed to transregional historical comparisons. In 1939, the Nazis defended their proliferating camps by pointing to British concentration camps in the South African War (1899–1902). That analogy does not excuse the Nazi camps any more than the invocation of Roman or Mughal example can excuse British abuses.

Analogies, especially to the most morally abject episodes of the twentieth century, are liable to being invoked excessively and inaccurately. But silencing an analogy out of regard for the alterity of the past and what is particular and new about the present risks denying the past's afterlife in the present (as Peter Gordon has also argued), the way it has structured the world we inhabit, the way our very writing, reading, and recalling of it has shaped and continues to shape our own actions—just as a sense of the past shaped British actions.[10]

Analogy is central to empirical inquiry, as Gordon rightly reminds us, but, in the era of colonialism, Enlightenment philosophers, such as Gibbon's great admirer Adam Smith, popularized the view of history as a collection of analogies whose study allowed one to discern "general principles" of moral conduct.[11] "The tradition of all dead generations weighs like a nightmare on the brains of the living," Marx described history's legitimating role in the modern era. "[J]ust as they seem to be occupied with revolutionising themselves and things . . . they anxiously conjure up the spirits of the past . . . to present this new scene in world history in time-honored disguise." Given this historical role of historical analogies, the question is not so much whether to analogize but whether the analogies we invoke serve ethical ends.

Eschewing comparisons to European fascism does not free us to understand our present discontents on their own terms but rather preserves undisturbed the anodyne analogies to ancient Rome and Greece that have legitimized American and British liberal empire since the Enlightenment, when invocations of history began to make history. Worse, it risks promoting myths of British and American exceptionalism. By changing our comparison set, we may more clearly grasp both what makes the present different from what came before and the way the past has habitually been repurposed in a manner inhibiting ethical accountability in the present.

Modern European imperialism was qualitatively different from ancient and contemporary land-based imperialisms (the theorists Eric

Hobsbawm's and Ernest Gellner's perception of a resemblance between the multinational U.K. itself and the Austro-Hungarian Empire is more persuasive). The propaganda about a "new Rome" that enabled the racist violence of empire cannot today redeem it. To dispel the idea that a political formation based on racism might nevertheless be a source of pride today, we might instead draw a comparison to the way racist despotisms in modern Europe have been evaluated. Apart from a fringe minority, no one touts the "pros" of Nazism. Since the 1970s controversy around Robert Fogel and Stanley Engerman's *Time on the Cross* (1974), respectable scholars no longer enumerate slavery's pros and cons either. We have agreed, together, that slavery was a moral wrong that cannot be redeemed. The fact that we have not arrived at such a consensus on the British Empire testifies to the success with which older palliating historical analogies enable it to be continually relegitimized, despite the anticolonial struggles of the last century.

Countless rebels, anticolonial thinkers, and historians left exhaustive testimony of the British Empire's calamitous record of continual racist violence. At the close of the nineteenth century, the poet Wilfrid Blunt described in *The Times*—the paper that is today so certain of empire's moral soundness—the "hundred years of violent fraud and crime" the empire had wrought around the world. He called on fellow Britons to "sit with ashes on our heads" in mourning.

The Johnson government seeks to smother the memory of such dissenting voices in favor of mythologizing Churchill. In 1937, while Hitler looked to the genocide of Native Americans as a model for his conception of lebensraum (the idea that expansion was essential to German survival), Churchill refused to admit "that a great wrong has been done to" Native Americans or Aboriginal Australians "by the fact that a stronger race has . . . taken their place." Churchill was rejecting the moral outrage of anti-imperialists, whose struggle to end imperialism has been partially honored by today's reparations movement: Australian Aboriginals have won the right to sue for colonial land loss, while conversations about reparations and restitution of objects to Greece, Nigeria, India, Easter Island, and other countries are intensifying.[12] France's apparently greater willingness to return its looted artifacts offers another comparison that might fruitfully shift British perceptions.[13]

Stepping out from behind Churchill's shadow and acknowledging the harms of empire does not imply that the British are existentially evil any more than Germans are for their Nazi past. It is not a call for British self-abasement but, as the term "reparation" indicates, for a process of repair that will benefit both Britain and its former colonies. Empire's racism and cruelties not only denied the humanity of the colonized but, as George Orwell recognized, depended on warping the humanity of the colonizer.[14] Today, Germans are more respected and functional as a society,[15] more capable of navigating their place in the European Union, because they have engaged in what Susan Neiman calls *Vergangenheit-saufarbeitung,* or "working-off-the-past."

Still, even Germany's redemption remains limited (as Mamdani and Scott also note) as long as Nazism is singled out as a criminal exception in an otherwise benign history of modern imperialism.[16] Monstrous as the Nazi regime was, the fact remains that slavery, apartheid, and Nazism shared common origins in the wider phenomenon of European imperialism. Black radical thinkers such as George Padmore recognized how colonialism and slavery had opened the way for European fascism in the 1930s, *as* Hitler was emulating American race laws.[17] Thinkers as diverse as Hannah Arendt and Aimé Césaire again traced those common roots in breathtaking indictments after World War II. British camps in Kenya may not have been the same as Nazi and Stalinist camps, but they were also "not wholly different," writes Caroline Elkins.

Rather than anxiously safeguard the empire from Nazi taint, we might more productively reckon with all this imperial past. By condemning its worst excesses—Nazism, slavery, apartheid—we not only have avoided condemning imperialism itself but have relegitimized it, as evident, for instance, in the imperial presumption that drove the 2003 invasion of Iraq and the paternalist power dynamics shaping the global response to climate change today. The scandal of modern imperialism was not Nazism, slavery, or the rogue activities of particular companies and generals;[18] it was imperialism itself, the enabling context of all these atrocities: a form of rule without consent aimed at coercive resource extraction on the racist presumption that Europeans alone were the bearers of historical progress.

Academic objections to the accuracy of an analogy are inevitably correct, given the irreproducible nature of all history,[19] but excessive pre-occupation with the fitness of an analogy distracts us from larger and more urgent problems arising from silencing certain pasts in our present, like the history of empire and slavery. Some discourage the fascist analogy for Trumpism out of a worry itself rooted in analogical thinking: that it will license reckless policing and militarization as the invocation of "Islamo-fascism" did after 9/11. But no necessary historical logic dooms every cry of fascist to the same outcome. The ends to which it is put are on us—as guided by our understanding of the past.

Analogizing Trumpism to fascism abnormalizes Trump as an aberration in American history only if we understand "fascism" as a unique evil unrelated to other troubling pasts. With a clear grasp of fascism's connection to empire, the comparison of Trumpism to fascism might inspire us to challenge the myths of liberal exceptionalism that blind so many to the realities of American and British imperialism.

That it has had this effect in some quarters is evidenced by the unprecedented support for Black Lives Matter and Rhodes Must Fall, movements calling on us to address inequities long predating Trump. Rather than abnormalizing Trump and normalizing, say, George W. Bush, it might increase awareness both of the path from the latter to the former and of the long complicity of American and British empire in the history of fascism. It is a historical comparison that reminds us of a historical connection. Rather than disguising Trump's quintessential Americanness or sullying Britain's self-image, the fascism analogy may help reveal what fascism always owed to Americanness and to empire.

NARENDRA MODI AND THE NEW FACE OF INDIA

PANKAJ MISHRA

In *A Suitable Boy*, Vikram Seth writes with affection of a placid India's first general election in 1951, and the egalitarian spirit it momentarily bestowed on an electorate deeply riven by class and caste: "the great washed and unwashed public, sceptical and gullible," but all "endowed with universal adult suffrage."[1] India's sixteenth general election (April 7, 2014), held against a background of economic jolts and titanic corruption scandals, and tainted by the nastiest campaign yet, announces a new turbulent phase for the country—arguably, the most sinister since its independence from British rule in 1947.[2] Back then, it would have been inconceivable that a figure such as Narendra Modi, the Hindu nationalist chief minister of Gujarat accused, along with his closest aides, of complicity in crimes ranging from an anti-Muslim pogrom in his state in 2002 to extrajudicial killings, and barred from entering the United States, may occupy India's highest political office.[3]

Modi is a lifelong member of the Rashtriya Swayamsevak Sangh (RSS), a paramilitary Hindu nationalist organization inspired by the fascist movements of Europe, whose founder's belief that Nazi Germany had manifested "race pride at its highest" by purging the Jews is by no means unexceptional among the votaries of Hindutva, or "Hinduness."[4] In 1948, a former member of the RSS murdered Gandhi for being too soft on Muslims. The outfit, traditionally dominated by upper-caste Hindus, has led many vicious assaults on minorities. A notorious executioner of dozens of Muslims in Gujarat in 2002 crowed that he had slashed open with his sword the womb of a heavily pregnant woman and extracted her fetus.[5] Modi himself described the relief camps housing tens of thousands of displaced Muslims as "child-breeding centers."

Such rhetoric has helped Modi sweep one election after another in Gujarat. A senior American diplomat described him, in cables disclosed by WikiLeaks, as an "insular, distrustful person" who "reigns by fear and intimidation"; his neo-Hindu devotees on Facebook and Twitter continue to render the air mephitic with hate and malice, populating the paranoid world of both have-nots and haves with fresh enemies— "terrorists," "jihadis," "Pakistani agents," "pseudo-secularists," "sicku-lars," "socialists," and "commies." Modi's own electoral strategy as prime ministerial candidate, however, has been more polished, despite his appeals, both dog-whistled and overt, to Hindu solidarity against men-acing aliens and outsiders, such as the Italian-born leader of the Con-gress Party, Sonia Gandhi, Bangladeshi "infiltrators," and those who eat the holy cow.[6]

Modi exhorts his largely young supporters—more than two-thirds of India's population is under the age of thirty-five—to join a revolution that will destroy the corrupt old political order and uproot its moral and ideological foundations while buttressing the essential framework, the market economy, of a glorious new India. In an apparently ungov-ernable country, where many revere the author of *Mein Kampf* for his tremendous will to power and organization, he has shrewdly deployed the idioms of management, national security and civilisational glory.[7]

Boasting of his fifty-six-inch chest, Modi has replaced Mahatma Gandhi, the icon of nonviolence, with Vivekananda, the nineteenth-century Hindu revivalist who was obsessed with making Indians a "manly" nation.[8] Vivekananda's garlanded statue or portrait is as ubiq-uitous in Modi's public appearances as his dandyish pastel waistcoats. But Modi is never less convincing than when he presents himself as a humble tea vendor, the son-of-the-soil challenger to the Congress's haughty dynasts. His record as chief minister is predominantly distin-guished by the transfer—through privatization or outright gifts—of national resources to the country's biggest corporations. His closest allies—India's biggest businessmen—have accordingly enlisted their mainstream media outlets into the cult of Modi as decisive administrator; dissenting journalists have been removed or silenced.[9]

Not long after India's first full-scale pogrom in 2002, leading corporate bosses, ranging from the suave Ratan Tata to Mukesh Ambani, the owner of a twenty-seven-story residence, began to pave Modi's ascent to respectability and power.[10] The stars of Bollywood fell (literally) at the feet of Modi.[11] In recent months, liberal-minded columnists and journalists have joined their logrolling right-wing compatriots in certifying Modi as a "moderate" developmentalist. The Columbia University economist Jagdish Bhagwati, who insists that he intellectually fathered India's economic reforms in 1991, and Gurcharan Das, author of *India Unbound*, have volunteered passionate exonerations of the man they consider India's savior.[12]

Bhagwati, once a fervent supporter of outgoing prime minister Manmohan Singh, has even publicly applied for an advisory position with Modi's government.[13] It may be because the nearly double-digit economic growth of recent years that Ivy League economists like him—India's own version of Chile's Chicago Boys and Russia's Harvard Boys—instigated and championed turns out to have been based primarily on extraction of natural resources, cheap labor, and foreign-capital inflows rather than high productivity and innovation, or indeed the brick-and-mortar ventures that fueled China's rise as a manufacturing powerhouse.[14] "The bulk of India's aggregate growth," the World Bank's chief economist Kaushik Basu warns, "is occurring through a disproportionate rise in the incomes at the upper end of the income ladder." Thus, it has left largely undisturbed the country's shameful ratios—43 percent of all Indian children below the age of five are undernourished, and 48 percent stunted; nearly half of Indian women of childbearing age are anemic, and more than half of all Indians still defecate in the open.

Absurdly uneven and jobless economic growth has led to what the economists Amartya Sen and Jean Drèze call "islands of California in a sea of sub-Saharan Africa."[15] The failure to generate stable employment—one million new jobs are required every month—for an increasingly urban and atomized population, or to allay the severe inequalities of opportunity as well as income, created, well before the recent economic setbacks, a large simmering reservoir of rage and frustration. Many Indians, neglected by the state, which spends less proportionately on health and education than Malawi, and spurned by private industry, which prefers cheap contract labor, invest their hopes in notions of free enterprise and individual initiative. However, old and new hierarchies of class, caste, and education restrict most of them to the ranks of the unwashed. As *The Wall Street Journal* admitted, India is not "overflowing with Horatio Alger stories."[16] Balram Halwai, the entrepreneur from rural India in Aravind Adiga's Booker-winning novel *The White Tiger*, who finds in murder and theft the quickest route to business success and self-confidence in the metropolis, and the social Darwinist Mumbai slum dwellers in Katherine Boo's *Behind the Beautiful Forevers* point to an intensified dialectic in India today: cruel exclusion and even more brutal self-empowerment.[17]

SUCH EXTENSIVE MORAL SQUALOR may bewilder those who expected India to conform, however gradually and imperfectly, to a Western ideal of liberal democracy and capitalism. But those scandalized by the lure of an indigenized fascism in the country billed as the "world's largest democracy" should know: this was not the work of a day, or of a few "extremists." It has been in the making for years. "Democracy in India," B. R. Ambedkar, the main framer of India's constitution, warned in the 1950s, "is only a top dressing on an Indian soil, which is essentially undemocratic."[18] Ambedkar saw democracy in India as a promise of justice and dignity to the country's despised and impoverished millions, which could be realized only through intense political struggle. For more than two decades that possibility has faced a pincer movement: a form of global capitalism that can enrich only a small minority and a xenophobic nationalism that handily identifies fresh scapegoats for large-scale socioeconomic failure and frustration.

In many ways, Modi and his rabble—tycoons, neo-Hindu techies, and outright fanatics—are perfect mascots for the changes that have transformed India since the early 1990s: the liberalization of the country's economy, and the destruction by Modi's compatriots of the sixteenth-century Babri mosque in Ayodhya. Long before the killings in Gujarat, Indian security forces enjoyed what amounted to a license to kill, torture, and rape in the border regions of Kashmir and the northeast; a similar infrastructure of repression was installed in central India after forest-dwelling tribal peoples revolted against the nexus of mining corporations and the state. The government's plan to spy on internet and phone connections makes the American National Security Agency's surveillance look highly responsible.[19] Muslims have been imprisoned for years without trial on the flimsiest suspicion of "terrorism"; one of them, a Kashmiri who had only circumstantial evidence against him, was rushed to the gallows last year, denied even the customary last meeting with his kin, in order to satisfy, as the supreme court put it, "the collective conscience of the people."[20]

"People who were not born then," Robert Musil wrote in *The Man Without Qualities* of the period before another apparently abrupt collapse of liberal values, "will find it difficult to believe, but the fact is that even then time was moving faster than a cavalry camel. . . . But in those days, no one knew what it was moving towards. Nor could anyone quite distinguish between what was above and what was below, between what was moving forward and what backward."[21] One symptom of this widespread confusion in Musil's novel is the Viennese elite's weird ambivalence about the crimes of a brutal murderer called Moosbrugger. Certainly, figuring out what was above and what was below is harder for the parachuting foreign journalists who alighted upon a new idea of India as an economic "powerhouse" and the many "rising" Indians in a generation born after economic liberalization in 1991, who are seduced by Modi's promise of the utopia of consumerism—one in which skyscrapers, expressways, bullet trains, and shopping malls proliferate (and from which such eyesores as the poor are excluded).

―――――――

PEOPLE WHO were born before 1991, and did not know what time was moving toward, might be forgiven for feeling nostalgia for the simpler days of postcolonial idealism and hopefulness—those that Seth evokes in *A Suitable Boy*. Set in the 1950s, the novel brims with optimism about the world's most audacious experiment in democracy, endorsing the Nehruvian "idea of India" that seems flexible enough to accommodate formerly untouchable Hindus (Dalits) and Muslims as well as the middle-class intelligentsia. The novel's affable anglophone characters radiate the assumption that the sectarian passions that blighted India during its partition in 1947 will be defused, secular progress through science and reason will eventually manifest itself, and an enlightened leadership will usher a near destitute people into active citizenship and economic prosperity.

India's first prime minister, Jawaharlal Nehru, appears in the novel as an effective one-man buffer against Hindu chauvinism. "The thought of India as a Hindu state, with its minorities treated as second-class citizens, sickened him." In Nehru's own vision, grand projects such as big dams and factories would bring India's superstitious masses out of their benighted rural habitats and propel them into first-world affluence and rationality. The Harrow- and Cambridge-educated Indian leader had inherited from British colonials at least part of their civilizing mission, turning it into a national project to catch up with the industrialized West. "I was eager and anxious," Nehru wrote of India, "to change her outlook and appearance and give her the garb of modernity." Even the "uninteresting" peasant, whose "limited outlook" induced in him a "feeling of overwhelming pity and a sense of ever-impending tragedy" was to be present at what he called India's "tryst with destiny."

That long attempt by India's ruling class to give the country the "garb of modernity" has produced, in its sixth decade, effects entirely unanticipated by Nehru or anyone else: intense politicization and fierce contests for power together with violence, fragmentation, and chaos, and a concomitant longing for authoritarian control. Modi's image as an exponent of discipline and order is built on both the successes and failures of the ancien régime. He offers top-down modernization, but without modernity: bullet trains without the culture of criticism, managerial efficiency without the guarantee of equal rights. And this streamlined design for a new India immediately entices those well-off Indians who have long regarded democracy as a nuisance, recoiled from the destitute masses, and idolized technocratic, if despotic, "doers" like the first prime minister of Singapore, Lee Kuan Yew.

But then the Nehruvian assumption that economic growth plotted and supervised by a wise technocracy would also bring about social change was also profoundly undemocratic and self-serving. Seth's novel, along with much anglophone literature, seems, in retrospect, to have uncritically reproduced the establishment ideology of English-speaking and overwhelmingly upper-caste Hindus who gained most from state-planned economic growth: the Indian middle class employed in the public sector, civil servants, scientists, and monopolist industrialists. This ruling class's rhetoric of socialism disguised its nearly complete monopoly of power. As D. R. Nagaraj, one of postcolonial India's finest minds, pointed out, "the institutions of capitalism, science and technology were taken over by the upper castes." Even today, businessmen, bureaucrats, scientists, writers in English, academics, think-tankers, newspaper editors, columnists, and TV anchors are disproportionately drawn from among the Hindu upper castes. And, as Amartya Sen has often lamented, their "breathtakingly conservative" outlook is to be blamed for the meager investment in health and education—essential requirements for an equitable society as well as sustained economic growth—that put India behind even disaster-prone China in human development indexes, and now makes it trail Bangladesh.

Dynastic politics froze the Congress Party into a network of patronage, delaying the empowerment of the underprivileged Indians who routinely gave it landslide victories. Nehru may have thought of political power as a function of moral responsibility. But his insecure daughter, Indira Gandhi, consumed by Nixon-caliber paranoia, turned politics into a game of self-aggrandizement, arresting opposition leaders and suspending fundamental rights in 1975 during a nationwide "state of emergency." She supported Sikh fundamentalists in Punjab (who eventually turned against her) and rigged elections in Muslim-majority Kashmir. In the 1980s, the Congress Party, facing a fragmenting voter base, cynically resorted to stoking Hindu nationalism. After Indira Gandhi's assassination by her bodyguards in 1984, Congress politicians led lynch mobs against Sikhs, killing more than three thousand civilians. Three months later, her son Rajiv Gandhi won elections with a landslide. Then, in another eerie prefiguring of Modi's methods, Gandhi, a former pilot obsessed with computers, tried to combine technocratic rule with soft Hindutva.

The Bharatiya Janata Party (BJP), a political offshoot of the RSS that Nehru had successfully banished into the political wilderness, turned out to be much better at this kind of thing. In 1990, its leader, L. K. Advani, rode a "chariot" (actually a rigged-up Toyota flatbed truck) across India in a Hindu supremacist campaign against the mosque in Ayodhya. The wildfire of anti-Muslim violence across the country reaped immediate electoral dividends. (In old photos, Modi appears atop the chariot as Advani's hawk-eyed understudy.) Another BJP chieftain ventured to hoist the Indian tricolor in insurgent Kashmir. (Again, the bearded man photographed helping his doddery senior taunt curfew-bound Kashmiris turns out to be the young Modi.) Following a few more massacres, the BJP was in power in 1998, conducting nuclear tests and fast-tracking the program of economic liberalization started by the Congress after a severe financial crisis in 1991.

The Hindu nationalists had a ready consumer base for their blend of chauvinism and marketization. With India's politics and economy reaching an impasse, which forced many of their relatives to immigrate to the United States, and the Congress facing decline, many powerful Indians were seeking fresh political representatives and a new self-legitimizing ideology in the late 1980s and 1990s. This quest was fulfilled by, first, both the post–Cold War dogma of free markets and then an openly right-wing political party that was prepared to go further than the Congress in developing close relations with the United States (and Israel, which, once shunned, is now India's second-biggest arms supplier after Russia). You can only marvel today at the swiftness with which the old illusions of an overregulated economy were replaced by the fantasies of an unregulated one.

According to the new wisdom—new to India, if already worn out and discredited in Latin America—all governments needed to do was get out of the way of buoyant and autonomous entrepreneurs and stop subsidizing the poor and the lazy (in a risible self-contradiction these Indian promoters of minimalist governance also clamored for a big militarized state apparatus to fight and intimidate neighbors and stifle domestic insurgencies). The long, complex experience of strong European as well as East Asian economies—active state intervention in markets and support to strategic industries, long periods of economic nationalism, investments in health and education—was elided in a new triumphalist global history of free markets. Its promise of instant and widespread affluence seemed to have been manufactured especially for gormless journalists and columnists. Still, in the last decade, neoliberalism became the common sense of many Indians who were merely aspiring as well as those who had already made it—the only elite ideology after Nehruvian nation building to have achieved a high degree of pan-Indian consent, if not total hegemony. The old official rhetoric of egalitarian and shared futures gave way to the media's celebrations of private wealth creation—embodied today by Ambani's twenty-seven-story private residence in a city where a majority lives in slums—and a proliferation of Ayn Randian cliches about ambition, willpower, and striving.

NEHRU'S PROGRAM of national self-strengthening had included, along with such ideals as secularism, socialism and nonalignment, a deep-rooted suspicion of American foreign policy and economic doctrines. In a stunning coup, India's postcolonial project was taken over, as Octavio Paz once wrote of the Mexican revolution, "by a capitalist class made in the image and likeness of U.S. capitalism and dependent upon it." A new book by Anita Raghavan, *The Billionaire's Apprentice: The Rise of the Indian-American Elite and the Fall of the Galleon Hedge Fund*, reveals how well-placed men such as Rajat Gupta, the investment banker recently convicted for insider trading in New York, expedited close links between American and Indian political and business leaders.[22]

India's upper-caste elite transcended party lines in their impassioned courting of likely American partners. In 2008, an American diplomat in Delhi was given an exclusive preview by a Congress Party factotum of two chests containing $25 million in cash—money to bribe members of Parliament into voting for a nuclear deal with the United States. Visiting the White House later that year, Singh blurted out to George W. Bush, probably resigned by then to being the most despised American president in history, that "the people of India love you deeply."[23] In a conversation disclosed by WikiLeaks, Arun Jaitley, a senior leader of the BJP who is tipped to be finance minister in Modi's government, urged American diplomats in Delhi to see his party's anti-Muslim rhetoric as "opportunistic," a mere "talking point," and to take more seriously his own professional and emotional links with the United States.[24]

A transnational elite of right-wing Indians based in the United States helped circulate an impression of an irresistibly "emerging giant"—the subtitle of a book by Arvind Panagariya, a New York–based economist and another aspiring adviser to Modi.[25] Very quickly, the delusional notion that India was, as *Foreign Affairs* proclaimed on its cover in 2006, a "roaring capitalist success-story" assumed an extraordinary persuasive power. In India itself, a handful of corporate acquisitions—such as Tata's of Jaguar and Corus—stoked exorbitant fantasies of an imminent "Global Indian Takeover" (the title of a regular feature once in India's leading business daily, the *Economic Times*). Rent seekers in a shadow intellectual economy—think-tank sailors, bloggers, and Twitterbots—as well as academics perched on corporate-endowed chairs recited the mantra of privatization and deregulation in tune. Nostrums from the Reagan-Thatcher era—the primary source of ideological self-indoctrination for many Americanized Indians—about "labor flexibility" were endlessly regurgitated, even though a vast majority of the workforce in India—more than 90 percent—toils in the unorganized or "informal" sector. Bhagwati, for instance, hailed Bangladesh for its superb labor relations a few months before the collapse of the Rana Plaza in Dhaka; he also speculated that the poor "celebrate" inequality, and, with Marie Antoinette–ish serenity, advised malnourished families to consume "more milk and fruits." Confronted with the World Health Organization's extensive evidence about malnutrition in India, Panagariya, ardent patron of the emerging giant, argued that Indian children are genetically underweight.

THIS PITILESS American free-marketeering wasn't the only extraordinary mutation of Indian political and economic discourse. By 1993, when *A Suitable Boy* was published, the single-party democracy it describes had long been under siege from low-caste groups and a rising Hindu-nationalist middle class. (Sunil Khilnani's *The Idea of India*, the most eloquent defense and elaboration of India's foundational ideology, now seems another posthumous tribute to it.[26]) India after Indira Gandhi increasingly failed to respect the Nehruvian elite's coordinates of progress and order. Indian democracy, it turned out, had seemed stable only because political participation was severely limited, and upper-caste Hindus effectively ran the country. The arrival of low-caste Hindus in mass politics in the 1980s, with their representatives demanding their own share of the spoils of power, put the first strains on the old patrimonial system. Upper-caste panic initially helped swell the ranks of the BJP, but even greater shifts caused by accelerating economic growth after 1991 have fragmented even relatively recent political formations based on caste and religion.

Rapid urbanization and the decline of agriculture created a large mass of the working poor exposed to ruthless exploitation in the unorganized sector. Connected to their homes in the hinterland through the flow of remittances, investment, culture, and ideas, these migrants from rural areas were steadily politically awakened with the help of print literacy, electronic media, job mobility, and, most important, mobile phones (subscribers grew from forty-five million in 2002 to almost one billion in 2012). The Congress, though instrumentally social-welfarist while in power, failed to respond to this electorally consequential blurring of rural and urban borderlines, and the heightened desires for recognition and dignity as well as for rapid inclusion into global modernity. Even the BJP, which had fed on upper-caste paranoia, had been struggling under its aging leaders to respond to an increasingly demanding mass of voters after its initial success in the 1990s, until Modi reinvented himself as a messiah of development, and quickly found enlarged constituencies—among haves as well as have-nots—for his blend of xenophobia and populism.

A wave of political disaffection has also deposited democratic social movements and dedicated individuals across the country. Groups both within and outside the government, such as those that successfully lobbied for the groundbreaking Right to Information Act, are outlining the possibilities of what John Keane calls "monitory democracy." India's many activist networks—for the rights of women, Dalits, peasants, and indigenous communities—or issue-based campaigns, such as those against big dams and nuclear power plants, steer clear of timeworn ideas of national security, economic development, and technocratic management, whether articulated by the Nehruvians or the neo-Hindus. In a major environment referendum last year, residents of small tribal hamlets in a remote part of eastern India voted to reject bauxite mining in their habitats. Growing demands across India for autonomy and bottom-up governance confirm that Modi is merely offering old—and soured—lassi in new bottles with his version of top-down modernization.

Modi, however, has opportunely timed his attempt to occupy the commanding heights of the Indian state vacated by the Congress. The structural problems of India's globalized economy have dramatically slowed its growth since 2011, terminating the euphoria over the Global Indian Takeover. Corruption scandals involving the sale of billions of dollars' worth of national resources such as mines, forests, land, water, and telecom spectrums have revealed that crony capitalism and rent seeking were the real engines of India's economy. The beneficiaries of the phenomenon identified by Arundhati Roy as "gush-up" have soared into a transnational oligarchy, putting the bulk of their investments abroad and snapping up, together with Chinese and Russian plutocrats, real estate in London, New York, and Singapore. Meanwhile, those made to wait unconscionably long for "trickle-down"—people with dramatically raised but mostly unfulfillable aspirations—have become vulnerable to demagogues promising national regeneration. It is this tiger of unfocused fury, spawned by global capitalism in the "underdeveloped" world, that Modi has sought to ride from Gujarat to New Delhi.

"EVEN IN THE DARKEST OF TIMES," Hannah Arendt once wrote, "we have the right to expect some illumination." The most prominent Indian institutions and individuals have rarely obliged, even as the darkness of the country's atrocity-rich borderlands moved into the heartland. Some of the most respected commentators, who are often eloquent in their defense of the right to free speech of famous writers, maintained a careful silence about the government's routine strangling of the internet and mobile networks in Kashmir. Even the liberal newspaper *The Hindu* prominently featured a journalist who retailed, as an investigation in *Caravan* revealed, false accusations of terrorism against innocent citizens. (The virtues of intelligence, courage, and integrity are manifested more commonly in small periodicals such as *Caravan* and *Economic and Political Weekly*, or independent websites such as Kafila.org and Scroll.in.) The owners of the country's largest English-language newspaper, *The Times of India*, which has lurched from tedium to decadence within a few years, have innovated a revenue stream called "paid news." Unctuously lobbing softballs at Modi, the prophets of electronic media seem, on other occasions, to have copied their paranoid inquisitorial style from Glenn Beck and Rush Limbaugh. Santosh Desai, one of contemporary India's most astute observers, correctly points out that the "intolerance that one sees from a large section of society is in some way a product of a 'televisionised' India. The pent-up feelings of resentment and entitlement have rushed out and get both tacit and explicit support from television."

A spate of corporate-sponsored literary festivals did not compensate for the missing culture of debate and reflection in the press. The frothy glamour of these events may have helped obscure the deeper intellectual and cultural churning in India today, the emergence of writers and artists from unconventional class and caste backgrounds, and the renewed attention to Ambedkar, the bracing Dalit thinker obscured by upper-caste iconographies. The probing work of, among others, such documentary filmmakers as Anand Patwardhan (*Jai Bhim Comrade*), Rahul Roy

(*Till We Meet Again*), Rakesh Sharma (*Final Solution*), and Sanjay Kak (*Red Ant Dream*), and members of the Raqs Media Collective outlines a modernist counterculture in the making.[27]

But the case of Bollywood shows how the unraveling of the earliest nation-building project can do away with the stories and images through which many people imagined themselves to be part of a larger whole, and leave only tawdriness in its place. Popular Hindi cinema degenerated alarmingly in the 1980s. Slicker now, and craftily aware of its nonresident Indian audience, it has become an expression of consumer nationalism and middle-class self-regard; Amitabh Bachchan, the "angry young man" who enunciated a widely felt victimhood during a high point of corruption and inflation in the 1970s, metamorphosed into an avuncular endorser of luxury brands. A search for authenticity, and linguistic vivacity, has led filmmakers back to the rural hinterland in such films as *Gangs of Wasseypur*, *Peepli Live*, and *Ishqiya*, whose flaws are somewhat redeemed by their scrupulous avoidance of Indians sporting Hermès bags or driving Ferraris.[28] Some recent breakthroughs, such as Anand Gandhi's *Ship of Theseus* and Dibakar Banerjee's Costa-Gavras-inspired *Shanghai*, gesture to the cinema of crisis pioneered by Asian, African, and Latin American filmmakers.[29] But India's many film industries have yet to produce anything that matches Jia Zhangke's unsentimental evocations of China's past and present, the acute examination of middle-class pathologies in Kleber Mendonça Filho's *Neighboring Sounds*, or Nuri Bilge Ceylan's delicate portrait of the sterile secularist intellectual in *Distant*.[30]

THE LONG ARTISTIC DROUGHT results partly from the confusion and bewilderment of an older, entrenched elite, the main producers, until recently, of mainstream culture. With their prerogative to rule and interpret India pilfered by the "unwashed" and the "gullible," the anglophones have been struggling to grasp the eruption of mass politics in India, its new centrifugal thrust, and the nature of the challenge posed by many apparently illiberal individuals and movements. It is easy for them to denounce India's evidently uncouth retailers of caste and religious identity as embodiments of, in Salman Rushdie's words, "Caligulan barbarity"; or to mock Chetan Bhagat, the best-selling author of novels for young adults and champion tweeter, for boasting of his "selfie" with Modi.[31] Those pied-pipering the young into Modi-mania nevertheless possess the occult power to fulfill the deeper needs of their needy followers. They can compile vivid ideological collages—made of fragments of modernity, glimpses of utopia, and renovated pieces of a forgotten past. It is in the "mythological thrillers" and positive-thinking fictions—the most popular literary genres in India today—that a post-1991 generation which doesn't even know it is lost fleetingly but thrillingly recognizes itself.

In a conventional liberal perspective, these works may seem like hotchpotches, full of absurd contradictions that confound the "above" with the "below," the "forward" with the "backward." Modi, for instance, consistently mixes up dates and historical events, exposing an abysmal ignorance of the past of the country he hopes to lead into a glorious future. Yet his lusty hatred of the Nehru-Gandhi dynasty excites many young Indians weaned on the neoliberal opiates about aspiration and merit. And he combines his historical revisionism and Hindu nationalism with a revolutionary futurism. He knows that resonant sentiments, images, and symbols—Vivekananda plus holograms and Modi masks—rather than rational argument or accurate history galvanize individuals. Vigorously aestheticizing mass politics, and mesmerizing the restless young, he has emerged as the new India's canniest artist.

But, as Walter Benjamin pointed out, rallies, parades, and grand monuments do not secure the masses their rights; they give them no more than the chance to express themselves, and noisily identify with an alluring leader and his party. It seems predictable that Modi will gratify only a few with his ambitious rescheduling of India's tryst with destiny. Though many exasperated Indians see Modi as bearing the long awaited fruits of the globalized economy, he actually embodies its inevitable dysfunction. He resembles the European and Japanese demagogues of the early twentieth century who responded to the many crises of liberalism and democracy—and of thwarted nation building and modernization—by merging corporate and political power, and exhorting communal unity before internal and external threats. But Modi belongs also to the dark days of the early twenty-first century.

His ostensibly gratuitous assault on Muslims—already India's most depressed and demoralized minority—was another example of what the social anthropologist Arjun Appadurai calls "a vast worldwide Malthusian correction, which works through the idioms of minoritisation and ethnicisation but is functionally geared to preparing the world for the winners of globalisation, minus the inconvenient noise of its losers." Certainly, the new horizons of desire and fear opened up by global capitalism do not favor democracy or human rights. Other strongmen who supervised the bloody purges of economically enervated and unproductive people were also ruthless majoritarians, consecrated by big election victories. The crony-capitalist regimes of Thaksin Shinawatra in Thailand and Vladimir Putin in Russia were inaugurated by ferocious offensives against ethnic minorities. The electorally bountiful pogrom in Gujarat in 2002, too, now seems an early initiation ritual for Modi's India.

The difficulty of assessing his personal culpability in the killings and rapes of 2002 is the same difficulty that Musil identifies with Moosbrugger in his novel: how to measure the crimes, however immense, of individuals against a universal breakdown of values and the normalization of violence and injustice. "If mankind could dream collectively," Musil writes, "it would dream Moosbrugger." There is little cause yet for such despair in India, where the aggrieved fantasy of authoritarianism will have to reckon with the gathering energies below; the great potential of the country's underprivileged and voiceless peoples still lies untapped. But for now some Indians have dreamed collectively, and they have dreamed a man accused of mass murder.

POSTSCRIPT

In 2017, the third year of his domination of Indian politics and society, Narendra Modi walked hand in hand with Donald Trump at Houston's NRG Stadium to address a rapturous crowd of fifty thousand people. "I admire him," Modi said of Trump, for his "strong resolve to make America great again." But it would soon become clear that Trump admired Modi a lot more—for his unchallenged authority over every aspect of Indian life.

Announcing his visit to India in 2020, Trump claimed that Modi had promised him that "millions and millions of people" would greet him. Only about a hundred thousand people actually turned up in the new cricket stadium in Modi's home state of Gujarat to listen to Trump's speeches. Trump still looked impressed by the carefully orchestrated mass adulation for him—perhaps, also by the fact that the stadium was named after the Indian prime minister. And, later at a press conference, he could barely conceal his admiration for Modi's accomplishment when representatives of India's media, termed "North Korean" by critics for its propagandistic fervor, lobbed softball questions at the two leaders. Turning to Modi, Trump said, "You have great reporters, I wish I had reporters like this. . . . Where do you find these reporters? This is a great thing."

Trump would have envied, too, had he been a bit more curious, Modi's sway over India's judiciary and military, his preponderance on all social and legacy media platforms, his deft use of hyperpatriotic Bollywood films, and the emotional hold of his ressentiment-filled oratory over the Indian masses. From the seductive pageantry of fascism to a cravenly sycophantic media, Modi has enjoyed for nearly a decade now all that Trump longed for and was denied in the United States.

It is also true that his peculiar upbringing and education have given him a lot more political advantages than Trump, a nepo kid from Manhattan. Modi has since his teenage years worked for an organization inspired, aesthetically as well as ideologically, by the European fascist movements of the 1920s and 1930s. His spiritual and intellectual mentors admiringly quoted from the writings of Adolf Hitler on the role of minorities in a homogenized and militarized nation-state. *Mein Kampf* was mainstreamed in India as a text about nationalism and managerial efficiency long before Modi assumed supreme power.

Modi has achieved much more in his lifelong project since I first described his trajectory in the week of his epochal election in May 2014. He has cemented, as I predicted, fascism's crucial alliance between the state and capital, perfecting India's own model of regressive modernization. It has been bizarre, to say the least, after this experience of Modi's India to hear American claims—some sincere, others opportunistic, but always loud during Trump's tenure—that fascism is arriving, is here, or has always existed. The impassioned debate over this historical conjuncture of modernity has barely referred to its most explicit incarnation in our age. The preceding pages are an attempt to describe how a contemporary and indigenized derivative of fascism comes to triumph in a deficient democracy.

SO, IS RUSSIA FASCIST NOW?

Labels and Policy Implications

MARLENE LARUELLE

PUTIN'S SPEECHES: FASCISM OR A RETURN TO OLD SOVIET TROPES?

In his infamous speeches of February 21 and 24, 2022, which sought to justify the invasion of Ukraine, Vladimir Putin negated Ukraine's independent identity and legitimacy as a nation (a stance he had already expressed in a more verbose manner in a July 2021 article). Putin argued that Ukrainians have been "contaminated" by Nazism and are in a kind of "denial" of their supposed national unity with Russians and therefore need to be "de-Nazified" in order to regain an awareness of their "authentic" Russian identity.[1]

This preposterous rhetoric attests to the widespread disdain of a former imperial metropole for the supposed lack of autonomous identity of its former "subjects" more than it does to fascism. Indeed, fascism hopes for the revival of a *domestic* identity through violence, while in the Russian case, the point is not for Russians to regenerate themselves but for Ukraine's "false identity" to be crushed. Viewed in this light, the tenor of Putin's speech hews more closely to Xi Jinping's argument for rooting out Uyghur identity than to the classic fascist notion of self-regeneration.

To be sure, the current ideological production of the Russian regime is quite ludicrous and complex. It combines celebrating Russia's pre-Soviet imperial identity with strong criticisms of the Soviet nationalities policy that gave birth to Ukraine in its contemporary form, while simultaneously engaging in a redux of the Second World War and the fight against fascism to justify the war. It also blends in a mode of East Slavic imperialism by asserting the unity of the three Eastern Slavic nations of Russia, Ukraine, and Belarus with the cult of Russia's multinationality at home—and many of the Russian soldiers sent to Ukraine belong to minorities, such as Buryats and North Caucasians.[2]

The only discursive moment where one finds the fascist idea of Russian society becoming "purified" by war is expressed in Putin's March 16 speech calling for Russia's "self-purification" from "scums and traitors" to "be stronger."[3] This type of narrative is rooted in a totalitarian vision of the healthy body politic needing to be purged in order to remain so, and in the idea of violence to that end as redemptive.

But if the rhetorical components of Russia's self-regeneration comport with the idea of a possible fascist shift in Putin's discourse, they also recall many Soviet tropes. De-Nazification brings to mind Stalin's parallel policy of *de-kulakization*, along with other repressive social-engineering projects of Stalinism. Medical metaphors of purity and contamination, as well as the dehumanization of enemies, were classic tools of the Soviet Orwellian language.[4] Denouncing opponents as fifth columnists and "national traitors" is nothing new either.[5]

Another element that potentially connects the Russian president to the fascist tradition has been his cult of masculinity and the construction of "Putin" as a brand for the man-soldier, the man-defender of the nation, but also potentially the man-aggressor.[6] His metaphor of Ukraine as a beautiful woman who has to endure what she dislikes ("Like it or not, my beauty, bear with it") in reference to the implementation of the Minsk II agreements, with its rapist undertones, is revealing of Putin's deeply entrenched, gendered vision of strength and weakness on the international scene.[7]

So, is Putin moving more toward fascism, or merely resurrecting old Soviet tropes? The crucial role played by the sloganeering of antifascism as the flagship of Russia's war and the preposterous call for "de-Nazifiying" Ukraine lead me to read the transformation of Russia's political language as a return to old Soviet narratives, namely that the United States is fostering far-right groups in Europe to fight against communism and that Ukrainians are automatically "banderites."[8] One of Russia's leading sociologists, Lev Gudkov, has coined the idea of a "relapsing" or "recurrent" totalitarianism to express the concept of Russia reactivating Soviet habits of both vertical and horizontal repression.[9] Carnegie Moscow expert Andrei Kolesnikov, too, speaks of "hybrid totalitarianism."[10] Recent research by Maria Snegovaya and Kirill Petrov on the background of Russia's top one hundred elites found that the proportion of them with Soviet nomenklatura ties today, thirty years after the collapse of the USSR, is approximately 60 percent.[11]

Not surprising then, that old Soviet imagery and patterns of action can take hold again so rapidly. Proponents of totalitarianism theory would argue that both fascism and communism, or at least Stalinism, are equals in terms of their totalizing ideological commitments and the unitary nexus of state-regime-society that leads to this particular type of organic, exclusionary language, and that the nuances between them don't matter so much.[12] But the Soviet Union was not fascist: its ideology was based on a humanistic idea of progress and not of reaction, and there was no obsessive urge to regenerate the nation through violence, the goal being rather to build a more egalitarian society by force. Our framing of the new Russia thus clearly does matter, and suggesting that Putin is a fascist packs a bigger, but ultimately misleading, punch.

THE STATE-SOCIETY RELATIONSHIP: NO MASS MOBILIZATION

Even more central to the definition of fascism is the need for heavy mobilization of the population and the exultation in a cult of war. So far, Russia fits neither of the two requirements: the authorities do not celebrate war, but on the contrary hide it and have even passed a law that condemns those talking about a "war," and not a "special military operation," to up to fifteen years in prison. They try to avoid full military mobilization, as a large-scale draft of young men would force a recognition that the "operation" is indeed a "war" and could jeopardize the Russian people's passive consensus around the regime's "special operation." The Kremlin therefore does not celebrate war as regeneration of the nation, and wants to keep the population more demobilized than mobilized. And Russian society does appear indeed more amorphous than zealous.

So far, the signs of top-down pressures exerted on the population to display loyalty and support for war have been manufactured in a pretty poor, Soviet-inspired manner, and with a quite low degree of conviction on the part of much of the population.[13] We don't see any signs of mass mobilization, which would entail a fanaticized population exalting this ideology through rallies and parades. For instance, state-sector workers had to be forced to attend Putin's stadium speech on March 18, and hurried back home immediately after it was over.[14] Contrary to Timothy Snyder's claim, there is no cult of the dead in the Nazi sense, but instead a state-sponsored obsession with the memory of the Second World War forms the core social consensus of Russian society.

Moreover, while youth support is a central component of any fascist regime, in Russia, the youth are the most unreliable part of the population from the regime's point of view, and the least supportive of the war.[15] The renewal of old-fashioned patriotic-military inculcation is mostly limited to prevent undesired sentiments spreading among broader constituencies (especially schoolchildren and college students), rather than taking a tack of inculcating them with "the one and only true creed."[16]

One can of course identify some potentially fascist mobilization dynamics such as, for instance, the reporting that Z signs (Z has become the visual rally-'round-the-flag symbol of the pro-war camp) are painted on the doors of antiwar activists to expose and threaten them. However, this possible mobilization remains difficult to quantify and seems to be a pretty marginal movement at the grassroots level, and likely to be mostly a PR construction pushed by the authorities. The passivity of a large part of Russian society does allow for violence to take place, and this makes it indirectly complicit in Russia's actions in Ukraine, but this nonetheless differs from the sort of active grassroots collective mobilization seen in fascist regimes.[17]

Furthermore, Russian society does not seem to buy the most radical arguments advanced by the state media machine to justify the war. Even though one should look with caution at today's surveys conducted in Russia, they still give us some insights.[18] A survey conducted on March 22 by the very official FOM (Funds for Public Opinion) on the reasons for the "special operation" gives the following results: the Russian public sees the war as an issue of strategic security for Russia to avoid the installation of NATO bases on Ukrainian territory (71 percent), and as the defense of the population of the two self-proclaimed republics of Donetsk and Luhansk (52 percent).[19] Only 21 percent think the "special operation" aims at changing the political course of Ukraine and 10 percent think one of its goals is "liquidating Ukraine's statehood and integrating it into Russia." A Levada Center survey (the last independent poll agency in Russia) conducted a few days later gives slightly different results (43 percent to protect Russians in Donbas, 25 percent to protect Russia, 21 percent to de-Nazify Ukraine, and only 3 percent to integrate Ukraine into Russia).[20] Both surveys confirm that the Russian population reads the conflict mostly as a geopolitical struggle with the West and does not show any particular enthusiasm for the more cultural, political, and genocidal aims of liquidating Ukraine's statehood and nationhood.

One way to assess Russia's possible move toward fascism will be to see how its militia culture evolves in the war context. As stated by the American University and University of Melbourne political scientists Lucas Dolan and Simon Frankel Pratt, "fascism starts with paramilitary ties to mainstream parties."[21] The Putin regime has cultivated a large militia space ranging from Cossacks to paramilitary groups to Orthodox vigilantes, and even including mixed martial arts and other trained fighters. Russian mercenary groups, including the most infamous of them, the Wagner Group (its name itself a reference to Hitler's favorite composer), have taken to displaying Nazi-inspired symbols.[22] If militia culture were to gain a new status in post–February 24 Russia and become a larger vigilante movement, it would constitute compelling evidence that the Russian state apparatus is becoming fascist.

DANGEROUS POLICY IMPLICATIONS: NEAR AND BEYOND

Another critical component of our discussion relates to the usefulness of the label "fascism" for policymaking purposes. What political ends does the term serve as far as Western policy toward post–February 24 Russia is concerned?

Referring to Russia as fascist feeds into the historical metaphor that today's Russia is repeating Nazi Germany's actions in Ukraine, a metaphor that both Volodymyr Zelensky and many Central and Eastern European leaders put forth regularly. In March, the Western public's reactions to a Russian missile hitting the Babi Yar memorial site (where some thirty-three thousand Jews were executed by the Nazis), and the death of one of the last Ukrainian (non-Jewish) survivors of Buchenwald in the Kharkiv bombings, drew immediate parallels with fascism not simply as a broad category of regime, but with Nazi Germany and the Holocaust in particular. Since the discovery of the mass killings of civilians in the Kyiv suburbs, illustrated by the Bucha massacre, as well as the release of more information on filtration camps and reportage on rapes of Ukrainian women by Russian soldiers, the notion of genocide has been raised to qualify Russia's war crimes and crimes against humanity, often paired with an implicit or explicit reference to the Holocaust.[23]

But genocide and fascism should not be conflated, for genocide can emerge under different types of murderous regimes. In his book *The Dark Side of Democracy: Explaining Ethnic Cleansing*, the UCLA sociologist Michael Mann rightfully insists on genocide's diversity of ideological contexts.[24] Some scholars, such as the Johns Hopkins University political scientist Eugene Finkel, consider that the threshold for using the term "genocide" in the case of Russia's actions in Ukraine has been reached; others, like the University of Amsterdam Professor of Holocaust and Genocide Studies Ugur Üngör, argue that it has not.[25] The issue of intentionality, top-down orders, and the relationship between the killing of civilians, rapes, filtration camps, and cultural annihilation will have to be investigated by international justice authorities in order to confirm or negate the genocidal nature of these murderous events.[26]

The parallel with Nazi Germany is problematic for many other reasons. First, tracing the historical metaphor of the Second World War to its end implies that the war should end for Russia the way it ended for Nazi Germany in 1945: with total capitulation, collective guilt, foreign military occupation, and a Nuremberg-style trial for its leaders. This is more than improbable: the likelihood of Putin killing himself in his bunker amid the ruins of Moscow is null. The war is not being fought on Russian territory and therefore the parallel with Germany's total defeat that would allow for a profound transformation of Russian political culture is not to be expected. If regime change in Moscow is perceived as the West's endgame—as bellicose statements by President Biden or Defense Secretary Lloyd Austin that Putin "cannot remain in power" and Russia "must be weakened" would seem to suggest—this may only reinforce the perception by Russian leaders that victory is an existential question for the regime.[27]

Second, while the war is, to be sure, the full and sole responsibility of the Putin regime, the strategic deadlock that preceded it is not. It has been a cocreated dynamic in which the West has its own share of responsibility, primarily for sending mixed signals about NATO expansion.[28] As in any human relationship, which is what relationships between countries ultimately boil down to, communication problems are a two-way street. These mixed signals on NATO directly clashed with Moscow's "red lines": that any Western military presence on Ukraine's territory (whether directly through NATO enlargement or indirectly through EU agreement, which allows for foreign troops to be stationed there) would be seen as an existential threat.[29]

But Western ambiguities also impacted the Ukrainians themselves, who are still trying to understand to which degree they are "in" or "out" of the transatlantic community, now at the price of their own lives. Moving forward, Ukraine's grievances toward Western partners, already increasingly expressed by Zelensky, will continue to grow once the war reaches its stalemate, the country's reconstruction will be slow, and Western opinion will undoubtedly show some Ukraine fatigue. These outcomes will in part be the result of the West's two decades of mixed signaling.

Third, the parallel with the Second World War is also analytically wrong because it presupposes a clear, Manichaean triumph of good over evil. The war in Ukraine creates the illusion of a rejuvenated liberal order to come, of the type Francis Fukuyama expressed. But blithely predicting that liberalism will find a new legitimacy only because it is united against an enemy does not prefigure a happy ending: Viktor Orbán's and Aleksandar Vučić's recent electoral victories in Hungary and Serbia, respectively, as well as Marine Le Pen's garnering of an unprecedented 41 percent of the vote in the French presidential election, serve to remind us that illiberalism remains highly attractive to a substantial swath of the European electorate. It may be toxic to refer to Putin as a role model now, but that doesn't mean that the homegrown elements of illiberalism in Europe and the United States have miraculously disappeared—or that illiberal leaders will not continue to partner with Russia, even if more discreetly.[30]

Moreover, the West is denouncing Russia's language of an existential civilizational conflict even as it itself employs a civilizational vision of the world order (Biden's 2021 Democracy Summit was an unfortunate example of this) and frames the war in ideological terms of democracy versus dictatorship.[31] A Manichaean polarization between friend and foe and enforcing a reading of the war as being a fight for the "free world" reveals an inability to conceptualize the new world (dis)order outside of outdated Cold War references, and the naïve hope that liberalism can reinvent itself just by creating a new existential threat to battle.[32]

Furthermore, while the war may have awakened (at least temporarily) a renewed sense of European unity, it has not automatically made "the West" more legitimate in other regions. For the Global South, the war is an internal conflict belonging to the Global North that distracts the world community from much more important and long-term issues such as fair redistribution of the planet's wealth, fair representation in international organizations, climate change, etc.[33] The fact that thirty-five nations abstained at the U.N. General Assembly vote condemning the Russian invasion does not mean they are neutral toward Russia's aggression and indifferent to Ukraine's unjustified and unjustifiable suffering. It does mean that they consider the West partly responsible for the war because of its own normative imperialism and thus will not condone playing the sanctions card. Seen from the Global South, Russia's behavior, while unacceptable, does not in and of itself make the West any more legitimate.[34]

PART V

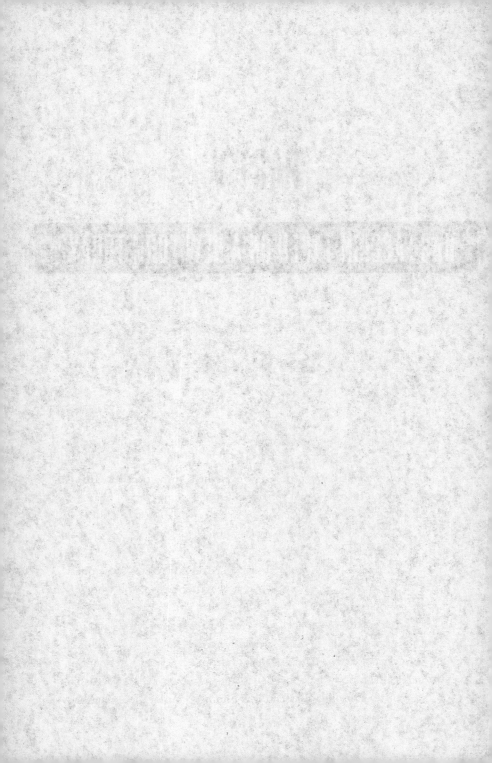

ARE WE APPROACHING A NEW WAVE OF FASCISM?

GEOFF MANN

Until recently, we could talk about "the politics of climate change." The belief was that climate, like trade, was an "issue," a problem that could be contained and addressed by targeted institutions and regulations. This view is no longer tenable. We have crossed a threshold—it's not that climate change is the only "issue," but rather that nothing escapes it. All politics are climate politics.

The upshot of this is an inchoate condition of permanent emergency, and the extraordinary uncertainty that follows. Economic growth projections and demographic models are still based on the assumption that the next century will be much like the last, but no one really knows what is going to happen to the world over the coming decades. This is especially true for the social impacts of global temperature changes. How will human communities be organized? How will societies react to climate-induced "shocks" as they accumulate? Will existing political and economic institutions and relations survive? That the effects of planetary warming will vary across time and space only makes these questions harder to answer. Who will live, how will they live, and who will decide? No one knows.

This uncertainty produces fears, even expectations, of a dark age. Climate-induced scarcities, mass migrations, and desperation will only intensify existing trends and disorders: Europe's far-right ethnonationalist parties vie for power; demagogues rule in India, Brazil, and Russia; totalitarianism consolidates itself in Xi Jinping's China; and unabashed white supremacy saturates the U.S. Republican Party. Add "climate chaos" to all of this and the prospect of an incipient "fascism" seems credible—and if we aren't exactly sure what we mean when we say fascism, we are sure we will know it when we see it. As the Uruguayan journalist Eduardo Galeano said when surveying the Latin American dictatorships in 1974, "If all this is not fascism, let's acknowledge it looks a lot like it."

For some historians, the problem is not that fascism can never happen again, but rather that it has specific characteristics. Donald Trump's brutal buffoonery seems particularly ill described: as the intellectual historian Enzo Traverso argues, "Trump is as distant from classical fascism as Occupy Wall Street, the 15-M movement in Spain and the Nuit debout movement in France are from the communism of the 20th century."

Yet what if such confident dismissals about the present-day threat of fascism let us relax, precisely when we shouldn't? What if an "incipient" fascism turns out to be more than a few hundred white boys with homemade swastikas glued to their Boy Scout uniforms? Maybe every past fascist "success" was preceded by a refusal to acknowledge the scale of the threat on the horizon: in *No Name in the Street* (1972), the American writer James Baldwin recounts that listening to liberals intellectualize over cocktails the perils of McCarthyism brought to mind "German Jews sitting around debating whether Hitler was a threat to their lives until the debate was summarily resolved for them by a knocking at the door." If the price of anticipating (and preventing) fascism is mislabeling not-quite fascism, there is good reason to set aside analytical quibbles.

The problem with demanding a precise definition of fascism is that it exaggerates both the "exceptional" character of fascist politics, and the distance between us and its historical calamities. In thinking about fascism, we can't just be on the lookout for its original form as it emerged in interwar Europe—dandies and thugs pursuing the renewal of the racial-national body through party-organized violence and imperialism. Nor does fascism necessarily require a historical rupture or crisis moment such as the economic and political chaos after 1918, even if those conditions helped Mussolini and Hitler rise to power.[1] Fascism can be, and today is quite likely to be, far less precise, less total, and far more "everyday" than that.

The banality of fascism was highlighted in the decades following the Second World War, when anticolonial thinkers identified the terrifying parallels between the supposed historical novelty of European fascism and the colonialism that long predated it. In 1950, Aimé Césaire, the Martinican poet, playwright (and later, politician), declared that the quotidian barbarism of colonization had "ensavaged" Europe, so much so that Europeans became immune to their own barbarity: "And then one fine day the bourgeoisie is awakened by a powerful *choc en retour*: the gestapos are busy, the prisons are filling up, the torturers around the racks invent, refine and discuss." Ten years later, Frantz Fanon asked: "What is fascism but colonialism amid the traditionally colonial countries?"

The centuries-old domestic fascism in the United States has also been widely noted. The prison abolition scholar and activist Ruth Wilson Gilmore and the Italian social theorist Alberto Toscano have recently shown how, from the 1960s, the Black liberation movement saw fascism as a "preventative counterrevolution"—similar to the capitalist response to the Communist movement in Europe after the First World War. The difference is that unlike Nazism or Italian fascism, which were organized around a movement or party arisen in an act of defiant reaction, American fascism is a long-standing and violent project to dominate and exploit Black and Indigenous people—to deny them freedom and autonomy; to keep them as close as possible to death.

The Black radical militant and intellectual Angela Davis always insisted that "Blacks and other Third World peoples are the first and most deeply injured victims of fascism," and neither Algiers nor Philadelphia required some of the integral features that defined European fascism in the twentieth century to produce their regimes: there was no obvious crisis trigger (a lost war, hyperinflation, or a depression), nor an animating vision of an idealized New Man in a purified nation reborn. Instead, there was a robust and responsive structure of state-sponsored or state-coordinated racist violence and terror that could be effectively militarized when a conflagration called for it: think of the century-long "pacification" of Algeria, or the U.S. police-prison system. Fascism on this count does not even necessarily need an openly fascist state. Some Europeans noted the same possibility after 1945: as Theodor Adorno remarked in 1959, "The survival of National Socialism *within* democracy" is likely "more menacing than the survival of fascist tendencies *against* democracy."

This is where an attachment to a "precise" definition of fascism misses the point. It is not that the defining features of mid-twentieth-century fascism are not fascist, but rather that fascism can be far more boring and indeterminate, a "fuzzy totalitarianism," as Umberto Eco put it. It can easily become part of the everyday rhythms of history. Lynchings, pogroms, seemingly "random" violence, the detailed bureaucratic schemata of hierarchy, category, punishment, and death: all are catastrophic for those subjected to fascist oppression, but they are hardly unfamiliar to the fascist going about his day, nor to the citizens of many a liberal democracy. In Canada, where I write, the government continues its militarized invasions of unceded Indigenous land to ensure the construction of another gas pipeline; there are now restrictions in the U.S. state of Georgia on providing water to citizens waiting in line to vote; and a teenage white supremacist, Kyle Rittenhouse, was invited to meet Donald Trump after he killed two Black Lives Matter protesters in August 2020. These are commonplace features of life in "Western civilization." In these conditions, it is easy to be a nonfascist fascist.

This is potentially the most troubling possibility in the internecine conflict between "Western civilization" and climate change. As Adorno also said, "For countless people life was not at all bad under fascism. Terror's sharp blade was aimed only at a few and relatively well-defined groups." For many of the people outside those groups, one had merely to get out of the way and get by. With far-right political movements ready to take advantage of conditions easily presented as an existential threat, expectations of fascism hardly seem far-fetched.

Writing in 1943, the Polish economist Michał Kalecki, a colleague of John Maynard Keynes, argued that fascism has always promised the most radical fix to the threat of capitalist collapse, a stability that virtually no other order can deliver. "In a democracy one does not know what the next government will be like. Under fascism there is no next government," Kalecki wrote. "[O]ne of the basic functions of Nazism was to overcome the reluctance of big business to large-scale government intervention." Keynes himself once called fascism "the capitalist branch of the totalitarian faith," which has always involved a coordinated relationship between the state, elites, and big business. As the Swedish activist-scholar Andreas Malm and his co-authors in the Zetkin Collective make terrifyingly clear in *White Skin, Black Fuel: On the Danger of Fossil Fascism* (2021), the extreme right's commitment to fossil-fuel-based corporate capitalism means that the larger its role in politics today, the more likely climate catastrophes become.

On bleak days, then, it can seem as if there's nowhere to run, with fascism the darkness at either end of the tunnel. In the permanent emergency, either we let society descend into the crisis conditions that have solicited fascist violence in the past, or we reconstruct society so thoroughly it demands a form of total and unyielding state power to see the project through. Fossil fascism or climate fascism: either would surely involve the imposition of violent order, partly through the vilification of an internal enemy—immigrants, but also other oppressed or outcast peoples—whose very existence must be contained, even obliterated, in the interests of protecting fascism's true subjects.

The point is that fascism's advance does not solely depend on a world of increasing fires, floods, and droughts. In the capitalist societies that dominate the planet, in conditions of uncertainty and instability, a radical program to mitigate the effects of climate change—one that does not involve the redistribution of political and economic power—could well take fascist form. A perusal of the ideas behind so-called ecofascism, such as the "patriotic ecology" of the National Rally's "green" wing, "Nouvelle Écologie," or the evil Malthusianism behind the 2019 massacre at the Al-Noor mosque in New Zealand, makes it clear that for some, radical climate action does not involve Green New Deals or international climate cooperation, but rather cages, vigilantes, and border patrols facing refugees across snarls of barbed wire.

All of these phenomena already exist, and are proliferating at border crossings and ports. Many of the key features of what we might call fascism in the age of climate change are things we, in the West, already do.

As climate-related calamities intensify and become more prevalent, so, too, will the political institutions and rationales with which governments "manage" them. There is no reason to expect that contemporary fascisms will not organize the response to climate change. Insofar as climate politics need not be principally about climate, they are already doing so. Immigration and pandemic policy, for example, have become two of the principal mechanisms for dealing with mass population movements that are in many cases substantially climate driven, especially by drought and acute weather events.

Those arriving in northern Europe and the southern United States from the Middle East and Central America confront harsh and unforgiving policy environments that are in many ways ethnonationalist climate policy by another name. The far right of Europe and North America has, of course, long justified anti-immigration politics as a defense of "nature" from hordes with no connection to the land. But in the era of climate change and the shrinking of the planet's "climate niche" where humans can live—to which migration is obviously one of the most important adaptation strategies—increasing barriers to immigration has also become a key mechanism for distributing the impacts of global heating.

The greatest risk is that as these kinds of institutional models proliferate, many will accede to the progress of fascism in the same way they have accepted the draconian policies that precede it. And if, as Keynes said, many of us love order more than we hate fascism, we might also sympathize with this acceptance, even if it makes us ashamed to admit it.[2] We can, of course, denounce the injustice, proclaim with Greta Thunberg that "history will judge." But that is an empty admonition when it is clear that many have no intention of sharing others' histories, and even resent the idea that history should be shared. The fascist's is a eugenicized past, the one Baldwin saw in a photograph of fifteen-year-old civil rights pioneer Dorothy Counts bravely making her way to a white school through a seething mob in North Carolina in 1957, an "unutterable pride, tension, and anguish in that girl's face as she approached the halls of learning, with history, jeering, at her back."

This is a world in which any emergent fascism draws much of its energy from the dark and bitter nostalgia that fuels the contemporary right. For all its "Make X Great Again" sloganeering, the fascism of our times is no longer committed to the rebirth of classical fascism's New Man, but to the reverse engineering of history and a cartoonish, mythical past, when France was French, or Britain belonged to the British. When you could be proud of the empire, feel no guilt about your gas-guzzling car, and no shame in being white.

In stark contrast to the most compelling demands of contemporary climate movements, which emphasize a moral obligation to future generations and the nonhuman world, today's emergent fascism is a political program that indicts the present as a crime against the past. For much of its white base, the point is that the life they have "always lived" was not a disaster, that they are being "replaced" on the stage of history, that progressive politics turns what was a source of pride into an object of shame.

As Republican legislatures across the United States enact laws attacking voting rights, criminalizing protest, and limiting school curricula, the philosopher Jason Stanley has argued that the country is now in fascism's "legal phase," a reminder that history can just as readily jeer us as judge us.[3] Climate change is in some ways the ultimate rebuke to the promises these competing pasts made to the future, a jeering history none of us can escape, even if for many it was never their own, but imposed upon them.

But if nothing else, it is also a reminder that history, however much some might try to take it for their own, is something we must live with together. Whatever the future holds, however a changing climate leads us to push and pull our individual and collective lives in unknown directions, the task of entangling and interweaving our histories will be essential to the struggle against fascism. The one thing fascism cannot survive is a world in which the parts understand themselves as inextricable from the whole. This condition is also essential to our attempts to come to grips with climate change; at this moment in history, the fight against fascism is also a struggle for climate justice.

FIGHTING FASCISM IN THE TWENTY-FIRST CENTURY

The Adorno Algorithm

MOIRA WEIGEL

To revisit *The Authoritarian Personality* in the hopes of adapting its insights to our time is to confront the irony that its most famous methodological innovation achieved full flowering at Cambridge Analytica. The Frankfurt School has long served as a source of phobic fascination and perhaps improbable inspiration for right-wing activists. And at least some leftists have long criticized its most prominent members for overemphasizing psychic and cultural factors at the expense of material ones. But, insofar as its "F-scale" for measuring potential fascism prototyped a form of political forecasting based on personal data, *The Authoritarian Personality* poses a particularly acute version of the problem of unanticipated consequences. The flourishing of quantitative propaganda and personality research that the study both built on and extended not only did not cure prejudice in the United States—they ultimately proved expedient for cultivating it. A second irony, which may or may not contradict the first, is that to repeat the claim that Cambridge Analytica swung the 2016 election is to take the sales pitch of interested and unscrupulous actors as fact. As many critics of *The Authoritarian Personality* were quick to point out, and Theodor Adorno acknowledged in its pages, prediction based on personality typing does not really work.[1]

In recent years, the rise of Donald Trump and the rise of right-wing movements and leaders worldwide have inspired spirited debates about whether it is appropriate to call them "fascist." At the same time, a more specialized set of conversations has considered how useful the work of the Frankfurt School remains for analyzing them. In many ways, the Frankfurt School account of fascism has become ever more anachronistic. This is not only because of the cultural elitism and historical pessimism that set Theodor Adorno in conflict with the student movement after he returned to Germany. Nor is it only because Black, decolonial, and Third Worldist scholars and activists theorizing and fighting "racial fascism" provincialized Eurocentric interpretations of the phenomenon.[2] Both of those things are true. But a Frankfurt School account of the *new* new right-wing extremism also fails on its own terms, just as members of the Frankfurt School would have predicted.

The authors and editors of *The Authoritarian Personality* emphasized from the outset that the phenomenon they were investigating was historically specific. The historically specific context for the forms of fascism and latent fascism that members of the Frankfurt School analyzed, as well as for their analysis itself, was mass society. The psychotechnics they examined had their material basis in mass production and mass media technologies that applied the logics of monopoly capital to culture: analog recording, vertically integrated production, one-to-many broadcasting, and so on. As a result, the theories that Theodor Adorno, Max Horkheimer, and their colleagues advanced about fascism and the latent fascist tendencies within liberal democracies placed a great deal of explanatory power in features of culture and political economy that no longer obtain. They feel anachronistic because today's fascisms, or latent fascisms, are not mass, but networked, movements. They are taking place not in a mass society, but in a networked one. It is ruled not by monopoly capital but by surveillance capital; its work rhythms are not Taylorist but agile; its cultural logic is not standardization but personalization; it does not "infect everything with sameness," as Horkheimer and Adorno's *The Dialectic of Enlightenment* accused the midcentury culture industry of doing, but optimizes everything, including pleasures, based on actuarial assessments of opportunity and risk.[3]

I should not overstate the distinctions that I am sketching. Despite the emphasis that members of the Frankfurt School placed on historical specificity, they also understood fascism as expressing timeless human drives toward domination and self-subjugation. For Adorno and Horkheimer, the paradigmatic bourgeois subject was the ancient hero Odysseus. And despite breathless headlines to the contrary, there were in fact white supremacists in the United States before YouTube. Still, if the premise of *The Authoritarian Personality* was that industrial modernity produced distinctive dispositions, the broad transformations from industrialism to postindustrialism and Cold War liberalism to neoliberalism have transformed all the fundamental categories that the Frankfurt School used in their analyses: class structure, governmentality, interpersonal communications, and affect.

Many passages from *The Authoritarian Personality* and from other Frankfurt School texts on "the American agitator" could now be mistaken for descriptions of Tucker Carlson or Alex Jones. However, there are some features of new right-wing movements that clearly depart from the mold that the study described. Conventionalism, for instance, is not what it was. If the fascist personality exhibited a "conflict of surface conventionality and underlying rebelliousness," the contemporary right inverts this tendency, presenting familiar forms of prejudice, which correspond to deeply entrenched forms of inequality, as countercultural. Nor do straightforward sexual repression and homophobia play the same role they once did. Much work remains to be done in order to interpret how such cultural and ideological changes relate to the rise of "platform"[4] or "surveillance capitalism."[5] But it seems safe to say that they reflect changes in the total organization of society which also change both what it means to be authoritarian and what it means to have a personality—a curious thing that, like sexuality, is at once a property endowed to each of us at birth and a potential that we must develop.

If there is such a thing as an authoritarian personality today, it must, by its own logic, be an Authoritarian Personality 2.0. It must have been *updated to remain the same*, which, as the media theorist Wendy Hui Kyong Chun points out, is both the general function of software updates and a distinctive mode of crisis management under neoliberalism.[6] Adorno can speak to the AP 2.0, despite his obvious untimeliness. But, to make him do so, we must turn to the margins of his canon.

THE MEANS THAT the authors of *The Authoritarian Personality* devised to measure susceptibility to fascist propaganda was the F-scale. This scale had not been part of their initial plan. As Adorno et al. related in the chapter describing its design, the idea for it emerged after the team had already done considerable work on the more conventional Likert scales measuring anti-Semitism ("A-S"), ethnocentrism ("E"), and political and economic conservatism ("PEC"). Following well-established protocols of opinion-attitude research, these measured consciously held views. The F-scale was originally intended to create an alternative that could replace A-S and E, if it correlated strongly enough with them. However, the authors gradually arrived at a different aim. Rather than attitudes or opinions, the F-scale would measure "underlying antidemocratic trends at the level of the personality."[7] It focused on variables in personality structure that could be "related functionally to various manifestations of prejudice."[8]

The value of the entire endeavor depended on a fundamental assumption: that there was such a thing as a *type* of person, that people could be grouped into meaningful categories based on their positions in statistical distributions of traits, and that such constructs could meaningfully anticipate not only other traits but also their future behavior. Adorno knew that this assumption would strike many of his readers as problematic. "Hardly any concept in contemporary American psychology has been so thoroughly criticized as that of typology," he began.[9] Moreover, by the 1940s, methods of measuring human character that had emerged from nineteenth-century anthropometry, and been institutionalized in the United States through intelligence testing, were tainted by their association with Nazi eugenics. Nonetheless, Adorno proposed, the "problem of typology" did not allow itself to be easily dispensed with. "Not all typologies are devices for dividing the world into sheep and buck, but some of them reflect certain experiences which, though hard to systematize, have, to put it as loosely as possible, hit upon something."[10]

The looseness of the language, here, might sound like an evasion, but it turns out to be the point. For Adorno, it was the vagueness of the type, its "halfway" status or ambiguous wavering between the uniqueness of the individual and the statistical generalizability of mass society, that rendered it a valuable source of knowledge. However, one had to be precise about what typology offered knowledge *about*. For Adorno, "the kind of subsumption of individuals under pre-established classes which has been consummated in Nazi Germany, where the labeling of live human beings, independently of their specific qualities, resulted in decisions about their life and death" was clearly indefensible.[11] The typology that he aimed to recuperate was of a different, even opposing, sort. "The reason for the persistent plausibility of the typological approach," he wrote, "is not a static biological one, but just the opposite: dynamic and social."

If popular typology seemed to reveal something about psychology, this was because "the fact that human society has been up to now divided into classes affects more than the external relations of men. The marks of social repression are left within the individual soul."[12] The proper object of typological knowledge was not the individual psyche, nor yet the social totality, but the standardizing pressures that the latter exerted on the former, and the reactions they produced. That is, the process and consequences of typing itself.

Adorno saw his typology as a means of studying *social mediation*, in other words. From this perspective, "the construction of psychological types does not merely imply an arbitrary, compulsive attempt to bring some 'order' into the confusing diversity of human personality." Rather, "it represents a means of 'conceptualizing' this diversity according to its own structure." Its imprecision reflected the status of any given "type" as an abstraction, and such an abstraction remained necessary for the purpose of healing. The goal of *The Authoritarian Personality* was that its findings *not* be replicated. If typology combined classification with prediction, Adorno's critical typology did so for the purpose of intervention. For him, the F-scale did not reveal facts but, rather, likely futures— and it did so, so that they might be averted.

THE AUTHORS OF *The Authoritarian Personality* noted that several of the items with the highest discriminatory power—that is, the strongest ability to predict a subject's overall score—concerned superstition. Adorno, who was the author of these items, had long been interested in the subject. During a brief sojourn in California in 1954, he undertook a more detailed analysis of the *Los Angeles Times* astrology column, which provided the basis for his short book *The Stars Down to Earth*. In the process, he identified two features that distinguished popular astrology from other mass media: the apparent personalization that it offered and the formal abstraction that it involved. Both qualities anticipated features of later algorithmic media.

At the core of Adorno's analysis of astrology was the idea of its "pseudo-rationalism." While astrology was premised on a blatantly irrational form of typing—the division of individuals into cohorts depending on the constellations under which they had been born—the advice that it tendered was startlingly commonsense. Adorno's content analysis revealed that the recommendations in "Astrological Forecasts" primarily focused on suggestions about what time of day to perform various tasks, and moreover that following these suggestions would generally keep a reader at work approximately nine to five, tidying up and enjoying leisure afterward. "Make your appearance more charming early." "Contact all and complete business and correspondence early. Later, pitch in and make home, family and property conditions more satisfactory through cooperative measures." "In the PM have fun; be happy."[13] Adorno considered such advice was proto-authoritarian, rather than simply banal, because of the relationship to authority that it fostered.

The astrology column took seemingly inexorable social forces by which people consciously or unconsciously felt oppressed and externalized them, projecting them onto the stars, which it characterized as having already determined everything in advance. By misrepresenting social forces as natural, and placing them at such remove, it rendered them impervious to human questioning or action. At the same time, astrology encouraged readers to turn to these very symbols of the forces that oppressed them for aid. When they did, the help they received came in the form of commands to adjust themselves to the rhythms of alienated life and work. By encouraging readers to exercise the prerogatives of narrow instrumental rationality, astrology thus conditioned them to reproduce the irrational contradictions under which they lived. Finally, to the extent that astrology offered a sense of transgressing modern norms, it conditioned them to take pleasure in this experience of being coerced.

In the content analyses that he conducted for the Princeton Radio Project, Adorno had identified an "ideology of personality" at work in fascist propaganda. Astrology, however, worked in the opposite direction. Rather than conjuring the personality of the fascist leader to broadcast it to an undifferentiated mass, it used mass media to create the illusion of addressing each reader individually. The astrology columnist had to "sound as though he had concrete knowledge of what problems beset each of his prospective followers born under some sign at a specific time," Adorno wrote. "Yet he must always remain non-committal enough so that he cannot be easily discredited."[14] The rhetorical solution lay in "some rather rigid stereotypes of style." These included combining imperative verbs with abstract nouns ("'Follow up that intuition of yours' or 'Display that keen mind of yours'") as well as grammatical shifters ("The word 'that' seems to imply that the columnist, on the basis of astrological inspiration, knows exactly what the individual addressee who happens to read the column is like or was like at some particular time"). These "nice little tricks" made "apparently specific references . . . so general that they can be made to fit all the time."[15] In order to target them effectively, the astrologer had to conduct the very kind of socio-psychological analysis that Adorno himself was engaged in. Just as Adorno had characterized the radio demagogue Martin Luther Thomas as a "practical psychologist," he observed that the astrology columnist "really has to be what is called in American slang, a homespun philosopher."[16] Both the fascist demagogue and the astrology columnist succeeded because they found ways to manipulate people according to the typedness of their personalities, and the psychological dynamics that produced it.

Like other forms of contemporary mass culture, astrology employed what he called the "threat-help" or "threat-relief" pattern, depicting scenarios of danger from which individuals could then be saved, or save themselves. Adorno noted that the astrology column shared this tactic with advertising: "Only if some mild terror is exercised, will [the reader] seek help—analogous to advertising of drugs against body odor."[17] "The ideal of social *conformity* [was] promoted throughout the column and expressed by the implicit, but ubiquitous rule that one has to adjust oneself continuously to the commands of the stars at a given time."[18] This conformity, however, was the product of a deeper psychological defense: compulsivity. Through its pseudo-personalized mode of address, astrology simultaneously excited a sense of helplessness and encouraged readers to take small, meaningless actions to assuage it. It emphasized the freedom of the individual to choose but constrained his choices to a highly structured set of options.

While the threat-help pattern appeared across mass culture, Adorno argued that a second feature distinguished astrology from other forms of mass communication: the highly abstract nature of the identifications that it elicited. "Soap operas, television shows, and above all movies are characterized by heroes, persons who positively or negatively solve their own problems," Adorno observed. "They stand vicariously for the spectator." The astrology column eliminated representations of humans and human agency. "For the column, the hero is replaced by either the heavenly signs or, more likely, by the omniscient columnist himself." While the genre was ostensibly more proactive or interactive than radio or cinema, it in fact promoted *greater* psychological passivity. "Since the course of events is referred to as something pre-established, people will not have the feeling, still present in hero worship, that by identification with the hero, they may have to be heroic themselves."[19] The reader targeted or caught up in astrology's "makeshift of pseudo-personalization" was thus "trained to identify themselves with the existent *in abstracto* rather than with heroic persons, to concede their own impotence and thus be allowed as a compensation to go on living."[20]

While the pseudo-personalization of astrology excited compulsivity, its abstraction drew on, and heightened, paranoia. Attachment to astrology constituted a form of "cruel optimism," and as with any cruel optimism, critique was no real fix. A person could not give up compulsively acting, and the sensations of agency that such action provided, except at a steep psychic cost.[21] This was true even if the astrology enthusiast did not take the "Forecasts" entirely seriously. For Adorno, this lack of seriousness was a common feature of fascism, and one that did not make it any less dangerous. Indeed, it could make fascists more dangerous: to prove their own beliefs to themselves, they would commit violence.

IN SOME RESPECTS, these grim conclusions read almost like a parody of Adorno. Yet, personalization is a key objective force producing new types today. And it is in urgent need of demystification. I noted in my introduction that personalization has recently gone from being regarded as a solution to being regarded as the problem—from a supposed remedy to the authoritarian tendencies latent in mass society and media to a supposedly authoritarian force. Both claims are paranoid, as the ease of flipping between them suggests. They project what they already believe about liberalism and neoliberalism onto technologies, to which they then attribute the power to make things so. By reinterpreting personalization through the lens of Adorno's critical typology, we can arrive at a clearer analysis of its status and role in driving new authoritarian movements. Such an analysis clarifies that, for all the concern pundits and politicians have expressed about Russian bots and Chinese malware, such movements are not primarily external threats. They are pathologies of democracies under digital capitalism.

The techniques that make contemporary algorithmic personalization possible are considerably more complicated than the "little tricks" that Adorno's astrology columnist played with language. However, despite its greater complexity, algorithmic personalization is not magic. Algorithmic personalization does not address users directly, as individuals, any more than "Astrological Forecasts" did. Personalization is a mirage, an effect, and a paradoxical one, insofar as it depends on, and drives, unprecedented forms of standardization and massification. In a narrow sense, algorithms produce this effect by making a series of automated predictions about the behavior of a given person—what content they are likely to engage with, what zip code they are likely to grocery shop in, what percentage of their student debt they are likely to be able to repay next month—based on their similarities to vast numbers of other people or, more precisely, to the data subjects to whom they are taken to be similar. Mass personalization did not eliminate the forms of typing that monopoly capital and mass society deployed, even if machine learning can refine and remix them. Mass personalization produced, and is producing, new social types that provide the objective basis for new right-wing movements.

Crucially, this is not just a question of "content," of filter bubbles and fake news. In the society of algorithms, these questions involve every aspect of social life. Personalized algorithms determine not just what memes or videos a person sees, but their access to credit and health care, how their employer schedules their work, and how the state surveils them. For algorithmic predictions to be any good requires a vast amount of training data; the greater the data monopoly a firm holds, the better its predictions will be, the more people who therefore use it, the more powerfully network effects will drive more people to use it, and the more the dominance of these few firms means you will *have* to do so, or face social deprivation or exclusion. The compulsivity of the social media user or gig worker is, like the compulsivity of their midcentury ancestor, rational. Or, pseudo-rational. Today we call this pleasurable coercion *optimization*.

If we widen the aperture, we quickly recognize that "data colonialism" is built on the material infrastructures and practices of historical colonialisms and exploitations. Any digital materialism, and any serious account of the socio-psychology of fascism today must reckon with personalization as an expression of these objective contexts. Personalization is a core process of contemporary social mediation. As such, it is implicated in forms of social domination.

Adorno warned, in "Types of Syndromes" that while he was sympathetic to the "humane" impulse of many psychologists to reject typology as a method, "individualism, opposed to inhuman pigeonholing, may ultimately become a mere ideological veil in a society which actually *is* inhuman and whose intrinsic tendency toward the 'subsumption' of everything shows it by the classification of people themselves."[22] Amid the crises of neoliberalism, the humane desire to reconstitute public discourse and common sense may obscure how profoundly the historical bases of publicity and commonness have been eroded. The increasing commodification of social life, the end of state regulation or subsidy of news, the replacement of knowledge production by profit seeking, society by network, democracy by markets, citizens by consumers— the trends driving radicalization within contemporary platforms are also examples of those platforms' working as designed. They cannot be simply wished away. Most online harm, the cybersecurity expert (and former chief security officer at Facebook) Alex Stamos recently argued, comes not from failures but abuse, or "the technically correct use of products . . . to cause harm."[23] While many citizens may find the activities of, say, Cambridge Analytica abhorrent, they are not aberrant. What the scandal around them revealed was the nature of Facebook's business as usual.

To speak of personalized media causing online radicalization is to engage in a form of technological determinism, which is always a form of fetishism—to grant technology the agency of humans and reduce humans to its objects. Like all fetishisms, it is also othering. To say that others are "being radicalized" by targeted propaganda is to assume the position of a "God's eye view," able to perceive foreign enemies and their domestic dupes—and, moreover, to set the parameters to legitimate political contention on this basis. As critical scholars of disinformation and propaganda have observed, these field-organizing concepts attempt to sidestep thorny questions. If a person showed up to a rally against abortion rights or in favor of reparations to Black Americans because they saw a Facebook "event" created by a "sock puppet" account created by Russia's Internet Research Agency, does that second fact invalidate their political claim?[24] The frame of "algorithmic radicalization" is a way of repressing insight into the systemic nature of current crises and one's own implication in them. If social scientists want to treat forms of new right-wing extremism as a social pathology, we cannot afford to dismiss its content simply as a "mistake." As Adorno remarked in his 1967 lecture on the subject: "By no means all elements of this ideology are simply untrue, but . . . true elements are also used in the service of an untrue ideology . . . the art of opposing this lies substantially in picking out the abuse of truth for untruth and resisting it."[25] For this, there is no easy "technofix."

At the same time, the point of demystifying popular forms of technological determinism is not to replace them with radical constructivism. As the media scholar John Durham Peters has observed, disparaging technological determinism has become a fetish itself.[26] Data-driven technologies do determine a great deal, too much, about human life today. That there were white supremacists in the United States before YouTube does not mean that YouTube has done nothing to and for white supremacy. The point is to figure out what. If technological determinism others the potential fascist, to obscure fascist potentials within neoliberalism, too radical constructivism sustains a fantasy of political agency in which it would be possible simply to walk away. Materialist analysis needs to develop an alternative to both approaches.

Here, we begin to see how Adorno's philosophy of method—his vision of critical typology as an immanent critique of social mediation—might reframe the fascism debates of the present. As many of the participants in these debates have observed, they have fundamentally focused on analogy—and, more specifically, the proper use of historical analogizing in public life. At stake is not only the legitimacy of making comparisons, but the pragmatic question of whether doing so in public might rouse ordinary citizens. My figure of the update—the AP 2.0—offers an alternative way of conceptualizing the difficulties that both analogy and continuity present—and, thus, hopefully moving the debate beyond its impasses.

Analogy is often characterized as way of claiming likeness. However, in so doing, it also instates difference. This has been a core complaint of critics of the fascism analogy. The gesture of picking one point of resemblance across time obscures others. So, for instance, comparing Trump to Hitler disavows Trump's similarity to more proximate figures. "'Whoever is not prepared to talk about Bushism should also remain silent about Trumpism.'—Max Horkheimer," the political theorist Corey Robin quipped.[27] While emphasizing continuities constitutes one strategy for avoiding these pitfalls, it risks rendering analytical categories static, taking the effects of historical processes as their cause. As a concept, the update offers an alternative to the opposition between analogy and continuity, by foregrounding change in continuity and vice versa. As Wendy Hui Kyong Chun has put it, systems must always be updating to remain the same.

In her book of that title, Chun argues that the systems update embodies the "twinning of habit and crisis" that characterizes network temporality.[28] For Chun, network temporality coincides with the time of neoliberalism. Networks are images of neoliberalism insofar as they eliminate society in favor of nodes and edges; they replace representation with a form of mapping, at once empirical and theoretical, produced by constant habitual action, driven by desire to connect. Within this context, the update becomes the paradoxical means by which technical and political systems persist precisely by being regularly eclipsed—as segments of new code are deployed to debug and patch their programs. "Nothing remains, even though everything does," Chun writes. "Program (x) + exception (x) = program $(x+1)$."[29] In the era of "new" or interactive "media," which constantly create crisis, insofar as they constantly elicit user action, this pattern becomes the norm. "A true sign of trouble is the lack of signs of updates."[30]

This situation reflects a distinctive mode of exercising power, with a distinct relationship to time. "If some things stay in place, it is not because they are unchanging and unchangeable, but rather because they are constantly implemented and enforced. What remains is not what is static, but instead what constantly repeats and is repeated."[31] For this reason, the update also creates distinctive possibilities for resistance. For Chun, the updates that stabilize a system by replacing the same with more of (almost) the same simultaneously introduce opportunities for change. However, this change must take place through tweaks, or the formation of new habits, rather than heroic acts. The significance of the update as a concept or figure for the AP 2.0 is twofold. It helps us cognize the forms of similarity and difference from historical fascism that contemporary right-wing movements exhibit. And it helps us conceive what kinds of agency are in fact available to respond to such movements from within a society of algorithms.

Both sides of the fascism debate implicitly embrace a model of political agency, and of the relationship between thinking and action, where an intellectual speaking in public makes their audience recognize *something* that they had not seen before. It is by making this thing conscious that critique inspires action. The update defines a different scope for both thinking and political work. If contemporary right-wing movements have updated potential fascism, stabilizing its overall dynamics by adjusting its features, analyses of fascist potentials must answer in kind. To prevent critical theory from becoming paranoid, projecting old preoccupations on, and bringing old methods to, the present, we must adjust its habits, too.

To frame what we are talking about when we talk about *The Authoritarian Personality* today as a problem of analogy is to suggest that we know what is being compared, more or less. The question becomes whether we, or they, are now as they were then. The answer becomes, always, yes and no; how analogy works is, it depends. To see the current conjuncture in terms of continuity is to presume we know what it involves, too. Now that the Trump era has officially ended, and yet stochastic acts of racist violence and the macabre strangeness of QAnon persist, it seems clear that there are still many social and psychological variables to map. Not all of them can be othered quite so easily as designations of "hate" and "extremism" attempt. Rather than telling us what the right today is like, an update of Adorno's critical typology would aim to tell us what it is, and why our systems continue to produce it.

FROM BOWLING ALONE TO POSTING ALONE

ANTON JÄGER

In June 2021, the Survey Center on American Life published a study tracking friendship patterns in the United States.[1] The report was anything but heartening. Registering a "friendship recession," the report noted how Americans were increasingly lonely and isolated: 12 percent of them now say they do not have close friendships, compared to 3 percent in 1990, and almost 50 percent said they lost contact with friends during the COVID-19 pandemic. The psychosomatic fallout was dire: heart disease, sleep disruptions, increased risk of Alzheimer's. The friendship recession has had potentially lethal effects.

The center's study offered a miniaturized model of a much broader process that has overtaken countries beyond the United States in the last thirty years. As the quintessential voluntary association, friendship circles stand in for other institutions in our collective life—unions, parties, clubs. In his memoirs, the French philosopher Jean-Claude Michéa said that one of the most disconcerting moments of his childhood was the day he discovered that there were people in the village who were not members of the Communist Party. "That seemed unimaginable," he recalled, as if those people "lived outside of society." Not coincidentally, in May 1968, French students sometimes compared the relationship of workers to the Communist Party with that of Christians to the Church. The Christians yearned for God, and the workers for revolution. Instead, "the Christians got the church, and the working class got the party."

The son of Communist parents, Michéa saw the party as an extension of a more primary social unit. Friendship patterns have always served as a useful indicator for broader social trends, and writers at *Vox* were quick to apply the data to political analysis.[2] The researchers invoked Hannah Arendt's dictum that friendship was the best antidote for authoritarianism. At the end of 1951's *Origins of Totalitarianism*, Arendt postulated that a new form of loneliness had overtaken Westerners in the twentieth century, leading them to join new secular cults to remedy their perdition. "What prepares men for totalitarian domination in the non-totalitarian world," she claimed, "is the fact that loneliness, once a borderline experience usually suffered in certain marginal social conditions like old age, has become an everyday experience." The conclusions were clear. As Americans become lonelier and more isolated in the new century, the same totalitarian temptation now lurks.

To social scientists, this refrain must sound tiredly familiar: it is the stock-in-trade of one of the classics of early-twenty-first-century political science, Robert Putnam's 2000 book *Bowling Alone: The Collapse and Revival of American Community*. That book noted a curious pattern: more and more Americans took up bowling toward the end of the twentieth century, but they increasingly undertook the activity *alone*, with the sudden decline of many bowling leagues the clearest explanation. Such a crisis was by no means limited to sports clubs. From churches to trade unions to shooting establishments to Masonic lodges, all experienced a dramatic contraction of membership in the 1980s and 1990s and began to disband. What remained was a wasteland of sociability.

Putnam surveyed a variety of causes for this great disengagement. The luring of the middle class from city centers to exurbs in the 1960s encouraged privacy. Removed from American cities, citizens ended up in suburbs designed mainly for motorists and without footpaths. Consumption was democratized in the postwar boom. People spent more time in their cars, a mobile privatization of public space. Corner stores were bulldozed in favor of shopping malls, and train tracks lost out to highways. With the steady entry of women into the labor market, voluntary associations lost a central base of support. Employees began working longer hours than their parents had and found little time for volunteering. Television locked citizens at home in the evening: the tombstone of postwar loneliness.

Putnam also debunked some powerful misconceptions about the crisis of civil society. The first was that the welfare state was the real culprit. The transfer of social services from the community to the state level, the argument ran, would threaten citizens' self-reliance. Putnam was skeptical: both strong (Scandinavia) and weak (United States) welfare states had seen a decline in civic capacity. In France and Belgium, a "red" civil society was even allowed to manage part of the social security budget. Battles over integration also proved an insufficient explanation: both Black and white Americans withdrew from clubs, while overall distrust between racial groups was declining.

Putnam had no use for panaceas either. Back in 2000, he had already presaged that the internet would offer a poor substitute for those old associations and reinforce antisocial tendencies. In 2020, holed up in his New Hampshire home during the pandemic, the social scientist added an afterword to a new edition of *Bowling Alone*. Its tone was characteristically melancholic: there was no "correlation between internet usage and civic engagement," while "cyberbalkanization" and not "digital democracy" was the future. The stock of "social capital" had not been replenished.

The weaknesses in this approach were already plain to see by the early 2000s. For one, *Bowling Alone* spent too little time investigating the structural transformation of its civil society—the rise of new NGOs as substitutes for mass membership organizations, the ascent of new sporting clubs, the revival of association in evangelical megachurches and schools.

Putnam also deployed a highly dubious notion of social capital. In this aspect, the book spoke to the market-friendly sensibilities of the late 1990s: civic ties were useful as a means for social mobility, not as expressions of collective power. They could adorn college applications or help people land trainee programs, not change nations or make revolutions. Such economism also explained a glaring gap in Putnam's book—the aggressive drop in union strength at the close of the century. In a book of more than five hundred pages, there was no index entry for "deindustrialization." With limited discussions of labor as well, *Bowling Alone* had little to say about how capital's offensive contributed to the decline of civil society—and how representative worker power was for civic life as a whole. The dwindling of union membership not only had dramatic consequences on the left but also disoriented the right—a side of the story that hardly appears in *Bowling Alone*.

Despite these evident faults, however, Putnam's book has stood the test of time. Statistics still point to a steady decline for many secular membership organizations. Despite growing public approval for union efforts, the U.S. unionization rate declined by 0.5 percentage points to a mere 10.3 percent in 2021, returning to its 2019 rate. The political developments of the last decade, from COVID-19 lockdowns to the escalating downsizing of classical parties, also validated Putnam's intuition. More than that, his book has now been used to explain the uncertainty of the Donald Trump years, in which the controlled demolition of the public sphere in the 1980s and 1990s drove a new form of resentment politics.

The so-called hyperpolitics of the 2010s also did not falsify Putnam's thesis. While the interactive internet has largely replaced the monological television set, the general crisis of belonging and place that the new media inaugurated has not abated. Even in a society ever more heavily politicized and riven by partisan conflict, the levers for collective action, from states to unions to community groups, remain brittle. Despite surges of militancy in some sectors, the "great resignation" ushered in by COVID's tight labor markets has not led to a politics of collective voice but rather to one of "individual exit," as the sociologist Daniel Zamora put it.[3] European unions have suffered a similar fate, losing members to self-employment. While Putnam noted the upswing in voter turnout in the 2020 election, this was "voting alone," vastly different from the organized bands that found their way to the ballot box in the nineteenth century.

There are both push and pull factors involved here. Since the 1980s, citizens have been actively ejected from associations through anti-union legislation or globalized labor markets. At the same time, passive alternatives to union and party power—cheap credit, self-help, cryptocurrency, online forums—have multiplied. The result is an increasingly capsular world where, as the commentator Matthew Yglesias warned, our home has become an ever greater source of comfort, allowing citizens to interact without ever leaving their house. "Sitting at home alone has become a lot less boring," he claims, ushering in a world where we could all "stream alone." The civic results will be dire.

Here, then, was the rational core of the Putnam thesis: far beyond the bowling alley, social life in the West had indeed become increasingly atomistic over the course of the 1980s and 1990s. The economic rationale for this restructuring was evident, and a Marxist interpretation proved a useful supplement to the Putnamite view: individualization was an imperative for capital, and collective life had to be diminished in order for the market to find new avenues for accumulation. By 1980, states could either cut ties with existing civil society organizations and let go of the inflationary threat or face ballooning public debt.

In the past thirty years, these pillars of party democracy have gradually eroded and been hollowed out. Two trends remain symptomatic of this process. The first is the declining membership of parties across the board, coupled with the increasing median ages of their members. On the left, the German Social Democratic Party went from one million members in 1986 to 660,000 in 2003; the Dutch Socialists went from 90,000 to 57,000. The French Communist Party tumbled from 632,000 members in 1978 to 210,000 in 1998; its Italian sister party went from 1,753,323 in the same year to 621,670 in 1998. The British Labour Party counted 675,906 members in 1978, falling to 200,000 in 2005.

While the trend remains more marked for the classical left—which has always relied more squarely on mass mobilization—it is no less striking on the right. The British Conservatives lost one million members between 1973 and 1994, while the French Gaullists dropped from 760,000 to 80,000. The Tories—the first mass party in European history—now receive more donations from dead members than from living ones, excluding their (now rebuffed) Russian oligarchs.

The United States has often served as a natural outlier to these European cases. Americans never had any true mass parties after 1896, the last major examples being the antislavery agitation of the 1850s and the rise of the original Populist movement in the 1880s and 1890s. After the People's Party's defeat—in the South with stuffed ballot boxes and guns, in the North by electoral inertia—America's bipartisan elites constructed a system that essentially neutered any third-party challengers. American parties nonetheless had a variety of bases and roots within society. These organizations effectively made, for example, the New Deal Democratic Party a mass party by proxy, tied to a hinterland of labor, union, and civil organizations that represented popular sectors. On both the left and the right, workers, employers, and shop owners have defended their interests in local clubs, committees, trade guilds, and syndicates.

This infrastructure was also a key launching pad for the revolts that detonated the civil rights revolution of the 1960s. Detroit labor leader Walter Reuther marched with Martin Luther King Jr early in the decade, while one of the foremost supporters of the 1963 March on Washington was A. Philip Randolph, the union radical who had begun by organizing workers under Jim Crow. The relation of these forces to the Democratic Party was always complicated and stepmotherly. Overall, however, they ensured that the party remained a "party of workers" without ever becoming a workers' party.

From the 1970s onward, this same landscape began to desiccate, both passively and actively. The Tocquevillian utopia portrayed by generations of European visitors to North America was replaced by the reality of bowling alone. Instead of mass membership organizations, voluntary associations increasingly turned to a nonprofit model to organize advocacy in Washington.

The shift to the nonprofit drastically changed the composition of these advocacy groups. Instead of relying on dues-paying members, they reached out to wealthy donors to fill their coffers. In a United States in which the government was increasingly giving up its redistributive role, this move created a natural constituency from new welfare recipients. The logic was self-evident: associations that practically operated as businesses but did not want to fulfill their tax obligations to the state saw an opportunity in the nonprofit model. The American political scientist Theda Skocpol casts them as "advocates without members": nonprofit organizations functioning as the lawyers of a mute defendant.

This has abiding consequences for our reading of the current moment. As the sociologist Dylan John Riley noted in 2012, "The contemporary politics of the advanced-capitalist world bears scant resemblance to that of the interwar period."[4] At the time, "populations organized themselves into mass parties of the left and right," not an era of "a crisis of politics as a form of human activity," where it was "unlikely that either [Eduard] Bernstein or Lenin can offer lessons directly applicable."

A view of today's politics as a direct product of the 2010s thus necessitates an emancipation from a series of frames we have inherited from an older age—and chief among them is a vision that sees our age as one of fascist resurgence. In the six years since Donald Trump's election, a waspish debate on whether he should be classified as a fascist has overtaken American and European academia. The January 6 riots proved shocking and unsurprising to these observers.

Putnam had already warned that social capital was never an unqualified good, and subsequent writers have regularly spoken about "bowling for fascism" as an adequate description of Nazi strength in the 1930s. As Putnam himself noted: "It was social capital, for example, that enabled Timothy McVeigh to bomb the Alfred P. Murrah Federal Building in Oklahoma City. McVeigh's network of friends, bound together by a norm of reciprocity, enabled him to do what he could not have done alone."

Ever since this warning, readings of Trumpism as heralding a new age of association have multiplied. In a recent paper, three social scientists have claimed that voters in flyover states have gone from bowling alone to "golfing with Trump," arguing that "the rise in votes for Trump has been the result of long-term economic and population decline in areas with strong social capital."[5] The conclusion seems inescapable: since Germans and Italians first went bowling for fascism in the 1930s, Trump is now deserving of the same term.

This reading has appeared in both prudent and imprudent versions. For academics such as the historian Timothy Snyder or the philosopher Jason Stanley, Trump and Jair Bolsonaro appear in perfect continuity with the strongmen of the 1930s, with the former president as "the original sin of American history in the post-slavery era, our closest brush with fascism so far." This was still "pre-fascism" to Snyder, and "for a coup to work in 2024, the breakers will require something that Trump never quite had: an angry minority, organized for nationwide violence, ready to add intimidation to an election. . . . Four years of amplifying a big lie just might get them this."[6] Journalists like Paul Mason and Sarah Kendzior have drafted texts instructing us in "how to stop fascism," while antifascist in chief Madeleine Albright published *Fascism: A Warning.*[7]

More subtle versions of this thesis are available. The writers Gabriel Winant and Alberto Toscano, for instance, have proposed a frame of "racial fascism" to read Trumpism on a broader timeline. In their view, white identity politics and fascism have always been interlinked. As Winant notes, "The primary factor of social cohesion in Tocqueville's America was nothing other than white supremacy. Given that this structure has endured . . . it makes little sense to imagine our society as formerly rich with association, but now bereft of it."[8] Referring to a 2020 incident in which a white couple in a Midwest gated neighborhood brandished weapons against Black Lives Matter protesters, Winant observed that, although "the gun-waving McCloskeys in St. Louis are presumably not members of the same kind of fraternal organizations that were popular in the 19th century . . . they are members of a homeowners' association," and they rely on "whiteness [as] a kind of inchoate associational gel, out of which a variety of more specific associations may grow in a given historical conjuncture." Hence, if Trump looks like a racial fascist, swims like a racial fascist, and quacks like a racial fascist, then he most probably is a racial fascist. Voices in high quarters have joined Winant on this point. In a September 1, 2022, speech, President Joe Biden castigated Trumpist Republicans as a "threat to the republic" and saw them tending toward "semi-fascism."

This reading now faces its own chorus of critics. To scholars like Riley and Corey Robin, Trumpism is better theorized as a form of Bonapartism that shares little with the "superpoliticized" fascisms of the interwar period. Above all, the two crucial preconditions for any fascist movement remain lacking: a prerevolutionary working class on the verge of power and a population's shared experience of total war, which would create a mass body. Fascism in power, they claim, has a hegemonic character and is not content to meddle on the margins. Just like pagans in a Christian world, they would have little purchase in the new order.

One of the most recurrent responses to this critique points at asymmetries between left and right. While the 1980s and 1990s saw a dramatic decline in left-wing civic life, the right has weathered Putnam's era fairly better, with police unions and neighborhood defense clubs surviving the neoliberal onslaught. Fascism, after all, is the mentality of rank-and-file police elevated to state policy, a type of countermobilization for a militant working class. It's no surprise that Marine Le Pen has received overwhelming support from French policemen.

A similar argument has been made for the British Conservative Party. This outfit has supposedly retained its bastions of strength across society in private schools, Oxbridge, and sporting clubs. As the journalist R. W. Johnson noted in 2015, "The atomisation and dispersal of the Labour vote" has led to "whole chunks falling off the side" to the Scottish National Party and the UK Independence Party, while "the institutional base of the Tory Party—private schools, the Anglican Church, wealthy housing districts, the expanded private sector and even home ownership in general—is as healthy as ever."[9] The result was "a one-sided decay of the class cleavage, with the Tories holding onto their old hinterland far better than Labour has." From Oxford's Bullingdon Club to the City guilds, conservative parties have managed to preserve their elite incubators and retain deeper pools of personnel.

It is difficult to see how such statements invalidate Putnam's original hypothesis, however. The metrics for social capital used by anti-Putnamites are, for instance, curiously indeterminate. Collapsing NGOs and homeowner associations into the same category as parties and unions tells us little about the relative strength of civil society institutions. Rather than civic fortresses, NGOs function as heads without bodies—finding it easier to attract donors rather than members. Even if Trump and other nationalists did rely on high associational density, this would not detract from the overall context of demobilization in which they operate. As islands in a minoritarian political system, they can retain power only by exploiting the Constitution's most antimajoritarian features. This is worlds removed from the anticonstitutionalism of the Nazis, who saw the Weimar Republic as born with socialist birthmarks. Fascist parties never were card-playing clubs, and golfing with Trump is a pallid replacement for fascist boot camps.

What about the right's other reserve institutions, from "whiteness" to homeownership? It is indeed true that many right-wing institutions have fared better in the neoliberal age. Yet an argument such as Winant's makes it unclear how we should distinguish between being white and being a member of the Ku Klux Klan, just like being an employer is hardly the same as paying dues to an employers' organization. In an age in which legal segregation has been abolished, racial status is barely the guarantee of civic inclusion that it used to be under the Jim Crow regime. And a homeowner's convention is no John Birch Society chapter, much like Bolsonaro's WhatsApp groups are not Benito Mussolini's *squadristi*.

The Ku Klux Klan and other white supremacist organizations might well count as the first properly fascist organizations in history. But as institutions, they have been on the wane for decades, and they hardly supply the shock troops for white supremacy that they did in the past. Militias like the Proud Boys and the boogaloo movement instead thrive as "individualized commandos," as Adam Tooze put it, far removed from the veterans that populated the Freikorps or the Black and Tans in the early 1920s. These were highly disciplined formations with direct experience of combat, not lumpen loners who drove out to protect car dealerships.

The same holds true in European cases. Giorgia Meloni's postfascist Brothers of Italy has grown precipitously in the last year and now presides over more than 100,000 members and leads a governing coalition. Still, it will not equal the 230,000 members that its predecessor, Italian Social Movement, had in the early 1960s, leading to a fascism with "no squads, uniforms or baseball bats."[10] Both numerically and qualitatively, the hard right remains a shadow of its former self—as does the center-right.

The Tory Primrose League was disbanded in 2004, and visitors to the British Isles will quickly be struck by the fading colors of the Conservative Club placards in the country's rural towns. Like the old Workingmen's Associations, these clubs scarcely function as mass mobilizers anymore, often appearing more like retirement homes (the median age of the Conservative Party membership is now estimated at seventy-two). As *New Left Review*'s Tariq Ali has noted, this self-immolation was itself a product of the neoliberal 1980s.[11] Margaret Thatcher's market reforms led to "the decimation of the Tories' provincial base of local gentry, bank managers and businessmen through the waves of trans-Atlantic acquisitions and privatizations she unleashed."

There are exceptions to this rule, of course—the anti-Obama Tea Party activists who met up in basements in the early 2010s, the Hindu youth clubs run by Narendra Modi's Bharatiya Janata Party, or the anti-immigrant "defense leagues" organized by the Scandinavian far right. In general, however, the civic pattern looks as disarticulated on the right as it does on the left.

Clear parallels between the current day and the 1930s need not be minimized, of course. Like Adolf Hitler and Mussolini, Trump was an eminently lazy regent, happy to leave his policies to specialists and high-ranking officials, while, like a digital Napoleon Bonaparte, he dabbles with the crowds. And like those leaders, Trump owes his power mainly to that group of compliant conservatives in the Republican Party who seek to deploy the far right as a wedge against rival oligarchs.

After that, the analogies quickly weaken. Trump built on the executive power unbound by Presidents Barack Obama and George W. Bush. Nor do Republicans owe their power to a mass movement in a tightly organized party. Senate minority leader Mitch McConnell regularly complains of slacking parliamentary discipline in the Majorie Taylor Greenes of the party. The Republicans thereby prefer to derive power from preexisting posts in the U.S. state, which has always exhibited aggressively elitist traits since the eighteenth century. Corey Robin rightly speaks of "gonzo constitutionalism": a merciless deployment of the most antidemocratic features of the U.S. political order.

The most unsettling fact about MAGA Republicanism is, as Robin writes, that it does not depend "upon the bogeymen of democracy—demagoguery, populism, or the masses—but upon the constitutional mainstays we learned about in high-school civics."[12] Only in 2004 did the GOP win the presidential election with a popular majority, when Bush Jr. took a narrow 50.7 percent of the vote. Otherwise, the Republican Party strengthened its grip on the state apparatus mainly through minority mechanisms: appointing judges to the Supreme Court, gerrymandering, and filibustering.

Rather than a fascist threat, the party offers a pared-down oligarchy—the wielding of the last antimajoritarian levers in the American ancien régime. "Nationalizing our elections is just a multi-decade Democratic Party goal in constant search of a justification," McConnell stated in Congress last year, openly admitting that low turnout is a boon to his party.[13] "Semi-fascism" might be a rhetorically grateful term for this behavior—but at the end of the day, not everything that is bad is the same.

In the past ten years, pundits across the political spectrum have scouted for technical fixes for Putnam's crisis. Undoubtedly the most appealing of these has been the new online world. This is an old story: two decades ago, when Putnam published his book, theorists were already wondering whether the internet's new global connectivity, conceived in the bosom of the American security state, could remake society. Today, the children of the internet retain little faith in Twitter or TikTok's capacity for good, much like Putnam doubted that online engagement could replace older civic mores. This skepticism is mirrored by a confusion about the internet's supposed political potential. If the Scylla of social media analysis was the naïve utopianism of the early 2000s, its Charybdis is our current digital pessimism, which sees so much of the world's problems—from political polarization to sexual impotence to declining literacy rates—as both the causes and consequences of being "too online."

Clearly, the internet becomes comprehensible only in the world of the lonely bowler. Online culture thrives on the atomization that the neoliberal offensive has inflicted on society—there is now ample research showing positive correlations between declining civic commitment and broadband access. At the same time, the internet accelerates and entrenches social atomization. The exit and entry costs of this new, simulated civil society are extremely low, and the stigma of leaving a Facebook group or a Twitter subculture is incomparable to being forced to move out of a neighborhood because a worker scabbed during a strike.

The extreme marketization of Putnam's 1980s and 1990s also made the world vulnerable to the perils of social media. The dissolution of voluntary organizations, the decline of Fordist job stability, the death of religious life, the evaporation of amateur athletic associations, the "dissolution of the masses," and the rise of a multitudinous crowd of individuals were all forces that generated the demand for social media long before there was a product like Facebook or Instagram. Social media could grow only in a void that was not of its own making.

The internet is thus best read as a *Pharmakon*—a Greek noun that denotes both a means of remedy and a poison, a supposed antidote that can only exacerbate the disease. This also poses sensitive issues for the right, particularly after European and American capitals became increasingly divided in the preceding decades. As Paul Heideman has noted about the GOP in *Catalyst*, the assault on working-class organizations of the 1980s removed the external sources of discipline that once grouped capitalists together and imposed a common policy agenda.[14]

Without this opponent, internal fractures are likely to widen. With the compounding "weakening of the parties since the 1970s, and the political disorganization of corporate America since the 1980s," it is, as the academic Cathie Jo Martin has argued, "much harder for U.S. employers to think about their collective long-term interests." And rather than a process of realignment in which Republicans have seized working-class votes, it is the ruthless march of "dealignment" that drives our age of political tumult.

Capital's disorganization provides a much more rewarding frame for the "populist explosion" than ahistorical references to the authoritarianism of the 1930s. The German author Heinrich Geiselberger has noted how, without "the enemies of socialism," the right "can only evoke its specter." Geiselberger, together with the left-wing intellectual Gáspár Miklós Tamás, prefers to speak of post-fascism: an attempt to make citizenship less universal and confine it to national borders, but without the organizational clout that fascists demonstrated in the twentieth century. The new right is therefore "atomised, volatile, swarm-like, with porous borders between gravity and earnestness, sincerity and irony."

Above all, the new politics is consistently informal. The mob that expressed unconditional support for Trump on January 6 does not even have membership lists. QAnon and the antilockdown movement are a subculture that thrives mostly on blogs, Instagram, and Facebook groups. There are, of course, more and less prominent QAnon figures—influencers, so to speak. Yet their leadership is not official or mandated by votes. Rather than a militarily drilled mass, we see a roving swarm, incited by a clique of self-selected activists.

This informality also manifests itself economically. In the past year, Trump extorted thousands of dollars from his followers and continued to rake in funds, without ever building a clear party structure. As early as 1920, the sociologist Max Weber noted how charismatic leaders did not pay their followers and backers with fixed salaries, but rather worked through "donations, booty or bequests."[15] Unsurprisingly, charismatic leadership was also a thoroughly unstable mode of rule: succession to the throne could not simply be guaranteed for the mob, which would now have to look for its next redeemer.

What would a viable alternative to this fascist frame look like? As Riley suggests, a far more powerful precedent for our situation can be found in Karl Marx's account of the 1848 revolution. Early that year, instead of giving in to this unrest, Napoleon III gathered an apathetic peasant population and ordered them to quell the revolution. Marx described these French peasants as a "sack of potatoes" whose "identity of their interests fosters no community spirit, no national association and no political organization." And since the peasants could not represent themselves, "they must be represented"—in this case by a king.

Rather than a politics pitting workers against bosses, structured by the capital-labor opposition, Bonaparte's was a politics of debtors and creditors—another shared feature with the 2010s, in which private debts transferred onto public accounts fueled the American and European debt crises. Bonaparte's peasants focused on circulation and taxes rather than on production. Instead of peering aimlessly at the 1930s, we would have to look at a much older, primal age of democracy for suitable parallels with our populist era.

Yet the fascist frame also carries an even graver risk: an overestimation of socialist strength. Fascism implies a popular front and strategic alliances with liberalism, including no-strike pledges. Rather than force focus, the fascist frame will distract and confuse us from the crisis of political engagement so typical of the twenty-first century. Putnam was right, but for the wrong reasons: associationism matters for democracy, but it hardly matters to capital—and might even threaten it. In the absence of this threat, both on left and right, we will keep on bowling alone.

MEN IN DARK TIMES

*How Hannah Arendt's Fans Misread
the Post-Truth Presidency*

REBECCA PANOVKA

In a 1959 letter to her friend Mary McCarthy, Hannah Arendt paused to commiserate on a harrowing experience they had in common: having their writing fact-checked by *The New Yorker*. In her previous correspondence, McCarthy had mused that the magazine's checking department was "invented by some personal Prosecutor of mine to shatter the morale," and Arendt shared her frustration. Fact-checking, she replied, was a "kind of torture," a "rigmarole," and "one of the many forms in which the would-be writers persecute the writer." Arendt's opposition to the practice of fact-checking ran deeper than personal irritation. Throughout her work, she was critical of the infiltration of scientific terminology and methods into all aspects of human life. Couching an argument in language that sounded scientific, she thought, was a way of claiming the ability to know or predict things that could never be predicted or known. Fact-checking was a part of that larger trend: the practice, she wrote to McCarthy, was a form of "phony scientificality."

This Arendt—snide, melodramatic, disdainful of the concept of factual verification—is not quite the picture that emerged after the election of Donald Trump, when she was rebranded as something of a patron saint of facts. "Welcome to the post-truth presidency," the *Washington Post* opinion editor Ruth Marcus wrote, crediting Arendt as the thinker who had "presciently explained the basis for this phenomenon." Michiko Kakutani, in an article titled "The Death of Truth: How We Gave Up on Facts and Ended Up with Trump," likewise cast Arendt as a prophet whose "words increasingly sound less like a dispatch from another century than a chilling description of the political and cultural landscape we inhabit today." "How Hannah Arendt's Classic Work on Totalitarianism Illuminates Today's America," ran a headline in *The Washington Post*. In Arendt's work, the scholar Richard Bernstein declared in *The New York Times*, "we can hear not only a critique of the horrors of 20th-century totalitarianism, but also a warning about forces pervading the politics of the United States and Europe today." The think pieces proliferated, reciting the same handful of Arendt quotations from her 1967 *New Yorker* essay "Truth and Politics" and her 1951 opus *The Origins of Totalitarianism*. Soon enough, Amazon sold out of *Origins*. "How could such a book speak so powerfully to our present moment?" asks a blurb at the top of its product page.

Arendt was deemed relevant when Trump was elected, relevant when he refused to wear a mask, relevant even in his defeat—with each successive crisis cast as confirmation of the predictions extrapolated from her prose. "As Congress is set to affirm the outcome of the 2020 presidential election," wrote the *Times* columnist Thomas Edsall, "the words of Hannah Arendt, who fled Nazi Germany after being arrested in 1933, acquire new relevance." In a *New York Times Magazine* cover story following the January 6 Capitol riot, the historian Timothy Snyder invoked Arendt to place Trump's "big lie"—that he had won the election—on a spectrum with Hitler's "big lies" that Jews ran the world and had sabotaged Germany during World War I. "Post-truth is pre-fascism," Snyder wrote, "and Trump has been our post-truth president."

As the scholar Samuel Moyn has observed, Arendt was "the most used and abused philosophical source to interpret [Trump's] presidency." Quoting Arendt, he argued, "gave many a think piece the patina of a famous name and pseudo-profundity." In the slew of essays preaching the Arendt gospel, the content of her theories has often seemed extraneous—too elaborate to summarize in a paragraph or two, and ultimately unnecessary to the obvious argument that it is danger-ous for a sitting president to spout incorrect information. But though Arendt is not needed for a straightforward condemnation of Trump's lies, her thinking is useful in another, perhaps counterintuitive sense: as a reminder to look beyond Trump and his outlandish and constantly fact-checked distortions, and to think more carefully about the long-standing tradition of lies in American politics.

The Origins of Totalitarianism has a somewhat misleading title, tacked on only after the text was almost complete. (While she was draft-ing the manuscript, Arendt referred to it as "the imperialism-book.") Written in the years after World War II, *Origins* can be understood as an attempt to make sense of Hitler by tracing the "subterranean trends" that primed Europe for totalitarian rule. But it is a book in three parts, and the first two do not directly concern the rise of totalitarian lead-ers; they are about anti-Semitism and imperialism in the century pre-ceding the Third Reich. Arendt's most popular quotations come from the third part, "Totalitarianism," which discusses the regimes of Hitler and Stalin. But even here, her analysis is difficult to apply to Trump. As Arendt defines it, totalitarianism attempts to "transform the nature of man." It is a "perpetual motion" machine, an engine that must exert absolute control over its subjects and requires for that control a state of constant expansion. "Wherever it rose to power," she writes, totalitari-anism "destroyed all social, legal and political traditions of the country" and "supplanted the party system, not by one-party dictatorships, but by a mass movement." Totalitarianism always "shifted the center of power from the army to the police, and established a foreign policy openly directed toward world domination."

Origins evangelists, to be fair, do not tend to claim that the United States lapsed into a totalitarian dictatorship under Trump—only that Trump's brand of politics displays some of the warning signs Arendt identified. ("Post-truth" is "pre-fascism," not full-blown fascism.) And some of Arendt's descriptions of totalitarian subjects as vulnerable to conspiratorial thinking do bear an uncanny resemblance to a liberal car-icature of Trump's supporters. Take this passage, one of the most fre-quently quoted in contemporary pieces about Arendt:

> The ideal subject of totalitarian rule is not the convinced Nazi
> or the convinced Communist, but people for whom the dis-
> tinction between fact and fiction (*i.e.,* the reality of experience)
> and the distinction between true and false (*i.e.,* the standards of
> thought) no longer exist.

To Arendt, the "ideal subject" for a regime intending to exercise
totalizing control is one who does not ask questions. A thinking subject,
even one sympathetic to the aims of the movement, can always dissent.
(Arendt's mentor and onetime lover, Martin Heidegger, was a "convinced Nazi," an intellectual who supported the rise of the Third Reich,
but not an ideal subject once the regime came to power: he publicly criticized Hitler's government for betraying the "inner truth and greatness"
of the movement.) When Arendt claims that totalitarianism transforms
human nature, what she means is that a regime can establish absolute
control only by dissolving its subjects into something like a single organism, ridding individuals of the capacity for independent thought.

In interwar Europe, Arendt believed, social atomization and the
breakdown of communal bonds had engendered a pervasive loneliness.
Ideology is tempting to lonely minds, she writes, because it knits the
arbitrariness that characterizes modern life into a single, fully explained
narrative, promising to "eliminate coincidences by inventing an all-
embracing omnipotence which is supposed to be at the root of every
accident." Where reality feels fragile and contingent, totalitarian movements can "conjure up a lying world of consistency which is more adequate to the needs of the human mind than reality itself."

Arendt saw Nazism and communism as endeavoring to fashion
history into a science, something that acts according to universal laws
and can therefore be predicted. A totalitarian leader, she writes, styles
himself as the fulfillment of historical destiny and therefore its oracle.
She cites Hitler's announcement to the Reichstag in January 1939: "I
want today once again to make a prophecy," he said. "In case the Jewish financiers...succeed once more in hurling the peoples into a world
war, the result will be...the annihilation of the Jewish race in Europe."
What Hitler means, according to Arendt, is: "I intend to make war and

I intend to kill the Jews of Europe." Totalitarianism voids the distinction between a prophecy and a declaration of intent. As Arendt puts it, once a totalitarian movement has seized power, "all debate about the truth or falsity of a totalitarian dictator's prediction is as weird as arguing with a potential murderer about whether his future victim is dead or alive." Just as the murderer can kill his victim to substantiate his claim, a government with total control can, in theory, ensure the accuracy of its predictions.

But total control is a chimera—a prediction about human affairs can be infallible only in a world expunged of all human agency—so its pursuit necessarily culminates in both outward aggression and internal terror. The organization of a totalitarian regime—its concentric circles of power, its bureaucratic systems, its elevated police force, its plans for world conquest—is designed to create "a society whose members act and react according to the rules of a fictitious world." For adherents of the totalitarian movement, its lies grow impossible to challenge, "as real and untouchable an element in their lives as the rules of arithmetic"—and even the leaders "are convinced that they must follow consistently the fiction and the rules of the fictitious world which were laid down during their struggle for power." According to Arendt, Hitler felt compelled to play along with his predictions, following conspiracies to their inevitable conclusions, often against reason and even self-interest; he was not content to lie without reorganizing the actual world accordingly.

To accuse Trump of anything so sophisticated is to misread his lies altogether. From the start, Trump's lies were incidental and reactive, unconstrained by the need for coherence or the pressure to position himself as the culmination of historical trends. Though he retweeted QAnon-linked accounts, he did not explicitly endorse the conspiracy, which he could have harnessed to achieve the kind of "lying world of consistency" Arendt outlines. He invented facts as he needed them, flooding the field with misinformation. He tossed off a lie, and by the time the media had scrambled to fact-check him, he had already moved on to the next one. For the most part, his supporters were undeterred when his lies were unveiled, because they understood he was saying whatever was advantageous, not speaking as an absolute authority. In the end, Trump's lies were less grand theory than self-aggrandizement—corporate bluster intended to artificially boost his own stock. He tended to inflate the numbers: how much money he was worth, how many people had attended his inauguration, how many votes he had received.

Mapping Arendt's framework onto Trump obscures the way his lies operated, and what they were: not totalitarian world building so much as boardroom bullshit. Far from resorting to terror, Trump made only paltry efforts to convert his lies into action. He antagonized the press but never made moves to dismantle it. Even when he contested the 2020 election result, he made his case through lies and lawyers rather than recruiting the kind of organized military force that might have executed a bona fide coup. On January 6, there was no serviceable plan because Trump never made the defining totalitarian effort to bend reality to his fictional world. His lies never progressed beyond the singular goal of saving face.

In the oft quoted "Truth and Politics," Arendt is not ringing alarm bells at the blurring of facts and falsehoods in the political realm; she is acknowledging that lies have always been a part of politics. "The story of the conflict between truth and politics is an old and complicated one," she writes, "and nothing would be gained by simplification or moral denunciation." Though it is placed in conversation with *Origins*, "Truth and Politics" was written decades after the war and has relatively little to do with totalitarianism. Its immediate subtext is Arendt's perception of herself as a besieged truth teller.

In 1963, two years after she traveled to Israel to cover the trial of Adolf Eichmann for *The New Yorker*, Arendt ignited a controversy with the publication of *Eichmann in Jerusalem*. Mossad operatives had captured Eichmann and flown him to Jerusalem for prosecution, but now, Arendt was appalled to discover, the Israeli government displayed little interest in passing accurate judgment on the man or his crimes. Eichmann was one of the organizers of the Final Solution, but Arendt saw that he did not come across as a monster with evil designs; he seemed to her like an ordinary bureaucrat. Evil, she determined, could be carried out in mundane, boring ways, not by people with sadistic intentions, but by those who drifted along, forgetting to think about what they were doing. An evildoer in the Eichmann mold was a person who had neglected to judge for himself, failing to evaluate the rightness or wrongness of the systems he helped to invent. In demonizing Eichmann, the Israelis had failed to recognize "the banality of evil."

Many Jewish observers were offended by what they saw as Arendt's sympathetic portrayal of Eichmann and unsympathetic portrayal of the heads of the Jewish Councils, the leaders who she felt could have done more in the face of impending disaster. Her thesis, interpreted by some as a defense of Eichmann, was attacked, and her assertion that the councils had cooperated with the Nazis treated as a blasphemous lie. Scores of pieces (and even a book) were written to fact-check and refute her claims, and Arendt, together with McCarthy and Daniel Bell, wrote several essays refuting those refutations.

Occasioned by the outcry, "Truth and Politics" was Arendt's attempt to work through her indignation. Despite the animus that undergirds it, the essay provides a systematic and impersonal account of the way truth and lies operate in the political arena. Arendt first distinguishes rational truth (mathematical truth, philosophical truth—anything that can be proven by axiom) from factual truth. The difference here is between a statement like "$2 + 2 = 4$" and one like "It rained in Reykjavík yesterday." Whereas rational truth *must* be the case, Arendt writes, "facts have no conclusive reason whatever for being what they are." Believing them requires a degree of trust in witnesses, historians, and scientists. If rational truth provides the basis for philosophical speculation, then facts perform an analogous role for political thought. When we enter the public sphere to debate a policy or decision, proper participation is possible only if we rely on a shared set of facts.

Because factual truth is not self-evident, it is "easy to discredit factual truth as just another opinion." In a war of opinion against opinion, lies—which are crafted to maximize credibility and reduce the appearance of arbitrariness—carry the advantage. When the truth teller confronts the liar, the real facts will often sound paltry, incidental, random; the liar "will usually have plausibility on his side." If the truth sounds implausible, it is vulnerable to denialism and willful ignorance, and Arendt is particularly concerned with facts that are publicly known but treated as secrets. Though she brings up Hitler and Stalin to note that under their regimes it was taboo to discuss concentration camps, the phenomenon she describes is not limited to totalitarianism. She writes, "Contemporary history is full of instances in which tellers of factual truth were felt to be more dangerous, and even more hostile, than the real opponents." The truth-degrading culprits she points to in the essay are not Hitler and Goebbels but Charles de Gaulle and Konrad Adenauer.

The postwar European governments, Arendt holds, were built on myths—on "such evident non-facts as that France belongs among the victors of the last war and hence is one of the great powers," and that the "barbarism of National Socialism had affected only a relatively small percentage of the country." These untruths are evidence of what Arendt calls "image-making." Image-making goes beyond altering facts and skewing perceptions, and instead offers entirely new narratives constructed to replace reality wholesale. According to Arendt, modern political lies are "so big that they require a complete rearrangement of the whole factual texture." Politicians must create a new reality into which their lies "will fit without seam, crack, or fissure, exactly as the facts fitted into their own original context." Though this language is reminiscent of the "lying world" from *Origins,* Arendt is referring here to the ordinary operations of modern governments, not the state of exception in Nazi Germany. In *Origins,* Arendt asserted that totalitarian governments replaced the real world with a fictional world, but "Truth and Politics" clarifies that this kind of image-making does not, on its own, amount to totalitarianism: liberal democracies are implicated in the same game of defactualization.

For Arendt, power is ultimately incapable of producing an adequate substitute for factual reality. Even totalitarian regimes are unable to render their lies airtight or their narratives all-encompassing. As facts change and history progresses, the totalizing system struggles to adapt to new data, and those who believe the official story notice as inconsistencies develop. The sense of a shifting reality gives rise to a "trembling, wobbling" feeling; eventually, it amounts to a disorientation that Arendt compares to the effects of brainwashing. After victims of brainwashing have been reacquainted with reality, she writes, they tend to experience "a peculiar kind of cynicism—an absolute refusal to believe in the truth of anything, no matter how well this truth may be established." Once a regime's lies are unveiled, its subjects become deeply distrustful, incapable of distinguishing between truth and lies.

A brainwashing victim, by this account, looks something like the "ideal subject" of totalitarian rule. In another ubiquitously cited passage, she writes,

> The result of a consistent and total substitution of lies for factual truth is not that the lies will now be accepted as truth, and that the truth be defamed as lies, but that the sense by which we take our bearings in the real world—and the category of truth vs. falsehood is among the mental means to this end—is being destroyed.

It is easy to gloss over the words "consistent" and "total" and conflate the kind of lie Arendt describes with the Trump administration's "alternative facts." But by definition, alternative facts cannot be total: the term itself implies conflicting data. In "Truth and Politics," Arendt is not warning about liars in Washington. She is worried, rather, about a state of affairs in which a singular, unquestioned image has been installed in place of reality, and in which, as cracks begin to appear, those who placed their faith in authority have no one left to trust—a state of affairs, as she made clear, that cannot coexist with a free and combative press.

"Truth and Politics" engages with American politics only obliquely, but a few years later, Arendt had the opportunity to retrofit her theory of image-making to the United States in an essay for *The New York Review of Books*. In "Lying in Politics," which recycles much of the material from "Truth and Politics," Arendt discusses the trove of lies revealed by the Pentagon Papers. She identifies a class of leaders in Washington who, like the totalitarians, had appropriated the language and logic of science to promote a fraudulent image. Borrowing the journalist Neil Sheehan's term, she calls these men "the problem-solvers." Administrators such as Secretary of Defense Robert McNamara, she writes, "were eager to find formulae, preferably expressed in a pseudo-mathematical language, which would unify the most disparate phenomena with which reality presented them," weaving chaos into order, reality into fiction. The problem-solvers were familiar to Arendt—allergic to contingency, hungry instead for consistent systems. She detects in them a "disdain for facts, and the accidental character of those facts." Rather, she writes, "they were eager to discover *laws* by which to explain and predict political and historical facts as though they were as necessary, and thus as reliable, as the physicists once believed natural phenomena to be."

According to Arendt, the problem-solvers saw politics as "a variety of public relations" and "lied not so much for their country, certainly not for their country's survival, which was never at stake, as for its 'image.'" She quotes Assistant Secretary of Defense John McNaughton, who was revealed in the Pentagon Papers to have summarized the principal American military aim in Vietnam as follows: "To avoid humiliating defeat (to our reputation ...)." For the government, defeat was not as problematic as the appearance of defeat. What the papers show, Arendt writes, is that the ultimate goal of the Vietnam War was not power or profit or any specific interest at all. There *was* no ultimate goal to which appearing as the "greatest power in the world" was proximate: "The goal was the image itself." Rather than striving for world conquest, the American government had set its sights on victory over the hearts and minds of the world's people. "Image-making as global policy," she writes, "is indeed something new in the huge arsenal of human follies recorded in history." For Arendt, Vietnam was yet another instance in which glorified bureaucrats failed to think for themselves. "The problem-solvers did not *judge*," she writes, "they calculated." Like Eichmann, they planned and executed a strategy without stopping to consider its rightness or wrongness.

Yet even in its most despicable crimes, Arendt clarified multiple times, the American government had not lapsed into totalitarianism. In the case of the Vietnam War, one mitigating factor was a strong investigative press, which prevented the problem-solvers' image from attaining a hegemonic hold on the public. "In the Pentagon Papers, we deal with people who did their utmost to win the minds of the people," she concludes, "but since they labored in a free country where all kinds of information were available, they never really succeeded." Arendt contends (somewhat controversially) that the Pentagon Papers were full of facts that had already been reported—secrets and lies that had been leaked years earlier. She argues, as she had in "Truth and Politics," that political participation depends on access to unmanipulated information. The Pentagon Papers demonstrated that the American press had protected that right, supplying the factual conditions for a free and informed debate about Vietnam.

Under Arendt's analysis, the terms of the post-2016 conversation about truth and lies grow slippery. If politicians have always lied, and the American government has a well-established habit of attempting to deceive its citizens, what is new about "post-truth"? Trump's hatred for reporters was hardly novel. (Arendt cites a rumor that the Nixon administration planned a campaign to "destroy the 'credibility' of the press before the 1972 Presidential election," which she deems "quite in line with the public relations mentality.") What was distinct, perhaps, was the way reporters responded to Trump's lies. Throughout the Trump administration, the press maintained an antagonistic pose, aggressively fact-checking the President. His narrative never had the chance to become monolithic, because an alternative story was always available.

Trump's lies were not more convincing than those of other presidents; they opened the curtain on an epistemic crisis because they were less convincing, more flagrant. Trump was often accused of "saying the quiet part out loud"—revealing the open secrets politicians generally avoid acknowledging. The rhetorical effectiveness of Trump's taboo breaking proved the same thing Arendt gleaned from the Pentagon Papers: the American people already know their politicians aren't telling them the truth. Trump did not need to create a make-believe world, because he appealed to those who had already lost confidence in the official representations of American political reality.

For Arendt, real government conspiracies are what give rise to outlandish conspiracy theories—it is fraudulent image-making, perpetrated by authority, that degrades the ability of the public to judge the difference between fact and fiction. Jerome Kohn, Arendt's longtime assistant and literary trustee, once argued that the lies of the George W. Bush administration echoed Arendt's warnings. The administration had forged documents stating that Saddam Hussein was in the process of obtaining yellowcake uranium, and the press had dutifully printed the lie. The absence of dissent to the passing of the Patriot Act and the invasion of Iraq afforded the government the opportunity to craft a singular fiction—exactly the kind of unquestioned image-making Arendt feared. Kohn pointed to a *New York Times Magazine* report by Ron Suskind in which an anonymous aide redressed the journalist for being insufficiently attuned to the way truth operates in the American empire. The aide, who is widely believed, despite his denials, to be Karl Rove, said that Suskind and his ilk were "in what we call the reality-based community," meaning they believed "that solutions emerge from your judicious study of discernible reality." For the aide, discernible reality was beside the point. "That's not the way the world really works anymore," he said. "We're an empire now, and when we act, we create our own reality."

Since Arendt's time, Kohn said, the United States had witnessed "a slide from a lot of lying for political expediency into domination by an ideology and the kind of worship of logical consistency that brings that ideology to the public." Though it was not overwritten with an officially sanctioned ideological system like Nazism or communism, the status quo of American politics in the aughts was not devoid of ideology. The Iraq War represented its own ideological project, an effort to export and enforce liberal democracy as the natural and inevitable end point of history. And in the half century since Arendt wrote "Lying in Politics," Washington largely continued its "image-making as global policy," checked only to varying degrees by the press.

Trump's loudest critics spent his time in office wringing their hands over "alternative facts," worshipping fact-checkers, and fetishizing factual truth—declaiming Trump as an exception and yearning for a return to normal. But amid the criticism, they did little to examine the status of truth under previous administrations. Trump was not the first liar in the Oval Office, and unlike some of his predecessors, he was fiercely challenged by an adversarial press and an opposition party keen to decry his every statement. Rather than a calculating liar with an all-embracing plan, Trump was an opportunist able to exploit a lack of public trust in the institutions charged with disseminating facts. The journalists who nitpicked his statements managed only to preach to the proverbial choir, while his most ardent supporters shrugged off authoritative facts altogether, convinced that the media was aligned with the "deep state." The press, after all, had already proved itself unequipped to dismantle the fictional reality constructed by the architects of American empire.

In her preface to the third edition of *Origins,* Arendt cautioned against prematurely crying totalitarianism in a U.S. context. Arendt had watched as protesters hurled accusations of fascism at the Johnson administration, and she thought they were preoccupied with the wrong war. In her view, the United States was closer to repeating the sins of British imperialism, but this "unhappy relevance," she warned, should not be taken to imply that history would inevitably repeat itself. To respect human freedom is to acknowledge that history does not operate according to scientific laws: "No matter how much we may be capable of learning from the past," she writes, "it will not enable us to know the future."

GENDER AND THE RADICAL RIGHT'S DEPARTURES FROM FASCISM

UDI GREENBERG

When Giorgia Meloni, the Italian far-right firebrand, concluded her election campaign on September 25, 2022, her closing pitch was revealing. Rather than speaking on immigration or economics, she posted a video of herself on Tiktok, holding two melons in front of her chest and winking at the camera. With crude sexual undertones (Meloni in Italian is slang for "breasts"), the video exemplified the radical right's political messaging. On the one hand, it sought to draw attention to Meloni's uniqueness as a female political leader (and a proud single mother at that). Her party, the Brothers of Italy, was the only major force with a woman at its head, and Meloni has often noted that it elevated women candidates across the country. On the other hand, the video is dripping with sexism. Meloni's wink was intended to convey irony, but the image reduced the Italian leader to her function as a sexual object; Meloni is also a vocal opponent of feminism.[1] This cocktail—celebrating women's participation in public affairs while reinforcing an antifeminist message—is now typical for the radical right in Europe. At least in the continent's central and western parts, what some scholars call "femonationalism" has become the mainstream of the right's agenda.[2]

Scholars have increasingly recognized how central conceptions of gender and sexuality are for today's radical right. Policies regarding reproduction, family structures, and gender education take much space in right-wing parties' platforms, and imagery that focuses on gender norms and sexuality is central to their political mobilization.[3] But when debating the links between the contemporary radical right and fascism, gender has received relatively scant attention. Commentators note the persistence of antifeminism and heteronormativity, but mostly focus on similarities and divergences in the right's thinking about immigration, pluralism, economics, or race.[4] In what follows, I seek to briefly chart the evolution of the European far right's thinking about gender and sexuality. I argue that despite some meaningful continuities with the fascist past, especially in understanding reproduction, the contemporary radical right has developed a profoundly nonfascist vision of gender norms. In fact, understanding the far right's thinking on the roles of men and women can help illuminate how far it has broken with fascist thinking on other issues, especially labor and militarism. This, in turn, may help explain a major puzzle surrounding the contemporary right: its sustained electoral expansion, even at moments in which some economic benchmarks (such as unemployment rates) seem to improve.

AT FIRST GLANCE, it may seem like European fascism and the contemporary radical right's approach to gender and sexuality are eerily similar. Both view reproduction as a communal matter, part of the collective body's quest to preserve and increase its strength. As is well known, fascist and semi-fascist regimes based much of their legitimacy on promises to increase the nation's birthrates, the decline of which they often attributed to the rise of feminism and sexual liberation movements. Many of their welfare programs, such as reduced taxation loans to families with young children, were designed to encourage the departure of women from the workforce to raise as many children as possible. In some cases, regimes were so anxious to accelerate their racist natalism that they were ready to compromise the institution of marriage. Christian conservatives, who profusely praised fascist antifeminism, grumbled about the Third Reich's active encouragement of premarital sex or Vichy's granting of rights to children born out of wedlock. This fixation on reproduction was also one explanation for fascist regimes' homophobia and opposition to contraception and abortion (though in these they were of course hardly unique). As Mussolini famously put it, "The most fundamental, essential element of the political, and therefore economic, and moral, influence of a nation lies in its demographic strength."[5]

A similar understanding of reproduction is very much central to the contemporary radical right. In speeches and platforms, its leaders routinely bemoan Europe's declining birthrates, promising a reversal with targeted welfare policies, such as interest-free loans to couples with young children. France's National Front (renamed National Rally in 2018) was perhaps most ambitious in this regard, offering in 2017 to provide minimum wage and pensions for stay-at-home mothers.[6] Hungary under Viktor Orbán's Fidesz Party similarly provided gifts, housing, and tax emptions for mothers of multiple children.[7] Many claim that reproduction is the key to reducing immigration, the right's most galvanizing political issue. The German Alternative for Germany (AfD) 2017 platform, for example, outlined its family policy under the title "larger families instead of mass immigration," claiming that only a surge in births would allow the German economy to survive without depending on "foreign" labor.[8] The radical right also shares with its interwar predecessors the conviction that declining birthrates are the result of antipatriarchal ideologies, especially feminism. The right-wing German sociologist Gabriele Kuby proclaimed that women who choose to stay home to focus on child-rearing should gain the same respect as their working counterparts.[9] Natalism is also part of the logic that informs the radical right's assault on what its leaders call "gender ideology," by which they mean any questioning of heteronormativity, whether in academic gender studies or campaigns for LGBTQ+ rights.[10] As the Italian Meloni explained in a fiery 2019 speech to the World Council of Families in Verona, "The low birthrate is the biggest problem facing Europe. If we do not address this, everything else we do is pointless."[11]

These important similarities, however, can obscure important differences, and not only because natalism and heteronormativity were shared by many movements and regimes, including antifascist ones. This is especially true in the social functions that fascists and contemporary right-wing politicians assign to the two sexes. For fascist movements and regimes, there was an irreconcilable conflict between motherhood and work. Not only was motherhood too time-consuming and emotionally demanding to leave space for work; drawing on long antifeminist traditions, fascist theoreticians assumed that women's bodies and mentalities rendered them less capable of the self-discipline and rationality required for labor. Their "natural" inclination and talents lay in taking care of children (who also lacked full self-control and rationality). This was the spirit in which Joseph Goebbels explained in a landmark speech that the Third Reich's efforts to push women out of the workforce were not oppressive, but in fact emancipatory, allowing women to realize their "true" calling. As he put it, "women have a different mission, a different value, than that of the man."[12] In practice, fascist success on this front was always partial, and many women, especially from the working class, continued to work. Still, the goal of reducing female participation was central to these regimes' logic; women's contribution to racial health was not in the assembly line or the store.

The contemporary radical right, in contrast, shows a far more ambiguous approach to women's work that is both less rigid and less consumed by notions of gendered "essence." Even as far-right parties lament the decline of "traditional" families and state their respect for women who stay at home, they accept female work as a central feature of modern life.[13] Many, in fact, back policies that are explicitly designed to enable it. The Belgian Vlaams Blok, for example, supports public childcare, which would enable women to join the workforce.[14] The Danish People's Party, the Italian Brothers of Italy, and the Dutch Party for Freedom similarly deviate from their otherwise neoliberal economic platforms (which focus on cutting aid to the poor) to accept state support for female employment.[15] The German AfD's platform states that "the economy is calling for women as part of the workforce," and that state support for this trend is crucial.[16] And even in Hungary, Fidesz sought to assist working women by expanding municipal childcare.[17] In this regard, the right in the United States can be seen as an outlier, wedded as it is to arrangements that limit or prohibit women's access to the labor market (most obviously, resistance to subsidized childcare). To be sure, one should not overstate the right's support for female work. Its publications steer clear of references to the language of women's empowerment, and its platforms oppose many policies designed to increase female employment, such as quotas and affirmative action. Hungary's Minister of Family Affairs Katalin Novák (since 2022, the nation's president) was revealing when she commented that women should not allow work to eclipse their "privilege" of delivering children.[18] Yet the right's approach to this topic should not be understood merely as a pragmatic compromise with the realities of double-income families or single-parent households. Its policies and rhetoric demonstrate its acceptance of women as legitimate actors in the public sphere, a notion that would have been unimaginable for its fascist predecessors.

Equally important, and often less recognized, is the divergence between the fascist and radical right's conceptions of masculinity. As a movement born in war and post–World War I violence, one of fascism's main missions was the militarization of civil life. By organizing multiple organs, from factories to youth clubs, along military lines with marches, uniforms, and hierarchical command, its leaders sought to infuse society with the discipline and power they associated with military service. Like the fighting that so deeply shaped fascism, militarism was to be a very male undertaking. In fact, this was fascism's main definition of the task facing men: to be soldiers, which meant fighting in war or realizing the values of obedience, sacrifice, and violence in everyday life. As Hitler explained in a 1935 speech to the party, German boys were to grow into men who were "swift as a greyhound, as tough as leather, and as hard as Krupp steel."[19] As in all aspects of fascist ideology, these ideas often built on earlier codes that were not unique to fascism (infatuation with military prowess was also central to authoritarian and liberal regimes). And even their most ardent promoters always left some room for caveats (SS publications explained for example that cuddling one's children in public was not a sign of weakness but of healthy love). But it is beyond doubt that fascism's conception of masculinity as militaristic service was one of its core features.[20]

The contemporary radical right, on the other hand, no longer defines masculinity in military terms. While some of its more extreme activists are veterans (and in the case of France, even high-ranking officers), its publications and speeches mostly discuss men in the context of deindustrialization (and competition over jobs with immigrants) or strengthening fathers' rights. There is very little talk of military-style male bonding or military acumen. When the German AfD launched an advent calendar in 2018 under the title "yes to white men," to celebrate people who "significantly influenced our Western civilization," it included religious leaders (Martin Luther), neoliberal politicians (Ronald Reagan), and entrepreneurs (Steve Jobs), but no military figures.[21] Indeed, one of the most striking features of today's nationalists is the marginality of military affairs to their vision. They are very much the products of one of modern Europe's most remarkable shifts: the end of compulsory military service in most large economies over the last few decades.[22] Here, too, the United States can be viewed as somewhat of an outlier, at least when compared to Europe. Its prolonged wars and the vast veteran body they created retain an important presence in far-right networks.[23]

———

OVER THE LAST FEW YEARS, observers have repeatedly debated how to explain the right's continuous radicalization. Because its meteoric rise so clearly followed the economic crisis of 2008 and the harsh austerity that followed, most commentary assumed the right gained new followers by speaking to economic and social anxieties. Its racialized and xenophobic discourse, so the story went, was a convenient framework to explain the consequences of deindustrialization, globalization, and aging populations. Yet the radical right continued to gain traction even after economic conditions improved, at least by some measures. In some European countries, such as France or Germany, unemployment rates have in fact reached historic lows in the late 2010s and early 2020s (with a short interruption due to the pandemic), but this seems to have little impact on voting patterns.

There are many reasons for this trend, from a changing media landscape to shifts in voters' loyalty to institutional parties, but one that has not received as much attention is the radical right's capacity to make inroads with women. Even as its electoral base and political leadership remains heavily male (less than a quarter of the French National Rally or German AfD's parliamentarians are women, substantially less than other major parties), the radical right has meaningfully improved its showing with female voters. This was achieved in part by highlighting its departure from older visions of gender roles, and especially by insisting that both men and women have equal access to the same public functions.[24] In fact, as recent sociological research has shown, this messaging has been central to some voters, especially younger ones. As one supporter of Marine Le Pen explained, "She's a modern woman because she isn't the only one who cooks. It's Aliot [her romantic partner] who's in charge of that. We aren't stuck like we used to be in the kitchen, cooking or cleaning. Marine Le Pen is a good example." Some even go so far to associate the radical right with the blurring of gender distinctions. "I don't see Marine as either a woman or a man," said one of Le Pen's young supporters. "She's something more. She's a leader. It goes beyond the question of sexual identity."[25] As Meloni's election-day videos demonstrates, this stance is hardly universal in far-right circles, which often still traffic in sexism. It is, however, sexism that is very different from its fascist precedents, and which may require a very different response.

TRUMP AND THE TRAPPED COUNTRY

COREY ROBIN

Before the storming of the Capitol, it seemed as if Donald Trump might leave the White House the way he had come in—tweeting an average of thirty-five times a day and promising the world, "See you in court."[1] But that Trump, the Trump of litigation and bluster, lawsuits and tweets, disappeared on January 6.

In a democratic election, candidates must will their way to victory or accept defeat. Trump could do neither, leaving him with the option that observers had long feared he would take: a violent assault on democracy itself. That the assault failed, and probably had nowhere to go had it succeeded, is important. That it was tried at all is also important.

The attack on the Capitol was the latest, and most significant, data point supporting the claim that Trump has practiced strongman politics, variously described as authoritarian, fascist, or tyrannical. The strongman thesis was supposed to capture something novel on the right: not its cruelty or racism, which had long been observed by scholars and journalists, but its potential to end democracy itself. For many liberals and leftists, Trump threatened the people's power to determine their future. While this idea provoked much debate during the Trump years, January 6 seemed to settle it. Even the sharpest critics of the thesis were shaken from their skepticism.[2]

Yet if the fear behind the strongman thesis was the eclipse of democracy, we still have reason for concern—less because of a tyrant looming on the right than because of a paralysis of political agency across the board. The signal quality of Trump's presidency was not how unusual it was but how emblematic it was. In all likelihood, the first two years of the Biden administration will see little transformative legislation and a lot of executive orders. (The stimulus bill may augur fundamental changes down the road, but its most redistributive provisions are temporary and will face major challenges upon their expiration.³) It will look, in other words, like Trump's presidency and all but the first two years of Obama's. It will mark twelve years of an era in which the call of the voters is answered by the palsy of our institutions.

The possibility of this convergence across three presidencies—where a flurry of executive orders masks the failure of legislative will, and the absence of legislative will belies the presence of a majority will—offers a novel twist on the strongman thesis. In retrospect, the theory appears useful not for what it helped us to see but for what it prevented us from seeing. Behind its shadows is a reality we've been facing for some time: not the concentration of power in the hands of one person, but the dispersal of power across the polity; not the conversion of popular preferences into partisan will, but the inability of parties to legislate those preferences; not the threat of a tyrannical white majority to the Constitution, but the way in which a minority of mostly white voters depends upon the Constitution to stop the multiracial majority.

Strongman Trump was supposed to rule in one of two ways: either he would gather the force of white voters to impose his will on the GOP and, from there, the American state, or he would use the rhetorical power of his office, the brutality of his words, to transform American political culture.

Behind each fear lay a vision of democratic power that we only wish were true. One vision depicts the president, as the leader of a political party, translating the voters' will into a legislative program. That long had been the dream of American political observers, who envied the parliamentary systems of midcentury Europe, where unified parties offered clear alternatives to the voters, voters cast their ballots for parties, and parties controlled the state.⁴ The other vision idealizes a democracy in which words matter and leaders use them to rouse the citizenry. Language becomes an instrument of power.

With Trump, the democratic wish returned as a liberal nightmare. The responsible party leader appeared as a cruel tyrant, the inspiring rhetorician as a vicious demagogue. The wish didn't generate the reality of Trump. But, like all frustrated desires, its traces remain in our distorted vision of that reality.

The belief that Trump mastered the Republican Party, and that he and the GOP dominated the American polity, was shared by Trump's defenders and critics alike. That belief was lent added credence when more than half the Republican members of Congress refused to certify Biden's election, and the overwhelming majority of Republican senators voted to acquit Trump in his second impeachment trial.

Yet whenever Republicans wanted to oppose Trump on matters of policy or political importance to them, they did. Before the pandemic, thirteen Senate Republicans joined the Democrats to defeat Trump's immigration bill.[5] Republicans refused to pay for his wall.[6] In July 2020, the same month that *Vox* criticized "Trump's authoritarian impulses and near-total control of the Republican Party," the GOP forced Trump to back down on cutting payroll taxes;[7] his defense secretary banned the Confederate flag at military bases;[8] and Senate Republicans, in defiance of a threatened veto, passed a bill requiring the Pentagon to rename military bases honoring Confederate generals.[9]

Less than a week before they abased themselves on January 6, Republicans in Congress voted, overwhelmingly, to override Trump's veto of the National Defense Authorization Act (NDAA), which is the annual military-spending bill.[10] That vote alone was unprecedented. Jimmy Carter, Ronald Reagan, Bill Clinton, George W. Bush, and Barack Obama vetoed the NDAA.[11] Each time, Congress was forced to back down and revise its position. Not only did Congress, under Trump, not back down but it also imposed restrictions on presidential power that any strongman would bridle at. It limited the president's ability to use emergency declarations to divert military funds, as Trump had done with the border wall.[12] It constrained the Pentagon's ability to transfer military weapons to local police, as critics of the police have long demanded. And, in response to Trump's handling of the Black Lives Matters protests, the bill required federal law enforcement officers and members of the armed services, when responding to civil disorders, to wear insignia identifying themselves.

Even when Trump and the Republicans controlled all the elected branches of government, they were routinely unable to exercise the power that they had. They failed to repeal Obamacare. Though the Republican Senate did vote to appoint three Supreme Court justices who struck down *Roe v. Wade*, the Republican Congress was never able to ban federal funds for abortion or enact a federal ban on abortion after twenty weeks.[13] Nor were they able to expand the death penalty,[14] change immigration law,[15] or enact other items on their legislative agenda. Their one major legislative achievement was tax cuts.[16]

On the heels of those cuts, the House Speaker, Paul Ryan, said that he was coming for Medicare and Social Security;[17] Trump promised something he called "welfare reform." What the two men, along with Mitch McConnell, the Senate majority leader, delivered instead was "a domestic budget to make Barack Obama proud."[18] Rather than slash liberal programs, Trump, McConnell, and Ryan were forced to pass a budget that included $1.3 trillion in increased funding for Pell Grants, Head Start, Health and Human Services, the National Endowment for the Arts, the Department of Education, renewable energies, and the National Science Foundation, and made no cuts to the Environmental Protection Agency or Planned Parenthood. All this before Nancy Pelosi recovered her Speaker's gavel, in January 2019.

The consequences of Trump's rhetoric were also more contradictory than Trump and his critics supposed. Trump certainly aggravated the racism and violence of his base, preparing the mob for the actions it took on January 6. But the underlying fear that he would transform the broader political culture through the mere fact of his words turned out to be a kind of inverted democratic wish.[19] In the face of Trump's bully pulpit, the public fled in the opposite direction.

"On nearly every major policy issue," Catherine Rampell reported in *The Washington Post* in October 2020, Trump "has pushed the country to the left."[20] That was certainly true of trade, immigration, and Obamacare (formally known as the Affordable Care Act, or ACA). As four researchers noted, in March 2020, "The ACA is now more popular than at any other point in its ten-year history."²¹ Reversing a public opinion trend under Obama, this rise in popularity owed less to the increasing number of people helped by the ACA than it did to Trump's attack on the law, which inspired Democrats and independents to support it.

As we descend from the higher sphere of policy to the viscera of race, the effect is even stronger. Two of the lowest polling moments of Trump's presidency came in August 2017, just after his "both sides" remarks on the white supremacist rally at Charlottesville, and in June 2020, amid his crackdown on the Black Lives Matter protests.²² (His lowest moment was the week that followed January 6.) As support for Trump plummeted over the summer of 2020, support for Black Lives Matter peaked, with a record number of Americans claiming that the criminal justice system discriminated against African Americans and other people of color.²³ Support for Black Lives Matter would then begin to drop, prompting anticipation, across the spectrum, of a Trump-led white backlash à la Richard Nixon, centered in the suburbs. But instead of riding to power on the specter of Black criminality, Trump lost support among white and suburban voters, leading to his defeat. It was 1968 in reverse.

Although Trump never dominated the American state, and never transformed the GOP's economic or social agenda, he did intensify the right's long-standing hostility to democracy.²⁴ Like most American presidents, in other words, he had an impact on his party. Whether that portends a Trump 2.0 in the future, more savvy and skilled than the first, or recalls the ultra-left's violent turn in the 1970s, when a diminished cadre of radicals sought to push politics leftward as the ground beneath it shifted right, remains to be seen.

The strongman thesis did register a shift on the right, which had been gestating since the presidency of George W. Bush but which got obscured by all the talk of fascism and right-wing populism. While that talk posits an unsettling affinity between master and masses, the right has been losing its popular touch for decades. In the last eight presidential elections, the Republican candidate has won the popular vote just once. Nixon, Reagan, and George W. Bush all rode the wave of racial backlash, yet each wave was smaller than the last. Nixon was reelected with 61 percent of the vote, Reagan with 59 percent, and Bush with 51 percent. Trump was forced to join that small, sad fraternity of losers who fail to win a second term at all.[25]

The diminishing returns of right-wing populism can be seen in the decreasing potency of GOP rule. The innovations that Nixon, Reagan, and Bush pioneered—the "silent majority," law and order, the end of big government, the Department of Homeland Security—defined the political grammar of both parties and the common sense of the nation. Trump's legacy is the rejection of his party's premises by more than half the country. Where Reagan and Bush respectively got 168 and 40 Democrats to vote for their tax cuts, Trump got none. Asked to name her most significant achievement, Margaret Thatcher replied, "Tony Blair." Trump's will be Arizona, Georgia, and A.O.C.

Seeking to counter their waning position, the Republican Party and the conservative movement have come to depend upon three pillars of countermajoritarian rule: the Senate, the Electoral College, and the Supreme Court.[26] These institutions are not authoritarian or fascist—indeed, they are eminently constitutional—but they are antidemocratic. They are also mainstays of the right. In a remarkable statement, now forgotten, issued three days before January 6, seven conservative members of the House warned their Republicans colleagues that GOP presidential candidates have depended on the electoral college for nearly all presidential victories in the last generation:

> If we perpetuate the notion that Congress may disregard certified electoral votes—based solely on its own assessment that one or more states mishandled the presidential election—we will be delegitimizing the very system that led Donald Trump to victory in 2016, and that could provide the only path to victory in 2024.[27]

This is the reality that the strongman thesis, in all its guises, mischaracterizes yet records. Fascism's most resonant image—of a triumphant will bending the nation to its vision—was born in the long shadow of the French Revolution. Against the mass movements of the left and the constitutional state of the center, fascism called the young to the cause of novelty and creation. Today's right is nothing like that. It is an artifact of the world's most ancient and extant legal order, holding on to the Constitution, and the institutions it authorizes, for dear life.

If these institutions promise life to the right, they spell death for the left. In 2020, a majority of the voters cast their ballots for Biden and for the Democrats in the House. Yet their preferences could go ignored, thanks to the parties' near standoff in the Senate. That standoff hardly reflects the popular will; according to statistics compiled by *Jacobin*'s executive editor, Seth Ackerman, the Senate's Democratic bloc represents 56 percent of the population. But that is the design of our institutions, which privilege the interests of states with small populations, often white and rural, that can block the will of the majority.

The current moment is less reminiscent of the last days of Weimar than of Britain in the years before the Reform Act of 1832. With a scheme of representation dating back to the twelfth century, Parliament was the playground of grandees from rural and sparsely populated regions of the South. Growing cities in the Midlands and the North had no representation at all.

Standing atop this "aristocracy of mere locality," in the words of the historian and Whig politician Thomas Macaulay, were the Tories. For six decades, virtually without interruption, they leveraged this Senate-like system of rotten boroughs to keep the Whigs out of power, enabling an increasingly isolated group of aristocrats and gentry to maintain their privileges. While "the natural growth of society went on" among the middle classes and in the cities, Macaulay said, "the artificial polity continued unchanged."

Other features of this system will sound familiar. Polling places were few and far between; one of the leading items on the reform agenda was to increase their number. Electoral laws were so byzantine, and generated results so murky, that an army of well-paid lawyers was on the payroll for years, sorting out the returns and arguing over their validity. The "artificial polity" kept politics frozen in time, discouraging both parties from taking up vital economic questions of the day, and preventing new social forces and the partisan realignment that was eventually to come.

This is the situation we now find ourselves in. One party, representing the popular majority, remains on the outskirts of power, thanks to the Constitution. The other party, representing the minority, cannot wield power when it has it but finds its position protected nonetheless by the very same Constitution.

We are not witnesses to Prometheus unbound. We are seeing the sufferings of Sisyphus, forever rolling his rock—immigration reform, a Green New Deal—up a hill. It's no wonder everyone saw an authoritarian at the top of that hill. When no one can act, any performance of power, no matter how empty, can seem real.

ACKNOWLEDGMENTS

I wish to thank my editor at W. W. Norton, Alane Mason, who provided me with much needed guidance in putting together this anthology. I'm grateful as well for her excellent line editing. Many thanks to Victoria Smolkin, Samuel Moyn, Udi Greenberg, Peter Gordon, Thomas Meaney, and Daniel Bessner for either commenting on early drafts of my introduction to this anthology or helping me think through the main stakes of today's fascism debate. They all have different ways of thinking about this debate, so I appreciate their pushback against my various lines of argumentation and for encouraging me to develop certain ideas further. And much appreciation to all the contributors for agreeing to participate and for supporting this project. I am indebted to my two research assistants, Reed Schwartz and Ben Sheriff, who, under short notice, offered their services. I'm thankful to the College of Social Studies at Wesleyan University for funding this assistance, and to Martha Crebbin for arranging it. Much appreciation to Samuel Moyn and Jason Stanley for encouraging me to pursue this anthology, to Alane Mason for agreeing to take it on, and to Victoria Smolkin for her encouragement and support from beginning to end.

NOTES

INTRODUCTION: MAKING SENSE OF THE FASCISM DEBATE

1. Bruce Kuklick, *Fascism Comes to America: A Century of Obsession in Politics and Culture* (Chicago: University of Chicago Press, 2022).
2. I thank Udi Greenberg for raising these points to me.
3. Yascha Mounk, *The People vs. Democracy: Why Our Freedom Is in Danger and How to Save It* (Cambridge, Mass.: Harvard University Press, 2018).
4. Edward Luce, *The Retreat of Western Liberalism* (New York: Atlantic Monthly Press, 2017); Patrick Deneen, *Why Liberalism Failed* (New Haven: Yale University Press, 2018).
5. Noam Chomsky, Robert Pollin, and C. J. Polychroniou, *Climate Crisis and the Global Green New Deal* (London: Verso, 2020).
6. Chas Danner, "How the U.S. Is Trying to Stave Off a Banking System Crisis," *New York*, March 13, 2023.
7. Sarah Butrymowicz and Pete D'Amato, "A Crisis Is Looming for U.S. Colleges—and Not Just Because of the Pandemic," NBC News, August 4, 2020.
8. Adam Tooze, *Shutdown: How Covid Shook the World's Economy* (New York: Viking, 2021).
9. Anton Troianovski, "In Ukraine Crisis, the Looming Threat of a New Cold War," *New York Times*, February 19, 2022.
10. Adam Tooze, "Welcome to the World of the Polycrisis," *Financial Times*, August 28, 2022.
11. On the origins of the word "polycrisis," see Andreas Kluth, "So We're in a Polycrisis. Is That Even a Thing?," *Washington Post*, January 21, 2023.
12. For more on George W. Bush's framing of the "war on terror" through the prism of "Islamo-fascism," see Kuklick, *Fascism Comes to America*, 181. For liberals who defended the war on terror, viewing it through the prism of antifascism and totalitarianism, see Tony Judt, "Bush's Useful Idiots," *London Review of Books* 28, no. 18 (September 21, 2006).
13. Michael Brenes and Daniel Steinmetz-Jenkins, "Legacies of Cold War Liberalism," *Dissent*, Winter 2021.
14. Gideon Rachman, "The Global Democratic Recession: Democracy Is in Retreat Around the World—for Now," *Financial Times*, August 8, 2016.
15. Daniel A. Bell, *The China Model: Political Meritocracy and the Limits of Democracy* (Princeton, N.J.: Princeton University Press, 2015).
16. Eric Foner, "The Professional," *The Nation*, January 14, 2010.
17. Kuklick, *Fascism Comes to America*, 173.
18. Alexander Burns, "Obama a 'Fascist'?," *Politico*, April 15, 2009; Roy Edroso, "How Rightbloggers Made 'Fascist' the New 'Socialist,'" *Village Voice*, April 6, 2009.
19. Josh Katz, "Who Will Be President," *New York Times*, November 8, 2016.

20. See, in particular, Jonathan Chait, "Why Liberals Should Support a Trump Republican Nomination," *New York*, February 5, 2016.

21. Timothy Snyder, *On Tyranny: Twenty Lessons from the Twentieth Century* (New York: Tim Duggan Books/Crown, 2017).

22. The post-2016 crisis of democracy literature is substantial. See, for instance, Steven Levitsky and Daniel Ziblatt, *How Democracies Die* (New York: Crown, 2018); Yascha Mounk, *The People Versus Democracy: Why Our Freedom Is in Danger and How to Save It* (Cambridge, Mass.: Harvard University Press, 2018); David Frum, *Trumpocracy: The Corruption of the American Republic* (New York: HarperCollins, 2018); William A. Galston, *Antipluralism: The Populist Threat to Liberal Democracy* (New Haven: Yale University Press, 2018); E. J. Dionne Jr., Norman J. Ornstein, and Thomas E. Mann, *One Nation After Trump: A Guide for the Perplexed, the Disillusioned, the Desperate, and the Not-Yet-Deported* (New York: St. Martin's, 2017).

23. Ta-Nehisi Coates, "The First White President," *The Atlantic*, October 2017.

24. Anne Applebaum, "The Bad Guys Are Winning," *The Atlantic*, November 15, 2021.

25. Joseph E Stiglitz, *Globalization and Its Discontents* (New York: W. W. Norton, 2002).

26. See, in particular, Charles W. Mills, *The Racial Contract* (Ithaca, N.Y.: Cornell University Press, 1997).

27. See Adam Tooze, "1922/2022—The Centenary of Mussolini's 'March on Rome' and the Dilemmas of the Liberal Expert Class," Chartbook, October 20, 2022, https://adamtooze.substack.com/p/chartbook-166-19222022-the-centenary; Tom Nichols, "A Longish and Quixotic Thread on the Misuse of 'Fascism,'" Twitter, April 15, 2023, https://twitter.com/RadioFreeTom/status/1647337063543365635. For Müller, see his contribution in this anthology, "Is it Fascism?"

28. Dinesh D'Souza, *The Big Lie: Exposing the Nazi Roots of the American Left* (Washington, D.C.: Regnery, 2017).

29. On the history profession's turn to presentism, see Daniel Steinmetz-Jenkins, "Beyond the End of History," *Chronicle of Higher Education*, August 14, 2020.

30. Jacob Mikanowski, "The Bleak Prophecy of Timothy Snyder," *Chronicle of Higher Education*, April 12, 2019.

31. Chauncey DeVega, "Historian Timothy Snyder: 'It's Pretty Much Inevitable' That Trump Will Try to Stage a Coup and Overthrow Democracy," *Salon*, May 1, 2017.

32. Timothy Snyder, "The American Abyss," *New York Times Magazine*, January 9, 2021; Timothy Snyder, "January 6: The Facts," Thinking About It, December 28, 2022, https://snyder.substack.com/p/january-6-the-facts.

33. See also Geoff Eley, "What Is Fascism and Where Does It Come From?," *History Workshop Journal* 91, no. 1 (Spring 2021): 1–28. See also John Ganz's many interventions available via his Substack site, Unpopular Front: https://johnganz.substack.com/p/the-fascism-debate-e72.

34. Robert O. Paxton, *The Anatomy of Fascism* (New York: Alfred A. Knopf, 2004), 49.

35. See also Alberto Toscano, "The Long Shadow of Racial Fascism," *Jacobin*, October 28, 2020, https://www.bostonreview.net/articles/alberto-toscano-tk/.

36. Geoffrey Barraclough, *An Introduction to Contemporary History* (London: C. A. Watts, 1964), 28.

37. Ibid.

38. Gary Gerstle, "The Age of Neoliberalism Is Ending in America. What Will Replace It?," *The Guardian*, June 21, 2021; Gary Gerstle, "Biden's Infrastructure Success Is a Historic—and Sorely Needed—Win," *The Guardian*, November 8, 2021.

39. Nils Gilman, "A New Dawn, a New Day, a New Life," Small Precautions, April 18, 2021.

40. For a piece that connects right-wing authoritarian rejections of gender fluidity and LGBTQ+ activism to fascism, see Gabriel Winant, "We Live in a Society," *n+1*, December 12, 2020.

41. See, for instance, David Frum, "If Liberals Won't Enforce Borders, Fascists Will," *The Atlantic*, April 2019; Olivia Solon, "Artificial Intelligence Is Ripe for Abuse, Tech Researcher Warns: 'A Fascist's Dream,'" *The Guardian*, March 13, 2017; Nicolas Guilhot, "Bad Information," *Boston Review*, April 23, 2021.

42. On how the George Floyd riots inspired a global history war, see Alaina M. Morgan, "Historical Sankofa: On Understanding Antiblack Violence in the Present Through the African Diasporic Past," *Modern Intellectual History* (forthcoming). On how historical disputes over what constitutes Russia informed Putin's decision to go to war, see Victoria Smolkin, "Fantasy Is Not History," *Meduza*, February 24, 2022.

43. See also Dylan Riley, "What Is Trump," *New Left Review* 114 (November/December 2018): 5–31.

44. For a cultural approach, see Kristin Kobes Du Mez, *Jesus and John Wayne: How White Evangelicals Corrupted a Faith and Fractured a Nation* (New York: W. W. Norton, 2020). For a sociological approach, see Philip Gorski and Samuel Perry, *The Flag and the Cross: White Christian Nationalism and the Threat to American Democracy* (New York: Oxford University Press, 2022). For a theological reckoning with Trumpism and evangelicals, see Mark A. Noll, David W. Bebbington, and George M. Marsden, eds., *Evangelicals: Who They Have Been, Are Now, and Could Be* (Grand Rapids, Mich.: William. B. Eerdmans, 2019), as well as Daniel Steinmetz-Jenkins, "The Nationalist Roots of White Evangelical Politics," *Dissent*, Spring 2021.

45. Matt Karp, "History as End," *Harper's*, July 2021.

POLITICAL PRISONERS, PRISONS, AND BLACK LIBERATION

1. Report to the Seventh Congress of the Communist International, 1935.

WHAT IS FASCISM?

1. Benito Mussolini, "Fascismo," *Enciclopedia Treccani* (Milan: Istituto Treccani, 1932), http://www.treccani.it/enciclopedia/fascismo_%28Enciclopedia-Italiana%29/.

2. Robert O. Paxton, *The Anatomy of Fascism* (New York: Vintage, 2005), 9; Michael Mann, *Fascists* (Cambridge: Cambridge University Press, 2004), 9.

3. Paxton, *Anatomy of Fascism*, 218.

4. Robert O. Paxton, "I've Hesitated to Call Donald Trump a Fascist. Until Now," *Newsweek*, January 11, 2012.

5. Jason Stanley, *How Fascism Works: The Politics of Us and Them* (New York: Random House, 2018).

6. Benito Mussolini, "Stato, anti-Stato, e fascismo," *Gerarchia*, June 25, 1922.

7. Ibid.; Mussolini, "Fascismo."

8. "Extracts from the Theses of the Thirteenth ECCI Plenum on Fascism, the War Danger and the Tasks of Communist Parties (December 1933)," in *Communist International: Documents, 1919–1943*, ed. Jane Degras (London: Routledge, 2014), 296.

9. Neal M. Rosendorf, *Franco Sells Spain to America: Hollywood Tourism and PR as Postwar Spanish Soft Power* (New York: Palgrave Macmillan, 2014).

10. Ruth Ben-Ghiat, *Strongmen: From Mussolini to the Present* (New York: W. W. Norton, 2021).

11. Hannah Arendt, *The Origins of Totalitarianism* (New York: Harcourt Brace Jovanovich, 1973), 308.

12. Gianfranco Fini, interview by Alberto Statera, "Il migliore resta Mussolini," *La Stampa*, April 1, 1994; Piero Ignazi, *Postfascisti? Dal Movimento sociale italiano ad Alleanza Nazionale* (Bologna: Il Mulino, 1994); Salvatore Merlo, *La conversione di Fini* (Florence: Vallecchi, 2010).

13. Silvio Berlusconi, interview by Boris Johnson and Nicholas Farrell, *Spectator*, September 11, 2003.

14. Timothy Snyder, "We Should Say It. Russia Is Fascist," *New York Times*, May 19, 2022.

15. Ruth Ben-Ghiat, "'Kanye. Elon. Trump.' Hate Speech Is Protected Speech for Republican Extremists," *Lucid: Substack*, December 3, 2022.

IS IT FASCISM?

1. Natasha Lennard, *Being Numerous: Essays on Non-Fascist Life* (New York: Verso, 2019), 9.

2. Udi Greenberg, "What Was the Fascism Debate?," *Dissent*, Summer 2021. The fact that the concept also mobilizes—and that there are overlaps between social scientific and political concepts—does not warrant the conclusion that fascism necessarily "expresses loathing more than it identifies a reality or a growing series of realities" or that fascism "does not so much isolate a thing as it does some stigmatizing." For these views, see Bruce Kuklick, *Fascism Comes to America: A Century of Obsession in Politics and Culture* (Chicago: University of Chicago Press, 2022), 3.

3. Gavriel D. Rosenfeld, "An American Führer? Nazi Analogies and the Struggle to Explain Donald Trump," *Central European History* 52, , no. 4 (2019): 554–87.

4. Alec Ryrie, "Martin Luther Was the Donald Trump of 1517," *Foreign Policy*, May 23, 2017.

5. Jason Stanley, "American Fascism?," *El País*, August 1, 2020.

6. For a similar exercise with different assumptions, see Dylan Riley's "What Is Trump?," *New Left Review* 114 (November/December 2018): 5–31. It uses "four comparative axes: geopolitical context, economic crisis, relations of class and nation, and, finally, the character of civil society and political parties."

7. I leave aside here the further (and important) aspect of distinguishing between different phases (such as movement and regime phase); Paxton has analyzed this aspect most fruitfully; for right-wing populism, Nadia Urbinati has also drawn a helpful distinction between movement and regime phases. See Robert O. Paxton, *The Anatomy of Fascism* (London: Allen Lane, 2004), and Nadia Urbinati, *Me the People: How Populism Transforms Democracy* (Cambridge, Mass.: Harvard University Press, 2019). On "incitement capitalism," see William Callison and Quinn Slobodian, "Coronapolitics from the Reichstag to the Capitol," *Boston Review*, January 2021.

8. Roger Griffin, *Fascism* (Cambridge: Polity, 2018).

9. Geoff Eley, "What Is Fascism and Where Does It Come From?," *History Workshop Journal* 91, no. 1 (Spring 2021): 10.

10. Paxton, *Anatomy of Fascism*, 23.

11. Kathleen Belew, *Bring the War Home: The White Power Movement and Paramilitary America* (Cambridge, Mass.: Harvard University Press, 2018).

12. Cas Mudde, *The Far Right Today* (Cambridge: Polity, 2019) and Spencer Ackerman, *Reign of Terror* (New York: Penguin, 2021).

13. See Larry Bartels, *Democracy Erodes from the Top* (Princeton, N.J.: Princeton University Press, 2023).

14. David Bell, "Fascism or Caesarism?," *Eurozine*, September 2020, https://www.eurozine.com/fascism-or-caesarism/, last accessed October 21, 2021).

15. Griffin, *Fascism*, 87.

16. Ibid.

17. Joachim Fest, *Gesichter des Dritten Reichs* (Frankfurt: Büchergilde Gutenberg, 1965).

18. I have tried to explain this notion of a formation of "new peoples" in *Contesting Democracy: Political Ideas in Twentieth-Century Europe* (London: Yale University Press, 2011).

19. See Tali Mendelberg's response to "Forum: The Logic of Misogyny" at Tali Mendelberg responds to Kate Manne | Boston Review, https://www.bostonreview.net/forum_response/tali-mendelberg-responds-kate-manne/, accessed October 21, 2021.

20. Adam Serwer, *The Cruelty Is the Point: The Past, Present, and Future of Trump's America* (New York: Random House, 2021).

21. Eley, "What Is Fascism?," 18.

22. Klaus Theweleit, *Männerphantasien*, 3rd ed. (Berlin: Matthes @ Seitz, 2020).

23. I am grateful to Erika A. Kiss for pointing me to Woolf in this context.

24. Sara R. Farris, *In the Name of Women's Rights: The Rise of Femonationalism* (Durham, N.C.: Duke University Press, 2017).

25. Juan Linz, *Totalitarian and Authoritarian Regimes* (London: Lynne Riener, 2000).

26. Isabel Best, "Should We Even Go There? Historians on Comparing Fascism to Trumpism," *The Guardian*, December 1, 2016.

27. Kate Manne, "Forum: The Logic of Misogyny," *Boston Review*, July 11, 2016, http://bostonreview.net/forum/kate-manne-logic-misogyny, last accessed May 17, 2020.

28. Larry M. Bartels, "Ethnic Antagonism Erodes Republicans' Commitment to Democracy," *Proceedings of the National Academy of Sciences* 117, no. 37 (September 15, 2020): 22752–22759. Available at: www.pnas.org/content/pnas/early/2020/08/26/2007747117.full.pdf.

29. Federico Finchelstein, Pablo Piccato, and Jason Stanley, "Alexandria Ocasio-Cortez Is Right to Warm of 'Fascism in the United States,'" *New Republic*, August 20, 2020.

30. Kim Lane Scheppele, "Autocratic Legalism," *University of Chicago Law Review* 85 (2018): 545–83.

31. Bartels, "Ethnic Antagonism."

I'VE HESITATED TO CALL DONALD TRUMP A FASCIST. UNTIL NOW

1. Robert O. Paxton, "American Duce," *Harper's*, April 13, 2017.

WHY TRUMP ISN'T A FASCIST

1. Timothy Snyder, "America and the Politics of Pain," *New Statesman*, October 28, 2020; Sarah Churchwell, "The Return of American Fascism," *New Statesman*, September 2, 2020.

WHY HISTORICAL ANALOGY MATTERS

1. Anika Walke et al., "An Open Letter to the Director of the U.S. Holocaust Memorial Museum: Omer Bartov," *New York Review of Books*, July 1, 2019.

2. Andrea Pitzer, "'Some Suburb of Hell': America's New Concentration Camp System: Andrea Pitzer," *New York Review of Books*, June 21, 2019.

3. Jan-Werner Müller, "Populism and the People," *London Review of Books* 41, no. 10 (May 23, 2019).

4. Ernst Cassirer, *The Myth of the State* (New Haven: Yale University Press, 2013).

5. Robert O. Paxton, "The Future of Fascism," *Slate*, April 6, 2017.

THE TROUBLE WITH COMPARISONS

1. Aaron Blake, "This New York Times 'Hitler' Book Review Sure Reads like a Thinly Veiled Trump Comparison," *Washington Post*, September 28, 2016; Chauncey DeVega, "Historian Timothy Snyder: 'It's Pretty Much Inevitable' That Trump Will Try to Stage a Coup and Overthrow Democracy," *Salon*, May 1, 2017.

2. Tamsin Shaw, "William Barr: The Carl Schmitt of Our Time," *New York Review of Books*, January 15, 2020.

3. Charles Maier, *The Unmasterable Past: History, Holocaust, and German National Identity* (Cambridge, Mass.: Harvard University Press, 1998), 83–84.

4. Ibid., 96.

5. Peter E. Gordon, "Why Historical Analogy Matters," *New York Review of Books*, January 7, 2020.

6. Jason Stanley, *How Fascism Works: The Politics of Us and Them* (2018; repr., New York: Random House, 2020).

WILLIAM BARR: THE CARL SCHMITT OF OUR TIME

1. Michael T. Flynn, *The Field of Fight: How We Can Win the Global War Against Radical Islam and Its Allies* (New York: St. Martin's, 2016), 8.

2. "Attorney General William P. Barr Delivers the 19th Annual Barbara K. Olson Memorial Lecture at the Federalist Society's 2019 National Lawyers Convention," U.S. Department of Justice, November 15, 2019, https://www.justice.gov/opa/speech/attorney-general-william-p-barr-delivers-19th-annual-barbara-k-olson-memorial-lecture.

3. "Attorney General William P. Barr Delivers Remarks to the Law School and the De Nicola Center for Ethics and Culture at the University of Notre Dame," U.S. Department of Justice, October 11, 2019, https://www.justice.gov/opa/speech/attorney-general-william-p-barr-delivers-remarks-law-school-and-de-nicola-center-ethics.

4. Tara Subramaniam, Marshall Cohen, and Holmes Lybrand, "Fact-Checking Bill Barr's Comments on the Russia Investigation IG Report," CNN Politics, December 11, 2019; "Trump Calls FBI 'Scum' at Rally," *Hardball*, MSNBC, December 10, 2019.

5. David Johnston, "F.B.I. to Shift from Cold War to Crime War," *New York Times*, January 9, 1992.

6. Tim Elfrink, "William Barr Says 'Communities' That Protest Cops Could Lose 'the Police Protection They Need,'" *Washington Post*, December 4, 2019.

7. Thomistic Institute, "Perspective of a Catholic Prosecutor: Honorable John Durham," SoundCloud, November 13, 2018, https://soundcloud.com/thomisticinstitute/perspective-of-a-catholic-prosecutor-honorable-john-durham.

8. Scott Shane, "Amid Details on Torture, Data on 26 Who Were Held in Error," *New York Times*, December 12, 2014.

WHAT'S IN A WORD?

1. Julian Emiridge, "The Forgotten Interventions," *Jacobin*, January 12, 2017; Joseph Grosso, "Killing Guatemala," *Jacobin*, November 18, 2015.

2. Timothy Snyder, "The American Abyss," *New York Times*, January 9, 2021; Leila Fadel, "'How Fascism Works' Author on Trump's Attempts to Overturn Election Results," NPR, November 21, 2020; Sean Illing, "Fascism: A Warning from Madeleine Albright," *Vox*, February 14, 2019.

3. Branko Marcetic, "Give Me Liberty—No, Wait, Give Me Death," *Jacobin*, May 13, 2020.

4. David Klion, "'Almost the Complete Opposite of Fascism,'" *Jewish Currents*, December 4, 2020; Corey Robin, "Corey Robin: What Trump's Impeachment Could Mean," *Jacobin*, September 1, 2021.

5. Micah Uetricht and Meagan Day, "The U.S. Cannot Retaliate Against Iran's Strikes in Iraq," *Jacobin*, January 7, 2020.

6. John Feffer, "John Bolton Is Gone. The Threat of War Is Not," *Jacobin*, September 21, 2019.

7. Helen Lackner, "How Yemen's Dream of Unity Turned Sour," *Jacobin*, May 22, 2020.

8. Norman Ornstein, "The House Must as an Immediate Step Pass a Domestic Terrorism Statute,

with a Focus on White Supremacist Terrorism, and Send It to the Senate," Twitter, January 9, 2021, https://twitter.com/NormOrnstein/status/1347969828854910979.

9. Katie Halper, "Is Trump 'Fascist'? A Debate with Jason Stanley, Samuel Moyn, Jodi Dean, Dan Bessner and Eugene Puryear," YouTube, January 14, 2021, https://www.youtube.com/watch?v=dXeswiXTsII.

10. "Officer Appears to Pose for Selfie with Rioter," The Lead, CNN Politics, January 7, 2021.

AMERICAN FASCISM: IT HAS HAPPENED HERE

1. José Antonio Primo de Rivera, "Total Feeling" [1934], in *Fascism (Oxford Readers)*, ed. Roger Griffin (Oxford: Oxford University Press, 1995), 187.

2. Samuel Moyn, "The Trouble with Comparisons," *New York Review of Books*, May 19, 2020.

3. Amiri Baraka, "Black Reconstruction: Du Bois and the U.S. Struggle for Democracy and Socialism," *Conjunctions* 29 (1997): 62–80.

4. Philip Bump, "In 1927, Donald Trump's Father Was Arrested After a Klan Riot in Queens," *Washington Post*, February 29, 2016.

5. A. G. Sulzberger, "As Survivors Dwindle, Tulsa Confronts Past," *New York Times*, June 19, 2011.

ONE HUNDRED YEARS OF FASCISM

1. Blaine Taylor, "Benito Mussolini and the Fascist March on Rome," Warfare History Network, December 2009, https://warfarehistorynetwork.com/article/benito-mussolini-the-fascist-march-on-rome/.

2. Robert O. Paxton, "Is Fascism Back?," Project Syndicate, January 7, 2016, https://www.project-syndicate.org/magazine/is-fascism-back-by-robert-o--paxton-2016-01.

3. Jason Stanley and Federico Finchelstein, "Op-Ed: White Replacement Theory Is Fascism's New Name," *Los Angeles Times*, May 24, 2022.

4. Sarah Churchwell, *Behold, America: The Entangled History of "America First" and "the American Dream"* (New York: Basic Books, 2018).

5. "Ford's Anti-Semitism," *American Experience*, PBS, https://www.pbs.org/wgbh/americanexperience/features/henryford-antisemitism/, accessed March 22, 2023.

6. Patrick Young, "When America's Racist Immigration Law Inspired Hitler," *Long Island Wins*, August 30, 2018, https://longislandwins.com/immigration-history/when-americas-racist-immigration-law-inspired-hitler/; Jill Weiss Simins, " 'America First': The Ku Klux Klan Influence on Immigration Policy in the 1920s," *Hoosier State Chronicles*, June 20, 2019, https://blog.newspapers.library.in.gov/america-first-the-ku-klux-klan-influence-on-immigration-policy-in-the-1920s/.

7. Smithsonian American Art Museum, "Manifest Destiny and Indian Removal," American Experience, Smithsonian Institution, https://americanexperience.si.edu/wp-content/uploads/2015/02/Manifest-Destiny-and-Indian-Removal.pdf, accessed March 22, 2023; U.S. Holocaust Memorial Museum, "Lebensraum," Holocaust Encyclopedia, https://encyclopedia.ushmm.org/content/en/article/lebensraum, accessed March 22, 2023; Jennifer Rosenberg, "Hitler's Search for More German Living Space," ThoughtCo, March 23, 2020, https://www.thoughtco.com/lebensraum-eastern-expansion-4081248.

8. Timothy Snyder, *Black Earth: The Holocaust as History and Warning* (New York: Tim Duggan Books/Crown, 2015).

9. Kimberlé Crenshaw, "Mapping the Margins: Intersectionality, Identity Politics, and Violence Against Women of Color," *Stanford Law Review* 43, no. 6 (July 1991): 1241–99.

10. Jelani Cobb, "The Man Behind Critical Race Theory," *New Yorker*, September 13, 2021.

11. Janel George, "A Lesson on Critical Race Theory," American Bar Association, January 11, 2021, https://www.americanbar.org/groups/crsj/publications/human_rights_magazine_home/civil -rights-reimagining-policing/a-lesson-on-critical-race-theory/.

12. U.S. Holocaust Memorial Museum, "1935 Nuremberg Laws," Holocaust Encyclopedia, https://encyclopedia.ushmm.org/content/en/article/the-nuremberg-race-laws, accessed March 22, 2023.

13. James Q. Whitman, *Hitler's American Model: The United States and the Making of Nazi Race Law* (Princeton, N.J.: Princeton University Press, 2018); James Q. Whitman, "Are Nazis as American as Apple Pie?," Project Syndicate, August 17, 2017, https://www.project-syndicate .org/commentary/charlottesville-nazis-american-democracy-by-james-q--whitman-2017-08.

14. Erin Blakemore, "A Ship of Jewish Refugees Was Refused U.S. Landing in 1939," History, A&E Television Networks, June 4, 2019, https://www.history.com/news/wwii-jewish-refugee-ship -st-louis-1939.

15. Charles A. Lindbergh, "Aviation, Geography, and Race," *Reader's Digest*, November 1939.

16. Charles A. Lindbergh, "Des Moines Speech," PBS, http://www.shoppbs.pbs.org/wgbh/amex/ lindbergh/filmmore/reference/primary/desmoinesspeech.html, accessed March 22, 2023.

17. Alan de Bromhead, Barry Eichengreen, and Kevin H. O'Rourke, "Political Extremism in the 1920s and 1930s: Do German Lessons Generalize?," *Journal of Economic History* 73, no. 2 (June 2013): 371–406.

18. Douglas F. Dowd, "Economic Stagnation in Europe in the Interwar Period," *Journal of Economic History* 15, no. 3 (September 1955): 273–80.

19. U.S. Holocaust Memorial Museum, "The Path to Nazi Genocide," Holocaust Encyclopedia, https://www.ushmm.org/learn/holocaust/path-to-nazi-genocide/the-path-to-nazi-genocide/ full-film, accessed March 22, 2023.

20. Richard J. Evans, "German Women and the Triumph of Hitler," *Journal of Modern History* 48, no. 1 (March 1976): 123–75.

21. "Today in Labor History: Nazis Destroy Unions," *People's World*, May 2, 2014, https://www .peoplesworld.org/article/today-in-labor-history-nazis-destroy-unions/.

22. Vladimir Tismaneanu, review of *Lenin, Stalin, and Hitler: The Age of Social Catastrophe*, by Robert Gellately, *Kritika: Explorations in Russian and Eurasian History* 10, no. 3 (Summer 2009): 724–29.

23. "Between World Wars, Gay Culture Flourished in Berlin," *Fresh Air*, NPR, December 17, 2014, https://www.npr.org/2014/12/17/371424790/between-world-wars-gay-culture-flourished-in -berlin.

24. "The First Institute for Sexual Science (1919–1933)," Magnus Hirschfeld und das Institut für Sexualwissenschaft, https://magnus-hirschfeld.de/ausstellungen/institute/, accessed March 22, 2023.

25. U.S. Holocaust Memorial Museum, "Magnus Hirschfeld," Holocaust Encyclopedia, https:// encyclopedia.ushmm.org/content/en/article/magnus-hirschfeld-2, accessed March 22, 2023.

26. "Iron Guard," *Encyclopedia Britannica*, https://www.britannica.com/topic/Iron-Guard, accessed March 22, 2023.

27. Centro de Pesquisa e Documentação de História Contemporânea do Brasil—Fundação Getúlio Vargas and Enciclopédia Mirador Internacional, "Plínio Salgado," UOL, July 24, 2008, https:// educacao.uol.com.br/biografias/plinio-salgado.htm.

28. Stephen Minas, "The Patriarch Who's in Lockstep with Putin," EUobserver, March 7, 2022, https://euobserver.com/opinion/154488.

29. Chris Hedges, "Jesus, Endless War and the Irresistible Rise of American Fascism," *Salon*, May 10, 2022.

30. James K. Pollock, "The German Reichstag Elections of 1930," *American Political Science Review* 24, no. 4 (November 1930): 989–95.

31. "Adolf Hitler Is Named Chancellor of Germany," History, A&E Television Networks, January 11, 2023, https://www.history.com/this-day-in-history/adolf-hitler-is-named-chancellor-of-germany.

32. "Howard University 128th Anniversary," C-SPAN, March 3, 1995, https://www.c-span.org/video/?63683-1%2Fhoward-university-128th-anniversary.

33. "States of Incarceration: The Global Context 2021," Prison Policy Initiative, September 2021, https://www.prisonpolicy.org/global/2021.html.

34. "Arguments for and Against Allowing Felons to Vote While Incarcerated," Ballotpedia, December 2019, https://ballotpedia.org/Arguments_for_and_against_allowing_felons_to_vote_while_incarcerated.

35. "Voting Rights Restoration Efforts in Florida," Brennan Center for Justice, February 14, 2023, https://www.brennancenter.org/our-work/research-reports/voting-rights-restoration-efforts-florida; "Election Results: 2020 Florida Results," *Politico*, January 6, 2021.

36. "Ron DeSantis Signs Bill to Create Florida Voter-Fraud Police Force," *The Guardian*, April 25, 2022; "Exhaustive Fact Check Finds Little Evidence of Voter Fraud, but 2020's 'Big Lie' Lives On," *PBS NewsHour*, PBS, December 17, 2021.

37. Lawrence Mower, "Police Cameras Show Confusion, Anger over DeSantis' Voter Fraud Arrests," *Tampa Bay Times*, October 18, 2022.

38. "Literacy Tests," National Museum of American History, https://americanhistory.si.edu/democracy-exhibition/vote-voice/keeping-vote/state-rules-federal-rules/literacy-tests, accessed March 22, 2023.

39. Chetna Sharma, "National Register of Citizens Assam, India: The Tangled Logic of Documentary Evidence," *Journal of Immigrant and Refugee Studies* (forthcoming), https://doi.org/10.1080/15562948.2021.2018084.

40. Nicole Winchester, "India's Citizenship (Amendment) Act 2019," House of Lords Library, U.K. Parliament, February 12, 2020, https://lordslibrary.parliament.uk/research-briefings/lln-2020-0058/.

41. Tobias Hübinette, "Race and Sweden's Fascist Turn," *Boston Review*, October 19, 2022.

42. Steven Erlanger and Christina Anderson, "How the Far Right Bagged Election Success in Sweden," *New York Times*, September 17, 2022.

43. Moussa Bourekba, "The Fight Against Islamophobia in Catalonia: A Challenge to Coexistence," IEMed, https://www.iemed.org/publication/the-fight-against-islamophobia-in-catalonia-a-challenge-to-coexistence/, accessed March 22, 2023.

44. Patrik Szicherle and Péter Krekó, "A Propaganda Machine at the Service of Viktor Orbán," *VoxEurop*, November 18, 2021, https://voxeurop.eu/en/hungary-propaganda-machine-at-the-service-of-viktor-orban/.

45. Diane Jeantet, Mauricio Savarese, and Débora Álvares, "Brazilians Rally for Democracy, Seek to Rein in Bolsonaro," Associated Press, August 12, 2022; Dom Phillips, "Brazil: Tortured Dissidents Appalled by Bolsonaro's Praise for Dictatorship," *The Guardian*, March 30, 2019.

46. "Brazil Election Goes to Runoff Between Bolsonaro and Lula," *Al Jazeera*, October 3, 2022.

47. Alice Ritchie and Gaël Brancherau, "Italy's Giorgia Meloni: From Teen Activist Who Praised Mussolini to Brink of Power," *Times of Israel*, September 26, 2022; Isaac Chotiner, "'I'm a Woman, I'm a Mother, I'm Christian': How Giorgia Meloni Took Control in the Italian Election," *New Yorker*, September 28, 2022.

48. Thucydides, "Pericles' Funeral Oration," University of Minnesota: Human Rights Library, http://hrlibrary.umn.edu/education/thucydides.html, accessed March 22, 2023.

BELLUM SE IPSUM ALET

1. Alexi Jones and Wendy Sawyer, "Not Just 'a Few Bad Apples': U.S. Police Kill Civilians at Much Higher Rates than Other Countries," Prison Policy Initiative, June 5, 2020, https://www.prisonpolicy.org/blog/2020/06/05/policekillings/.

2. Federica Romaniello, "U.S. Accounts for 40% of World's Defence Spending," Forces Network, February 25, 2021, https://www.forces.net/news/us-accounts-40-worlds-defence-spending.

3. Rick Pluta, "2 Men Acquitted in 2020 Plot to Kidnap Michigan Gov. Gretchen Whitmer," NPR, April 9, 2022.

4. Raymond Geuss, "A Republic of Discussion," *The Point Magazine*, June 18, 2019.

5. Elizabeth Hinton, "'A War Within Our Own Boundaries': Lyndon Johnson's Great Society and the Rise of the Carceral State," *Journal of American History* 102, no. 1 (June 2015): 100–112.

6. Christian Bay, "'Extremism in the Defense of Liberty Is No Vice': A Humanist Interpretation of a Rightist Manifesto," *Bulletin of Peace Proposals* 16, no. 2 (1985): 145–54.

7. Newt Gingrich, "Building the Conservative Movement After Ronald Reagan," Heritage Foundation, August 28, 1988, https://www.heritage.org/political-process/report/building-the-conservative-movement-after-ronald-reagan.

8. John J. Pitney, *The Art of Political Warfare* (Norman: University of Oklahoma Press, 2001), 90.

9. Steven Rattner, "Volcker Asserts U.S. Must Trim Living Standard," *New York Times*, October 18, 1979.

10. Robert D. Putnam, "Bowling Alone: America's Declining Social Capital," *Journal of Democracy* 6, no. 1 (January 1995): 65–78.

THERE ARE NO LONE WOLVES: THE WHITE POWER MOVEMENT AT WAR

1. Lisa Lowe, *The Intimacies of Four Continents* (Durham, N.C.: Duke University Press, 2015), 173.

2. Kathleen Belew, *Bring the War Home: The White Power Movement and Paramilitary America* (Cambridge, Mass.: Harvard University Press, 2018).

3. These numbers, drawn from Southern Poverty Law Center and Center for Democratic Renewal estimates, appear in Betty A. Dobratz and Stephanie L. Shanks-Meile, *The White Separatist Movement in the United States: "White Power, White Pride!"* (New York: Twayne, 1997); Raphael S. Ezekiel, *The Racist Mind: Portraits of American Neo-Nazis and Klansmen* (New York: Penguin, 1995); Abby L. Ferber and Michael Kimmel, "Reading Right: The Western Tradition in White Supremacist Discourse," *Sociological Focus* 33, no. 2 (May 2000): 193–213.

4. D. J. Mulloy, *The World of the John Birch Society: Conspiracy, Conservatism, and the Cold War* (Nashville: Vanderbilt University Press, 2014), 2–3, 15–41.

5. On leaderless resistance changing movement attitudes toward recruitment as a measure of success, see Dobratz and Shanks-Meile, *White Separatist Movement*, 25. On membership numbers as secondary to a movement's structure of struggle, see Sidney Tarrow, *Power in Movement: Social Movement, Collective Action and Politics* (Cambridge: Cambridge University Press, 1994), 15.

6. Quoted from FBI internal documents in Andrew Gumbel and Roger G. Charles, *Oklahoma City: What the Investigation Missed—and Why It Still Matters* (New York: William Morrow, 2012), 262. See also Edward T. Linenthal, *The Unfinished Bombing: Oklahoma City in American Memory* (New York: Oxford University Press, 2001).

7. On transnational activity, see Robert W. Balch, "The Rise and Fall of Aryan Nations: A Resource Mobilization Perspective," *Journal of Political and Military Sociology* 34, no. 1 (Summer 2006): 81–113; Mattias Gardell, *Gods of the Blood: The Pagan Revival and White Separatism* (Durham,

N.C.: Duke University Press, 2003); Abby L. Ferber, *White Man Falling: Race, Gender, and White Supremacy* (Lanham, Md.: Rowman and Littlefield, 1998).

8. *The Turner Diaries* was first printed in serial in National Alliance, *Attack!*, 1974–1976 (available at Stimely Collection, University of Oregon, Eugene, box 31, folder 9) and then in book form as Andrew Macdonald, *The Turner Diaries* (Hillsboro, W. Va.: National Vanguard Books, 1978).

9. Ideas about outlasting the so-called Tribulations also appeared in mainstream evangelical accounts such as Tim LaHaye's popular *Left Behind* novels, the first of which appeared in 1995.

FROM CRISIS TO CATASTROPHE: LINEAGES OF THE GLOBAL NEW RIGHT

1. Robert O. Paxton, *The Anatomy of Fascism* (New York: Vintage, 2005), 206.

2. Guillaume Faye, "Europeans and Americans: Brothers in Arms," American Renaissance Conference, YouTube, 0:55:41, https://www.youtube.com/watch?v=pYc-IEFVU2E; Wilmot Robertson, *The Ethnostate* (Cape Canaveral, Fla.: Howard Allen Enterprises, 1992).

3. See Philip Murkowski, *Machine Dreams: Economics Becomes a Cyborg Science* (Cambridge: Cambridge University Press, 2002); Philip Murkowski and Dieter Plehwe, eds., *The Road from Mont Pèlerin: The Making of the Neoliberal Thought Collective* (Cambridge, Mass.: Harvard University Press, 2009); Quinn Slobodian, *Globalists: The End of Empire and the Birth of Neoliberalism* (Cambridge, Mass.: Harvard University Press, 2018).

4. Shane Burley, *Fascism Today: What It Is and How to End It* (Chico, Calif.: AK Press, 2010); Roger Griffin, *Fascism: Key Concepts in Political Theory* (Cambridge: Polity, 2018); Alexander Reid Ross, *Against the Fascist Creep* (Chicago: AK Press, 2017); Timothy Snyder, *On Tyranny: Twenty Lessons from the Twentieth Century* (New York: Tim Duggan Books/Crown, 2017).

5. Georges Bataille, "The Psychological Structure of Fascism," trans. Carl R. Lovitt, *New German Critique* 16 (Winter 1979): 64–87.

6. See Kathleen Belew, *Bring the War Home: The White Power Movement and Paramilitary America* (Cambridge, Mass.: Harvard University Press, 2018); Nicos Poulantzas, *Fascism and Dictatorship: The Third International and the Problem of Fascism*, trans. Judith White (1970; repr., London: Verso, 1979), 331–35.

7. Jean Raspail, *Camp of the Saints* (1973; repr., Petoskey, Mich.: Social Contract Press, 2013); Guillaume Faye, *Archeofuturism: European Visions of a Post-Catastrophic Age*, trans. Sergio Knipe (1999; repr., London: Arktos, 2010); Faye, "Europeans and Americans."

8. Benjamin Noys, *Malign Velocities: Accelerationism and Capitalism* (London: Zero, 2014).

9. See Faye, "Europeans and Americans."

LOSING THE PRESENT TO HISTORY

1. Many instances of this narrative can be found in Osama bin Laden, *Messages to the World: The Statements of Osama bin Laden*, ed. Bruce B. Lawrence (London: Verso, 2005).

2. See Mahatma Gandhi, *"Hind Swaraj" and Other Writings*, ed. Anthony Parel (New York: Cambridge University Press, 2003).

3. For Gandhi's emphasis on the present, see Mahatma Gandhi, *The Bhagvadgita* (New Delhi: Orient, 1980).

4. Mohammad Iqbal, *The Reconstruction of Religious Thought in Islam* (New Delhi: Ahsan, 2013).

5. Hannah Arendt, "Karl Jaspers: Citizen of the World?," in *Men in Dark Times* (San Diego: Harcourt Brace Jovanovich, 1995), 83.

6. Marshall G. S. Hodgson, *The Venture of Islam: Conscience and History in a World Civilization*, vol. 3 (Chicago: University of Chicago Press, 1977), 433–34.

7. See, for instance, Dipesh Chakrabarty, *The Climate of History in a Planetary Age* (Chicago: University of Chicago Press, 2021).

FASCISM AND ANALOGIES—BRITISH AND AMERICAN, PAST AND PRESENT

1. Samuel Moyn, "The Trouble with Comparisons," *New York Review of Books*, May 19, 2020.
2. Maya Wolfe-Robinson, "U.K. Government Should Focus on Covid, Not Statues, Campaigners Say," *The Guardian*, January 17, 2021.
3. "The Times View on Returning Artefacts: Spoils of History," *The Times*, February 10, 2020.
4. Jamie Doward, "I've Been Unfairly Targeted, Says Academic at Heart of National Trust 'Woke' Row," *The Guardian*, December 20, 2020; "The Myth and Reality of Britain's Role in Slavery," *The Economist*, November 12, 2020.
5. Jessica Elgot, "Boris Johnson: U.K. Must Not Return to Status Quo After Covid-19 Pandemic," *The Guardian*, October 6, 2020.
6. Jacob Rees-Mogg, "Labour Ashamed of Our History and Abhors Its Culture," *Express*, November 2, 2020.
7. "The Guardian View of Israel and Apartheid: Prophecy or Description?," *The Guardian*, January 17, 2021.
8. Marc Parry, "Uncovering the Brutal Truth About the British Empire," *The Guardian*, August 18, 2016.
9. Richard J. Evans, "Why Trump Isn't a Fascist," *New Statesman*, January 13, 2021.
10. Daniel Steinmetz-Jenkins, "Beyond the End of History," *Chronicle of Higher Education*, August 14, 2020; Peter E. Gordon, "Why Historical Analogy Matters," *New York Review of Books*, January 7, 2020.
11. Priya Satia, "Why Do We Think Learning About History Can Make Us Better?," *Chronicle of Higher Education*, October 23, 2020.
12. Bill Code, "Australia Aboriginals Win Right to Sue for Colonial Land Loss," *Al Jazeera*, March 15, 2019.
13. Anna Sansom, "France's National Assembly Votes to Return Colonial-Era Artefacts to Benin and Senegal," *The Art Newspaper*, October 7, 2020.
14. Priya Satia, "What's Really Orwellian About Our Global Black Lives Matter Moment," *Slate*, June 30, 2020.
15. Peter Gumbel, "Britain Has Lost Itself," *New York Times*, January 1, 2021.
16. Katrin Bennhold, "She Called the Police Over a Neo-Nazi Threat. But the Neo-Nazis Were Inside the Police," *New York Times*, December 21, 2020.
17. Alberto Toscano, "The Long Shadow of Racial Fascism," *Boston Review*, October 28, 2020.
18. Priya Satia, "An Epic Struggle for Mastery of a Subcontinent," *Los Angeles Review of Books*, March 3, 2020.
19. Zeynep Tufekci, "'This Must Be Your First,'" *The Atlantic*, December 7, 2020.

NARENDRA MODI AND THE NEW FACE OF INDIA

1. Jeremy Gavron, "A Suitable Joy," *The Guardian*, March 26, 1999.
2. Jason Burke and Guardian Interactive Team, "Indian Election 2014: Your Interactive Guide to the World's Biggest Vote," *The Guardian*, April 7, 2014.
3. Jason Burke, "Narendra Modi: India's Saviour or Its Worst Nightmare?," *The Guardian*, March 6, 2014; Pankaj Mishra, "The Gujarat Massacre: New India's Blood Rite," *The Guardian*, March 14, 2012.

4. Tina Parekh, "Modi's Gujarat Worships Hitler," *Times of India*, July 23, 2005.

5. "Gujarat Riots: 'Babu Bajrangi's Brutal Act Done out of Irrational Hatred,'" *DNA India*, September 4, 2012, https://www.dnaindia.com/india/report-gujarat-riots-babu-bajrangi-s-brutal -act-done-out-of-irrational-hatred-1736590.

6. Sujoy Dhar and PTI, "Narendra Modi Rails Against Illegal Immigrants After Assam Killings," *mint*, May 5, 2014, https://www.livemint.com/Politics/NbdTwVHXB4Eld8eKziqgyO/ Narendra-Modi-takes-jibe-at-Mamata-Banerjee-over-her-paper.html.

7. Bella Jaisinghani, "Hitler Fame in B-Schools Prompts Holocaust Exhibit," *Times of India*, November 6, 2012.

8. "Swami Vivekananda," Vedanta Society, https://vedantasociety.net/vivekananda, accessed April 6, 2023.

9. Sumit Galhotra, "Modi's Rise Does Not Bode Well for Indian Press Freedom," Committee to Protect Journalists, March 5, 2014, https://cpj.org/2014/03/modis-rise-does-not-bode-well-for -indian-press-fre/.

10. Kounteya Sinha, "Ratan Tata Awarded Knight Grand Cross of the Order of the British Empire," *Times of India*, May 6, 2014; "Mukesh Ambani," *Forbes*, https://www.forbes.com/profile/ mukesh-ambani/?sh=15c1a4c7214c, accessed April 6, 2023.

11. Raksha Kumar, "Narendra Modi Gets Support from Salman Khan and Salim Khan," *Time*, April 23, 2014.

12. Pankaj Mishra, "Which India Matters?," *New York Review of Books*, November 21, 2013.

13. "Outgoing Manmohan Singh Warns Against Narendra Modi as India's Next PM," *The Guardian*, January 3, 2014.

14. Christopher Hitchens, "11 September 1973," *London Review of Books* 24, no. 11 (July 2002); Janine R. Wedel, "The Harvard Boys Do Russia," *The Nation*, May 14, 1998.

15. Alex von Tunzelmann, "*An Uncertain Glory: India and Its Contradictions*, by Jean Drèze and Amartya Sen: Review," *The Telegraph*, August 1, 2013.

16. Geeta Anand, "Indian Private-School Education Experiment Tests Rich and Poor," *Wall Street Journal*, June 4, 2011.

17. Stuart Jeffries, "Aravind Adiga's Debut Novel, *The White Tiger*, Provokes Roars of Anger in India," *The Guardian*, October 15, 2008; Amit Chaudhuri, "*Behind the Beautiful Forevers: Life, Death and Hope in a Mumbai Slum* by Katherine Boo—Review," *The Guardian*, June 29, 2012.

18. Asbah Farooqui, "B. R. Ambedkar's Three Warnings on Democracy and Where India Stands Today," *DNA India*, April 14, 2014, https://www.dnaindia.com/analysis/standpoint-br -ambedkar-s-three-warnings-on-democracy-and-where-india-stands-today-1976571.

19. Geoffrey King, "On Internet Freedom, India's Perilous Trajectory," Committee to Protect Journalists, January 13, 2014, https://cpj.org/2014/01/on-internet-freedom-indias-perilous -trajectory/.

20. Arundhati Roy, "Afzal Guru's Hanging Has Created a Dangerously Radioactive Political Fallout," *The Guardian*, February 18, 2013.

21. Jane Smiley, "Robert Musil: The Man Without Qualities," *The Guardian*, June 16, 2006.

22. Frank Partnoy, "Inside Men," *New York Times*, June 27, 2013; Dominic Rushe, "Former Goldman Sachs Director Rajat Gupta Guilty of Leaking Insider Secrets," *The Guardian*, June 15, 2012.

23. Anand Giridharadas, "India Has a Soft Spot for Bush," *New York Times*, January 10, 2009.

24. "Home," Arun Jaitley, https://www.arunjaitley.com/, accessed April 6, 2023.

25. Arvind Panagariya, *India: The Emerging Giant* (New Delhi: Oxford University Press, 2018).

26. Sunil Khilnani, *The Idea of India* (New York: Farrar Straus Giroux, 2017).

27. Georgia Korossi, "Portraits of India: Interview with Anand Patwardhan," British Film

Institute, February 21, 2013, https://www.bfi.org.uk/interviews/earth-vision-interview-anand -patwardhan; South Asian Masculinities, "Till We Meet Again Trailer," YouTube, September 16, 2013, https://www.youtube.com/watch?v=OhEOI0A1zWQ; Dissent Videos, "Mati Ke Laal—Red Ant Dream by Sanjay Kak—Full Documentary," YouTube, August 1, 2013, https:// www.youtube.com/watch?v=pJc1vXFdB7g; Skye Sherwin, "Artist of the Week 182: Raqs Media Collective," *The Guardian*, March 22, 2012.

28. Viacom18 Studios, "Gangs of Wasseypur Trailer," YouTube, May 3, 2012, https://www.youtube .com/watch?v=j-AkWDkXcMY; "Peepli Live Trailer," IMDb, 2010, https://www.imdb.com/ video/vi3254060569/.

29. Team LongLiveCinema, "Dibakar Banerjee's *Shanghai* Official Theatrical Trailer," YouTube April 5, 2012, https://www.youtube.com/watch?v=wJV5p0EO1Gc.

30. A. O. Scott, "The Leisure Class Bears Its Burden," *New York Times*, August 23, 2012; Mert Candarli, "Uzak—Distant," YouTube, September 4, 2006, https://www.youtube.com/ watch?v=nAju9EZlt5w.

31. "Chetan Bhagat: Bollywood's Favourite Author," *The Guardian*, April 24, 2014.

SO, IS RUSSIA FASCIST NOW? LABELS AND POLICY IMPLICATIONS

1. Vladimir Putin, "Address by the President of the Russian Federation," Kremlin, February 21, 2022, http://en.kremlin.ru/events/president/news/67828; "On the Historical Unity of Russians and Ukrainians," Kremlin, July 12, 2021, http://en.kremlin.ru/events/president/news/66181.

2. Adam Charles Lenton, "Who Is Dying for the 'Russian World'?" *Riddle*, April 26, 2022, https:// ridl.io/en/who-is-dying-for-the-russian-world/.

3. Michael Rossi Poli Sci, "Vladimir Putin Addresses on Socioeconomic Strategy for Russia," YouTube, March 17, 2022, https://www.youtube.com/watch?v=7FyFkAyqn4Q.

4. Ilia Budraitskis, "Pereizobretenie natsizma dlia nuzhd gospropagandy: Kak moral' zameniaetsia siloi," *Mneniia*, April 14, 2022.

5. Scott Radnitz and Harris Mylonas, "Putin's Warning About Russian 'Fifth Columns' Has a Long, Sordid Lineage," *Washington Post*, March 30, 2022.

6. Andreya Pertseva, "Istoriia stanovleniia voennogo agressora Vladimira Putina," *Tvёrstka*, May 5, 2022, https://verstka.media/putin-voyna-ukraina/.

7. "Putin ob yasnil slova 'terpi moya krasavitsa'" *Vedomosti*, February 10, 2022, https://www .vedomosti.ru/politics/news/2022/02/10/908783-putin-obyasnil-slova.

8. The word "banderites" comes from Stepan Bandera (1909–1959), who was the main leader of the two nationalist organizations, Organization of Nationalist Ukrainians (OUN) and the Ukrainian Insurgent Army (UPA), that fought against the Soviet regime and collaborated with Nazi Germany. They were responsible for pogroms against Ukrainian Jews and the Polish minority. Bandera has become a contested symbol, seen by some as embodying Ukraine's far-right nationalism, by others as a national hero personifying the nation's struggle for its sovereignty.

9. Lev Gudkov, *Vozvratnyi totalitarizm* (Moscow: NLO, 2022).

10. Andrei Kolesnikov, "Gibridnyi totalitarizm: V rossiiskom avtoritarizme poiavili element total-itarnykh praktik, predpolagaiushchikh eshche bol'she konformizma, agressivnosti i nenavisti, schitaet columnist NT Andrey Kolesnikov," *Novoe vremya*, April 4, 2022, https://newtimes .ru/articles/detail/211258.

11. Maria Snegovaya and Kirill Petrov, "Long Soviet Shadows: The Nomenklatura Ties of Putin Elites," *Post-Soviet Affairs* 38, no. 4 (2022): 329–48.

12. Timothy Snyder, *Bloodlands: Europe Between Hitler and Stalin* (New York: Basic Books, 2010).

13. Marlene Laruelle and Ivan Grek, "Manufacturing Support for War: Russia's Preppers, Fellow

Travelers, and Activist Networks," PONARS Eurasia Policy Memo, April 4, 2022, https://www.ponarseurasia.org/manufacturing-support-for-war-russias-preppers-fellow-travelers-and-activist-networks/.

14. From Russian into English, "Interview with Russian Sociologist Grigory Yudin at Skazhi Gordeyevoy (Tell Gordeveva) Channel," YouTube, April 18, 2022, https://www.youtube.com/watch?v=BuuCeY9YwuY.

15. "The Conflict with Ukraine" (Russian public opinion poll), Yuri Levada Analytical Center Moscow, April 11, 2022, https://www.levada.ru/en/2022/04/11/the-conflict-with-ukraine/.

16. Redakstiya, "Kak v rossiiskie shkoly vozvrashchaetsia patrioticheskoe vospitanie," YouTube, April 21, 2022, https://www.youtube.com/watch?v=iIjBdlX-tsM.

17. Andrei Kolesnikov, "How Silent Assent Made Bucha Possible," Carnegie Endowment for International Peace, April 6, 2022, https://carnegieendowment.org/2022/04/06/how-silent-assent-made-bucha-possible-pub-86822.

18. Denis Volkov, "Can You Trust Russia's Public Support for a 'Military Operation' in Ukraine?," *Riddle*, April 12, 2022, https://ridl.io/en/can-you-trust-russia-s-public-support-for-a-military-operation-in-ukraine/.

19. "Ukraina—Opros 20 marta: Predstavleniia o tseliakh Rossii na Ukraine," FOM, March 28, 2022, https://fom.ru/Politika/14706.

20. "The Conflict with Ukraine."

21. Lucas Dolan and Simon Frankel Pratt, "Fascism Starts with Paramilitary Ties to Mainstream Parties," *Foreign Policy*, March 10, 2021.

22. Lukas Andriukaitis, "Signs of Neo-Nazi Ideology Amongst Russian Mercenaries," Res Publica—The Center for Civil Resistance, March 25, 2021, https://en.respublica.lt/signs-of-neo-nazi-ideology-amongst-russian-mercenaries.

23. Annabelle Timsit and Jennifer Hassan, "Signs of Massacre in Bucha Spark Calls for War Crimes Probes," *Washington Post*, April 3, 2022; Pjotr Sauer, "Hundreds of Ukrainians Forcibly Deported to Russia, Say Mariupol Women: Troops Ordered Women and Children on to Buses and Sent Them to 'Filtration Camps,' According to Witness Accounts," *The Guardian*, April 4, 2022; Mia Bloom, "Rape by Russian Soldiers in Ukraine Is the Latest Example of a Despicable Wartime Crime That Spans the Globe," *The Conversation*, April 7, 2022, https://theconversation.com/rape-by-russian-soldiers-in-ukraine-is-the-latest-example-of-a-despicable-wartime-crime-that-spans-the-globe-180656; "Israeli Lawmakers Tear into Zelensky for Holocaust Comparisons in Knesset Speech: Cyberattackers Attempt to Disrupt His Zoom Address," *Times of Israel*, March 20, 2022.

24. Michael Mann, *The Dark Side of Democracy: Explaining Ethnic Cleansing* (Cambridge: Cambridge University Press, 2004).

25. Andrew Buncombe, "Killings in Ukraine Amount to Genocide, Holocaust Expert Says: Several Factors Required to Match Legal Definition Ukraine-Born Academic Tells Andrew Buncombe," *Independent*, April 4, 2022; Dirk Wolthekker, "UvA-hoogleraar genocidestudies: 'Poetin moet voor tribunal gebracht worden,'" *Folia*, April 4, 2022, Actueel, https://www.folia.nl/actueel/151221/uva-hoogleraar-genocidestudies-poetin-moet-voor-tribunaal-gebracht-worden.

26. "Loose Language on Atrocities Will Not Help Ukraine: Biden's Allegation of Genocide Against Russia Is Too Hasty," *Financial Times*, April 20, 2022.

27. "What Joe Biden's Gaffe Says about His End-Game in Ukraine: Nine Ad-Libbed Words Mask His Caution in Dealing with Vladimir Putin," *The Economist*, April 2, 2022.

28. Timothy J. Colton and Samuel Charap, *Everyone Loses: The Ukraine Crisis and the Ruinous Contest for Post-Soviet Eurasia* (London: Routledge, 2017).

29. Max Seddon, Henry Foy, and Aime Williams, "Russia Publishes 'Red Line' Security Demands for Nato and U.S.," *Financial Times*, December 17, 2021.

30. Alexander Cooley and Daniel Nexon, "A False Dawn for Liberalism? Why the War in Ukraine May Not Revive the West," *Foreign Affairs* 101, no. 3 (March 29, 2022); Roger Cohen, "Le Pen Backs NATO-Russia Reconciliation and Reduced French Role in Alliance," *New York Times*, April 13, 2022.

31. Anatol Lieven, "Why It Would Be Better if This Democracy Summit Never Happened," *Responsible Statecraft*, Quincy Institute for Responsible Statecraft, December 7, 2022, https:// responsiblestatecraft.org/2021/12/07/why-it-would-be-better-if-this-democracy-summit-never -happened/.

32. Peter Slezkine, "The Trouble with 'the Free World': Why It's a Bad Idea to Revive a Cold War Concept," *Foreign Affairs* 101, no. 3 (May 6, 2022).

33. David Adler, "The West v. Russia: Why the Global South Isn't Taking Sides," *The Guardian*, March 28, 2022.

34. Shivshankar Menon, "The Fantasy of the Free World: Are Democracies Really United Against Russia?," *Foreign Affairs* 101, no. 3 (April 4, 2022).

ARE WE APPROACHING A NEW WAVE OF FASCISM?

1. Lucy Hughes-Hallett, "Mussolini and the Rise of Fascism," *New Statesman*, June 2, 2021.

2. Robert Skidelsky, "What Would Keynes Do?," *New Statesman*, September 10, 2020.

3. Emily Tamkin, "Joe Biden's Failure on Voting Rights Could Cost the Democrats the White House," *New Statesman*, January 18, 2022.

FIGHTING FASCISM IN THE TWENTY-FIRST CENTURY: THE ADORNO ALGORITHM

1. Adorno observed that the typology *The Authoritarian Personality* study developed did not "afford productive heuristic tools"—that is, it could not reliably generate predictions about any given individual. Theodor W. Adorno, Else Frenkel-Brunswik, Daniel J. Levinson, and R. Nevitt Sanford, *The Authoritarian Personality* (1950; repr., New York: Verso, 2019), 744. Academic audits of contemporary ad-targeting software have demonstrated that the third-party consumer data that they use is often of poor quality and that their algorithms are "correlation machines" with a negligible or even negative effect on sales. Tim Hwang, *Subprime Attention Crisis: Advertising and the Time Bomb at the Heart of the Internet* (New York: Farrar Straus Giroux, 2020). Historically, the concepts of "disinformation" and "misinformation" have been defined in relation to intent. But, as David Karpf points out, "strategic intent is not strategic impact." It is trivially easy for an entity like Russia's Internet Research Agency to manufacture engagement on social media platforms using bots and the services of "click farms." It is substantially harder to demonstrate that engagements motivate political activism or change voter behavior. David Karpf, "On Digital Disinformation and Democratic Myths," *MediaWell*, Social Science Research Council, December 10, 2019, https://mediawell .ssrc.org/expert-reflections/on-digital-disinformation-and-democratic-myths/. As for Cambridge Analytica, specifically, computational social scientists have disputed the extravagant claims that the firm made about the power of its "psychographic" methods. Elizabeth Gibney, "The Scant Science Behind Cambridge Analytica's Controversial Marketing Techniques," *Nature*, March 29, 2018.

2. Alberto Toscano, "The Long Shadow of Racial Fascism," *Boston Review*, October 27, 2020.

3. Max Horkheimer and Theodor W. Adorno, *Dialectic of Enlightenment*, trans. Gunzelin Noeri (Stanford, Calif.: Stanford University Press, 2002), 94.

4. Nick Srnicek, *Platform Capitalism* (Cambridge: Polity, 2017).

5. Shoshana Zuboff, *The Age of Surveillance Capitalism: The Fight for a Human Future at the New Frontier of Power* (New York: Public Affairs, 2019); Shoshana Zuboff, "Big Other: Surveillance Capitalism and the Prospects of an Information Civilization," *Journal of Information Technology* 30, no. 1 (March 2015): 75–89.

6. Wendy Hui Kyong Chun, *Updating to Remain the Same: Habitual New Media* (Cambridge, Mass.: MIT Press, 2016).

7. Adorno et al., *The Authoritarian Personality*, 223.

8. Ibid., 228.

9. Ibid., 744.

10. Ibid., 746.

11. Ibid., 745–46.

12. Ibid., 747.

13. Ibid., 65–66.

14. Ibid., 70.

15. Ibid.

16. Theodor W. Adorno, *The Psychological Technique of Martin Luther Thomas' Radio Addresses* (Stanford, Calif.: Stanford University Press, 2000), 3; Theodor W. Adorno, *The Stars Down to Earth*, ed. Stephen Crook (London: Routledge, 1994), 71.

17. Adorno, *The Stars Down to Earth*, 72.

18. Ibid., 80.

19. Ibid., 77.

20. Ibid., 78.

21. As Lauren Berlant put it, "what's cruel about these attachments, and not merely inconvenient or tragic, is that the subjects who have *x* in their lives might not well endure the loss of their object/scene of desire, even though its presence threatens their well-being, because whatever the content of the attachment is, the continuity of its form provides something of the subject's sense of what it means to keep on living on and to look forward to being in the world." Lauren Gail Berlant, *Cruel Optimism* (Durham, N.C.: Duke University Press, 2011). 24.

22. Adorno et al., *The Authoritarian Personality.*, 747.

23. Alex Stamos, "Tackling the Trust and Safety Crisis," 28th Usenix Security Conference, Santa Clara, Calif., 2019, https://www.usenix.org/conference/usenixsecurity19/presentation/stamos. Thanks to Matt Goerzen and Gabriella Coleman for drawing my attention to Stamos's presentation in their article "Hacking Security," *Logic* 4, no. 2 (2020): 135–49.

24. This example was first suggested to me by the journalist Ava Kofman.

25. Theodor Adorno, *Aspects of the New Right-Wing Extremism*, trans. Wieland Hoban, (Cambridge: Polity, 2020), 26.

26. John Durham Peters, " 'You Mean My Whole Fallacy Is Wrong': On Technological Determinism," *Representations*, no. 140 (2017): 10–26.

27. Corey Robin, " 'Whoever Is Not Prepared to Talk About Bushism Should Also Remain Silent About Trumpism.' —Max Horkheimer," Twitter, October 20, 2017, https://twitter.com/coreyrobin/status/921368631514148865.

28. Chun, *Updating to Remain the Same*, 3.

29. Ibid., 52, 70.

30. Ibid., 73.
31. Ibid., 89–90.

FROM BOWLING ALONE TO POSTING ALONE

1. Daniel A. Cox, "The State of American Friendship: Change, Challenges, and Loss," Survey Center on American Life, AEI, June 8, 2021, https://www.americansurveycenter.org/research/the-state-of-american-friendship-change-challenges-and-loss/.
2. Alissa Wilkinson, "The Radical Political Power of Friendship," *Vox*, August 23, 2022.
3. Daniel Zamora, "Why Your Flights Keep Getting Cancelled," *New Statesman*, July 14, 2022.
4. Dylan Riley, "Bernstein's Heirs," *New Left Review* 76 (July/August 2012): 136–50.
5. Andrés Rodríguez-Pose, Neil Lee, and Cornelius Lipp, "Golfing with Trump. Social Capital, Decline, Inequality, and the Rise of Populism in the U.S.," *Cambridge Journal of Regions, Economy and Society* 14, no. 3 (November 2021): 457–81.
6. Timothy Snyder, "The American Abyss," *New York Times*, January 9, 2021.
7. Paul Mason, *How to Stop Fascism: History, Ideology, Resistance* (London: Penguin Books, 2022); Madeleine Albright, *Fascism: A Warning* (New York: HarperCollins, 2019).
8. Gabriel Winant, "We Live in a Society," *n+1*, December 12, 2020.
9. "Letters," *London Review of Books*, November 19, 2015.
10. Maciej Zurowski, "Atlanticist Post-Fascist," *Weekly Worker*, October 6, 2022.
11. Tariq Ali, "Adieu Boris, Adieu," Sidecar, *New Left Review*, July 12, 2022.
12. Corey Robin, "The Gonzo Constitutionalism of the American Right," *New York Review of Books*, November 1, 2022.
13. Mike DeBonis, "Senate Republicans Block Debate on a Third Major Voting Rights Bill," *Washington Post*, November 4, 2021.
14. Paul Heideman, "Behind the Republican Party Crack-Up," *Catalyst*, September 9, 2021.
15. Max Weber, *Max Weber: Selections in Translation*, ed. W. G. Runciman, trans. Eric Matthews (Cambridge: Cambridge University Press, 1978), 234.

GENDER AND THE RADICAL RIGHT'S DEPARTURES FROM FASCISM

1. The video is available at https://www.tiktok.com/@giorgiameloni_ufficiale/video/714726391 3200045317?is_from_webapp=v1&refer=embed&referer_url=https%3A%2F%2Fwww .indy100.com%2Fpolitics%2Fgiorgia-meloni-melons-election-day-2658346240&referer_ url=https%3A%2F%2Fwww.indy100.com%2Fpolitics%2Fgiorgia-meloni-melons-election-day -2658346240&referer_video_id=7147263913200045317. On Meloni's gender politics, see, for example, Angela Giuffrida, "Italy Giorgia Meloni Denies She Is Anti-Women as Credentials Questioned," *The Guardian*, September 29, 2022.
2. The term is taken from Sarah R. Farris, *In the Name of Women's Rights: The Rise of Femonationalism* (Durham, N.C.: Duke University Press, 2017).
3. See, for example, Katrine Fanger and Lisanne Lichtenberg, "Gender and Family Rhetoric on the German Far Right," *Patterns of Prejudice* 55, no. 1 (2021): 71–93; Elżbieta Korolczuk and Agnieszka Graff, "Gender as 'Ebola from Brussels': The Anticolonial Frame and the Rise of Illiberal Populism," *Sign* 43, no. 4 (2018): 797–821; Tjitske Akkerman, "Gender and the Radical Right in Western Europe: A Comparative Analysis of Policy Agendas," *Patterns of Prejudice* 49, no. 1 (2015): 37–60.
4. See, for example, Jason Stanley, *How Fascism Works* (New York: Random House, 2018), 127–40. A relatively rare exception, which focuses on Germany, is Isabel Heinemann, "Volk and Family:

National Socialist Legacies and Gender Concepts in the Rhetoric of the Alternative for Germany," *Journal of Modern European History* 20, no. 3 (2022): 371–88.

5. See, for example, Dagmar Herzog, *Sex After Fascism* (Princeton, N.J.: Princeton University Press, 2005); W. D. Halls, *Politics, Society, and Christianity in Vichy France* (Oxford: Berg, 1995); Francine Muel-Dreyfus, *Vichy and the Eternal Feminine* (Durham, N.C.: Duke University Press, 2001). Mussolini's quote is taken from Lauren E. Forcucci, "Battle for Births: The Fascist Pronatalist Campaign in Italy, 1925–1938," *Journal of the Society for the Anthropology of Europe* 10, no. 1 (2010): 2.

6. Alexandra Snipes and Cass Mudde, "France's (Kinder, Gentler) Extremist: Marine Le Pen, Intersectionality, and Media Framing of Female Populist Radical Right Leaders," *Politics and Gender* 16, no. 2 (2020): 438–70.

7. Orsolya Bajnay, "Financial Incentives Meet Moral Imperatives in Viktor Orbán's 'Social Contract' with Hungarian Women," Heinrich Böll Stiftung, December 9, 2022, https://cz.boell.org/en/2022/12/09/Orban-Viktors-social-contract-women.

8. "Manifesto for Germany: The Political Programme of the AfD," April 2017, https://www.afd.de.

9. Gabriele Kuby, *The Global Sexual Revolution: Destruction of Freedom in the Name of Freedom* (Brooklyn: Angelico, 2015).

10. A good overview is provided by Sahar Abi-Hassan, "Populism and Gender," in *The Oxford Handbook of Populism*, ed. Cristobal Rovira Kaltwasser, Paul Tassart, Paulin Ochoa Espejo, and Pweew Ostiguy (New York: Oxford University Press, 2017), 426–44.

11. Giorgia Meloni, "Speech at the World Council of Families (2019)," YouTube, https://www.youtube.com/watch?v=VdfNSF-U6zc.

12. Joseph Goebbels, "German Women (1934)," in *The Third Reich Sourcebook*, ed. Sander Gilman and Anson Rabinbach (Berkeley: University of California Press, 2013), 316–19.

13. Eric Fassin, "Gender and the Problem of Universals: Catholic Mobilizations and Sexual Democracy in France," *Religion and Gender* 6, no. 2 (2016).

14. Tjitske Akkerman, "Gender and the Radical Right in Western Europe: A Comparative Analysis of Policy Agendas," *Patterns of Prejudice*, 49, no. 1–2 (2015): 47.

15. Cas Mudde and Cristóbal Rovira Kaltwasser, "*Vox Populi* or *Vox Masculini?* Populism and Gender in Northern Europe and South America," *Patterns of Prejudice* 49, no. 1–2 (2015): 16–36.

16. "Manifesto for Germany," 40.

17. Bajnay, "Financial Incentives."

18. This episode is discussed in Eva Fodor, "A Carefare Regime," in *The Gender Regime of Anti-Liberal Hungary* (New York: Springer, 2021), 29–64.

19. The quote is recorded in Leni Riefenstahl's *Triumph of the Will* (1935).

20. Sandro Ellassai, "The Masculine Mystique: Antimodernism and Virility in Fascist Italy," *Journal of Modern Studies* 10, no. 3 (2005): 314–35; Thomas Kühne, "Protean Masculinity, Hegemonic Masculinity: Soldiers in the Third Reich," *Central European History* 1, no. 3 (2018): 390–418.

21. Jenipher Camino Gonzalez, "AfD's 'White Men' Calendar Sparks Controversy," DW, December 11, 2018, https://www.dw.com/en/germany-afds-white-men-advent-calendar-sparks-controversy-and-ridicule/a-46672403.

22. James Sheehan, *Where Have All the Soldiers Gone? The Transformation of Modern Europe* (Boston: Houghton Mifflin, 2008).

23. Kathleen Belew, *Bring the War Back Home: The White Power Movement and Paramilitary America* (Cambridge, Mass.: Harvard University Press, 2018).

24. Trevor J. Allen and Sara Wallace Goodman, "Individual and Party Level Determinants of

Far-Right Support Among Women in Western Europe," *European Political Science Review* 13, no. 2 (2020): 1–16.

25. Dorit Geva, "Daughter, Mother, Captain: Marine Le Pen, Gender, and Populism in the French National Front," *Social Politics: International Studies in Gender, State and Society* 27, no. 1 (2020): 18, 19.

TRUMP AND THE TRAPPED COUNTRY

1. Michelle Broder Van Dyke, "Trump Tweeted 'See You in Court' and People Turned It into a Huge Meme," *BuzzFeed News*, February 9, 2017.

2. Robert O. Paxton, "I've Hesitated to Call Donald Trump a Fascist. Until Now," *Newsweek*, January 11, 2021.

3. Nicholas Lemann, "The Stimulus Bill Is the Most Economically Liberal Legislation in Decades," *New Yorker*, March 13, 2021.

4. "Toward a More Responsible Two-Party System. A Report of the Committee on Political Parties," *American Political Science Review* 44, no. 3 (September 1952).

5. Roll Call Vote 115th Congress—2nd Session, On the Cloture Motion, February 15, 2018, https://www.senate.gov/legislative/LIS/roll_call_votes/vote1152/vote_115_2_00036.htm.

6. Betsy Klein, "Trump Blames Former Speaker Paul Ryan for Not Getting Border Wall Funding," CNN Politics, January 31, 2019.

7. Zack Beauchamp, "Portland, Polarization, and the Crisis of the Republican Party," *Vox*, July 24, 2020; Erica Werner, Seung Min Kim, and Jeff Stein, "White House, GOP Kill Payroll Tax Cut but Flounder on Broader Coronavirus Bill," *Washington Post*, July 24, 2020.

8. Dan Lamothe, "Defense Secretary Effectively Bans Confederate Flags from Military Bases While Rejecting 'Divisive Symbols,'" *Washington Post*, July 17, 2020.

9. Karoun Demirjian, "Senate Passes Defense Bill by Veto-Proof Majority, Despite Trump's Warnings over Confederate-Named Bases," *Washington Post*, July 23, 2020.

10. Matthew Daly, "In a First, Congress Overrides Trump Veto of Defense Bill," Associated Press, January 1, 2021.

11. Pat Towell, "Presidential Vetoes of Annual Defense Authorization Bills," Congressional Research Service Reports, provided by UNT Libraries Government Documents Department, October 1, 2015, https://digital.library.unt.edu/ark:/67531/metadc795557/; "Statement by the President," National Archives and Records Administration, November 25, 2015, https://obamawhitehouse.archives.gov/the-press-office/2015/11/25/statement-president.

12. Karoun Demirjian, "Bipartisan Defense Bill Includes Several Rebukes of Trump's Record as Commander in Chief," *Washington Post*, December 3, 2020.

13. "H.R.7: To Prohibit Taxpayer Funded Abortions," ProPublica, August 12, 2015; "H.R.36: To Amend Title 18, United States Code, to Protect Pain-Capable Unborn Children, and for Other Purposes," ProPublica, August 12, 2015.

14. "H.R.115: To Amend Title 18, United States Code, to Provide Additional Aggravating Factors for the Imposition of the Death Penalty Based on the Status of the Victim," ProPublica, August 12, 2015.

15. "Rejects Republican Leadership-Backed . . . —H.R.6136: To Amend the Immigration Laws and Provide for . . . ," ProPublica, August 12, 2015.

16. "H.R.1180: To Amend the Fair Labor Standards Act of 1938 to Provide Compensatory Time for Employees in the Private Sector," ProPublica, August 12, 2015.

17. Kate Zernike and Alan Rappeport, "Heading Toward Tax Victory, Republicans Eye Next Step: Cut Spending," *New York Times*, December 2, 2017.

18. Corey Robin, "The Future of the GOP Currently Is a Long, Painful Decline. Paul Ryan Saw the Writing on the Wall—Who's Next?," NBC, May 18, 2018; Russell Berman, "A Domestic Budget to Make Barack Obama Proud," *The Atlantic*, March 25, 2018.

19. Jacob T. Levy, "The Weight of the Words," Niskanen Center, February 7, 2018, https://www .niskanencenter.org/the-weight-of-the-words/; Jeet Heer, "Presidents' Words Can Be Lasting Deeds," *New Republic*, February 12, 2018.

20. Catherine Rampell, "Trump Has Shifted the Country to the Left—or at Least Away from His Own Views," *Washington Post*, October 19, 2020.

21. Mollyann Brodie et al., "The Past, Present, And Possible Future of Public Opinion on the ACA," Health Affairs, March 2020, https://www.healthaffairs.org/doi/10.1377/hlthaff.2019.01420.

22. "Presidential Approval Ratings—Donald Trump," Gallup, September 21, 2022, https://news .gallup.com/poll/203198/presidential-approval-ratings-donald-trump.aspx.

23. Nate Cohn and Kevin Quealy, "How Public Opinion Has Moved on Black Lives Matter," *New York Times*, June 10, 2020; Gary Langer, "63% Support Black Lives Matter as Recognition of Discrimination Jumps," ABC News, July 21, 2020.

24. Corey Robin, *The Reactionary Mind: Conservatism from Edmund Burke to Donald Trump* (New York: Oxford University Press, 2018).

25. Gabe Alpert, "Presidents Who Didn't Win a Second Term," Investopedia, January 16, 2022, https://www.investopedia.com/financial-edge/0812/5-presidents-who-couldnt-secure-a-second -term.aspx.

26. Corey Robin, "The Gonzo Constitutionalism of the American Right," *New York Review of Books*, November 1, 2022.

27. James Hohmann, "Conservatives Fear Trump's Plot to Overturn Loss Will 'Imperil the Electoral College,'" *Washington Post*, January 5, 2021.

CONTRIBUTORS

HANNAH ARENDT (October 14, 1906–December 4, 1975) was a German-born American historian and political theorist. She is the author of *The Origins of Totalitarianism*, *The Human Condition*, *Eichmann in Jerusalem*, and other works of philosophy and politics.

RAYMOND ARON (March 14, 1905–October 17, 1983) was a French philosopher and sociologist, and one of France's most prominent liberal thinkers of the twentieth century.

KATHLEEN BELEW is an associate professor of history at Northwestern University. In her first book, *Bring the War Home: The White Power Movement and Paramilitary America* (2018), she explores how white power activists created a social movement through a common story about betrayal by the government, war, and its weapons, uniforms, and technologies. Belew is co-editor of *A Field Guide to White Supremacy* (2021) and has contributed essays to *The Presidency of Donald J. Trump: A First Historical Assessment* (2022) and the *New York Times* bestseller *Myth America: Historians Take on the Biggest Lies and Legends About Our Past* (2023).

RUTH BEN-GHIAT is a professor of history and Italian studies at New York University and author and television commentator on fascism, authoritarianism, and propaganda. She is the recipient of a Guggenheim and other fellowships and an adviser to Protect Democracy. Her latest book, *Strongmen: Mussolini to the Present* (2020; paperback, 2021), looks at how illiberal leaders use propaganda, corruption, violence, and machismo—and how they can be defeated.

DANIEL BESSNER is an associate professor of international studies in the Henry M. Jackson School of International Studies at the University of Washington. He is author of *Democracy in Exile: Hans Speier and the Rise of the Defense Intellectual* (2018) and co-editor, with Nicolas Guilhot, of *The Decisionist Imagination: Sovereignty, Social Science, and Democracy in the Twentieth Century* (2019).

BEN BURGIS is a columnist for *Jacobin* magazine, an adjunct philosophy professor at Rutgers University, and the host of the "Give Them an Argument" podcast. He is the author of several books, most recently *Christopher Hitchens: What He Got Right, How He Went Wrong, and Why He Still Matters*, and a regular opinion writer at *The Daily Beast*.

SARAH CHURCHWELL is a professor of American literature and chair of Public Understanding of the Humanities at the School of Advanced Study, University of London. She is the author of *Careless People: Murder, Mayhem and The Invention of The Great Gatsby*; *The Many Lives of Marilyn Monroe*; *Behold, America: A History of America First and the American Dream*; and *The Wrath to Come: Gone with the Wind and the Lies America Tells*.

ANGELA DAVIS is a professor at the University of California, Santa Cruz. She is the author of *Women, Race, and Class* and *Are Prisons Obsolete?*

FAISAL DEVJI is professor of Indian history and a fellow of St. Antony's College, Oxford, where he is also director of the Asian Studies Centre. The author of four books, on Al-Qaeda, global Islam, Gandhi's nonviolence, and Pakistan as a political idea, he is an intellectual historian interested in globalization and political thought.

UMBERTO ECO (January 5, 1932–February 19, 2016) was an Italian medievalist, philosopher, novelist, and political commentator. He is the author of *The Name of the Rose* and *Foucault's Pendulum*.

RICHARD J. EVANS is the author of *The Coming of the Third Reich* and other books on Nazi Germany, including *The Hitler Conspiracies*. He is Regius Professor Emeritus of history at the University of Cambridge and, from 2014 to 2020 he was provost of Gresham College, London.

LEAH FELDMAN is an associate professor of comparative literature at University of Chicago. She is the author of *On the Threshold of Eurasia: Orientalism and Revolutionary Aesthetics in the Caucasus* (2018). She is currently working on a new book, *Feeling Collapse,* which explores waning attachments to internationalist feelings amid the collapse of the Soviet empire. Her work has appeared in *Slavic Review*, *The Drama Review*, *The Global South*, and *Comparative Literature*.

PETER E. GORDON is the Amabel B. James Professor of history and a faculty affiliate in philosophy and German studies at Harvard University. He is the author of many books on the history of European philosophy and critical theory, including *Continental Divide: Heidegger, Cassirer, Davos* (2010); *Adorno and Existence* (2016); *Migrants in the Profane: Critical Theory and the Question of Secularization* (2020); and *A Precarious Happiness: Adorno and the Sources of Normativity,* based on his 2019 Adorno-Vorlesungen at the Goethe Universität Frankfurt (forthcoming in German and English, 2023–2024). He is also co-editor of several volumes, including *A Companion to Adorno* (2020) and *The Routledge Companion to the Frankfurt School* (2018), co-edited with Espen Hammer and Axel Honneth.

VICTORIA DE GRAZIA is Moore Collegiate Professor Emerita at Columbia University; the author, recently, of *The Perfect Fascist: A Story of Love, Morality and Power in Mussolini's Italy* (2020); and co-editor with Burcu Baykurt of *Soft Power Internationalism*.

UDI GREENBERG is an associate professor of European history at Dartmouth College. He is the author of *The Weimar Century: German Emigres and the Ideological Foundations of the Cold War* (2015) and, with Elizabeth Foster, he is the co-editor of *Decolonization and the Remaking of Christianity* (2023). His articles on politics, religion, and sexuality have appeared in many academic journals, as well as in venues like *The New Republic, Dissent, Boston Review, n+1,* and elsewhere. He is currently completing a book on the history of European Christians' approaches to politics, sexuality, and colonialism.

ANTON JÄGER is a postdoctoral research fellow at the Catholic University of Leuven. He has published widely on populism, basic income, and the contemporary crisis of democracy.

ROBIN D. G. KELLEY is the Gary B. Nash Endowed Chair in U.S. History at UCLA. His books include *Hammer and Hoe: Alabama Communists During the Great Depression*; *Race Rebels: Culture Politics and the Black Working Class*; *Yo' Mama's DisFunktional!: Fighting the Culture Wars in Urban America*; and *Freedom Dreams: The Black Radical Imagination*. His essays have appeared in several publications, including *The Nation, Monthly Review, The New York Times, American Historical Review, American Quarterly, Social Text, Metropolis, Black Music Research Journal*, and *The Boston Review*, for which he also serves as contributing editor.

MARLENE LARUELLE is Research Professor of international affairs and political science at the Elliott School of International Affairs, George Washington University, and director of the Illiberalism Studies Program at GW. Trained in political philosophy, she explores how nationalism and conservative values are becoming mainstream in different cultural contexts. She focuses on Russia's ideological landscape and its outreach abroad. She has been also working on Central Asia's nationhood and regional environment, as well as on Russia's Arctic policy. She has widely published on Russia's ideologies and nationalism, and on Russia's foreign policy and soft power strategies. She is the editor of the *Oxford Handbook of Illiberalism*, to be released in 2024

GEOFF MANN teaches geography at Simon Fraser University and is a senior fellow at the Institute for New Economic Thinking. His writing appears in *London Review of Books, The New York Review of Books*, and *Dissent*, among other places; his most recent books are *In the Long Run We Are All Dead: Keynesianism, Political Economy and Revolution* and, with Joel Wainwright, *Climate Leviathan: A Political Theory of Our Planetary Future*.

PANKAJ MISHRA is an essayist and novelist, a frequent contributor to *The New York Review of Books, London Review of Books*, and *The New Yorker*, and the author of two books of intellectual history, *From the Ruins of Empire* and *Age of Anger: A History of the Present*. His most recent book is *Run and Hide: A Novel*.

SAMUEL MOYN is Chancellor Kent Professor of law and history at Yale University. His latest book is *Liberalism Against Itself: Cold War Intellectuals and the Makings of Our Time*.

AAMIR R. MUFTI is Research Professor of English at Johns Hopkins University. In 2023, he co-edited "Crisis to Catastrophe: Lineages of the Global Right," a special issue of *boundary2*. His *Forget English! Orientalisms and World Literatures* was published in 2016.

JAN-WERNER MÜLLER is Roger Williams Straus Professor of social sciences at Princeton University. His books include *What is Populism?* (2017) and *Democracy Rules* (2021).

REINHOLD NIEBUHR (June 21, 1892—June 1, 1971) was a leading twentieth-century Protestant theologian who taught at Union Theological Seminary in New York City. He is the author of *Moral Man and Immoral Society* and *The Nature and Destiny of Man*.

REBECCA PANOVKA is a writer and co-editor of *The Drift*, a magazine of culture, politics, and literature she founded with Kiara Barrow in the summer of 2020. Her essays and criticism have appeared in *Harper's, The New Yorker, The New York Times, Bookforum*, and elsewhere.

ROBERT O. PAXTON is professor emeritus of modern European history at Columbia University. His works include *Parades and Politics at Vichy, Vichy France: Old Guard and New Order, Vichy France and the Jews* (with Michael Marrus), *French Peasant Fascism, The Anatomy of Fascism*, and *Europe in the Twentieth Century* (with Julie Hessler).

COREY ROBIN is Distinguished Professor of political science at Brooklyn College and the CUNY Graduate Center. He is the author of *Fear: The History of a Political Idea, The Reactionary Mind: Conservatism from Edmund Burke to Donald Trump*, and *The Enigma of Clarence Thomas*.

PRIYA SATIA is the Raymond A. Spruance Professor of international history and professor of history at Stanford University and author of three prize-winning books: *Spies in Arabia: The Great War and the Cultural Foundations of Britain's Covert Empire in the Middle East* (2008), *Empire of Guns: The Violent Making of the Industrial Revolution* (2018), and *Time's Monster: How History Makes History* (2020). Satia writes frequently for popular media, such as *The Washington Post, Time, The New Republic, The Nation, Foreign Policy,* and other outlets.

TAMSIN SHAW is associate professor of philosophy and European studies at NYU. She previously taught in the Politics Department at Princeton University and has held fellowships at the Institute for Advanced Study and King's College, Cambridge. She is the author of *Nietzsche's Political Skepticism* and has been a regular contributor to *The New York Review of Books* since 2013.

NIKHIL PAL SINGH is professor of history and chair of the Department of Social and Cultural Analysis at New York University. His most recent book is *Race and America's Long War* (2017).

JASON STANLEY is the Jacob Urowsky Professor of philosophy at Yale University and the author of six books, including, most recently, *How Fascism Works: The Politics of Us and Them* (2018) and *The Politics of Language* (2023), co-authored with David Beaver.

DANIEL STEINMETZ-JENKINS is an assistant professor in the College of Social Studies at Wesleyan University. His forthcoming book is titled *Impossible Peace, Improbable War: Raymond Aron and World Order*. He runs a regular interview series for *The Nation*.

LEON TROTSKY (November 7, 1879—August 21, 1940) was a leading Marxist revolutionary of the first half of the twentieth century. He played key roles in the Russian revolutions of 1905 and 1917. In the 1920 and 1930s, he was an important figure in the Marxist opposition against Joseph Stalin.

MOIRA WEIGEL is an assistant professor of communications studies at Northeastern University, a faculty associate of the Berkman Klein Center at Harvard Law School, and a founder of *Logic* magazine. She is also the author of *Labor of Love: The Invention of Dating* (2016); co-editor, with Ben Tarnoff, of *Voices from the Valley: Tech Workers Talk About What They Do and How They Do It* (2020); and a regular contributor to *The Guardian, The New Republic,* and *The New York Times*, among other publications.

CREDITS

Udi Greenberg, "Gender and the Radical Right's Departures from Fascism," written for this edition. Reprinted by permission of the author.

Anton Jäger, "From Bowling Alone to Posting Alone," *Jacobin*, December 5, 2022. Reprinted by permission of the author.

Robin D. G. Kelley, "U.S. Fascism v. Angelo Herndon," in *Four Hundred Souls: A Community History of African America, 1619–2019*, ed. Ibram X. Kendi and Keisha N. Blain (London: Penguin Press, 2021), 292–96. Reprinted by permission of the author.

Marlene Laruelle, "So, Is Russia Fascist Now? Labels and Policy Implications," *Washington Quarterly* 42, no. 2 (July 2022): 149–68. Reprinted by permission of the author.

Geoff Mann, "Are We Approaching a New Wave of Fascism?," *New Statesmen*, February 11, 2022. Reprinted by permission of the author.

Pankaj Mishra, "Narendra Modi and the New Face of India," *Guardian*, May 16, 2014. Reprinted by permission of the author.

Samuel Moyn, "The Trouble with Comparisons," *New York Review of Books*, May 19, 2020. Reprinted by permission of the author.

Jan-Werner Müller, "Is It Fascism?," from "Far-Right Populism Is Bad Enough," *Eurozine*, October 16, 2020. Reprinted by permission of Project Syndicate.

Reinhold Niebuhr, "Pawns for Fascism," *American Scholar* 6, no. 2 (Spring 1937): 145–52. Copyright © 1937 by the Phi Beta Kappa Society. Reprinted with permission.

Rebecca Panovka, "Men in Dark Times: How Hannah Arendt's Fans Misread the Post-Truth Presidency," *Harper's*, August 21, 2021. Reprinted by permission of the author.

Robert O. Paxton, "I've Hesitated to Call Donald Trump a Fascist. Until Now," *Newsweek*, January 11, 2021. Reprinted by permission of the author.

Corey Robin, "Trump and the Trapped Country," *The New Yorker*, May 13, 2021. Reprinted by permission of the author.

Priya Satia, "Fascism and Analogies—British and American, Past and Present," *Los Angeles Review of Books*, March 16, 2021. Reprinted by permission of the *Los Angeles Review of Books*.

Tamsin Shaw, "William Barr: The Carl Schmitt of Our Time," *New York Review of Books*, January 15, 2020. Reprinted by permission of the author.

Nikhil Pal Singh, "Bellum Se Ipsum Alet," from "America's Crisis-Industrial Complex," *New Statesman*, June 30, 2022. Reprinted by permission of the author.

Jason Stanley, "One Hundred Years of Fascism," *Project Syndicate*, October 28, 2022. Reprinted by permission of Project Syndicate.

Leon Trotsky, "Bonapartism, Fascism, and War" [October 1940], in Leon Trotsky Internet Archive (2002); https://www.marxists.org/archive/trotsky/1940/08/last-article.htm.

Moira Weigel, "Fighting Fascism in the Twenty-First Century: The Adorno Algorithm," from "The Authoritarian Personality 2.0," *Polity* 54, no. 1 (January 2022): 146–80. Reprinted by permission of Project Syndicate.

INDEX

Aboriginal Australians, 216
abortion, 162, 170, 182, 300
accelerationism, 194
Ackerman, Seth, 311
Adenauer, Konrad, 292
Adiga, Aravind, 222
Adorno, Theodor
    on astrology, 261–64
    on banality of fascism, 252
    transhistorical analyses and,
        191
    Trumpism prediction and,
        59
    Western civilization existen-
        tial threats and, 252
    See also Authoritarian Per-
        sonality, The
Advani, L. K., 226
Affordable Care Act, xiii, 192,
    308–9
Afghanistan war, 126–27
Albright, Madeleine, 58, 79,
    111, 125, 277
Algeria, 252
algorithmic personalization,
    264–66
Ali, Tariq, 280
Al-Qaeda, 199
Alternative for Germany (AfD),
    300, 303
alt-right, 176, 190, 196
Ambani, Mukesh, 221
Ambedkar, B. R., 222, 231
America First movements, 80,
    95, 144–46, 155, 156,
    157–58
American democracy
    antidemocratic constitu-
        tional design, 310–11,
        312

fascist solutions for problems
    in, 160
image-making and, 293–94,
    296
institutional weakness and,
    305–6
presidential power expansion
    and, 114–18, 119–20,
    206, 280
resilience of, 83
strongman thesis on, 305,
    306–7, 309–10
structural threat to, 130
See also democracy; oppres-
    sion and violence in
    American culture; Trump
    and fascism
American exceptionalism
Global South on, xvii
historical analogy and, 96,
    112–13, 215, 218
indigenous nature of fascism
    and, 136
January 6, 2021, Capitol
    attack and, 105, 206
right-wing populism and,
    66–67
World War II and, 137–38
See also Eurocentrism
American Fascisti Association,
    151
American interwar fascism,
    138–43, 145–46
America First movements
    and, 144–45, 146
anti-Semitism and, 137–38,
    140, 141, 142, 143, 145,
    146, 155–56
apocalypticism and, 194
capitalism and, 143–44

Jim Crow America and,
    140–45
Ku Klux Klan and, 7, 140,
    141, 143
Huey Long and, 142–43
Nazism and, 141–42
populism and, 142–43
possibility of, xiv, 3–10, 12,
    13, 16
racism and, 151–52
Trump and fascism and,
    145–46, 147–48
uniforms and, 68, 140–41,
    147
warnings about, 135–36,
    143–44
American Legion, 150
American oppression as
    fascism
    Black radical tradition on,
        xiii, xvii, 251–52
    Black resistance and, 33–34,
        123
    capitalism and, 33, 59
    criminal justice system and,
        32–33, 160, 252
    critical humanities on, 196
    hate crimes and, 57
    immigration policies and, 97,
        252–54
    indigenous nature of fascism
        and, 97, 135–36, 137–38,
        143–44
    Jim Crow America and, ix,
        xvi, 139–40, 151, 160
    Ku Klux Klan and, xvi,
        138–41, 279
    militias and paramilitary
        groups and, 61, 148
    peripherality and, 193

American oppression as fascism (*continued*)
    right-wing populism and, 137–38, 148
    Vietnam War and, 33
    voter suppression and, 160
    white Christian nationalism and, 159
    See also historical analogy; oppression and violence in American culture; Trump and fascism
American racism
    adaptive political nomenclature and, 95–96
    capitalism and, 27–28, 31–32
    emergent fascism and, 254–55
    as fascism, 212, 277
    historical analogy as apologetics for, 96
    interwar fascism and, 140, 141, 146, 151–52
    legal practices and, 157
    lynchings, 138, 150, 151, 152, 153, 252
    mass incarceration and, xvii, 31, 32–33, 120, 160, 168, 252
    mass shootings and, 167
    policing and, 30–31, 135, 165–66, 251–52, 309
    scientific racism, 155
    Trump and, 67, 127, 146–47, 308
    Tulsa Massacre, 146–47
    voter disenfranchisement and, 160, 170, 252, 255
    See also American oppression as fascism; Black resistance; Ku Klux Klan; oppression and violence in American culture
American Revolution, 206
American right wing
    alt-right, 176, 190, 196
    civil society and, 280
    civil war rhetoric and, 169–70
    critical humanities and, 196–97
    global new far-right movements and, 196
    great replacement theory and, xi
    military and, 303
    nativism and, xiii, 148, 197
    neo-Nazis, 56–57, 127, 175, 177, 181, 187, 189
    Republican Party and, xi, 57, 162, 192, 255, 280
    See also American interwar fascism; American oppression as fascism; January 6, 2021, Capitol attack; right-wing populism; Trump and fascism; white nationalism; white power movement
American slavery
    Civil War interpretations and, 166
    as fascist, 126, 137
    historical analogy and, 206
    imperialism/colonialism and, 217
    as model for Nazism, 156
    as moral wrong, 216
    oppression and violence in American culture and, 28
analogy, 87–88, 109
    See also historical analogy
anarchism, 14
Anatomy of Fascism, The (Paxton), 53, 140
Anders, Gunther, 203
Andrews, Kehinde, 212
Anglin, Andrew, 56
anthropology, 89
anti-Catholicism, 141
anti-colonialism, 153, 200, 202, 203, 210
anti-communism, 61–62, 77, 151, 156, 178
antidemocratic institutions, 310
Antifa, 58
antifascist mobilization. *See* resistance to authoritarianism
antifeminism, 190, 299–300, 301
anti-intellectualism, 44–45, 137, 147
antiliberalism, 189, 195
antilockdown movement, 283
antimodernism, 44, 45, 137, 189
antipluralism, 65–66
anti-Semitism
    American interwar fascism and, 137–38, 140, 141, 142, 143, 145, 146, 155–56
    anti-Communism and, 156
    Arendt on, 22–23, 24–25, 287
    The Authoritarian Personality and, 259
    as characteristic of fascism, 137
    Christianity and, 137, 140
    Communist International and, 24
    conspiracy theories and, 45
    domestic terrorism and, 177
    global new far-right movements and, 189
    historical persistence of, 100
    indiscriminate references to fascism and, 76
    interwar years, 77
    Ku Klux Klan and, 155–56
    Lindbergh and, 145, 146
    lower middle classes and, 7, 8
    nationalism and, 8
    Nazism and, 8, 22–23, 24–25, 26, 137, 156, 158, 259
    Schmitt and, 119
anti-unionism, 141, 273
anti-Vietnam war movement, 32
apartheid South Africa, 182
apocalypticism, 183–84, 193–94
Appadurai, Arjun, 234
Applebaum, Anne, xiii
Arab Spring, xi, 207
Archeofuturism (Faye), 193
Arendt, Hannah, 22–26
    analysis of fascism and, 191
    on apathy, 104
    on banality of evil, 92, 290–91
    on boomerang effect, 67
    on civil society, 271, 288

on illumination, 231
on imperialism/colonialism, 26, 137, 217, 287
on Nazism as totalitarian, 55
nuclear extinction and, 204
on nuclear weapons development, 203
The Origins of Totalitarianism, xviii, 271, 286, 287–90, 297
See also Arendt on truth and lies
Arendt on truth and lies, 285–97
George W. Bush and, 295–96
factual vs. rational truth, 291–92
Hitler and, 286, 288–89
image-making and, 292, 293–94, 296
"Lying in Politics," 293–94, 296
postwar democracies and, 292
Trump and, xviii, 285–88, 289–90, 295, 296–97
"Truth and Politics," 286, 290, 291–93, 295
Arizona Patriots, 180
Arktos, 196
Armenian genocide, 92
Armitage, David, 165
Aron, Raymond, 17–21
Aryan Nations, 182
astrology, 261–62
Atlanta Six, 151, 152
Atwater, Lee, 145
Auerbach, Erich, 191
Austin, Lloyd, 243
Australian Aborigines, 212
Austro-Hungarian Empire, 215
authoritarianism
authoritarian-populist regimes, 94
comparative analysis of, 99
cult of personality, xviii
current growth of, 54, 56–57
dictatorships and, 65
enemy-threat perception and, 120
vs. fascism, 65, 137

friendship as antidote for, 271
global comparisons of, 99–100
historical analogy and, 59
legalism within, 67
as systemic in democracies, 104
variations within, 65
See also global new far-right movements; resistance to authoritarianism; right-wing populism
Authoritarian Personality, The (Adorno et al.), 256–69
as anachronistic, 257–58
critical typology and, 259–60, 264, 265–66, 267
fascism as elastic term and, 102
fascism debate and, xix
historical analogy and, 267–69
networked society and, 257, 268
personalization and, 264–66
political forecasting and, 256
superstition and, 261, 264
systems update concept and, 258, 267, 268–69
technological determinism and, 266–67
Ayodhya mosque destruction (1992), 223, 226

Bachchan, Amitabh, 232
Bachelard, Gaston, 89
Badiou, Alain, 19–20
Badoglio, Pietro, 35
Baldwin, James, 250, 254
Balkan fascism, 42
banality of evil/fascism, 92, 251, 252, 290–91
Banerjee, Dibakar, 232
Bannon, Steve, 57, 116
Baraka, Amiri, 139
Barr, William, 107, 114, 116–21
Barraclough, Geoffrey, xvii
Bartels, Larry, 67
Bartha, Paul, 88
Basu, Kaushik, 221

Bataille, Georges, 191, 193
Beck, Glenn, 231
Beer Hall Putsch (1923), 82, 83–84, 85
Behind the Beautiful Forevers (Boo), 222
Behold, America: The Entangled History of "America First" and the "American Dream" (Churchwell), 155
Belew, Kathleen, xvii, 173–84
Belgium, 301
Bell, Daniel, 291
Bell, Derrick, 157
Bengal famine (1943), 213
Ben-Ghiat, Ruth, xvi, 53–57, 79
Benjamin, Walter, 102, 103, 189, 233
Berlin Olympics, 139
Berlusconi, Silvio, 55–56
Bernanos, Georges, 18
Bernstein, Richard, 286
Bessner, Daniel, xiv, xvi, 122–31
Beveridge, William, 108
Bhagat, Chetan, 233
Bhagwati, Jagdish, 221
Bharatiya Janata Party (BJP), 190, 226, 229, 280
Biden, Joe
civilizational vision and, 244
crisis of neoliberalism and, xvii
election of, 70, 83, 112, 122, 126, 307, 311
immigration/migration and, 104
institutional weakness and, 306
national security state and, 124
Russian regime change and, 243
Trumpist Republicans and, 277
Billionaire's Apprentice: The Rise of the Indian-American Elite and the Fall of the Galleon Hedge Fund (Raghavan), 227
bin Laden, Osama, 199, 200
birtherism conspiracies, xi
Black and Tans, 279

Black Earth: The Holocaust as History and Warning (Snyder), 156
Black Legion, 141
Black Lives Matter protests
  civil society and, 277
  civil war rhetoric and, 166
  crisis rhetoric and, xiii
  historical analogy and, 198
  oppression and violence in American culture and, 218
  Trump responses, 135, 146, 148, 252, 307–8, 309
Black Panther Party, 30
Black radical tradition, xiii, xvii, 123, 149–53
Black Reconstruction in America (Du Bois), 139
Black resistance
  American oppression as fascism and, 33–34, 123
  capitalism and, 31, 32
  classical European fascism and, 138, 139, 153
  communism and, 150–53
  crime and, 28, 29
  economic inequality and, 29–30
  Jim Crow America and, 149–53, 275
  mass incarceration and, xvii, 31, 32
  See also Black Lives Matter protests
Bloch, Marc, 108
Blum, Léon, 9, 70
Blunt, Wilfrid, 216
Boehner, John, xii
Bollywood, 221, 232, 235
Bolsheviks, 74
Bolsonaro, Jair, 161–62, 276
Bolton, John, 129
Bonaparte, Napoleon, 280
Bonapartism, 15–16
Boo, Katherine, 222
boogaloo movement, 279
boomerang effect, 67
Bottai, Giuseppe, 40
Bowling Alone: The Collapse and Revival of American Community (Putnam),

271–73, 274, 276, 278, 281, 284
Braxton, Eugene Angelo. *See* Herndon, Angelo
Braxton, Paul, 150
Brazil, 64, 159, 161–62, 276
Breivik, Anders, 184
Brexit, x, 196, 212
Bring the War Home (Belew), 175, 176, 178
Britain's Gulag (Elkins), 212–13, 217
British Conservative Party, 274, 278, 279–80
British exceptionalism, 215
British Labour Party, 274
Brockway, Fenner, 213
Broszat, Martin, 108
Brothers of Italy, 279, 298, 301
Brown, Michael, 166
Brown, William Montgomery, 152
Buchanan, Pat, 128–29, 192
Bund. *See* German American Bund
Burgis, Ben, xvi, 122–31
Burlak, Ann, 151
Bush, George H. W., 117
Bush, George W., and administration
  Arendt on truth and lies and, 295–96
  executive power extensions, 280
  fascism label as political accusation and, 124, 125
  India and, 228
  National Defense Authorization Act and, 307
  normalization of, 218
  strongman thesis and, 309, 310
  war on terror and, x–xi, 115–16, 119, 120–21, 126, 198, 206
Bush v. Gore, 125

Cambridge Analytica, 256, 266
Camp of the Saints (Raspail), 193
Canada, 252
Canguilhem, Georges, 89

capitalism
  accelerationism and, 194
  algorithmic personalization and, 264
  American interwar fascism and, 143–44
  American oppression as fascism and, 33, 59
  American racism and, 27–28, 31–32
  appeal of fascism and, 73
  civil society and, 282–83, 284
  classical European fascism and, 11, 14, 63, 69, 149, 158
  crime and, 28–30
  crises of, 191–92
  digital, 264
  Eurocentrism and, 199
  fascism as remedy for collapse of, 252–53
  fossil-fuel-based, 253
  global new far-right movements and, 189
  human rights and, 27–28
  incitement model, 60
  India and, 222, 227–28, 230
  as intrinsic to fascism, 33, 103, 253
  Marx on, 13–14
  Nazism opposition and, 158
  postwar resistance to fascism and, 78
  white supremacy and, 188
  See also neoliberalism
Capitol insurrection. *See* January 6, 2021, Capitol attack
Carlson, Tucker, 258
Carr, Joseph, 151
Carter, Jimmy, 307
Cassirer, Ernst, 94
Caste (Wilkerson), 212
Catalyst (Heideman), 282
CEF. *See* classical European fascism
Césaire, Aimé, 67, 137, 217, 251
Charleston church shooting (2015), 184

Cheney, Liz, 86
China, 249
Christchurch mosque attack (2019), 177, 181, 187, 253
Christian Democratic Party (Austria), 62
Christian Front, 142
Christian Identity, 184
Christianity
  American interwar fascism and, 140
  American right wing and, 159, 184
  anti-Semitism and, 137, 140
  classical European fascism and, 17, 159, 299
  definition of fascism and, 42
  fascism and, 140
  postwar resistance to fascism and, 78
  presidential power expansion and, 118
  Putin and fascism and, xix, 159
Christian nationalism, 140, 143, 161
Christians, George W., 141
Chun, Wendy Hui Kyong, 258, 268
Churchill, Winston, 211, 216
Churchwell, Sarah, xvi, 79, 135–48, 155
CIA (Central Intelligence Agency), 126
CIA torture tapes, 120–21
civil rights movement, ix, 169, 275
civil society, 270–83
  Arendt on, 271, 288
  capital and, 282–83, 284
  communism and, 270–71
  conservatives and, 278, 279–80
  COVID-19 pandemic and, 270, 273
  crisis of, 271–73, 274, 278–79, 281
  domestic terrorism and, 276
  internet and, 281–82
  interwar years, 276
  masculinity and, 302

NGOs and, 272, 275, 278–79
  policing and, 278
  political parties and, 274–75
  right-wing populism and, 282–83
  social capital and, 272–73, 276, 278
Civil War, 117, 164, 165, 166, 206, 207
civil war rhetoric, 163–66, 167, 168, 169–70, 172
classical European fascism, 124–27
  apathy and, 104
  The Authoritarian Personality and, 257, 259
  business and, 69, 82, 158, 253
  capitalism and, 11, 14, 63, 69, 149, 158
  Christianity and, 17, 159, 299
  comparisons and, 215
  conservative support for, 159–60
  definitions of, 54–55
  elite collaboration and, 61, 62, 73
  Eurocentrism and, 198
  European Resistance and, 36–37
  French Veterans Riot (1934) and, 69–70
  gender and, xviii, 64, 158–59, 299–301
  genocide and, 55, 76
  global new far-right movements and, 161
  ideology and, 63, 155–56, 158
  imperialism/colonialism and, 54–55, 74, 75–76, 80, 137, 156, 217, 250, 251
  importance of understanding, 71
  institutional domination and, 82, 125–26
  internationalization and, 22–26, 74

interwar resistance to, 77–78, 135, 137
  Ku Klux Klan and, 139, 154–56
  legal practices and, 156–57
  legitimacy and, 19
  lower middle classes and, 5
  Marxist cycle of history and, 13–14
  masculinity and, 302
  militias and paramilitary groups and, 81, 84, 125, 128, 154
  Modi and, 235
  opportunistic nature of, 74, 136, 147
  propaganda and, 22–23, 24, 156, 259, 262
  as secular religion, 17–19, 20–21
  as synecdoche for totalitarianism, 39–40
  Trump differences from, 69, 81–83, 94, 98, 214, 250
  Trump parallels with, ix, 59, 68–69, 79, 83–84, 107, 188–89, 276–77, 280
  uniforms and, 39, 68, 147
  violence and, 59–60, 63, 64, 68, 81, 154, 158
  women's work and, 301
  See also fascism, defining characteristics of; historical analogy; historical conditions for classical European fascism; Holocaust; Italian fascism; Nazism
climate politics, xviii, 72, 217, 249–50, 252–55
Clinton, Bill, 124, 125, 307
Clinton, Hillary, xii, xiv, 81
Coates, Ta-Nehisi, xii
Cold War
  apocalypticism and, 183
  definitions of fascism and, 55
  end of, 72
  fragility of democracy and, xii–xiii, 244
  historical analogy and, 204, 205–6
  Islam and, 199

Cold War (*continued*)
national security state and,
168
neoliberalism and, 258
nuclear weapons develop-
ment and, 203–4
Schmitt and, 114
colonialism. *See* imperialism/
colonialism
Columbine High School attack
(1999), 184
communism
Arendt and, 288
Black resistance to Amer-
ican oppression and,
150–53
civil society and, 270–71
enemy-threat perception and,
61–62, 77
European Resistance and, 37
postwar resistance to fascism
and, 78
resistance to fascism and, 37,
38, 54–55
secular religion and, 19–20
Soviet tropes in modern era
and, 239
See also anti-communism
Communist International, 24,
54–55, 150, 191
Communist Party (France),
19, 270
Communist Party (Germany),
69
Communist Party (Italy), 41
Communist Party (United
States), 150–51, 152
comparative political science, 99
Concept of the Political, The
(Schmitt), 114
Congress Party (India), 225,
227–28
conservatives
civil society and, 278,
279–80
classical European fascism
and, 16, 158, 159–60
lower middle classes and, 6
United Kingdom, 274, 278,
279–80
conspiracy theories, 45–46,
85, 295

contemporary radical right.
See global new far-right
movements
conventionalism, 258
Convergence of Catastrophes
(Faye), 193
Coolidge, Calvin, 155
Coughlin, Charles E. (Father),
6, 142
Council of Economic Advisers, 126
Counts, Dorothy, 254
COVID-19 pandemic
British memory wars and,
212
civil society and, 270, 273
crisis as condition for fascism
and, 72
crisis of neoliberalism and,
xvii
historical analogy and, 198
political impact of, 165
Trump administration
response, 67, 107, 127,
192
Crenshaw, Kimberlé, 156–57
crime
capitalism and, 28–30
economic inequality and,
28–31
hate crimes and, 57, 66
national security state and,
169
See also criminal justice system; mass incarceration;
policing
criminal justice system
American oppression as
fascism and, 32–33, 160,
252
mass incarceration, xvii, 31,
32–33, 120, 160, 168,
252
white power movement and,
178–80
See also policing
crises
Barr on, 117, 121
of capitalism, 191–92
civil society and, 271–73,
274, 278–79, 281
climate politics and, 249

as condition for fascism, 11,
18, 69, 72–73, 75, 76,
78, 158
hyperbolic political forecasting and, 164–65
of neoliberalism, xvii–xviii
presentism and, xv,
100–101
rhetoric of, x–xiv
See also climate politics
critical humanities, 188, 196–97
critical race theory (CRT),
157
Crusaders for Economic Liberty, 140–41

Dalton, Mary, 151
Danish People's Party, 301
D'Annunzio, Gabriele, 40
Dark Side of Democracy:
Explaining Ethnic Cleans-
ing, The (Mann), 242
Das, Gurcharan, 221
data colonialism, 265
Davis, Angela, xvii, 27–34,
251
Davis, Benjamin, Jr., 152
de Benoist, Alain, 194
decolonization, 200, 210
defactualization, 290–97
Defenders of the Christian
Faith, 143
de Gaulle, Charles, 292
de Grazia, Victoria, xvi, 71
deindustrialization, 272–73,
303
de Maistre, Joseph, 44
democracy
associationism and, 284
authoritarianism as systemic
in, 104
civil society and, 274
crisis rhetoric and, xi,
xii–xiii
vs. dictatorship, 244
division within, 65–66
enemy-threat perception
and, 95
far-right campaigns against,
161
fragility of, xii–xiii, 100, 105,
161–62, 244, 305

India and, 222–24, 229
latent fascist tendencies in, 95, 163, 252, 257
mechanisms of used in fascism, 19, 56, 94, 158, 159–60
multiracial, 169
National Socialism within, 252
oppression coexistence with, 109–11
preemptive political preservation of, 111–12
shallow European roots of, 83
See also American democracy; liberal democracy; social democracy
Democratic Party
fascism as political accusation and, xv, xvi
historical analogy and, 112, 124
migrant policies and, 104
national security state and, 170–71
neoliberalism and, xiii, xiv, 192
New Deal and, xiii, 275
southern strategy, 145
Democratic Socialists of America (DSA), 127
Department of Defense, 126
Desai, Santosh, 231
DeSantis, Ron, xix, 160
Devji, Faisal, xvii, 198–210
Dialectic of Enlightenment, The (Adorno and Horkheimer), 257
digital capitalism, 264
digital pessimism, 281
Dilling, Elizabeth, 144–45
Dimitrov, Georgi, 33
disanalogy, 108–10
disinformation, 85
Distant (Ceylan), 232
Dolan, Lucas, 241
domestic terrorism
civil society and, 276
national security state and, 131
peripherality and, 193

presidential power expansion and, 119
white power movement and, 173–74, 175, 177, 180–81, 182–83, 184
Drèze, Jean, 221
D'Souza, Dinesh, xv, xvi
Du Bois, W. E. B., xvi, 139
Dugin, Aleksandr, 194
Duke, David, 127
Durham, John, 120–21
Dutch Party for Freedom, 301
Dutch Socialists, 274

Eastman, Max, 14–15
Eco, Umberto, 35–49, 137, 252
eco-fascism, 253
economic globalization, xiii
economic inequality, xiii, xiv, 28–31, 72, 221–22
economic racism, 30–31
economic security, 5
Edsall, Thomas, 286
Eichmann, Adolf, 290–91
Eichmann in Jerusalem (Arendt), 290–91
Eisenhower, Dwight, 125
Electoral College, 128, 310
Eley, Geoff, 60, 64
elitism, mass, 46–47
Elkins, Caroline, 212–13, 217
El Paso shooting (2019), 177, 184, 187
emergent fascism
American racism and, 254–55
climate politics and, 253–54
definitions of, 56
global new far-right movements and, 56, 162–63
lack of coherent movements, 59–60
myths and avoidance, 255
networked society and, xviii, 257
right-wing populism and, xi
See also American oppression as fascism; Putin and fascism
enemy-threat perception
as characteristic of fascism, 45–46, 95, 253

as condition for classical European fascism, 61–62, 77
fascist tendencies in democracy and, 95
immigrants and, 45, 253
Islamophobia and, xi, 62, 115–16
presidential power expansion and, 114–16, 119–21
war and, 46
World War I and, 156
See also anti-Semitism; conspiracy theories
Engels, Friedrich, 14
Engerman, Stanley, 216
Enlightenment, 215
environmentalism, 194
Erdoğan, Recep Tayyip, xi, 94
ethnocentrism, 259
ethnonationalism, 191, 195, 254
ethnostate, 190
eugenics, 75, 77, 137, 146, 194, 259
Eurocentrism
fascism debate and, xvii
Frankfurt School and, 257
historical analogy and, 198–99, 200, 206–7, 209–10
See also American exceptionalism
European Resistance, 36–37
European Union, 217
Evans, Richard John, xvi, 79–85, 214
Evola, Julius, 43, 44, 193

factual truth, 291–92
Falangism, 38, 42, 47, 136
Fanon, Frantz, 251
Farinacci, Roberto, 40
fascio-modernism, 193
fascism
appeal of, 73, 75, 162
vs. authoritarianism, 65
capitalism as intrinsic to, 33, 103, 253
climate politics and, 252–55
global empowerment of, 195–97
India and, 60, 67, 235–36

fascism (*continued*)
  indigenous nature of, 97,
    135–36, 137–38, 143–44
  indiscriminate references
    to, 58–59, 71–72, 76,
    123–25
  individual social psychology
    of, 102
  as latent in democracy, 95,
    163, 252, 257
  as remedy for capitalist col-
    lapse, 252–53
  white identity politics and,
    277
  See also American oppres-
    sion as fascism; classical
    European fascism; fas-
    cism as political label/
    accusation; fascism
    debate; historical anal-
    ogy; Putin and fascism;
    Trump and fascism
fascism, defining characteristics
    of, 43–48, 136–38
  anti-intellectualism as,
    44–45, 137, 147
  anti-Semitism as, 137
  attacks on free press as, 137
  citizen disenfranchisement
    as, 161
  collective grievance/victim-
    hood as, 137
  dehumanization as, 137
  enemy-threat perception as,
    45–46, 95, 253
  genocide as, 55, 137
  vs. historical conditions, 60
  identity weaponization as,
    137, 147, 157, 161
  ideology and, 63–64, 147
  masculinity and, 47, 64,
    137, 302
  mass mobilization as,
    240–41
  nationalism as, 45–46, 94,
    136
  nativism as, 45, 94
  nostalgic regeneration as,
    43–44, 63, 137, 147, 161,
    162, 277
  Paxton on, 53, 189
  peripherality, 193

  political myths as, 94–95,
    137
  populism as, 94, 189
  racism as, 24, 26, 33, 45,
    137–38
  self-sacrifice as, 76, 82
  violence as, 59–61, 63, 64,
    68, 69–70, 140, 147
  war as, 46, 63, 80, 147,
    239–40
fascism, definitions of, 53–56
  Cold War and, 55
  Communist International
    on, 54–55, 191
  fuzziness of, 42–43, 136–37,
    188–89, 250–51, 252
  historical conditions and,
    71, 94
  historical vs. transhistorical,
    191
  Italian neofascists on, 55–56
  Mussolini and, 53, 54, 56
  population mobilization in a
    cult of war and, 239
  resistance and, 58–59
  World War II and, 54–55
Fascism: A Warning (Albright),
    111, 277
fascism as political label/
    accusation
  George W. Bush administra-
    tion and, 124, 125
  Cold War and, 55
  Democratic Party and, xv, xvi
  indiscriminate use of, 71–72,
    123, 124
  as justification for military
    action, 76
  Obama and, ix, xi–xii, 124
  Ukraine war and, 237, 239
Fascism Comes to America (Kuk-
    lick), ix
fascism debate, ix–xv, xvii–xx,
    127–29, 276
  American exceptionalism
    and, xvii
  The Authoritarian Personality
    and, 256–57
  crisis rhetoric and, x–xiv
  critical typology and, 267
  Eurocentrism and, xvii
  global perspectives and, xvii

  historical analogy and,
    xv–xviii
  hyperbolic political forecast-
    ing and, xv–xvi, xix–xx
  methodological approaches
    to, xix
  national identity and, xviii
  neoliberalism and, xiv,
    xvii–xviii
  systems update concept and,
    258, 267, 268–69
  See also historical analogy;
    Putin and fascism; Trump
    and fascism
Faye, Guillaume, 190, 191, 193
Federal Bureau of Investigation,
    126
Federalist Society, 114, 116,
    117, 121
Feldman, Leah, xvii, 187–97
Feldman, Matthew, 79
feminism, 64, 298
femonationalism, 64, 298
Feyerabend, Paul, 90
Fidesz Party (Hungary). *See*
    Orbán, Viktor
Field of Fight, The (Flynn), 116
15-M movement, 250
Final Solution (Sharma), 231
Fini, Gianfranco, 56
Finkel, Eugene, 242
Floyd, George, xiii, 146, 166
Flynn, Michael, 116
Fogel, Robert, 216
Foner, Eric, xi
Ford, Henry, 146, 155–56
Fort Smith trial (1987–88),
    178–80
For Whom the Bell Tolls (Hem-
    ingway), 38
fossil-fuel-based corporate capi-
    talism, 253
Foucault, Michel, 89–90, 100,
    174
Fourteen Words slogan, 181
Fox News, xi, 68, 171
France
  Communist Party, 19, 274
  far-right apocalypticism
    in, 193
  imperialism/colonialism,
    252

National Front/National
Rally, 194–95, 300
Pétain regime, 15–16
Popular Front, 9, 77
Veterans Riot (1934), 69–70
Franco, Francisco, 42, 55, 74
Frankfurt School, 102–3, 256,
257, 258
*See also Authoritarian
Personality, The*; Neo-
Marxist Institute for
Social Research
freedom of the press, 41, 294
Freedom Party (Austria), 62
Freikorps, 279
French Revolution, 310
Friedberg, Edna, 92–93
Friedländer, Saul, 106
Friedman, Thomas, 164
"friendship recession," 270
See also civil society
Friends of New Germany, 141
Fuentes, Nick, 57
fugitive slave laws, 28
Fukuyama, Francis, 244

Gaidar, Yegor, 194
Galeano, Eduardo, 250
Gandhi, Anand, 232
Gandhi, Indira, 225, 229
Gandhi, Mohandas, 200–202,
219
Gandhi, Rajiv, 226
Gandhi, Sonia, 220
Geer, John H., 152
Geiselberger, Heinrich, 282–83
Gellner, Ernest, 215
gender
antifeminism, 190, 299–300,
301
classical European fascism
and, xviii, 64, 158–59,
299–301
global new far-right movements and, 190, 298–304
great replacement theory
and, 193
reproduction and, 299–300
right-wing critiques of, xviii
white power movement
and, 181
women's work, 301–2

See also LGBTQ+ issues;
masculinity
gender ideology, 300
See also LGBTQ+ issues
genealogies of history. *See* historical analogy
Génération Identitaire, 190
genocide
Australian Aborigines and,
212, 216
Bucha massacre and, 242
as characteristic of fascism,
55, 137
classical European fascism
and, 55, 76
multiple instances of, 92
Native Americans, 156,
214, 216
Ukraine war and, 56, 162,
242–43
white power movement
and, 181
See also Holocaust
Gentile, Giovanni, 39, 63
German American Bund, 141–
42, 146
German Social Democratic
Party, 274
Germany
contemporary far right,
300, 303
repair efforts, 212, 217
See also Nazism
Gerstle, Gary, xvii
Geuss, Raymond, 169
Gibbon, Edward, 213, 214
Gilman, Nils, xvii
Gilmore, Ruth Wilson, 251
Gingrich, Newt, 169–70
global capitalism, 189, 222
globalization, 72, 196
global new far-right movements
American exceptionalism
and, 105
antifascism as oppositional
movement and, 191
apocalypticism and, 193–94
attacks on humanities studies, 188
authoritarianism and, xi
The Authoritarian Personality
on, 264

capitalism and, 189
citizen disenfranchisement
and, 161
civil wars and, 207–8
classical European fascism
connections, 161
climate politics and, 249–50,
253–54
comparative political science
on, 99–100
crisis rhetoric and, xi
critical humanities on, 197
culture and, 189, 190
definitions of fascism and,
55–56
emergent fascism and, 56,
162–63
extremists and, 167
fascism empowerment,
195–97
gender and, 190, 298–304
great replacement theory
and, 62, 161, 187, 193,
255
growth of, 161–63, 244
Hindu nationalism and, 189
ideology and, 189–90
January 6, 2021, Capitol
attack and, 208–9
lack of emphasis on military
and, 303
masculinity and, 302–3
neoliberalism and, 194–95
nostalgic regeneration and,
161, 162
reproduction and, 300
resistance to, 191
right-wing populism and, xi,
58, 105
Russia and, 194, 195–96,
244
social media and, 189
white nationalism and, 187,
189–91, 196
white power movement
and, 182
white supremacy and, 189
women's support and, 303–4
women's work and, 301–2
See also India
Global North, 244
global present, 203–6, 207

Global South, xiii, xvii, 244, 245
Go-Between, The (Hartley), 88
Goebbels, Joseph, 82, 301
Golden Dawn, 190
Goldwater, Barry, 145, 169
Gordon, Peter E., xii, xvi, 86–105, 110, 215
Göring, Hermann, 44, 63, 82
Gosar, Paul, 57
Gramsci, Antonio, 41, 44, 63
Grant, Madison, 138, 155, 194
Great Depression, x, 69, 70, 74, 75, 76, 149, 158, 192
  See also New Deal
Great Recession, 192
great replacement theory
  American interwar fascism and, 155
  American right wing and, xi
  global new far-right movements and, 62, 161, 187, 193, 255
  Islamophobia and, 62, 181, 182
  peripherality and, 193
  white power movement and, 181, 182–83
great resignation, 273
Great Society, 169
Greenberg, Udi, xviii, 298–304
Greene, Marjorie Taylor, 57, 280
Griffin, Roger, 63, 79, 136
Gropius, Walter, 40
Guantánamo Bay, 126
Gudkov, Lev, 239
Guenon, René, 44
Gupta, Rajat, 227
Guzmán, Jacobo Arbenz, 123

Hacking, Ian, 90
Halwai, Balram, 222
Harding, Warren G., 146
Harris, Kamala, 209
Hartley, L. P., 88
hate crimes, 57, 66
Heidegger, Martin, 288
Heideman, Paul, 282
Heimbach, Matthew, 196
Hemingway, Ernest, 38
Herero and Nama genocide, 92
Herndon, Angelo, 149–53

Herndon, Harriet, 150
Herndon, Milton, 153
Herndon, Sallie, 150
heroism, 47
heteronormativity. *See* LGBTQ+ issues
Heyer, Heather, 193
Himmler, Heinrich, 82
Hindenburg, Paul von, 69
Hindu nationalism, 161, 219–20, 224–25, 226, 229, 233, 280
Hirschfeld, Magnus, 157–58
historical analogy
  adaptive political nomenclature and, 95–96, 104–5
  American cultural superficiality and, 76–77
  American exceptionalism and, 96, 112–13, 215, 218
  anticolonialism and, 202, 203
  as apologetics, 96, 102, 103, 107–9, 216
  appeal of, 79–80, 106–7, 188
  British imperialism/colonialism and, 211–18
  Cold War and, 204, 205–6
  communist threat perception and, 61–62
  comparative political science discipline and, 99–100
  disanalogy and, 108–10
  elite collaboration and, 61, 62
  Eurocentrism and, 198–99, 200, 206–7, 209–10
  fascism debate and, xv–xviii
  fascism vs. right-wing populism and, 65–67
  Frankfurt School on, 102–3
  Historikerstreit on, 106, 109
  Holocaust and, 56, 86–87, 91, 92–93, 109, 212
  hyperbolic political forecasting and, xix–xx
  ideology and, 63–64
  incommensurability thesis and, 88–91
  Islam and, 199–200, 204–5

Italy and, 38
January 6, 2021, Capitol attack and, 206–7
  media encouragement of, 59
  misuses of, 112, 215, 217–18, 267–68
  Nazi use of, 214–15
  necessity of, 86–87, 93–94
  9/11 and, 198
  nominalism on, 98–99
  nuclear weapons development and, 203–4
  oppression and violence in American culture and, 96, 104, 109–10, 111, 112, 211, 218
  polarized interpretations and, 97–98
  presentism and, xv, 91, 100–101
  resistance to authoritarianism and, 85, 101–2, 107–8, 110–11, 112
  sloppiness of, 92–93
  stigma and, 56, 94
  strengths of, 96
  Ukraine war and, 242–44
  usefulness of, 94–96, 98, 103–4, 250
  violence and, 200–202
  violence as characteristic of fascism and, 59–60, 63, 64, 68
  violence as condition for fascism and, 59, 277
  war on terror and, 198, 206
  See also Trump and fascism
historical conditions for classical European fascism
  communist threat perception as, 61–62, 77
  conservative labor parties and, 16
  crisis as, 11, 18, 69, 72–73, 75, 76, 78, 158
  definition of fascism and, 71, 94
  experience of violence as, 11, 59, 61, 277
  experience of war as, 60–61, 73, 76, 80, 277–78

Great Depression as, 69, 75, 76, 158
Marx on, 60–61
Trotsky on, 11–12
working class and, 14, 277
histories of the present. *See* historical analogy
Historikerstreit (historian's dispute), 106, 109
history wars, xviii
Hitler, Adolf
  as analogical fascist, 124
  Beer Hall Putsch and, 82, 83–84
  Franco and, 55
  "freedom from interest servitude" and, 6
  German conservatives and, 159–60
  Indian reverence for, 220
  Jim Crow America and, 138–39
  racialized nationalism and, 156
  rise to power, 159
  Stalin and, 15, 106
  state organization and, 82
  suicide of, 76, 82, 243
  Trump parallels, 59, 68, 79, 83–84
  truth and lies and, 286, 288–89
  See also Nazism
Hitler Movement, 141
Hitler's American Model: The United States and the Making of Nazi Race Law (Whitman), 157, 214
Hitler-Stalin Pact (1939), 15
Hobsbawm, Eric, 215
Hodgson, Marshall, 199, 204–5
Holocaust
  dehistoricization of, 86–87, 91–93, 189
  Eco on, 36
  Eichmann trial and, 290
  historical analogy and, 56, 86–87, 91, 92–93, 109, 212
  Italian fascism and, 41–42
  Jewish refugees and, 157–58

"never again" moral imperative and, 76, 97
Trump administration and, 57
homophobia, 190, 258, 300
  See also LGBTQ+ issues
Hoover, Herbert, 125
Hoover, J. Edgar, 32
Horkheimer, Max, 102, 191, 257, 258, 268
How Democracies Die (Ziblatt and Levitsky), 99
How Fascism Works (Stanley), 94, 111
Hübinette, Tobias, 161
Hudson, John, 152
Hughes, Langston, xvi, 139
humanities. *See* critical humanities
Hungary
  nostalgic regeneration and, 161
  Orbán's electoral victory, 244
  reproduction and, 300
  right-wing authoritarianism and, xi
  Russia and, 195–96
  stigma of fascism label and, 56, 94
  women's work and, 301, 302
  See also Hungary; Orbán, Viktor
Hussein, Saddam, 76, 295

Idea of India, The (Khilnani), 229
illiberalism. *See* global new far-right movements
image-making, 292, 293–94, 296
Immigration Act (1924), 146
Immigration and Customs Enforcement (ICE), 125
immigration/migration
  Biden policies, 104
  Civil War historical interpretations and, 166
  climate politics and, 252–55
  global new far-right movements and, 195, 197, 300
  great replacement theory and, 155, 161, 181, 182, 300

Hindu nationalism and, 161
historical analogy and, 86, 93, 97
India and, 229
Italian fascism and, 162
legislative reform and, 308
masculinity and, 303
Muslim immigrants, 161, 181–82
national security state and, 168
race and, 209
Trump policies and rhetoric, 66, 86, 93, 97, 116, 119, 125, 128, 146, 307
US Muslim travel ban, 116, 119, 125, 128
imperialism/colonialism
  Arendt on, 26, 137, 217, 287
  boomerang effect and, 67
  classical European fascism and, 54–55, 74, 75–76, 80, 137, 156, 217, 250, 251
  colonial reparations and, 112
  data colonialism, 265
  definitions of fascism and, 42
  Eurocentrism and, 199
  as fascist, 137
  historical analogy and, 211–18
  historical conditions for fascism and, 73
  Russia and, 238, 245
  Trump and, 80
  Ukraine war and, 245
  violence in American culture and, 166
  See also anti-colonialism
incitement capitalism, 60
incommensurability thesis, 88–91
India, 219–36
  activist networks in, 230
  Bollywood, 221, 232, 235
  British imperialism and, 213, 214
  citizen disenfranchisement and, 161
  culture, 231–33
  democracy and, 222–24, 229
  economic inequality, 221–22

India (*continued*)
fascism as plausible designation in, 60, 67, 235–36
globalized economy and, 230
Hindu nationalism in, 161, 219–20, 224–25, 226, 229, 233, 280
informal economic sector in, 228, 229
journalism and news media in, 231, 235
Kashmir oppression, 223, 225, 226, 231
media, 231, 235
modernism and, 224–25
Muslims in, 161, 219–20, 223, 224, 226, 234
Nehru-Gandhi dynasty, 225–26, 229
neoliberalism and, 221, 222, 226–27, 228, 233
political violence in, 219–20, 223, 225–26, 234
right-wing populism in, 229
technocratic rule in, 224–25, 226
US capitalism and, 227–28, 229
India Unbound (Das), 221
individualism, 5–6, 9
International Jew, The (Ford), 146, 156
International Labor Defense (ILD), 151, 152
internet, 281–82
interpretative sociology, 101
interwar American fascism. *See* American interwar fascism
Intimacies of Four Continents, The (Lowe), 174
Iqbal, Mohammad, 202
Iran-Contra affair, 117–18
Iraq War, 115–16, 126–27, 217, 295–96
irrationalism, 44, 63
ISIS, 199
Islam, and historical analogy, 199–200, 204–5
"Islamo-fascism." *See* Islamophobia
Islamophobia

George W. Bush administration and, xi
Christchurch mosque attack (2019), 177, 181, 253
enemy-threat perception and, xi, 62, 115–16
great replacement theory and, 62, 161, 181, 182
historical analogy and, 198–99
Indian anti-Muslim violence and, 219–20, 223, 226, 234
racism and, 119
United States and, 62, 115–16, 119, 121, 125, 128
white power ideology and, 177
Israel, 131, 212, 226, 290–91
Italian Communist Party, 41, 274
Italian fascism
American newspapers and, 149–50
appeal of, 39
Christianity and, 159
culture and, 40–41
development of, 73–74
elite collaboration and, 61, 62, 73
historical conditions for, 73
identification with Roman Empire and, 41, 48, 74, 80
ideology and, 37–38, 39, 63
imperialism/colonialism and, 54–55, 80
Ku Klux Klan comparisons and, 140
national nature of, 23
qualitative populism and, 48
radical anticapitalism and, 42–43
rehabilitation and, 55
repression and, 41–42
resistance to, 77
Third Reich alliance, 74
vs. totalitarianism, 39, 40
youth and, 35–36, 48–49
See also classical European fascism; Italian neofascism

Italian neofascism, 55–56, 64, 162, 279, 298, 300
Italian Social Movement, 279
It Can't Happen Here (Lewis), ix, 105, 135, 143, 148

Jackson, Andrew, 138
Jäger, Anton, xix, 270–84
Jai Bhim Comrade (Patwardhan), 231
Jaitley, Arun, 228
James, C. L. R., 137
January 6, 2021, Capitol attack
American exceptionalism and, 105, 206
Arendt on truth and lies and, 286
attempted coup rhetoric and, 83, 123–24, 130–31
Civil War and, 207
civil war rhetoric and, 168
fragility of democracy and, 105
global new far-right movements and, 208–9
historical analogy and, 206–7
Hitler parallels, 83–85
hyperbolic political forecasting and, xv–xvi, 164
ineffectiveness of, 83, 122–23, 130, 283
police and, 83, 85, 131
Republican Party and, 57, 85, 131
strongman politics and, 305
Trump and fascism and, 54, 69, 70, 83–85, 122, 123, 127, 193
Trump's social capital and, 276
Japan, 74
expansion and, 77
Jaspers, Karl, 203, 204
Jewish Councils, 291
Jim Crow America
American interwar fascism and, 7, 140, 141, 143
Black resistance and, 149–53, 275
communist organizing against, 150–51

as fascist, ix, xvi, 126, 139–
40, 151, 160
historical analogy and, 206
institutional domination
and, 126
legal practices in, 157
Nazi connections with, 138–
39, 156, 157, 214, 217
persistence of, 160
See also Ku Klux Klan
Jobbik, 190
Jobs, Steve, 303
John Birch Society, 178
Johnson, Boris, 211, 212
Johnson, James, 34
Johnson, Lyndon, 169
Johnson, Matthew Raphael,
196
Johnson, R. W., 278
Jones, Alex, 258
Juneteenth, 146–47

Kak, Sanjay, 232
Kakutani, Michiko, 106, 286
Kalecki, Michał, 252, 253
Karp, Matt, xx
Keane, John, 230
Kelley, Robin Davis Gibran,
xvii, 149–53
Kendzior, Sarah, 277
Kenya, 212–13, 217
Keynes, John Maynard, 252–53,
254
Khilnani, Sunil, 229
King, Martin Luther Jr., 275
Kohn, Jerome, 295–96
Kolesnikov, Andrei, 239
Kristallnacht, 128, 142
Kuby, Gabriele, 300
Kuhn, Thomas, 90
Kuklick, Bruce, ix
Ku Klux Klan
as America First movement,
146, 155
American interwar fascism
and, 7, 140, 141, 143
American oppression as
fascism and, xvi, 138–41,
279
Black antifascism and,
149–50
civil society and, 279

classical European fascism
and, 139, 154–56
Nazi connections, 139
Trump and, 127, 146
white power movement and,
175, 181
See also Jim Crow America
Kunze, Gerhard, 142

labor unions, 6, 12, 41, 155,
272–73
Lane, David, 181
Laruelle, Marlene, xvii, xix,
237–45
Latin American dictatorships,
250
League of Nations, 73, 74,
145
Learning from the Germans
(Neiman), 212
left-wing antifascism, 126
Legion of the Archangel
Michael (Romania), 159
Leibniz, G. W., 99
Lenin, V. I., 14
Le Pen, Marine, 64, 196, 244,
278, 304
Levinas, Emmanuel, 191
Levitsky, Steven, 99
Lewis, Sinclair, ix, 105, 135,
143, 148
LGBTQ+ issues, xviii, 56, 158–
59, 182, 197, 300
See also gender
liberal antifascism, 126
liberal democracy
banality of fascism and, 252
Barr as threat to, 121
complicity of, 58
defactualization and, 292
emergent fascism and,
257–58
image-making and, 296
World War I discrediting
of, 80
See also democracy
liberalism, 119, 126, 194, 196
Limbaugh, Rush, 231
Lindbergh, Charles, 95, 128–
29, 145, 146, 158
Lonely Crowd, The (Riesman),
xix

lone wolf myth, 173–74, 175,
177, 180
Long, Huey, 6–7, 10, 142–43,
144
Lowe, Lisa, 174
lower middle classes, 3–10
demagogic appeals to, 6–7
individualism of, 5–6, 9
modern capitalism contraction and, 6
nationalism and, 7–8
1930s possibility of American fascism and, 3–4,
5, 9–10
racism and, 7
Luccock, Halford, 144
Luce, Edward, 164
Luther, Martin, 303
"Lying in Politics" (Arendt),
293–94, 296
lynchings, 138, 150, 151, 152,
153, 252

Macaulay, Thomas Babington,
311
MAGA hats, 68
Maier, Charles, 108–9
Male Phantasies (Theweleit), 64
Malm, Andreas, 253
Mamdani, Mahmood, 214, 217
Manifest Destiny, 156
Mann, Geoff, xviii, 249–55
Mann, Michael, 242
Manne, Kate, 66
Manson, Charles, 123
Man Without Qualities, The
(Musil), 223
Marche, Stephen, 164–65
Marcus, Ruth, 285
Marinetti, Filippo Tommaso,
41, 193
Martin, Cathie Jo, 282
Marx, Karl
on cycle of history, 13–15
on historical analogy, 215
historical analogy and,
102–3
on historical conditions for
classical European fas-
cism, 60–61
on imperialism/colonialism,
214

Marx, Karl (*continued*)
  on lumpenproletariat, 29
  materialism of, 18
  on French revolution of
    1848, 283
masculinity, 47, 64, 137, 197,
  238, 302–3
Mason, Paul, 277
"Mass Demonstration for True
  Americanism" (1939),
  141
mass incarceration, xvii, 31,
  32–33, 120, 160, 168,
  252
Matteotti, Giacomo, 41
Matteotti, Rosselli, 41
Mattis, James, 129
Maurras, Charles, 18
McCain, John, ix, 128
McCarthy, Mary, 285, 291
McCarthyism, 72, 250
McConnell, Mitch, xii, 280,
  281, 308
McMaster, H. R., 129
McNamara, Robert, 293
McNaughton, John, 294
McNeill, William H., 204
McVeigh, Timothy, 180, 276
  See also Oklahoma City
    bombing
media
  historical analogy and, 59
  incitement capitalism and,
    60
  India, 231, 235
  indiscriminate references to
    fascism and, 76
  Nazism and, 75
  personalization and, 264–66
  Russia, 241
  technological determinism
    and, 266–67
  Trump and, 68, 94, 295,
    296, 297
  Vietnam War and, 294–95
  See also social media
Meier, Heinrich, 119
Mein Kampf (Hitler), 38, 156,
  235
Meloni, Giorgia, 56, 64, 162,
  279, 298, 300
Michéa, Jean-Claude, 270, 271

middle-class frustration, 45
Mies van der Rohe, Ludwig, 40
migration. *See* immigration/
  migration
militias and paramilitary groups
  American oppression as
    fascism and, 61, 148
  as characteristic of fascism,
    137
  civil society and, 279
  classical European fascism
    and, 81, 84, 125, 128, 154
  far-right militias and, 67
  interwar American fascism
    and, 140–42
  masculinity and, 64
  modern uncoordinated
    nature of, 279–80
  oppression and violence in
    American culture and, 67,
    167, 180, 279
  Russia, 241–42
  Trump and, 68, 83, 105, 148
Mills, C. Wright, xix
Mishra, Pankaj, xvii, 219–36
misinformation, 85
misogyny. *See* gender
Mitchell, John N., 32
modernism, 44, 205, 224–25,
  258
Modi, Narendra
  anti-Muslim violence and,
    219–20, 234
  consumerism and, 220–21,
    223
  far right as political culture
    and, 190
  as fascist, 60, 67, 235–36
  global capitalism and, 230
  nativism and, 229
  Nehru-Gandhi dynasty
    and, 233
  right-wing authoritarian
    populism and, xi, 94
  stigma of fascism label and,
    94
  technocratic rule and,
    224–25
  Trump and, 234–36
  See also India
Monroe Doctrine, 75
Montale, Eugenio, 41

Moral Man and Immoral Society
  (Niebuhr), xix
Morrison, Toni, 160
Mossadegh, Mohammad, 123
Moyn, Samuel, xvi, 106–13,
  131, 136, 286
Mueller, Robert, 118
Mufti, Aamir R., xvii, 187–97
Mughal Empire, 213
Müller, Jan-Werner, xv, xvi,
  58–67, 94
multiculturalism, 190
Musil, Robert, 59, 223, 234
Musk, Elon, 56
Muslim immigrants, 161,
  181–82
Muslims
  as immigrants, 161, 181–82
  in India, 161, 219–20, 223,
    224, 226, 234
  US travel ban on, 116, 119,
    125, 128
Mussolini, Benito
  American finance capital
    and, 149
  Blackshirts and, 49, 125,
    128, 154, 158
  business and, 69, 82
  definitions of fascism and,
    53, 54, 56
  elite collaboration and, 61, 73
  Franco and, 55
  ideology and, 39
  imperialism/colonialism
    and, 139, 153
  on indigenous nature of
    fascism, 137
  Italian youth and, 35
  Ku Klux Klan and, 140
  March on Rome, 84, 130, 154
  Nazism and, 38
  personality of, 73–74
  populism and, 48
  reproduction and, 300
  resistance to fascism and, 77
  squadristi and, 68
  World War I and, 60
  See also Italian fascism;
    Order of Black Shirts

Nagaraj, D. R., 225
Napoleon III, 283–84

National Alliance (Italy), 56
National Defense Authorization
    Act (NDAA), 307
National Alliance (US), 180
National Front/National Rally
    (France), 194–95, 300
national identity, xviii
nationalism
    Arendt on, 25–26
    as characteristic of fascism,
        45–46, 94, 136
    global new far-right move-
        ments and, 189–90
    indigenous nature of fascism
        and, 136, 143–44
    interwar years, 77
    Italian fascism and, 54
    lower middle classes and,
        7–8
    opportunistic nature of fas-
        cism and, 147
    resistance to fascism and,
        77
National Labor Relations
    Board, 128
National Security Agency
    (NSA), 223
National Security Council, 126
National Socialism. *See* Nazism
Native American genocide, 156,
    214, 216
nativism
    America First movements,
        80, 95, 144–46, 155, 156,
        157–58
    American right wing and,
        xiii, 148, 197
    anti-immigrant violence and,
        177, 183
    as characteristic of fascism,
        45, 94
    civil society and, 280
    climate politics and, 254
    enemy-threat perception and,
        45, 253
    global new far-right move-
        ments and, 190, 195
    in India, 222, 229
    Ku Klux Klan and, 139
    mass shootings and, 167
NATO expansion, 243
Nazism

American interwar fascism
    and, 141–42
American slavery as model
    for, 156
anticonstitutionalism of,
    278–79
anti-Semitism and, 8, 22–23,
    24–25, 26, 137, 156,
    158, 259
attacks on free press and,
    94, 137
British imperialism and, 212,
    216, 217
Brownshirts and, 84, 125,
    128
business and, 158, 253
Christianity and, 17, 159
as complete political pro-
    gram, 38, 76
culture and, 40
gender and, 158–59
German efforts to repair,
    212, 217
Great Depression and, 75
Hindu nationalism and,
    219, 220
Historikerstreit on, 106, 109
identity weaponization and,
    157, 219
ideology and, 63, 155–56,
    158
imperialism/colonialism
    and, 54–55, 76, 80, 156
internationalization and,
    22–26, 74–75
Jim Crow America connec-
    tions, 138–39, 156, 157,
    214, 217
legitimacy and, 19
media and, 75
multiple constituencies of,
    159
Native American genocide as
    model for, 156, 214, 216
Putin's rhetoric and, 237
racism and, 18, 24, 38, 76,
    137, 157
rearmament of, 74, 75
religion and, 17–18, 39
rise to power, 19, 158, 159
Schmitt and, 114, 115
self-sacrifice and, 82

singular nature of, 42
as totalitarian, 38–39, 40, 55,
    74–75
traditionalism and, 43–44
Trump and, 146
truth and lies and, 286,
    288–89
use of historical analogy,
    214–15
violence and, 158
war experience and, 60
See also classical European
    fascism; Holocaust
Neal, Claude, 138
Nehru, Jawaharlal, 224, 225,
    226, 227, 229
Neighboring Sounds (Filho),
    232
Neiman, Susan, 212, 217
Neither Settler nor Native
    (Mamdani), 214
neoliberalism
    The Authoritarian Personality
        on, 258, 264, 266
    civil society and, 278–80,
        281–82
    Cold War and, 258
    crises of capitalism and,
        191–92
    crisis of, xvii–xviii
    critical humanities on, 197
    data colonialism and,
        265–66
    Democratic Party and, xiii,
        xiv, 192
    economic platforms of,
        301
    fascism debate and, xiv,
        xvii–xviii
    global new far-right move-
        ments and, 194–95
    hegemony of, 61–62
    India and, 221, 222, 226–27,
        228, 233
    network temporality and,
        268
    Obama and, xi
    oppression and violence in
        American culture and,
        171–72
    personalization and analysis
        of, 264

neoliberalism (*continued*)
    Trump administration and,
        192
    women's work and, 301
Neo-Marxist Institute for Social
    Research, 103
    See also Frankfurt School
neo-Nazis, 56–57, 127, 175,
    177, 181, 187, 189
Netherlands, 274, 301
networked society, xviii, 257
Never Trump Republicans, xii,
    112, 129
New Age of Empire, The
    (Andrews), 212
New Deal
    American interwar fascism
        and, 141
    Democratic Party and, xiii,
        275
    fascism as political label/
        accusation and, ix
    lower middle classes and, 9
    resistance to fascism and,
        77
    stereotypes of, 149
Newspeak, 48
Newton, Herbert, 151
New World Order, The (Robert-
    son), 45
Nichols, Tom, xv
Niebuhr, Reinhold, xiv, xix,
    3–10
Nietzsche, Friedrich, 17
Night at the Garden, A, 141
9/11, xi, 62, 115, 168, 198
1984 (Orwell), 48
Nixon, Richard M., 32, 33, 124,
    125, 295, 309–10
Nolte, Ernst, 106
No Name in the Street (Bald-
    win), 250
nongovernmental organiza-
    tions (NGOs), 272, 275,
    278–79
nonviolence, 201–2
Norway, Anders Breivik attack,
    184
Nouvelle Écologie, 253
Novák, Katalin, 302
Noys, Benjamin, 194
nuclear extinction, 204

Nuit debout movement, 250
Nuremberg laws, 139, 157

Obama, Barack, and
    administration
    BLM movement and, xiii
    crisis rhetoric and, x–xi
    fascism label as political accu-
        sation and, ix, xi–xii, 124
    immigration/migration
        and, 209
    institutional weakness and,
        306
    National Defense Authoriza-
        tion Act and, 307
    Tea Party and, 280
Obamacare, xiii, 192, 308–9
Ocasio-Cortez, Alexandria, xv,
    86, 101
Occupied Territories, 212
Occupy movement, xiii, 250
Oklahoma City bombing
    (1995), 173, 174, 175,
    180, 276
Old-Age Revolving Pensions
    plan (OARP), 6
online culture, 281–82
On the Judgment of History
    (Scott), 212
*On Tyranny: Twenty Lessons
    from the Twentieth Cen-
    tury* (Snyder), xv
opportunism, 74, 136, 147
oppression and violence in
    American culture
    anti-Communism and, 151
    arms industry and, 166, 167
    William Barr and, 115–16,
        119, 120–21
    Black radical tradition on,
        123
    George W. Bush administra-
        tion and, 126–27
    Cold War and, 206
    criminal justice system and,
        309
    historical analogy and, 96,
        104, 109–10, 111, 112,
        211, 218
    legal practices and, 156–57
    lynchings, 138, 150, 151,
        152, 153, 252

mass shootings and, 166–67
    militias and paramilitary
        groups and, 67, 167,
        180, 279
    national security state and,
        130–31, 167–71
    neoliberalism and, 171–72
    ongoing American civil war
        and, 165–66
    policing and, 30–31, 135,
        165–66, 251–52, 309
    presidential power expansion
        and, 206
    slavery, 28
    Trumpism as manifestation
        of, 122
    war on terror and, 206
    white supremacy and, 167
    See also American oppres-
        sion as fascism; domestic
        terrorism
Orbán, Viktor
    electoral victory of, 244
    nostalgic regeneration and,
        161
    right-wing authoritarianism
        and, xi
    Russian alignment of,
        195–96
    stigma of fascism label and,
        56, 94
    See also Hungary
Order (white power cell), 181
Order of Black Shirts, 141,
    151–52
    See also Mussolini, Benito,
        Blackshirts and
Origins of Totalitarianism, The
    (Arendt), xviii, 271, 286,
    287–90, 297
Orthodox nationalism, 190
Orwell, George, 48, 217
Owens, Jesse, 139

pacifism, 46
Padilla, José, 126
Padmore, George, 152, 217
Panagariya, Arvind, 228
Panovka, Rebecca, xviii, 285–97
Papadopoulos, George, 118
paradigm shift theory of scien-
    tific revolutions, 90

paramilitary groups. *See* militias and paramilitary groups
Pascal, Blaise, 118
Passing of the Great Race, The (Grant), 155
Patriot Act, x, 126, 296
Patwardhan, Anand, 231
Paxton, Robert Owen
 on characteristics of fascism, 53, 137, 189
 on indigenous nature of fascism, 136
 on Ku Klux Klan, xvi, 139–40, 154
 on rise of fascism, 61
 on Trump and fascism, 54, 68–70
 on unique nature of American fascism, 97
Payne, Stanley, 79, 136
Paz, Octavio, 227
Pécresse, Valérie, 62
Pelley, William Dudley, 141, 144
Pelosi, Nancy, 308
Pence, Mike, 122
Pentagon Papers, 293–95
People's Party (United States), 275
personality cults, 20–21
Pétain, Philippe, 15–16
Peters, John Durham, 267
Petrov, Kirill, 239
Pinochet, Augusto, 124, 125
Pioneer Home Protective Association, 141
Pittsburgh synagogue shooting (2018), 177, 184
Pitzer, Andrea, 93
policing
 Black Lives Matter protests and, 307
 civil society and, 279
 fascism and, 33, 125–26, 135, 278
 January 6, 2021, Capitol attack and, 83, 85, 131
 militarization and, 135, 167
 ongoing American civil war and, 165–66
 oppression and violence in American culture and,

30–31, 135, 165–66, 251–52, 309
 overreach by, 72, 152
 powers/authority of, 33, 170, 171
 protests of violence by, 32, 120, 166, 309
 racism and, 30–31, 165–66, 309
 state-sponsored violence by, 135, 165–66, 251–52
 totalitarianism and, 287, 289
 white supremacy and, 167
political myths, 94–95, 137
political parties, 13, 16, 274–75, 306
 See also specific parties
political polarization, 97–98, 164, 208
political theology, xix
political violence. *See* domestic terrorism; violence
polycrisis, x
 See also crises
Popular Front (France), 9, 77
Popular Front (Spain), 129
Popular Front (US), 77
Popular Front strategy, 78
populism
 American interwar fascism and, 142–43
 as characteristic of fascism, 94, 189
 crisis rhetoric and, xiii
 mass elitism and, 46–47
 qualitative, 47–48
 See also right-wing populism
post-fascism, 282–83
postindustrialism, 258
post-Reconstruction South. *See* Jim Crow America; Ku Klux Klan
poststructuralism, 89–90
Pound, Ezra, 43
Powell, Colin, xii
Power Elite, The (Mills), xix
Powers, Morris H., 151
Pratt, Simon Frankel, 241
presentism, xv, 91, 100–101
Priestley, Joseph, 87
Primo de Rivera, José Antonio, 136

proletariat. *See* working class
propaganda, 22–23, 24, 156, 259, 262
Protocols of the Elders of Zion, The, 44, 142, 146
Proud Boys, 68, 127, 190, 209, 279
pseudo-rationalism, 261
Putin, Vladimir
 political violence and, 234
 return to Russian presidency, xi
 US presidential election and, 118
 See also Putin and fascism; Ukraine war
Putin and fascism, 237–45
 Christianity and, xix, 159
 global new far-right movements and, 194, 195–96, 244
 historical analogies for Ukraine war and, 242–44
 masculinity and, 238
 mass mobilization and, 240–41
 militias and paramilitary groups and, 241–42
 nostalgic regeneration and, 162
 vs. right-wing populism, 58
 Snyder on, 56, 240
 Soviet tropes and, 238–39
 Ukraine "de-Nazification" rhetoric and, 237, 239
 war and, 239–40
Putnam, Robert, 271–73, 274, 276, 278, 281, 284

QAnon, 122, 127, 130, 269, 283, 289
qualitative populism, 47–48

Rabin, Yitzhak, 131
racial binary, 209
racial fascism, 257, 277
racial injustice protests (2020). *See* Black Lives Matter protests
racism
 British empire violence and, 215–16

racism (*continued*)
  as characteristic of fascism,
    24, 26, 33, 45, 137–38
  eugenic measures and, 75,
    137, 259
  far-right populism and, 67
  fear of difference and, 45
  historical analogy and,
    198–99
  historical persistence of,
    100, 160
  interwar years, 77
  Islamophobia and, 119
  lower middle classes and, 7
  Nazism and, 18, 24, 38, 76,
    137, 157
  protest rights and, 120
  stochastic acts of violence
    and, 269
  working-class role in fascism
    and, 34
  See also American racism;
    great replacement theory;
    white supremacy
Raghavan, Anita, 227
Rampell, Catherine, 308
Randolph, A. Philip, 275
Raqs Media Collective, 232
Rashtriya Swayamsevak Sangh
  (RSS), 219
Raspail, Jean, 193
rational truth, 291
Reagan, Ronald, 117–18, 124,
  169, 303, 307, 309, 310
Reconstruction, 206
Red Ant Dream (Kak) (docu-
  mentary film), 231
Rees-Mogg, Jacob, 212
Reform Act (1832), 311
Reich, Robert, 79
Reich, Wilhelm, 191
Reichstag fire, xvi, 106
religions, secular, 17–21
reparations movements, 216–17
reproduction, 299–300
  See also gender
Republican Party
  American right wing and, xi,
    57, 162, 192, 255, 280
  Biden election and, 83
  dangers of, 129
  ethnic antagonism and, 67

historical analogy and, 112
January 6, 2021, Capitol
  attack and, 57, 85, 131
national security state and,
  169–70, 171
oligarchy and, 281
oppression and violence in
  American culture and,
  129
right-wing populism and,
  310
strongman thesis and, 307
support for Trump, 83, 104,
  162, 280
Trump differences from
  classical European fascism
  and, 98
Trump election and, xii
US Constitution and, 281
white supremacy and, xi,
  162, 249–50
resistance to authoritarianism
  American democracy and,
    83
  Black role in, 33–34, 123,
    138, 139, 149–53
  communism and, 37, 38,
    54–55
  definitions of fascism and,
    58–59
  difficulty of development,
    76–77
  global new far-right move-
    ments and, 191
  historical analogy and, 85,
    101–2, 107–8, 110–11,
    112
  liberalism and, 126
  mass movement for, 33–34
  postwar society and, 71, 78
  Spanish Civil War and, 77
  working-class role in, 34
Reuther, Walter, 275
revolutionary activism, 12
revolution of 1848, French,
  283–84
Rhodes Must Fall movement,
  218
Riefenstahl, Leni, 81
Riesman, David, xix
Right to Information Act
  (India), 230

right-wing populism, 65–67
  American exceptionalism
    and, 66–67
  American oppression as
    fascism and, 137–38,
    148
  American Revolution and,
    207
  civil society and, 282–83
  diminishing returns of,
    309–10
  emergent fascism and, xi
  global new far-right move-
    ments and, xi, 58, 105
  India, 229
  Obama and, xii
  Republican Party and, 310
  strongman thesis and, 309,
    310
  Trump and, 65, 66, 94, 148,
    189, 192–93
Riley, Dylan John, 276, 277,
  283
Rittenhouse, Kyle, 252
Roberts, Andrew, 211
Robertson, Pat, 45
Robertson, Wilmot, 190
Robin, Corey, xiv, 128, 268,
  277, 280, 305–12
Roe v. Wade, 308
Rogers, Joel Augustus, 139
Roman *Divide et impera,* 214
Roman Empire, 213–14
Romania, 159
Romney, Mitt, 128
Roof, Dylann, 184
Roosevelt, Franklin D., 9, 38,
  49, 143, 144–45, 149
Rorty, Richard, 59
Rosenberg, Alfred, 63, 194
Rosenberg, Arthur, 191
Rove, Karl, 296
Roy, Arundhati, 230
Roy, Rahul, 231–32
Rubio, Marco, 129
Ruby Ridge, 180
Rushdie, Salman, 233
Russia. *See* Putin, Vladimir;
  Putin and fascism;
  Ukraine war
Russian Orthodox Church,
  xix

Rwandan genocide, 92
Ryan, Paul, 308

Said, Edward, 197
Salazar, António de Oliveira, 42
Salgado, Plínio, 159
Sanders, Bernie, xi, xiv, 128
Satia, Priya, xvii, 211–18
Scarborough, Joe, xii
Schama, Simon, 66
Schmitt, Carl, 107, 114–15,
    116, 117, 119, 120, 208
scientific racism, 155
Scott, Joan Wallach, 212, 217
Scottish National Party, 278
Scottsboro Nine, 139, 151
secularism, 119
secular religions, 17–21
Sen, Amartya, 221, 225
September 11, 2001, terror
    attacks, xi, 62, 115, 168,
    198
Serbia, 244
Seth, Vikram, 219, 223–24
sexism, 100, 304
    See also gender
sexual liberation movements,
    299
Shanghai (Banerjee), 232
Share Our Wealth movement,
    6–7
Sharma, Rakesh, 232
Shaw, Tamsin, xvi, 107, 114–21
Sheehan, Neil, 293
Shelly, Cameron, 88
Shinawatra, Thaksin, 234
Ship of Theseus (Gandhi), 232
Sikh fundamentalists, 225
Singh, Manmohan, 221, 228
Singh, Nikhil Pal, xvi, xvii,
    164–72
Skandza Forum, 190
skinheads, 175, 181
Skocpol, Theda, 275
slavery. *See* American slavery
Smith, Adam, 215
Smith, Gerald L. K., 145
Smith, Iain Duncan, 212
Snegovaya, Maria, 239
Snyder, Timothy
    on American slavery as
        model for Nazism, 156

Arendt and, 286
    on Putin, 56, 240
    on Trump, xv–xvi, 79, 80,
        125, 276–77, 286
social atomization. *See* civil
    society
social capital, 272–73, 276, 278
social change movements, 163
social conformity, 263
social democracy, xi, 16, 61, 77,
    78, 161
Social Democratic Party (Swe-
    den), 77, 161
socialism, 14–15, 73, 78
social media, 68, 85, 189, 282
social mediation, 260, 265
socioeconomic inequality. *See*
    economic inequality
sociology, 101
Sogno, Edgardo (Franchi), 37
Solnit, Rebecca, 79
Sontag, Susan, 76
South Africa, 93, 182, 212,
    214
Soviet Union
    fall of, 195, 199
    Nazi-Soviet Pact, 15
    Putin and, 238–39
    resistance to fascism and, 77
    Stalinism, 13, 39, 40, 55,
        217, 238
Spanish Civil War, 38, 55, 74,
    77, 153
Speer, Albert, 40
Spencer, Richard, 196
Spengler, Oswald, 20
Stalin, Joseph, 15, 77, 106
    See also Stalinism
Stalinism, 13, 39, 40, 55, 217,
    238
Stamos, Alex, 266
Stanley, Jason, 154–63
    Black radical tradition and,
        xvii
    definition of fascism and,
        65–66
    on enemy-threat percep-
        tion, 95
    on fascism as political
        method, 54
    legal phase of fascism and,
        255

on Trump and fascism, 94,
    111, 125, 276
Stars Down to Earth, The
    (Adorno), 261–64
Stoddard, Lothrop, 138, 194
Storey, Henry, 151
Strauss, Leo, 119
strongman thesis, 305, 306–7,
    309–10
Strongmen (Ben-Ghiat), 53
subsidized childcare, 301
Suitable Boy, A (Seth), 219,
    223–24, 225, 229
superstition, 261–64
Supreme Court (US), 152–53
surveillance, 33, 258
Suskind, Ron, 296
Sweden, 77, 161
syncretism, 43, 44
systemic racism, 95–96

Tamás, Gáspár Miklós, 282
Tanton, John, 194
Tata, Ratan, 221
Taylor, Jared, 196
Tea Party, xi, xii, 207, 280
technological determinism,
    266–67
terrorism
    9/11, xi, 62, 115, 168, 198
    war on terror, x–xi, 115–16,
        119, 120–21, 126, 198,
        206
    See also domestic terrorism
Thatcher, Margaret, 280, 310
Theweleit, Klaus, 64
Thomas, Martin Luther, 262
Thompson, Dorothy, 144
Three Faces of Fascism (Nolte),
    107
Thunberg, Greta, 254
Till We Meet Again (Roy) (doc-
    umentary film), 231
Time on the Cross (Engerman),
    216
Tocqueville, Alexis de, 275, 277
Tooze, Adam, x, xv, 279
Tory Party, 274, 278
Toscano, Alberto, 251, 277
totalitarianism
    Arendt on, 286, 287–89
    China, 249

totalitarianism (*continued*)
classical European fascism as synecdoche for, 39–40
definition of fascism and, 55
Nazism as, 38–39, 40, 55, 74–75
Russia and, 238, 239
Townsend, Francis, 6
Townsend Plan, 6
Toynbee, Arnold J., 204
trade union movement. *See* labor unions
traditionalism, 43–44, 190
Traditionalist Worker Party, 190
Trans-Pacific Partnership, 192
Traverso, Enzo, 250
Treaty of Versailles, 145–46
Trevelyan, G. M., 81
Triumph of the Will (Riefenstahl), 81
Trotsky, Leon, xiv, 11–16
Trotskyists, American, ix
True, James, 144
Trump, Donald J.
age of, 85
America First movements and, 80, 95, 145
apathetical response to, 104
Arendt on truth and lies and, xviii, 285–88, 289–90, 295, 296–97
aspirational fascism of, 94, 105, 127–28
attacks on free press and, 94
William Barr and, 107, 114, 116–21
Black Lives Matter protests and, 135, 146, 148, 252, 307–8, 309
business and, 69
Capitol attack and, 127
civic violence encouragement by, 68, 69, 81, 148
civil society and, 273
civil war rhetoric and, 163–66, 167, 168, 172
conjecture and, 59, 211
COVID-19 pandemic and, 67, 107, 127, 192
crisis rhetoric and, x, xii
election of, x, xii, xiv, xv–xvi, 164, 187

ethnic antagonism and, 67, 308
ethnic minorities and, 209
fascism as political accusation and, ix
fascism empowerment and, 196
foreign policy of, 80, 128–29
gender and, xviii
hate crimes and, 66
hyperpolitics and, 273
immigration/migration and, 66, 86, 93, 97, 116, 119, 125, 128, 146, 307
imperialism/colonialism and, 80
as ineffectual leader, 308
Islamophobia and, 116
masculinity and, 64
media and, 68, 94, 295, 296, 297
Modi and, 234–36
Muslim travel ban, 116, 119, 125, 128
National Defense Authorization Act and, 307
Nazism and, 146
neoliberalism and, 192
personal freedoms and, 81
political polarization and, 97–98, 164
as product of historical oppressions/privilege, 112–13
racism and, 67, 127, 146–47, 308
rejection of defeat, 81
Republican support for, 83, 104, 162, 280
resistance to, 83, 101–2, 106–7
right-wing populism and, 65, 66, 94, 127, 189, 192–93
Rittenhouse invite and, 252
social domination ideal and, 64
social media and, 85
strongman thesis and, 305, 306–7
tribal solidarity and, 95, 104
US Constitution and, 280–81

weakness of, 122–23, 128, 307–9
white nationalism and, 162
See also January 6, 2021, Capitol attack; Trump and fascism
Trump, Fred, 146
Trump and fascism
American interwar fascism and, 145–46, 147–48
Arendt on truth and lies and, xviii, 285–88, 289–90
aspirations and, 94, 105, 127–28
differences from classical European fascism and, 69, 81–83, 94, 98, 214, 250
global context of, 162
hyperbolic political forecasting and, xv–xvi, xix, 164–65
ideological differences and, 81–82, 250
institutional domination and, 82–83, 125–26
January 6, 2021, Capitol attack and, 54, 69, 70, 83–85, 122, 123, 127, 193
lack of coherent movement, 59–60
neo-Nazis and, 56–57, 127
parallels with classical European fascism, ix, 59, 68–69, 79, 83–84, 107, 188–89, 276–77, 280
Paxton on, 54, 68–70
right-wing populism and, 94, 148, 189, 192–93
social capital and, 276
stigma of fascism label and, 94
Trump election and, x, xii, xiv, xv–xvi
Trump's weakness and, 128
white nationalism and, 93, 127, 189
working class and, 277
Trump-Russia investigation, 118, 120
"Truth and Politics" (Arendt), 286, 290, 291–93, 295

Tulsa Massacre, 146–47
Turkey, xi, 94
Turner Diaries, The (Pierce), 180, 182, 183
2008 financial crisis, xiii, xvii, 198

UK Independence Party (UKIP), 278
Ukraine, 156
  See also Ukraine war
Ukraine war
  fascism and, 56
  fascism as political label/accusation and, 237, 239
  fascism empowerment and, 195, 196
  genocide and, 56, 162, 242–43
  Global South views on, 244–45
  historical analogy and, 242–44
  imperialism/colonialism and, 245
  masculinity and, 238
  mass mobilization and, 240–41
  political theology and, xix
  Western actions and, 243–44, 245
Üngör, Ugur, 242
United Kingdom
  British empire racial violence and, 215–16
  British Labour Party, 274
  Conservative Party, 274, 278, 279–80
  empire of, 73
  exceptionalism and, 215
  imperialism/colonialism, 73, 211–17
  Kenya and, 212–13, 217
  memory wars, 211–18
  Reform Act (1832), 311
  resistance to classical European fascism and, 77
United Nations, 115
United States
  Civil War, 117, 164, 165, 166, 206, 207

Constitution, 114–18, 166, 278–79, 280–81, 306, 310–11, 312
national security state, 33, 124, 126, 130–31, 167–71, 281
political elite of, 112
presidential power expansion, 114–18, 119–20, 206, 280
resistance to classical European fascism and, 77
  See also American democracy; American exceptionalism; American interwar fascism; American oppression as fascism; American racism; American slavery; criminal justice system; oppression and violence in American culture; Trump, Donald J.; Trump and fascism
United States Holocaust Memorial Museum, 86–87, 92
Unite the Right rally, Charlottesville (2017), 127, 176, 193, 309
US Central Intelligence Agency, 126
US Constitution, 166
  antidemocratic elements of, 310–11, 312
  civil society and, 278–79
  executive power and, 114–18
  institutional weakness and, 306
  Trump and, 280–81
"US Fascism v. Angelo Herndon" (Kelley), 149–53
US National Security Agency, 223
US Supreme Court, 152–53
US Supreme Court justices, 308

Vergangenheitsaufarbeitung (working-off-the-past), 217
Versailles peace conference, 73
Vichy France, 70
Vietnam War, 33, 72, 168, 181, 293–95

violence
  American culture and, 166–67
  anti-Muslim, in India, 219–20, 223, 226, 234
  as characteristic of fascism, 59–61, 63, 64, 68, 69–70, 140, 147
  classical European fascism and, 59–60, 63, 64, 68, 81, 154, 158
  experience of as condition for classical European fascism, 11, 59, 61, 277
  historical analogy and, 200–202
  Jim Crow America and, 140
  Trump's encouragement of, 68, 69, 81, 148
  See also domestic terrorism; oppression and violence in American culture
Vivekananda, Swami, 220, 233
Vlaams Blok (Belgium), 301
Volcker, Paul, 171
voting rights, 160, 255
Vučić, Aleksandar, 244

Waco siege, 180
Wagner Group, 241
Wagoner, Rick, xii
Wallace, Henry, 144
Walter, Barbara, 164, 165, 167, 168
war on terror, x–xi, 115–16, 119, 120–21, 126, 198, 206
Washington, George, 141
Watergate scandal, 125
Weber, Max, 100–101, 189, 283
Weigel, Moira, xviii, xix, 256–69
Weimar Republic, xix, 60, 83, 279
Weinberger, Caspar, 117
Weizmann, Chaim, 106
Wessel, Horst, 82
white nationalism
  Christianity and, 159
  on critical race theory, 157
  domestic terrorism and, 193
  far-right views and, 197

white nationalism (*continued*)
global context of, 187
global new far-right movements and, 187, 189–91,
196
Republican Party and, 162,
192
terminology and, 176
Trump and, 93, 127, 162,
189
See also great replacement
theory; white power
movement
white power movement,
173–84
apocalypticism and,
183–84
Christchurch mosques'
attack and, 181
diversity within, 175,
177–78
domestic terrorism and,
173–74, 175, 177, 180–
81, 182–83, 184
fears of racial extinction and,
181–82, 184
Fort Smith trial, 178–80
global context of, 182
goals of, 175, 182–83
great replacement theory
and, 181, 182–83
lone wolf myth and, 173–74,
175, 177, 180
misunderstandings of, 176,
177, 178
origins of, 181
piecemeal responses to,
175–76
strategies of, 175, 178, 180,
184
terminology and, 176–77
*White Skin, Black Fuel: On the
Danger of Fossil Fascism*
(Malm), 253
white supremacy
American interwar fascism
and, 151, 152
Black radical tradition on,
xiii
civil society and, 277
as fascist, 139
global context of, 187

global new far-right move-
ments and, 189
military and police connec-
tions with, 167
Republican Party and, xi,
162, 249–50
terminology and, 176–77
Trump and, 147
Unite the Right rally, Char-
lottesville (2017), 127,
176, 193, 309
See also American racism;
white nationalism; white
power movement
White Tiger, The (Adiga), 222
Whitman, James Q., 157, 214
Whitmer, Gretchen, 167–68
"Whose Country is This"
(Coolidge), 155
"Why Holocaust Analogies Are
Dangerous" (Friedberg),
92–93
Wilkerson, Isabel, 212
Will, George, xii
Wilson, Woodrow, 95, 145
Winant, Gabriel, 277
Windelband, Wilhelm, 91
Winrod, Gerald B., 143, 144
Wise, James Waterman, 135,
141
Wise, Stephen, 135
Wittgenstein, Ludwig, 42, 99
women
employment and, 301–2
support for global new far-
right movements, 303–4
See also gender
Woolf, Virginia, 64
working class
civil society and, 282
classical European fascism
and, 16
conditions for fascism and,
14, 277
1930s possibility of American fascism and, 4–5, 8,
12, 13
radicalization of, 11–12, 15
resistance to fascism and, 34
role in fascism, racism and,
34
See also labor unions

World Church of the Creator,
182
World Health Organization,
228
World War I
America First movements
and, 95
British imperialism/colonial-
ism and, 214
conditions for classical European fascism and, 60, 73,
76, 80, 277–78
enemy-threat perception
and, 156
French Veterans Riot (1934),
69–70
Italian Futurists and, 41
Nazi propaganda on, 156
twentieth-century global
crises and, 76
World War II
American exceptionalism
and, 137–38
anti-fascism as defining characteristic of, 38
Arendt and, 287
current fascist phenomenon
and, 72
definitions of fascism and,
54–55
French collapse during, 20
historical analogy with
Ukraine war, 242–44
postwar resistance to fascism,
77–78
refugees and, 25
Russia and, 238, 240
US entry and, 145
Wotansvolk, 182

xenophobia. *See* nativism
Xi Jinping, 237, 249

Yeltsin, Boris, 194
Yew, Lee Kuan, 224
Yglesias, Matthew, 274

Zamora, Daniel, 273
Zelensky, Volodymyr, 242,
243–44
Zhangke, Jia, 232
Ziblatt, Daniel, 99